D0857366

YALE CENTER FOR INTERNATIONAL AND AREA STUDIES

YALE
RUSSIAN AND EAST EUROPEAN
PUBLICATIONS

YALE
RUSSIAN AND EAST EUROPEAN
PUBLICATIONS

THE HUNGARIANS: A DIVIDED NATION

THE HUNGARIANS:
A DIVIDED NATION

Edited by
STEPHEN BORSODY

NEW HAVEN
YALE CENTER FOR INTERNATIONAL AND AREA STUDIES
1988

Library of Congress Card Catalog Number: 85-50189
ISBN: 0-936586-12-5 (paperback)
ISBN: 0-936586-07-9 (hardcover)
Typography by Brevis Press
Printed in the United States of America

DEDICATED
TO
OPPRESSED PEOPLES
EVERYWHERE

Contents

Part Three: Problems and Solutions

Appendix

Acknowledgments

The bronze medal of the jacket design, entitled "Pax 1919," is by Erzsébet Esseő. It is in the medal collection of the British Museum and is reproduced by permission of the Trustees of the British Museum, London.

In Chapter 11, the passages from Edvard Beneš's writings are excerpted by permission of *Foreign Affairs* (January 1942, October 1944, April 1946), copyrighted in 1941, 1944, 1946 by the Council on Foreign Relations, Inc., New York. The Smutný documents, in Vojtech Mastny's translations from the Czech, were originally published in *Jahrbücher für Geschichte Osteuropas* (September 1972). The excerpts from both the Beneš writings and the Smutný documents are the editor's selections.

Julian Schopflin, in collaboration with George Coulson, translated the following parts of the book: in chapter 5, from the French, the Introduction by François Fejtő; in chapter 8, from the Hungarian, Annex IV; in Chapter 10, from the Hungarian, Annex I; in chapter 13, from the Hungarian, the excerpts from an interview with Edgár Balogh, published by *Kritika* (Budapest, 1978, no. 3); in chapter 14, from the Hungarian, the essay by Pierre Kende, and Annex II; and in the Appendix, from the Hungarian, the statistical essay by Zoltán Dávid.

Chapter 8 was compiled from an article by Kálmán Janics ("Czechoslovakia's Magyar Minority: An Example of Diaspora Nationalism," *Canadian Review of Studies in Nationalism* [Fall 1975]), translated from the Hungarian and edited by Thomas Spira, and from two articles (in Hungarian) by Janics in *Új Látóhatár* (27/6 [1976],

34/3 [1983]), as well as from passages in Janics's book, *Czechoslovak Policy and the Hungarian Minority, 1945–1948* (New York, 1982), copyrighted in 1982 by Brooklyn College Studies on Society in Change. Annexes II and III of Chapter 8 were adapted from translations from the Hungarian by Elemér Bakó and George Olgyay, respectively. The editor is solely responsible for this work of compilation.

Andrew Ludanyi translated from the Hungarian the excerpts from László Rehák's book, *Kissebségtől a nemzetiségig* (Novi Sad, 1978), which appear in Annex I of Chapter 9 and Annex II of Chapter 12.

In Annex II of Chapter 10, Steven B. Vardy translated from the Hungarian the excerpts from a book by N. V. Arsentyev et al., *A boldogság felé,* itself a translation from the Russian by Zoltán Kulin et al. (Uzhgorod, 1975).

In Chapter 15, Lajos Für's essay was adapted from a translation prepared by Thomas Szendrey from the Hungarian.

The editor alone is responsible for the selection of the documentary material as well as for the editing of the material of the book as a whole, including translations and adaptations.

Our collective work has been a labor of love. A grant from the Committee for Danubian Research, Inc., Washington, D.C., as well as contributions to the MBK Book Fund and to the Boston Harvard Circle by private individuals (their wish is to remain anonymous), helped to defray the expenses of publication. We greatly appreciate their generosity. We are also grateful to the Yale Center for International and Area Studies for sponsoring our book in the prestigious "Yale Russian and East European Publications" series. I am particularly grateful to Professor Paul Bushkovitch, managing editor of the Yale series, for his editorial counsel; also, I greatly benefited from the comments of Professor Piotr S. Wandycz and Dr. Eva S. Balogh. However, neither of them should be identified with the views of this book in general, and with those expressed by me in particular. In fact, considering the highly controversial topics, this book is bound to provoke disagreements on all sides, including the Hungarian one. On the non-controversial side, I am much obliged to the copy editor, William B. Bidwell, and to Heather L. Nadelman for preparing the index.

It is a long way for a manuscript to get to the publisher. For much precious advice in that process I am indebted to my wife Zsóka, and to my daughter Éva. In preparing the final typescript, Elizabeth Kammen and Jacqueline Flaherty were most helpful. And, last but not least, I wish to express my gratitude to Brevis Press for the care and devotion with which they saw the book's production through from typescript to printed copy. S. B.

Preface

Our purpose with this book is to inform. We wish to call attention to a serious conflict that exists among the nations of the Danube region about which the people of the world—the younger generations in particular—know little or nothing. One of the main sources of this conflict is the existence of large Hungarian minorities in Hungary's neighbors.

Today one of every four Hungarians lives outside of Hungary. At the time of Hungary's partition after World War I, it was one in every three. The ratio was reduced as a result of concentration and growth of Hungarians in Hungary proper and their stagnation as minorities in the other countries. The Hungarian minority problem is one of sui generis, deserving, we believe, specific attention. It is a suppressed problem which will not politely go away just because it is treated as a nonexistent one. It is intertwined of course with the much broader—and quite well known—problem of half a continent, known since World War II as "Eastern Europe." But, despite the seriousness of the problem, the world seldom hears of the Hungarian minorities. The main reason for that is that the mother country, Hungary, hardly speaks about them. The official silence is imposed on Hungary, a member-state of the Soviet bloc, as a fraternal obligation to Communist solidarity.

Hungary's unfair territorial treatment that created the Hungarian minority problem was originally the work of the Western democracies. And it is not without irony that the status quo of the Danube region, denounced after World War I by the Communists as an evil product of imperialist bourgeois nationalism, now is regarded as just and in conformity with proletarian internationalism.

We are critical of the territorial settlement in the Danube region because it keeps an unduly large number of Hungarians in the inferior status of minorities. We also are critical of the nation-state policy, not only because it is hostile to minorities but because its ethnocentrism frustrates international reconciliation and cooperation. In our "revisionist" view of the future, we look toward the rise of a Danubian regional community of nations with equal rights for all and discrimination to none. This view may sound extraordinarily utopian, but it will take some unusual thinking to bring real peace to this region of unusual complexities.

In addition to Czechoslovakia, the Soviet Union, Romania, and Yugoslavia, Hungary's fifth neighbor, Austria, too, has a small Hungarian population. In our study, however, we do not discuss the Austrian minorities. Our topic is the Hungarian problem, as an aftermath of Hungary's territorial and ethnic partition. The Hungarians of Austria do not fit in with this theme. The ethnic division between Austria and Hungary is generally fair—with the minor exception of a couple of ancient Hungarian settlements in southern Burgenland. Fair, too, is the treatment of Hungarians in Austria. But, most importantly, the majority of Austria's Hungarians today are recent immigrants, post-World War II refugees. They belong to the Hungarian diaspora, along with countless similar groups of immigrants scattered all over the world. By contrast, the Hungarians in Czechoslovakia, the Soviet Union, Romania and Yugoslavia are ancient inhabitants of historic Hungary. They live where their ancestors had lived for centuries.

Our aim is to offer a fresh look at the Hungarian problem in the light of available information. To the best of our ability, we try to be objective. We also believe that discussing problems, rather than silencing them, serves the cause of peace among nations. Under normal conditions, a book of this sort might have been published long ago by Hungarians at home. Under the present circumstances, only Hungarians living abroad can do it. Whenever feasible, however, we engaged Hungarians living in Hungary as contributors.

As editor, I wish to express, first of all, my thanks to our contributors. To follow a design mapped out by an editor is not an easy way to write a reasonably coherent book. If we succeeded at all, it is due to the spirit of cooperation and the performance of the individual contributors. Our book has been planned as a collective work to emphasize the collective concern toward the subject. It should be pointed out, however, that the individual authors stand behind their own contributions only, and not necessarily behind the contents of the book as a whole.

Wellfleet, Massachusetts

Stephen Borsody

May 1987

Note on the Reprint Edition

In the wake of the 1989 European revolution, some aspects of the Hungarian problem have changed for the better. Hungary's new democratic regime is now genuinely concerned about the Hungarian people living forcibly divided in five countries. Also, the departure of Nicolae Ceausescu from the scene, the Romanian dictator who harbored genocidal plans against non-Romanians, has literally saved the collective existence of Transylvania's Hungarians, the single largest Hungarian community outside Hungary estimated at close to 2.5 million. But otherwise, there has been no fundamental improvement in the treatment of national minorities in the countries of the Danube region. The Hungarian question as such, which is the focus of this study, remains unchanged.

The Hungarians: A Divided Nation remains as timely today as it was when first published in 1988.

S. B.

Boston, May 1991

Introduction

John C. Campbell

The depth of national sentiments and the endurance of ethnic cultures are permanent facts in the history and life of the peoples of Central and Eastern Europe. Political structures may change, boundaries may be redrawn, war and revolution may disrupt societies, but consciousness of nationality, with language as its badge, remains. Nationalism, the exaggerated political expression of nationality, has been the curse of this area, in which ethnic groups are often so intermingled that no clear lines can be drawn between them. It has contributed to two world wars and has not been laid to rest by the two postwar peace settlements. Increasing our understanding of these phenomena helps to define the problem, although it provides no sure key to a solution.

This book should contribute to that understanding. Its focus is on the Hungarians and on their relation to their neighbors. It is in many ways a classic and instructive example. The Magyars of Hungary, after years of dominating other nationalities within the historic Hungarian state, found their own nation divided by the new frontiers drawn after World War I and confirmed after World War II. As a result of the postwar arrangements, many Hungarians now live under Czechoslovak, Soviet Ukrainian, Romanian, and Yugoslav rule. Yet the problem is not merely a Hungarian one; it is more general. In an age of nation-states, no matter where the frontiers are drawn in Central and Eastern Europe, conflict over territory and over the treatment of ethnic minorities is unavoidable. That age has not yet passed into history. The Soviet conquest of the entire area has not disposed of national rivalries. Neither the official cultivation of a common higher loyalty to Marxism-Leninism nor the emergence of resistance to nationalism based on solidarity against a common enemy have, as yet, successfully overcome national aspirations. In fact, the Communist regimes, particularly in Romania and in Slovakia, have made a point of using nationalism to bolster their own rule.

The political destiny of nations of this area has been determined in large measure by the interlocking of national aims with the policies and conflicts of the Great Powers. It was Hungary's misfortune that her leaders chose association with Germany in two world wars and had no friends among those who made the postwar settlements. The severe Hungarian ethnic and territorial losses inflicted by the Treaty of Trianon following World War I led almost inevitably to a revisionist foreign policy, which could succeed only with the help of the revisionist powers: Nazi Germany and Fascist Italy. Hungary's conservative leaders of the interwar period feared and distrusted Hitler, but they took what they could get of what they considered their rightful patrimony when Hitler smashed the status quo between 1938 and 1941. They acquired southern Slovakia and Ruthenia from Czechoslovakia, northern Transylvania from Romania, and a number of border areas from Yugoslavia. There was partial justification for these gains on ethnic grounds, but the decisions were fateful ones because, as war engulfed Central Europe, events passed beyond Hungary's control. Hungary could not avoid participation in Hitler's war and was the last of Hitler's satellites to get out. The war and the new configuration of power would determine the destiny of those territories Hungary had regained, and of their inhabitants, and indeed of Hungary itself.

The postwar settlement, which is well described in several chapters of this book, was bound to be unfavorable to Hungarian aspirations for boundaries more just than those of Trianon and for protection of the rights of Hungarians living outside Hungary. There was no conference of fair and like-minded statesmen dedicated to building a new Central Europe based on principles of freedom, justice, democracy, reconciliation, and cooperation. There were two competing forces, the USSR and the Western powers, already at odds over the fate of this part of Europe, and each saw the question of peace terms for Hungary in the light of that struggle. It was an unequal contest in that the Soviet Union was already in the process of establishing political preponderance in the entire area, to which the Western powers could oppose only words.

The Soviet leaders had no reason to be generous to Hungary. They were then trying to consolidate their influence in Czechoslovakia, Romania, and Yugoslavia, and did not wish to weaken the pro-Soviet regimes in those three countries by favoring Hungary against them. Their aims included eventual control of Hungary as well, but that could wait; they did not have to buy it with concessions to Hungary on peace terms. Two issues which came up for decision in the peace negotiations made the Soviet position quite clear. One was the Hungarian claim for a revision of the frontier with Romania; there, after some vague encouragement to the Hungarians, Moscow sided with Romania. The second was the Czechoslovak demand for expulsion of an additional 200,000 Hungarians from Slovakia; that demand was fully supported by the Soviet Union.

American sympathy for Hungary on these issues provided an interesting historical sidelight. Washington toyed with the idea of a minor revision of the Romanian frontier, but never took a firm position on it and eventually abandoned even the anodyne proposition that the two states might negotiate an agreed revision. On the question of population transfer the United States had a momentary success, keeping the Czechoslovak proposal out of the Hungarian peace treaty; but it was then left to be worked out bilaterally by the two states, and the United States by that time had no real influence with either.

The United States' relative benevolence toward Hungary in the peace negotiations of 1946 has two explanations. One had to do with principles. American diplomats believed that a more balanced boundary settlement with Romania, leaving fewer people under alien rule, was justified on grounds of self-determination and would make for greater stability and peace. Washington also took the position that the forcible uprooting and expulsion of Hungarians from Czechoslovakia was wrong in principle and would promote strife rather than peace. The other American motive was more practical and immediate. The Americans were trying to strengthen the position of the existing coalition government of Hungary against the threats and pressures of the local Communist party and of the Soviet Union. They could serve that aim by supporting the Hungarian government on popular national issues such as these.

These were not, however, matters of high priority. American influence in Central and Eastern Europe was limited. There was little point in expanding it except where it might help in the overall effort to save the area from Soviet domination, and in that regard the key issue was national independence for all those nations, not ideal frontiers between them. The United States was also trying to get a general peace settlement in Europe, where Germany and Italy were more important than the states of Eastern Europe. Washington had to decide, in the light of its broad strategy, on what specific matters it would take a stand against the Soviet Union. Territorial revision and protection of Hungarian minorities in neighboring states—sound propositions though they were at the time and have proved to be since—were not major issues for the United States and the West. In any event, when they lost on what was the major issue, that of Soviet domination of the entire area, they (and Hungary) lost on all the minor issues as well.

As after Trianon, Hungarians were bitter at the treatment meted out to their country after World War II. It seemed to belie the pledges of the Atlantic Charter and the bright promise of the newly founded United Nations. Not only were they bitter against the Soviet Union, which was occupying and dominating their country—that was to be expected—but they also resented the apparent indifference of the Western powers. The feeling was evident at the time—and is evident in this book—that the West had betrayed Hungary, and also its own professed ideals.

Hungary was, however, a victim of her own past, as well as of geography, the war, and the new balance of power. The country had been run, in the interwar period, by a reactionary and semi-fascist regime, and by the end of the war it was in the hands of the brutal fanatics of the outright fascist Arrow Cross party. It had, with Hitler's help, taken territory from neighboring states. The Allied Powers of World War II did not recognize those acquisitions and insisted in the armistice terms that Hungary withdraw from them. In theory, the map of Europe was on the table for redrawing in the formal negotiations for peace, and the world's interest in peace and stability might have been served by territorial changes, especially in the contested border areas. But Hungary's case for such changes, reasonable as it might have been, found few sympathetic listeners. Hungary had to pay for her past—and is still paying.

On the question of the protection of Hungarian minorities, the Soviet Union was unconcerned and the Western powers, while sympathetic, were opposed to a return to the old minority treaties of the interwar period. Those treaties had not worked well. They had produced endless bickering and international hearings and appeals, without beneficial results for the minorities. The treaties, moreover, had been imposed on some states and not on others; it would have been a discriminatory folly to recreate such a patchwork. The Western powers decided that it was far better to rely on the human rights clauses of the UN Charter and on the provisions of the peace treaties which incorporated the language of those clauses. Members of an ethnic minority would be entitled as individuals to certain human and political rights, but a minority group as such would have no collective right. It was a way of unhooking the question of minority protection from nationality conflicts and territorial disputes. Unfortunately, when it came to the test of practice, the Communist regimes which came to power in Central and Eastern Europe observed neither the national rights of ethnic minorities nor the human rights of the general body of their citizens.

How can we put in proper perspective this question of the Hungarians living beyond the borders of Hungary? If it is a festering sore, poisoning relations among the nations, what can be done about it? It is hard to deny the logic of a change in the frontiers whereby a substantial number of Hungarians could be reincorporated into Hungary without adding new minority groups to that country's population. At times some of the authors of this book seem to be pleading for that outcome. If we read only superficially, we may imagine ourselves back in the revisionist campaign of the interwar period, in which Hungarians, Czechoslovaks, Romanians, and Yugoslavs carried on their territorial disputes in the press and periodicals of the Western world. But there are significant differences. In the first place, the Western world has no prospect, in the foreseeable future, of playing any real role in these disputes, be it that of arbiter, judge, mediator, or interested party. Second, after two world wars it is clear that all nations will lose by endless agitation and reagitation over Europe's boundaries. A return to prewar revisionist propaganda would be pointless and senseless indeed.

This book is a combined effort by distinguished scholars (some in Hungary, but most of them in the West) to describe the historical origins of the problem, its changing shape over the years, and its present dimensions. This historical record would surely be written differently by authors from Czechoslovakia, the Soviet Union, Romania, or Yugoslavia. But the problem in its main lines is there, no matter what differences there may be in describing it. And new ways will have to be found to deal with it.

Today, the West is not the primary actor in this area. The Soviet Union is. But the Soviet Union has failed, both in ideology and in building its "socialist commonwealth," to cope with the problem. The Soviet leaders can contain "bourgeois nationalism" in its gross form by preventing their allies from attacking each other and from openly agitating for territorial change. They consider that to be necessary in order to maintain the solidarity of the bloc. Yet they have left each individual regime free to deal with national minorities as it sees fit. The regimes in Prague (more significantly, in Bratislava) and in Bucharest have seen fit to deal with them very harshly, in ways which do not differ from those of the past. Given the history of conflict among the nations of the region, that is not surprising. What is surprising—to some, anyway—is that the advent of Communist rule, under the aegis of a state that claims to have solved the "national question," has made so little difference. For minorities there is no court of appeal in Moscow.

A solution to the problem, or if that seems utopian, a start toward coping with it, can come only from steps toward reconciliation by the peoples themselves. If governments are incapable of it, then influence and action have to come from the peoples. As foresighted Hungarians (among them, the distinguished editor of this volume) have long seen, the Hungarian nation has no secure or promising future except through the reconciliation and cooperation of the area's peoples. One can argue about political forms and institutions, about what types of federation or confederation might work. The question is academic as long as an outside power has decisive power and makes the rules. Yet, a cultural and spiritual reconciliation can take place even under the hegemony of a foreign power. It is the only sound foundation for a shared political future combining national independence and free association.

Has the common experience of living under Communist rule and Soviet domination created that feeling of reconciliation and solidarity? There is no conclusive evidence that it has. Romanians and Hungarians in Transylvania have not reached deep understanding as the result of common dislike of the Russians or of living side by side under the tough Ceauşescu regime, which by its heavy stress on the themes of Romanian nationalism tends to keep them at odds. If by some miracle Soviet overlordship and Communist rule were suddenly removed, it is not likely that they would work together in harmony; they might well go back to fighting.

Nevertheless, we should not underestimate the possibilities of constructive change in this region where experience has nurtured both idealism and realism. We know that the USSR, while retaining ultimate control and the raw power to enforce it, has failed to impose its own order on Central and Eastern Europe. The regimes there are evolving uncertainly, each in a different way and at a different pace, all of them subject to instincts for self-preservation, to popular pressures for change, and to the facts of economics, as well as to the looming coercive power of the Soviet Union. Hungary has already undergone a transformation in which the regime, without changing its fundamental character, has partially come to terms with the people. Others may follow that pattern. In any event, the future of the region is unpredictable. Change is inevitable, and the peoples, as we have seen in Poland, will influence what form it takes.

They will gain if they can be mutually supportive. That is less likely, of course, if they are embittered by nationality conflicts. A vital question is whether the principle of self-determination can serve the end of reducing Soviet domination without at the same time leading to destructive conflict among the nations of the region. This is not just a theoretical question. The drama of Poland since 1980 has surely been watched with fascination by the other peoples of Central and Eastern Europe. The regimes, especially those dependent for their very existence on Moscow, have been properly scared, as was the case when Hungary erupted in 1956 and when Czechoslovakia tried to go her own way in 1968. But the peoples have not been unaware or indifferent. They are realistic enough to know that Soviet tolerance has its limits, but they have also seen the force which popular movements can generate and are aware of the pressure on governments to take account of such movements. National feeling, however, is often most strongly felt against neighbors, especially if they seem to be playing for their own national advantage.

This is the context in which I have read this volume about the

Hungarian nation and in which I recommend it to others. It should be read, above all, not as a brief for Hungarians subject to oppression or discrimination by other nations, not as a plea for revision of frontiers, but as an effort to expose a problem for all to see and to seek constructive solutions to it.

The West cannot do much about this problem now. The principal actors are the USSR, the Communist regimes, and the peoples of the region. What they do and what they refrain from doing will determine what happens. But the West cannot be indifferent. Western voices, official and unofficial, must speak out against the denial of human rights and of national identity and culture. Words will not change the facts of power, but words which strike a chord in the hearts and minds of those who are contending with the facts of power and creating conditions in which power is exercised may not be uttered in vain. Cultural ties between Western and Eastern Europe have survived the continent's political partition and continue to flourish. And economic crises beyond the curative powers of the existing regimes and of the Soviet Union may indeed bring the West into an unexpected and unprecedented position of influence. Whatever happens, we are well advised to take the long view, especially in these times when it is painfully clear that little can be done in the short term.

The concern of Hungarians, as of other peoples of the region, to preserve and protect their national culture is understandable and commendable. Only if the facts of the past and the present are known and recognized, and only if the need of mutual respect for national cultures is accepted, will there be a chance for these peoples to face and survive their present ordeal and to move forward, someday, into a brighter future.

✳ *PART ONE*

Historical Background

It has been found impossible to discover such lines, which would be at the same time just and practical. . . . obviously many of these difficulties would disappear if the boundaries were to be drawn with the purpose of separating not independent nations, but component portions of a federalized state. A reconsideration of the data from this aspect is desirable.

> The American Peace Commission to President Wilson on dividing Austria-Hungary into nation-states, 1918

The Saint-Germain, Versailles and subsequent treaties dictated by the victorious Entente powers, created a number of new small imperialist states. . . . These states were formed by the annexation of large territories with foreign populations and have become centres of national oppression and social reaction.

> "Resolution on National Question in Central Europe and Balkans," *The Communist International*, 1924

✳ 1

State- and Nation-building in Central Europe: The Origins of the Hungarian Problem

Stephen Borsody

L
ike the other older states of Europe, Hungary was founded during the great migrations of the Middle Ages. However, unlike the others, the Hungarian state was established by people who did not belong to any of the three principal linguistic families of Europeans—the Latin, Germanic, and Slavic. Arriving from Asia, the Magyar people who erected the Hungarian state in the ninth century were of Finno-Ugric stock. Among the Europeans, the Hungarians are related only to the Finns and Estonians by a common linguistic and anthropological heritage.[1]

The Magyar founders of Hungary arrived in Europe before "Europe" was formed. In fact, they took part in Europe's formation. Their Asiatic origin at that time was no handicap. But from the opening of the age of modern nationalism, that is, since the eighteenth century, the Hungarians' rival nations began to wish the Magyars "back to Asia."[2] And slurs denigrating the Hungarians as "barbarian intruders" are still to be heard from some "Europeans" at odds with their Hungarian neighbors.[3] The Hungarians do not think of themselves as Asiatics nor do they look different from other Europeans. In fact, their Asiatic Magyar forebears mixed fairly quickly and well with small scattered groups of people around them—mostly Slavs, but also a few remnants of some earlier visitors from Asia, mainly Avars. The Hungarians, however, never lost the language of their forebears, as did the Bulgarians, another people of Asiatic origin, who, after settling in the Balkans, became Slavic-speaking. If anything, the Magyars distinguished themselves, as successful state-builders usually do, by their ability to assimilate others. Originally, their numerical superiority in the land they conquered was also to their advantage. Today, however, most Hungarians are of mixed European rather than of original Magyar ancestry. It is their language and culture, as well as the collective sense of their history, that keeps them together.

After a series of savage raids in the tenth century on Western Europe—prompting their foes to associate the Magyars with the Huns—they settled down to constructive existence and nation-building on a European pattern. The medieval Hungarians built a state and a nation in the sparsely populated Carpathian Basin—no mean feat considering that no other people since the Romans had succeeded in creating a stable and lasting order in that part of Europe. Attaching themselves to the then rising and spreading Western civilization, the Hungarians accepted, around 1000 A.D., Christianity from Rome rather than from the Eastern center, Byzantium. Hungarian culture thus became distinctly Western, and during its formative stages Latin elements predominated.

The Kingdom of Hungary became one of the three distinguished members of medieval civilization in Central Europe, a peer of the Czech Kingdom of Bohemia-Moravia to the west and of the Kingdom of Poland to the north. However, geographic location, affecting political fortunes, pulled the three kingdoms in three different directions.

The medieval Czech Kingdom of Bohemia became part of the Holy Roman Empire, centered on latter-day Germany. Czech ambitions within the Empire achieved their highest fulfillment in the fourteenth century when Charles IV, a Czech king of the German Luxemburg family, became emperor of the Holy Roman Empire and Prague became the imperial capital. Medieval Czech good fortunes, however, did not continue into modern times. During the tumultuous age of the Reformation, the imperial throne (and the Czech crown as well) was already firmly in the hands of the Habsburgs, ardently Catholic and rabidly conservative. The Czechs, on the other hand, since the Hussite times of the fifteenth century, had been moving in the opposite direction toward reform and radicalism. The showdown between the two trends came when the Czech-German nobility of Bohemia rose against the Habsburgs, only to be defeated in the Battle of White Mountain in 1620. Under the restored Habsburg rule, guided by militant Catholicism, Germanization, and centralization, Bohemian-Moravian independence and the chances of Czech national statehood were extinguished for the next three hundred years.

Unlike Bohemia-Moravia, both Poland and Hungary successfully resisted the medieval pull of the Holy Roman Empire. Yet, due to the power of the Russian and Ottoman Empires, respectively, neither Poland nor Hungary escaped loss of national independence. Had Czechs, Hungarians, and Poles been united—some modern historians like to muse—they could have averted their respective national catastrophes.[4] Actually, toward the end of the Middle Ages, a loose personal union of the three kingdoms under the Polish-Lithuanian Jagiellonian dynasty did materialize briefly. But a union capable of averting the catastrophes of modern times was beyond the reach of these three leading Central European powers of sporadic glorious individual achievements.

All three of them, through the common religion that shaped their culture, belonged to Western civilization. But their individual fates were determined mainly by their geographical locations. Thus, medieval Bohemia-Moravia geopolitical destiny tied her, for better or worse, to her German neighbors. In the Polish case, Catholicism constituted an unbreakable Western tie. Yet its uncertain position on the crossroads between East and West prompted medieval Poland to turn eastward in search of power and security. She entered into a partnership with Lithuania, a grand duchy ruling over vast eastern Slav territories which, before the disastrous Mongolian invasion of the thirteenth century, belonged to Kievan Rus′. Through union with Lithuania, Poland became a great power of the European northeast. But Polish supremacy in that part of Europe lasted only as long as the Russians remained paralyzed by their misfortunes, brought upon them partly by Polish interference in their affairs. The animosity between Roman Catholic Poles and Orthodox Russians supplied the emotional fuel to their power struggle. It took several "times of trouble" before the Russian state, centered by that time on Moscow and brought under the rule of the Romanovs, made a spectacular come-back which turned out to be fatal for Poland. From the time of Peter the Great, tsarist Russia's power fast outstripped that of Poland. Internal instability added to Polish decline. By the end of the eighteenth century nothing was left of Poland's erstwhile greatness. Partitioned by her three powerful neighbors, Austria, Prussia, and Russia (the latter taking the largest part), Poland disappeared from the map of Europe, not to reappear until Russia's collapse and the Allied victory over Germany in World War I.

The medieval greatness of Hungary, too, eventually vanished. The Hungarian state achieved remarkable stability within the natural boundaries of the Carpathian Basin throughout the Middle Ages. Proof of its inner strength was its rapid recovery from the ravages of the thirteenth-century Mongolian invasion. In contrast to Hungarian stability were the unstable conditions in the neighboring Balkans where states rose and fell, and the Byzantine Empire continued its slow but steady decline toward demise. Lack of stability in the Balkans favored Hungary's fortunes for a while. Expanding southward, landlocked Hungary became an Adriatic power in the eleventh century when the Dalmatian coast of the Balkans came under its domination following Hungary's union with Croatia. A kingdom even older than the Hungarian, but much weaker by the eleventh century, Croatia remained constitutionally united under the Hungarian Crown until the end of World War I.

The pinnacle of Hungary's success as a medieval power was reached in the fourteenth century under King Louis the Great of the Anjou dynasty (a situation reminiscent of the Czech glory under another Western dynasty, the German Luxemburgs). Louis, the only Hungarian king called "great," actually was not the greatest of Hungarian kings. That distinction is usually accorded to Saint Stephen, who introduced Christianity to Hungary and is considered to be the founder of the Hungarian state, or to Mathias Corvinus, the popular native Renaissance king, who was remembered for his domestic achievements as "the just." Louis owed his exalted fame mainly to his foreign exploits. He added Poland's crown to the one he inherited from his father in Hungary. He also stood up for his family's dynastic rights as far south from Hungary as the Kingdom of Naples.

With the steady advance of the Ottoman Turks in the Balkans, the threat that ultimately ended Hungary's medieval independence came from the south, the same direction that had been for so long the scene of Hungarian triumphs. The common Moslem threat elicited some feeling of solidarity between Hungary and her Orthodox Christian Balkan neighbors, Slavs as well as Romanians (Vlachs, as they were known at that time). But Hungarian intervention was unable to save any of them from falling under Ottoman domination. In addition to defending their own Balkan dominions, the Magyars' warlike spirit against their distant Turkish relations was heightened by their medieval crusading conviction that the defense of Western Christendom was at stake. Ironically, in the heart of the West, the French were no longer fired by such medieval ambitions; they did not hesitate at the very height of the Ottoman threat to Europe to conclude a Turkish alliance against their Christian Habsburg rivals. And, for that matter, the Hungarians themselves were not uniformly committed to the defense of Western Christendom. At an early stage of the Turkish conflict there was a fairly significant peace party in Hungary which advocated accommodation with the Moslems. However, it was overpowered by the party of war and the ubiquitous papal intrigue, which traditionally played a prominent role in the councils of the Hungarian state.

Intermittently throughout the fifteenth century Hungary was at war with the Turks, often winning Christian acclaim but seldom military assistance. It looked for a while—at the time of János Hunyadi's famous victories—as if the Hungarian state would be strong enough to stem the westward tide of Ottoman power in Europe. However, when the Turks finally invaded Central Europe from their consolidated power base in the Balkans, the Kingdom of Hungary was in a pitiful state. Corruption and rivalry under weak kings prevailed at the top, while society at large was badly hurt when war preparations against the Turks turned, under György Dózsa's command, into a peasant uprising. The defeated peasants were cruelly punished and condemned to perpetual servitude, while the nobility rewarded itself through the legal provisions passed by the Diet and included in the *Tripartitum*, a work of codification of Hungarian law then in progress by István Verbőczy, a famous jurist of the time. As a result of this unfortunate coincidence, these punitive measures inflicted upon the great majority of the population served for centuries to come as a legal basis for narrowing down the very concept of the nation to the nobility. Indeed, Hungary had been humiliated by its own mean-spirited rulers even before it was defeated by the Turks in that disastrous battle at Mohács in 1526.

The Turks were stopped in their westward drive before they could capture Vienna, which was their Central European objective. For Hungary, however, the consequences of the Mohács defeat turned out to be catastrophic. The Hungarian state suffered severe blows from which it has never fully recovered. One of the immediate results of Mohács was Hungary's division into three parts. The Habsburgs took possession of the Hungarian Kingdom's western and northern parts. The central portion came under direct Turkish domination. Only Transylvania in the east, with some other territories west and north of it, remained in Hungarian hands (albeit under Ottoman suzerainty) to sustain the continuity of Hungarian independence.

Turkish rule lasted for a century and a half and it was followed by another one hundred and fifty years of Habsburg centralization attempts. The wars of conquest and reconquest devastated the ethnically most homogeneous Magyar heartland of multiethnic Hungary. The Magyars, enjoying comfortable ethnic majority before 1526, were reduced to a minority by the end of the eighteenth century. Apart from the enormous population losses in the Magyar heartland, two more reasons accounted for the diminution in relative numbers of Hungary's Magyar-speaking people. One was the natural increase of non-Magyars in the territories spared from the ravages of the Turkish wars; the other was the massive influx of foreign settlers after the expulsion of the Turks. The latter occurred partly as a spontaneous migration into underpopulated parts of Hungary from the Ottoman Balkans, but mainly as a planned policy of colonization by the Habsburgs. The dramatic shift, at the Hungarians' expense, in the ethnic composition of the Hungarian state led to the nineteenth-century nationality struggles which, if not the sole, were one of the principal causes of historic Hungary's demise.

Hungary's two neighbors, the Czech and Polish kingdoms, were also plagued by ethnic problems in the age of modern nationalism. But their efforts to regain their lost national independence took a different course from that of the Hungarians, and thus their multiethnicity resulted in different consequences. In 1867, Hungary made a seemingly profitable compromise with Austria, when the Hungarians' Habsburg-German archenemies had been weakened by defeats in wars against Italy and Prussia. With the Compromise (*Ausgleich*), the Austrian Empire became the dualist Austria-Hungary. With some limitations in matters of Austro-Hungarian "common affairs" (foreign and economic policy and national defense), dualist Hungary regained her national independence. But fifty years later, following Austria-Hungary's defeat in World War I, the Hungarians were punished as allies of the Germans, both of the Austrian and Prussian kind. Thus, when the twentieth-century reorganization came to pass according to the nationality principle, only Hungary's multiethnicity was judged a cause for partition in Central Europe. The kingdoms of the Czechs and Poles, no less mixed ethnically than the kingdom of the Hungarians, remained more or less recognizable on the map of Europe. New Czechoslovakia, as a matter of fact, became almost twice as large as the kingdom of the Czechs by the addition of Upper Hungary now called Slovakia. Historic Poland was greatly reduced but still contained large numbers of Ukrainians and Germans. Only Hungary was hacked up beyond recognition. The fall of the multinational Habsburg Monarchy sealed the fate of multinational Hungary as well.

The multinational Habsburg Monarchy tried to remain supranational in the age of modern nationalism. However, the Austro-Hungarian Compromise of 1867 became a turning point in the wrong direction when dualist Hungary turned into a nation-state. The Monarchy could not survive half national half supranational. Both the Habsburgs and the Hungarians failed miserably as modern federators of nations in Central Europe—and so have their successors since World War I. Yet the failure in the age of modern nationalism did not ruin altogether the Habsburg Monarchy's historical record. She has played a prominent role for centuries in the European balance of power, and she distinguished herself in both transmitting and generating Western culture among the peoples of Central and Southeastern Europe. Whether rulers or oppressed, all the Monarchy's nationalities benefitted to differing degrees from the common Habsburg heritage of a distinctly Central European brand of Western civilization. The benefits of the Monarchy's destruction, expected by the liberated nationalities, turned out to be of a much more questionable nature.

Of the two ruling nationalities, the Germans and Hungarians, hardest hit by the Monarchy's fall were the Hungarians. The Austrians lost an empire with a mixture of peoples of uncertain loyalties. The Hungarians lost their own country with many of their own people torn away from them by their neighbors. Hungary's partition following Austria-Hungary's defeat in World War I had taken place theoretically according to the principles of ethnicity and of national self-determination. In practice, however, these principles were not applied to the Hungarians. The fact of the matter is that historic Hungary's territory was up for grabs. Hungary's non-Magyar nationalities took whatever they pleased. Only their most absurd demands were rejected by the Western arbiters of this free-for-all, such as some Romanian territorial claims in eastern Hungary, and the Czech plan to connect newborn Czechoslovakia and Yugoslavia with a corridor across western Hungary.

The composition of the nation-states carved out from defeated Austria-Hungary duly reflected the double standard in applying national self-determination based on ethnic principles for the benefit of the victors. Defeated Austria and Hungary became ethnically almost homogeneous—96 and 90 percent respectively. But in Czechoslovakia, the Czechs, Slovaks, and Ruthenes—united in the hope of Slav solidarity—together amounted only to 69 percent of the total population. In Greater Romania—a composite new nation enlarged mainly by the annexation of multiethnic Transylvania—the Romanians made up only 72 percent of the population. In Yugoslavia—yet another untried fraternal Slav combination—the Serbs, Croats, and Slovenes together made up only 83 percent. (Incidentally, in all these states, the ethnic minorities claimed even larger percentages, arguing that official statistics favored the majorities.) In the case of restored Poland—not exactly a "successor" state, but treated with the same territorial generosity as Austria-Hungary's triumphant successors—boundaries were based broadly on historical rights and the population was ethnically only 69 percent Polish. And it should not be left unmentioned that Czech historical rights to the lands of the Bohemian-Moravian medieval kingdom (where one third of the population was German) was fully respected, whereas Hungarian historical claims were declared null and void.

As a result of this lopsided application of the celebrated Wilsonian principle of national self-determination, one-third of the Hungarians were divided among the three victorious neighboring states, newly formed or enlarged: Czechoslovakia, Romania, and Yugoslavia. The

Hungarian situation was further aggravated after World War II, when Subcarpathian Ruthenia, together with its Hungarians, was transferred from Czechoslovakia to the Soviet Union. From a nation divided into four after World War I, the Hungarians ended up after World War II as a nation divided into five parts.

After World War I, two European nations, the French and the English, with American assistance, presided over Hungary's partition. They showed no respect for Hungary's merits in Europe's history, nor for Hungarian rights according to modern principles of national self-determination. Their decision on Hungary, taken mostly under French pressure, reflected the emotional anti-Hungarian interpretations of the past and present, as propagated by Hungary's resentful Slavic neighbors, portraying the Hungarian state and nation as miscreations of European history. How did the Hungarians land in this hostile isolation?

Fundamentally, the Hungarian problem is intertwined with the peculiar general problems of state- and nation-building east of the Rhine. Farther east, in the belt of smaller nations from the Baltic to the Balkans, evolution of modern nations and states has been suppressed by the expansion of three empires—those of the Ottoman Turks in the Balkans, the Russian Romanovs in the Baltic region, and the German Habsburgs in Central Europe.

In the wake of the French Revolution and the Napoleonic wars, the ideas of modern nationalism penetrated this vast area of Central and Eastern Europe. The first crack in the old imperial order of this "unfinished part of Europe"[6] occurred in the Ottoman-dominated Balkans; hence the nineteenth-century term "Balkanization," a label for the breakup of empires into small nations, but also a derogatory term suggesting a breakup accompanied by ethnic rivalry and regional destabilization. "Balkanization" was a far cry from what the European champions of modern nationalism expected to happen. The liberated nations were supposed to be reunited under the banner of democratic equality.

The foremost prophet of modern European nationalism, the Italian Guiseppe Mazzini, was a champion of federal unions. His "Young Europe" plan envisioned regional democratic federations of nations—in Central Europe in particular.[7] But democratic federations have never materialized, either in Central Europe or elsewhere in the age of nationalism. As an international peacekeeping force, as Mazzini thought of it, nationalism has failed miserably. In retrospect, it even appears foolish that nationalism was ever thought of as possessing cosmopolitan qualities. As Edward Hallett Carr pointed out:

> [It was a puzzle] why the rugged individualism of nations would have been regarded as less self-assertive and menacing to peace than the rugged individualism of monarchs, why nations should have been expected to display the princely qualities of forebearance and sense of honour, but not the equally princely qualities of aggressiveness and greed, why nationalism should have been regarded as a stepping-stone to internationalism, and why, finally, it was rarely perceived that nationalism is not so much the apogee of individualism and of democracy as denial of them.[8]

Puzzling as it may seem, the age of nationalism did not quite extinguish the cosmopolitan ideal of European unity, handed down to the modern world from vague memories of universality under ancient Rome and medieval Christianity. Even Napoleon, who more than anyone else spread the nationalist idea across Europe, chose to pose as a universalist in exile, to foster the legend of himself as an apostle of a "United States of Europe."[9] And while sinking ever more deeply in the quagmire of nationalist rivalry, Europe of the nineteenth century hung on to the unifying dream of the "Concert of Europe." Even after the world wars of the twentieth century while shaping the world according to the nationality principle, the peacemakers went on believing in harmony among nation-states, first under the League of Nations and then under the United Nations.

To rationalize the failures of peace under nationalism, a distinction was invented in our time between good and bad nationalism. Of course, there is a world of difference between nineteenth-century humanist nationalism of Mazzini and the twentieth-century barbaric nationalism of Hitler, but distinguishing between good and bad does not resolve the problem at hand. In the peacemaking after World War I, in particular, dubious distinctions were drawn between the rival nationalisms of the defunct Habsburg Empire. The nationalism of the formerly oppressed was idealized, while that of the former oppressors was considered criminal. Exaggerated charges against Hungarians as oppressors of Hungary's non-Magyars, as well as allegations of a Hungarian menace to European peace on account of Austria-Hungary's alliance with Germany, served as prime justifications for the partition of the Hungarian state. This partition, in turn, resulted in the ethnic dismemberment of the Hungarian people, which has been the essence of the Hungarian problem ever since.

There was national oppression in Hungary in the age of modern nationalism, but it was neither of the kind nor duration that anti-Hungarian propaganda claimed. In fact, one of the main characteristics of Hungarian state-building had been the peaceful relationship among Hungary's different ethnic groups.

Turning into Europeanized Hungarians, the Magyars were builders of a state in the Carpathian Basin. Within that region, no rival ethnic state-building was attempted. Not even the catastrophe of the Turkish invasion, which split the medieval Hungarian Kingdom into three parts, altered the Hungarian political character of the Carpathian Basin. Although the northern and eastern parts of divided Hungary were the most ethnically mixed ones and were future strongholds of Romanian and Slovak separatism, in the sixteenth century, however, Slovaks of the north had no political consciousness to initiate separatist movements, while most of the Romanians in the east were not even living there at the time. Romanian ethnic preponderance in some parts of Hungary dates only from post-Turkish times and is due mainly to continuous migration from the Balkans.

During two centuries of Hungary's Turkish partition, the championing of the unity and continuity of the Hungarian state and nation could not unfold from the most homogeneously Hungarian part of the country, namely the Turkish-occupied central area. However, the champions of historic Hungary's continuity and indivisibility arose from the nonoccupied ethnically mixed western, northern, and eastern borderlands. In the west, the Habsburgs ruled as kings of Royal Hungary with Pozsony (Pressburg) as the Hungarian capital (renamed Bratislava, it became the capital of future Slovakia). In the east, Transylvania was an independent principality under local Hungarian rule, allied to the Turks against the Habsburgs. Both the Hungarians in Habsburg Hungary and the Hungarians in the Principality of Transylvania regarded themselves as legatees of Hungary's unity—the Transylvanians, in particular, as anointed heirs of Hungarian independence. Added to the Transylvanians' pride as champions of Hungarian liberty was their profession of religious freedoms. In fact, independent Transylvania had earned international recognition as an eastern outpost of European Protestantism and a pioneer of coexistence between Protestants and Catholics. In no sphere of life did the interests of Hungary's Magyars and non-Magyars clash yet.

Only after Hungary's liberation from the Turks and the restoration of the country's territorial integrity under Habsburg rule did the peaceful coexistence among Hungary's ethnic groups begin to break down—not because of Habsburg rule but as a result of the new spirit of the times. The process of ethnic disintegration began with ideas of modern nationalism spreading from the West to Central and Eastern Europe. Starting toward the end of the eighteenth century and accelerating throughout the nineteenth century, historic Hungary's nationality conflicts finally exploded in the twentieth century when they proved to be insoluble. These were the times, too, when the catastrophic consequences of the Turkish conquest of the sixteenth and seventeenth centuries were fully revealed. Gyula Szekfű, the prominent twentieth-century Hungarian historian, expressed it the most graphically—and also the most wistfully. Without the Turkish intervention, he wrote, Hungary, too, "could have entered the eighteenth century, like some of the other countries of Europe, as a nation of fifteen–twenty million . . . of which at least 80–90 percent could have been Magyar. . . . However, from the great people of European standing in the Middle Ages, the Hungarians have been reduced to the rank of a small people, similar to the Czechs, Serbs, Croats."[11]

The nationalist tone of Szekfű's description well reflects the spirit in which the Hungarians—to their undoing—met Hungary's nationality problems in the age of modern nationalism. They refused to recognize their own status of a small people. They avoided facing the fact that their fate is not only similar to, but common with, that of the Czechs, Serbs, and Croats, and the rest of Central Europe's small peoples. The Hungarians, of course, were not alone in violating the principle of national equality. Their neighbors turned out to be no better than they had been. The Hungarians simply found themselves sooner than the others did in a position to act the way nations usually do: without respect for the rights of others.

From the time that Western ideas of nation-state began to fire the imagination of the peoples of Europe's "unfinished part," everybody went to work correcting his nation's historical misfortunes. Since the eighteenth century, fables about the past have been planted in the minds of the smaller nations of Central and Southeastern Europe. This has resulted in mutually incompatible territorial aspirations. The Daco-Romanian theory about the origins of modern Romanians created an irreconcilable conflict with the Hungarians over the possession of Transylvania. The Slav conflict with the Hungarians came to be embedded in Romantic historical theories which challenged the very presence of the "Asiatic Magyars" on the sacred Slavic soil of Europe. The nineteenth-century Czech nationalist historian František Palacký bemoaned the Magyar invasion of the Danube region as the greatest tragedy of Slavdom. The Magyars, he believed, destroyed the Great Moravian Empire, they ruined Slavic unity by driving a wedge between the Western and Southern Slavs. But, even before Palacký, unfriendly views of German professors and philosophers putting down the "Asiatic Magyars" as an inferior race had found a lively response among the cultural elites of Hungary's ethnically awakening non-Magyar nationalities. Particularly pleasing to Slavic ears was the eighteenth-century Herderian prophecy about the great future of the Slavs and the inevitable doom of the Magyars.

Johann Gottfried von Herder's prophecy notwithstanding, the Magyars had one great advantage over their rivals in the age of modern national awakening. They were the only ones who had a state of their own. True, since the eighteenth century this Hungarian state of theirs was no longer theirs the way it was in the Middle Ages. Liberated from the Turks, Hungary was tied to Habsburg Austria. As kings of Hungary, the Habsburgs recognized the country's Diet as the representative body of the nation. And the nobility of the Diet prided itself on representing a "free kingdom." Yet, the Hungarians never reconciled themselves to the Habsburg curtailments of their independence. Nor did the Habsburgs forget the rebellious record of the Hungarians, in particular the wars the Transylvanian princes had fought against them. The last of these wars had ended only in 1711, resulting in the defeat and exile of Ferenc Rákóczi II, an ally of France against the Habsburgs during the War of Spanish Succession. Habsburg suspicion of Transylvania did not cease with the Peace of Szatmár that ended the Hungarian war against the Habsburgs in 1711. Transylvania had been placed under a separate Habsburg administration, partly for reasons of military security against the Turks, but no less as a measure of political security against the Hungarians. "Union" with Transylvania thus became one of the principal demands of Hungarian struggle against Vienna. But not until the Austro-Hungarian Compromise of 1867 did the Habsburgs finally relinquish their strategic foothold there.

Another factor, besides Habsburg centralizing tendencies, that curtailed Hungarian independent nationhood in post-Turkish times was the dramatic change in the ethnic composition of the Hungarian state. From the late medieval 80 percent majority, the Magyar ratio sank to an estimated 40 percent minority toward the end of the eighteenth century. Post-Turkish colonization schemes introduced by the Habsburg kings as well as uncontrolled massive population movements into depopulated areas accounted for the drastic ethnic shift to the detriment of the Magyars. Masses of Serbian and Croatian immigrants settled in the south of Hungary, changing the medieval ethnic boundary between Magyars and Southern Slavs. A no less substantial ethnic change was taking place in the east of Hungary in the wake of continuous Romanian immigration from Wallachia and Moldavia. According to some sources the so-called "Romanization" of Transylvania was the result of migration chiefly taking place as late as the eighteenth century.[12] And with the Habsburg domination came, of course, masses of German-speaking settlers, whose arrival added substantial numbers to the earlier Germans of medieval origin.

However, from a poor minority in the late eighteenth century, the ratio of the Magyar-speaking population in Hungary rose to a precarious 54 percent majority in 1910, the year of the last census prior to the collapse of the Hungarian state in the wake of defeat in World War I. Hungarian demographic success was an insult to the national sensitivities and aspirations of the non-Magyar nationalities of the Austro-Hungarian Monarchy. It has been seen by them as statistical proof of forcible Magyarization, an emotional issue which, to this day, defies any rational discussion between Hungarians and their neighbors.

In retrospect, of course, even the staunchest defender of the Hungarian cause must wish the Hungarians had embarked on a course different from blind chauvinism in their efforts to correct their historic misfortunes. The Hungarians made grave mistakes in trying to remake their multiethnic historical state into a unilingual modern nation-state on the West European model. There were abundant warning signs, reminding the Hungarians of their folly. But no warning was strong enough to divert the Hungarians from their single-minded nationalist goals. Not even the few Hungarians aware of the rising nationalist sentiments among Hungary's non-Magyars were willing to make sufficient concessions. And, as time went on, nothing less than recognition of national equality for all of its inhabitants could have saved historic Hungary from ethnic disintegration.

Lack of Hungarian sensitivity to the national rights of their non-Magyar-speaking countrymen was fostered by great gaps in national consciousness between Magyars and non-Magyars. The non-Magyars of Hungary only recently became affected by modern nationalist sentiments; the Magyars, by the virtue of their continuous statehood, in one form or another, needed no awakening although modern nationalism certainly contributed to national stirrings of a new kind by the beginning of the nineteenth century.

The Hungarian revolution of 1848–49 against Austria fully revealed both the superior power and the menacing weakness of the Hungarian national movement. Under Lajos Kossuth's leadership, the Hungarians were capable of staging a national uprising against Austria which nearly wrecked the Habsburg Empire. On the other hand, Hungary's non-Magyars turned against the liberal Hungarian revolutionary leadership and sided instead with reactionary Vienna. Nationalist feelings by that time were such that Austrian promises of special status for national groups were preferable to Hungarian liberalism which only belatedly acknowledged the national rights of the non-Magyars. Yet, in spite of an ensuing civil war within Hungary, the Hungarian war of independence was not quite hopeless. It was eventually crushed only with the help of tsarist Russia's intervention, Austria's faithful helper in keeping alive the reactionary legacy of the Holy Alliance. In the long run, Russia's intervention also heightened the Hungarians' fear of a Panslav danger. Panslavism in fact became one of the great obstacles to Slav-Magyar reconciliation in Central Europe. It filled the region's Slavs with exaggerated expectations and the non-Slav Magyars with exaggerated fears of the reactionary design to unite all Slavs into a great conservative commonwealth of nations under Holy Russia's imperial auspices.

Yet Hungary's defeat in 1849 did inject some element of realism into Hungarian political thinking. The successors of the fiery nationalist Kossuth in Hungarian politics were men of moderation. Kossuth himself began toying with plans for a Danubian federation with Hungary's Romanian and Serbian neighbors. But, as far as concessions went, neither Kossuth in exile nor the Hungarians at home, who concluded the Compromise (*Ausgleich*) of 1867 with Austria, were willing to go further than recognizing nationality rights in the context of individual civil rights. The territorial integrity of Hungary was not negotiable, not even with the most liberal of Hungarians, except one: Count László Teleki, a former exile and follower of Kossuth. But Teleki committed suicide.

Ferenc Deák and József Eötvös, architects of the Austro-Hungarian Compromise of 1867, went as far as any living Hungarians were ready to go at that time concerning Hungary's non-Magyars' nationality rights. The Nationalities Law of 1868 granted them individual language rights in matters of education, local administration, and justice. A separate compromise with Croatia (united with Hungary since the eleventh century) confirmed the autonomy of the Zagreb Diet. But the head (the "ban") of the autonomous administration of Croatia-Slavonia was appointed by the Hungarian government. The Croats also sent a delegation to the Hungarian parliament in Budapest. The Adriatic port city of Fiume (and the adjacent littoral) became a *corpus separatum* under the Hungarian crown, but Hungary made some territorial concessions in Lower Slavonia to Croatia in exchange.

The Nationalities Law of 1868 was quite an unusual act of generosity in contemporary nationalist Europe, when the idea of minority protection was generally shunned by the triumphant concept of the nation-state. Not even post-World War I Europe, committed to international protection of national minorities, went further than the Hungarian law of 1868 in granting individual language rights within the general framework of civil rights. On the other hand, neither prewar Hungary's non-Magyar nationalities nor the national minorities after World War I were satisfied with such concessions. They wanted national equality. They wanted collective rights. They wanted self-determination. They wanted territorial self-government.

Pre-World War I Hungary, instead of radically expanding the rights of the non-Magyars by granting them territorial autonomy, moved swiftly away even from the much smaller concessions of the Nationalities Law of 1868. The political passivity of the non-Magyars, as a protest against the inadequacy of the Nationalities Law, played into the hands of the Magyar opponents of the Law. Hungarian national restraint, incipient in the compromises of the 1860s, was soon over-powered by passions of nationalist narrowmindedness. From the 1870s, dualist Hungary embarked on an ambitious policy of Magyarization. This forcible drive toward assimilation (as distinguished from a spontaneous one) had no more than forty years to do real harm to Hungary's non-Magyars during the fifty years of Austria-Hungary's existence. But the relatively short period of national oppression was long enough for the oppressed to forget the centuries of Hungary's existence as their peaceful haven and even protector of their survival as modern nationalities. The Kingdom of Hungary in fact sheltered the national awakening of Romanians and Serbs at a time when their kinfolk in their Balkan homelands were still prostrate under Turkish domination. And without the shield of the Hungarian state two smaller Slavic people, the Slovaks and Subcarpathian Ruthenes, might have been absorbed by their stronger Slavic next of kin. Recent Czech and Ukrainian efforts to this effect are strong indications of such a likelihood. Yet, Hungary's former non-Magyar nationalities continue to view the Hungarian state solely in its role as an oppressor. Their historians and politicians have tarnished the record of the period of Hungary's ethnic peace that preceded the age of nationalism. To this very day, mythical beliefs in an alleged millennial Magyar crime of national oppression are among the foremost impediments frustrating the reconciliation between Hungarians and their neighbors.

Hungary's detractors gave an equally unfounded interpretation of Hungary's alliance with Germany in World War I. They turned it into another millennial crime, which was a truly outlandish distortion in view of the centuries of Magyar struggle against the Habsburg variety of German *Drang nach Osten*. True, in 1870, in collusion with Austria's Germans, the Hungarians torpedoed an Austro-Czech compromise plan, committing a tragic mistake, a senseless blow against the Danube region's chances to evolve into a federal union of nations. True, too, after 1878 dualist Austria-Hungary was an ally of Imperial Germany. Yet, against a few decades of Hungarian reliance on German power stood centuries of resistance: the Hungarian struggle against the dynastic imperialism of the German Habsburgs in Central Europe.[13]

To set the record of Hungarian state-building and nation-building straight, no other issue looms larger than the clarification of the much-maligned Hungarian policy of Magyarization. To speak of a "millennial oppression" of Hungary's non-Magyars, as Hungary's neighbors do, is utter nonsense. The Magyar founders of the Hungarian state in fact distinguished themselves by tolerance toward peoples of different languages and cultures. The roots of this tolerance, as some historians believe, may go back to the practices of Asiatic steppe people, like the Magyars, in leaving alone the social habits and fabrics of peoples they conquered. A no less commendable follow-up to this pagan liberalism was medieval Hungary's Christian policy of granting groups of peoples of non-Magyar tongues, whether natives or colonists, certain forms of "autonomy, headed by persons from their own ranks."[14] Spontaneous linguistic Magyarization has, of course, always taken place, since the Magyars have been recognized as builders and rulers of the Hungarian state. Similar assimilations had taken place everywhere else in Europe. Hungary was no exception to the rule.

Until the age of modern nationalism, only the Habsburgs tried to challenge the Magyar preponderance in the Kingdom of Hungary. But the Habsburg effort at Germanization in Hungary remained notably unsuccessful compared to similar efforts in other areas, particularly Bohemia-Moravia. The nobility in Hungary originally came from many ethnic groups but by modern times it was predominantly Hungarian-speaking despite Turkish dismemberment and subsequent Habsburg rule. Given the preponderance of Magyars within the ranks of the Hungarian nobility it is perhaps not surprising that when the demands of modern nationalism stirred up language conflicts, the ruling Hungarian nobility took it for granted that it was their birthright to make Hungary into a Magyar-speaking state and nation. The Magyar-speaking population enthusiastically followed suit. In fact, it was considered extremely unpopular for a Magyar to oppose Magyarization. Neophyte zeal of the recently assimilated Magyars, especially of Slovak and German origin, only fueled the flames of chauvinistic intolerance.

Magyarization in a way became too great a temptation following the Austro-Hungarian Compromise of 1867. After more than three centuries, the Magyars once again became masters of their own state. The Hungarian cause, though not fully triumphant in the eyes of Magyars yearning for independence from Austria, scored a great victory with the Compromise of 1867. The political moderation, evident in the 1860s, soon gave way to patriotic emotions embracing linguistic Magyarization as a sacred goal of national policy. The forcible Magyarization was launched under Kálmán Tisza's premiership. He introduced the 1879 Education Act which made the teaching of Magyar compulsory in state primary schools. Other measures to suppress the ethnic cultural and national aspirations of non-Magyars followed. A linguistically homogeneous Hungary was to be achieved through the system of education and administration. Whether this was an attainable goal is rather doubtful. The policy itself was cut short by Hungary's defeat in World War I. But the Magyar pressure seemed brutal enough to convince Hungary's nationally conscious non-Magyars that the policy of Magyarization threatened their people's linguistic survival. Only Croatia-Slavonia was spared the frenzy of Magyarization—though, with singular lack of wisdom, the Hungarian language was decreed mandatory on Croatian railroads in 1907, adding fuel to Hungary's worsening relations with the South Slavs.

Magyarization in Hungary became forcible, but the label does not fit all the facts to which it is applied. First of all, assimilation remained, as before, overwhelmingly spontaneous; if for no other reason than because there was not much opportunity to advance, above the village level, without knowledge of the Hungarian language. Spontaneous or forcible, Magyarization increased the number of Magyars, but it did not alter ethnic boundaries within Hungary. The towns may have been Magyarized, but in the countryside the territorial ethnic divisions remained basically the same as they had been for the last two centuries. Unlike Hungary's neighbors following Hungary's post-World War I partitions, the Hungarians never embarked on a policy of colonization in order to change the ethnic character of territories under their exclusive domination. Also, a closer look at the numerical results of assimilation during Hungary's dualist era may correct some of the misconceptions created by sweeping denunciations of Magyarization.

The increase in the number of Magyar-speaking inhabitants achieved by assimilation between 1850 and 1910 is put by recent research at two million. Well over half of this Magyarization, by all evidence, was spontaneous. The list of assimilated Magyars is led by Jews (700,000), whose enthusiasm to join the Magyar nation is best reflected in their outstanding contributions to Hungarian modernization in all aspects of life, both material and intellectual. The next largest group was Hungary's Germans, mostly scattered among Magyars in the central regions (500,000). Their assimilation, too, despite some anti-Hungarian Pan-Germanic agitation from Vienna, was spontaneous and smooth until Hitler's time. This leaves 800,000 newly assimilated Magyars belonging to ethnic groups whose nationally conscious elites opposed assimilation and fought Magyarization with ever growing determination. Resistance to Magyarization was strongest among the Romanians and South Slavs, weakest among the Slovaks. Between 1850 and 1910, an estimated 400,000 Slovaks became Magyar-speaking, but of Romanians and South Slavs, only 150,000 each. The remaining 100,000 newly assimilated Magyars belonged to the statistical "others"—among them the Magyarophile Ruthenes whose ethnically conscious national elite was even smaller than that of the Slovaks.[15]

This statistical mirror greatly reduces the alleged enormity of Magyar culpability for Magyarization, dramatized and exaggerated out of proportion by anti-Hungarian propaganda. It does not reduce, however, the seriousness of the nationality conflict as a whole. At least one third of Hungary's population (not counting Croatia) on the eve of World War I was potentially, if not actively, irredentist and separatist. Among them, broken down by nationalities, the Romanians represented 17 percent of Hungary's total population, the Slovaks 12 percent, and the other Slavs 5 percent. Thus, the potentially disloyal nationalities in pre-World War I Hungary represented about the same proportion of the country's population as did the disloyal Germans in post-World War II Czechoslovakia. After World War II these Bohemian and Moravian Germans were punished for their disloyalty by expulsion from Czechoslovakia. However, in Hungary, after World War I, the disloyal nationalities punished the Hungarians, which proves that circumstances indeed alter cases.

There were ugly aspects to Magyarization in pre-World War I Hungary which offended the non-Magyar people's human dignity: the haughtiness of the shallow "gentleman" class, the offensive harping on Hungarian cultural superiority. And there were several serious incidents which were shameful indeed, even without propagandistic exaggerations. On the other hand, as Hugh Seton-Watson has pointed out: "Judged by the methods of the mid-twentieth century, in Europe, or beyond, the forcible Magyarization of Kálmán Tisza and his successors was comparatively mild; yet in an age which was accustomed to humane standards in government, it was resented as unjust and brutal."[16]

The Hungarian ruling class bears grave responsibility for the chauvinistic nationalism which alienated the non-Magyar nationalities from the Hungarian state. Moreover, the fear of the alleged separatist tendencies of Hungary's non-Magyar inhabitants also affected Hungarian policy concerning the long overdue extension of suffrage which had been very narrowly defined in 1867. The great majority of the population, Magyars and non-Magyars alike, were deprived of a voice in political life. The parliament and the administration in general were run exclusively by the nobility and the "gentrified" upper-middle class.

The ruling classes, supported by Hungarian nationalist public opinion, opposed universal suffrage, arguing that it would strengthen the separatist-irredentist tendencies among the non-Magyar nationalities. Opposed to this reactionary-chauvinistic leadership, was the liberal-democratic and socialist-progressive school of thought. Its ideas were most memorably articulated by the sociologist-politician Oszkár Jászi. He maintained that, if there was a way to save historic Hungary from ethnic disintegration, it was through radical democratization.[17] In the best tradition of nineteenth-century Hungarian liberal thinkers—István Széchenyi and József Eötvös in particular—Jászi tried to alert his compatriots to the dangers of the nationality problem. His efforts, not unlike those of other farsighted Hungarians of his time, were entirely in vain. Yet, undaunted by the defeat of the Hungarian democratic revolution of 1918 (led by Jászi's disciple in nationality affairs, Count Mihály Károlyi), Oszkár Jászi remained, in his American exile, an untiring advocate of a democratic federalist Central European solution.

It may seem in retrospect as if any effort to save historic Hungary might have been doomed to failure. Yet Hungary was not a ramshackle state. (Austria-Hungary as a whole may have deserved to be called a "ramshackle empire," according to David Lloyd George's memorable epithet.) In the 1910 census 54 percent of Hungary's multiethnic population declared itself Magyar. But the percentage of loyalty to the Hungarian state was much higher. Forcible Magyarization did not significantly erode the sentiments of historical patriotism among Hungary's non-Magyars. Separatist irredenta sentiments were not widespread enough to threaten the Hungarian state with dissolution. In fact, it was Magyar success that angered the political elites of nationally conscious non-Magyars. And the Magyar failure to allay the anger of non-Magyars by timely compromise resulted in historical Hungary's demise only in combination with Austria-Hungary's defeat in World War I.

The peacemakers' solution to the nationality problems in the Danube region was the partition of Hungary and the establishment of either new or enlarged national states. Yet all these states continued to be plagued by nationality conflicts. A better solution would have been, as Jászi believed, a Hungary reorganized "on the model of Switzerland" within a federalized Central Europe which would have been "a better guarantee of democracy, of economic progress and of peace" than the new order of nation-states.[18] The new order was a work of vengeance. Yet faults and failures that initially triggered the vengeance do not account for the magnitude of injustice inflicted on Hungary following its defeat in World War I. To comprehend Hungary's territorial and ethnic partition, the brutality of war and its impact on wartime diplomacy as well as on the policy of peacemaking must be taken into consideration.

As the brutality of war in Europe intensified, the search for an ideal peace to justify the carnage increased apace. The Western democracies embraced the slogan that seemed to satisfy the wartime need: Liberation of the small and oppressed nations of Europe. They also found an exile from Austria-Hungary with extraordinary talent for articulating this slogan in an attractive peace plan which seemed satisfactory from both idealistic and pragmatic points of view. The man in exile was Tomáš G. Masaryk; the peace plan was called the "New Europe." Masaryk's success was proof of his extraordinary talents, but it also proved the tragic political aimlessness of the Western democracies in World War I. With considerable pride Masaryk recorded in his memoirs: ". . . we supplied the Allies with a political program. This is no exaggeration, as our friends from France, England and America admit. Nor did we give them only our program. We gave them programs for the liberation of other peoples and for the reconstruction of Europe as a whole."[19]

A compatriot of Masaryk, the Czech historian Otakar Odložilik, said of him: "Masaryk saw the principal enemy in the past."[20] This meant not just the Habsburgs, but perhaps even more the Hungarians. In fact, in the Danube region, the destruction of Hungary's historical statehood was the primary objective of the Masaryk plan. To Masaryk, a pupil of Palacký, the "meaning" of Czech history was the struggle with the Germans. A corollary of this philosophy of Czech history was the thesis that the Magyars were "invaders" who spoiled Slavic history. The plan Masaryk so successfully sold to his Western backers promised to make Europe safe against the Germans as well as their accomplices, the Magyars. It was to be achieved by liberating the Slavs, by creating a "Slavic barrier" of "buffer states" in Central and Eastern Europe. Poland, Czechoslovakia, Yugoslavia, and Romania—the latter an honorary member of the Slavic club on account of Romanian hostility to the Magyars—were to serve as pillars of this "Slavic bulwark" to which Masaryk had hoped eventually to add Russia as well.[21]

Strict adherence to facts is not in the nature of propaganda, least of all wartime propaganda. In his early wartime memoranda—written in 1915 for R. W. Seton-Watson who forwarded them to the British Foreign Office—Masaryk referred to "independent Bohemia" and "Greater Serbia" instead of "Czechoslovakia" and "Yugoslavia." The Slovaks he declared to be "Bohemians," Czechs, that is, eager for union with their brethren outside of Hungary. This might have come as a surprise to the Slovaks had they known of Masaryk's doings abroad on their behalf. According to Masaryk the Slovaks were also "for centuries the victims of the most brutal Magyarization,"[22] a notion which would have been news to the Magyars who themselves had been the victims of steady, and often brutal, oppression for centuries since the Mohács disaster in 1526. The Hungarian state itself was treated by Masaryk as something already non-existent. On his maps, accompanying his wartime memoranda, all that was reserved for the Magyars was an ethnic enclave smaller even than the future Trianon Hungary. While much of the success of Czech wartime propaganda was Masaryk's achievement, his junior partner, Edvard Beneš, far outdid Masaryk in denouncing the Hungarians as the source of all things evil in both the past and the present. Yet Beneš's eventual prominence in shaping Central European history was predicated on Masaryk's success. And Masaryk's success was also decisive in expediting the triumph of the Yugoslav and Romanian wartime plans.[23]

In the winter of 1917–1918, while the secret separate peace negotiations were going on between the Allies and Austria-Hungary, the "New Europe" plans were still in jeopardy. In his Fourteen Points address to Congress in January 1918, President Wilson still spoke only of the "freest opportunity of autonomous development" for the peoples of Austria-Hungary, to safeguard and assure their "place among the nations." This would have meant, in practical terms, federalization of Central Europe. But this was not what the Central European "New Europe" advocates had in mind. They wanted more than their ethnic due. They wanted nation-states built at the expense of their neighbors. They advocated territorial punishments for Germans and Hungarians, and territorial rewards for everybody else in Central Europe. The oppressed nationalities of Austria-Hungary, anticipating victory over their rivals in World War I, wished to do exactly what the Hungarians had been doing before the war: to build nation-states which would correct their real or presumed historical misfortunes.

Allied postwar plans merged with Masaryk's plans only in the last months of the war. It was a pragmatic move to serve Allied war interests without the historical-philosophical motivations that enthralled Masaryk's mind. The Allied decision to embrace officially the "New Europe" plan had a great deal to do with the loss of Russia as an ally following the Bolshevik Revolution in October 1917. The Slavic exiles from Austria-Hungary suddenly became more precious than ever before in the propaganda war against the Central Powers. They became, as Z. A. B. Zeman astutely observed, "a part of the great mobilization of forces that accompanied Russia's exit from the War."[24]

The "New Europe" plan became the peace settlement after World War I. By the time the victors of the war gathered in Paris to start the peace negotiations, sizeable Hungarian territories had been occupied by Hungary's neighbors in agreement with the Allied and Associated Powers. Some of these territories had been already promised to the smaller allies by the "gentlemen negotiators"[25] during the course of the war. The Magyars, the "invaders" of the ninth century, were defeated and the oppressed people, victims of a "millennial" Magyar yoke, were liberated. The survival of these poor victims was called a "miracle" by wartime propaganda. And while reminiscing over Hungary's punishment at the Paris Peace Conference, the British diplomat Harold Nicolson noted: "I confess that I regarded, and still regard, that Turanian tribe with acute distaste. Like their cousins the Turks, they had destroyed much and created nothing."[26] This Allied participant at the Paris Peace Conference did more than just express his unflattering opinion of the Hungarian people. He captured the biased political atmosphere of the international setting in which the historical Hungarian state met its death.

It would be far-fetched, of course, to suggest that Hungary and the "Asiatic" Hungarians were punished because of Western racist prejudice. But, as twentieth-century Europe knows only too well, racism and nationalism can engender similar emotions of hatred and prejudice.[27] And there is no denying that the Hungarian problem as we know it today has its origins in the national hatreds and nationalist prejudices of the world wars of our century.

Notes

1. In their own language, the Hungarians call themselves "Magyar," a designation used now in all languages to distinguish the Magyar and non-Magyar-speaking peoples of the historic kingdom of Hungary. In this volume, too, the term "Magyar" is being used for that particular purpose.

2. An influential English-language book by a Czech medievalist advanced the theory that the "invasion of the Magyars" destroyed the "bridge" built by the Moravian Empire between East and West. Unable "to take over the task of intermediaries and to transmit to the rest of Europe the treasures of Constantinople," the Magyars supposedly "severed" Western Europe from "its intellectual roots," thus delaying the rediscovery of antiquity that came with the Renaissance. See Francis Dvornik, *The Making of Central and Eastern Europe* (London, 1949), 183–84. Such views, smacking of twentieth-century nationalism, are similar to those advocated by František Palacký, Dvornik's nineteenth-century Czech compatriot. Palacký regarded the settlement of the Magyars in the Carpathian Basin as "the greatest misfortune" because it severed the Slavic North from the Slavic South. In addition, the Magyars separated the Czechs from the Slovaks who, supposedly, lived as "brethren" already at that time. Although sheer fantasy, these views, since World War I, have found wide acceptance in the West. See, for instance, R. W. Seton-Watson, *A History of the Czechs and Slovaks* (London, 1943), 15; Alfred Fichelle, "Le monde slave," in *Encyclopédie de la Pléiade: histoire universelle* (Paris, 1957), 2:1122. The Romanians have adjusted these anti-Hungarian Slav theories to their own nationalist fantasies, viewing the Hungarians as despoilers of "ancient Romanian soil of many millenia," in Ion Lăncrănjan's words, referring to Transylvania (see note 3 below). And some Soviet historians have become newcomers to interpretations of this sort by

inventing "ancient Slavic ties" between the Ukraine and Subcarpathian Ruthenia, following its Soviet annexation after World War II (see Annex II in Chapter 10, below).

3. Cf. Ion Lăncrănjan, *Cuvînt despre Transylvania* (Bucharest, 1982). See more on Lăncrănjan's book in Chapter 14, below.

4. For a detailed parallel history of the three Central European kingdoms deploring their disunity, see Oscar Halecki, *Borderlands of Western Civilization* (New York, 1952), in particular pp. 56, 126, 139, 147, 155, 201, and 222ff.

5. Cf. Hugh Seton-Watson, *Nations and States* (Boulder, Colo., 1977), chap. 4, "Europe: Multi-National Empires and New Nations."

6. The phrase "unfinished part of Europe," is Oszkár Jászi's; he used it in his pre-World War I writings in Hungarian.

7. Hans Kohn, *Prophets and Peoples* (New York, 1947), 93–94.

8. Edward Hallett Carr, *Nationalism and After* (London, 1945), 9.

9. H. Butterfield, *Napoleon* (New York, 1962), 117.

10. Slovak and Romanian historiographies treat the northern and eastern parts of Hungary primarily as scenes of their own national histories, playing down or even omitting the Hungarian presence. The Romanians in particular are fond of drawing farfetched nationalistic conclusions from Michael the Brave's brief appearance in Transylvania's history. Hugh Seton-Watson put the incident in its right place (*Nations and States,* 176): "For one year (1600–1601) Michael the Brave became ruler of Wallachia, Moldavia, and Transylvania at once. This was a result of international diplomacy and war, not of any national programme to unite the Orthodox people of Latin speech in one kingdom."

11. Gyula Szekfű, *Magyar történet* (Budapest, 1938), 3:498.

12. Oszkár Jászi, *A nemzeti államok kialakulása és a nemzetiségi kérdés* (Budapest, 1912), 367, 369–70. In support of his view on the controversial issue of eighteenth-century Romanian migrations, Jászi relies in part on a work by József Ajtay, *A magyarság fejlődése az utolsó 200 év alatt* (Budapest, 1905). Ajtay's credibility, Jászi points out, is enhanced by his use of Romanian sources (Ajtay, *A magyarság fejlődése,* 15). Estimates of Romanians migrating from Moldavia and Wallachia to Hungary in the first half of the eighteenth century range between a total of 350,000 and 500,000. Transylvania's estimated population alone before these migrations was 800,000 to 865,000, while that of Hungary's as a whole, according to the 1715–1720 conscriptions, was 2.5 million. Cf. László Makkai and Zoltán Szabó, eds., *Erdély története* (Budapest, 1986), 2:975–76. As for the estimates of the percentage of Magyars in Hungary toward the end of the eighteenth century: 29 percent is Jászi's figure (in *op. cit.* above), while 36–43 percent is a more recent one by István Szabó, *A magyarság életrajza* (Budapest, 1941), 230,

238. Today, Szabó's calculations are regarded as the more realistic ones. Cf. György Litván, Introduction to Jászi's *op. cit.,* an abridged edition (Budapest, 1986), 25–29. In view of these estimates, my choice of 40 percent seems a fair compromise.

13. Cf. Stephen Borsody, "Hungary in the Habsburg Monarchy: From Independence Struggle to Hegemony," in Steven B. Vardy and Agnes H. Vardy, eds., *Society in Change* (Boulder, Colo., 1983), 523–38.

14. Cf. Gyula Szekfű, *État et nation* (Paris, 1945), 111–17.

15. The figures on assimilation are quoted from László Katus, "Magyarok, nemzetiségek, a népszaporulat tükrében (1850–1910)," *História* 4:4/ 5 (1982): 18–21. It should be noted that the "Ruthenes" are called now "Transcarpathian Ukrainians." The name change occurred after World War II, when Czechoslovakia ceded to the Soviet Union the territory of "Subcarpathia," which she annexed from Hungary after World War I.

16. Seton-Watson, *Nations and States,* 164.

17. Oscar Jászi, *Revolution and Counter-Revolution in Hungary* (London, 1924), 38.

18. Ibid.

19. Thomas Garrigue Masaryk, *The Making of a State* (New York, 1927), 370. Great Britain and the United States seem to have been aware of the advantages of a federalist solution in Central Europe but the conviction was not strong enough to resist the wartime propaganda of the nation-state advocates, successfully conducted by the exiles from Austria-Hungary and by their Western supporters. See, in particular, D. Perman, *The Shaping of the Czechoslovak State* (Leiden, 1962), and Harry Hanak, *Great Britain and Austria-Hungary during the First World War* (London, 1962). Also, see note 11 in Chapter 16, below.

20. Otakar Odložilik, *Masaryk's Idea of Democracy* (New York, 1952), 12.

21. Cf. R. W. Seton-Watson, *Masaryk in England* (London, 1943), 109. (After World War II, Russia indeed became the head of a "Slavic bulwark" against German power in Europe, but neither in the democratic way Masaryk had anticipated nor in the spirit of Slavic brotherhood envisaged by President Edvard Beneš's wartime propaganda.)

22. Seton-Watson, *Masaryk in England,* 125–29.

23. Cf. Stephen Borsody, "Hungary's Road to Trianon: Propaganda and Peacemaking," in Béla K. Király et al., eds., *Essays on World War I: Total War and Peacemaking: A Case Study on Trianon* (New York, 1982), 23–28. For an exceptionally realistic recent view of Masaryk's and Beneš's work, as founders and builders of post-World War I Central Europe, see F. Gregory Campbell, "Empty Pedestals?," *Slavic Review* 44 (1985): 1–19.

24. Z. A. B. Zeman, *The Gentlemen Negotiators* (New York, 1971), 360.

25. The term "gentlemen negotiators" is Zeman's. A native of Central Europe, Professor Zeman wisely remarked: "None of the experts on whose advice the British Foreign Office drew pointed out that the national profile of the inhabitants in many parts of the Habsburg Empire was not as sharply defined as, say, that of the English and the French, and that, for better or worse, viable communities arose in central and eastern Europe out of the simple fact of people living in one place at the same time rather than because they belonged to one particular nation." Zeman, *The Gentlemen Negotiator,* 361. Some of the territorial dispositions made by the "gentlemen negotiators" caused consternation, but few of them have been corrected. The wartime territorial promises to Romania in particular were subject to criticism. R. W. Seton-Watson was filled with "horror" when he learned about them in 1916, and later described them as "scandalously immoderate." See Hugh Seton-Watson, "R. W. Seton-Watson and the Trianon Settlement," in Király, *Essays on World War I,* 7; and R. W. Seton-Watson, *A History of the Roumanians* (London, 1934), 490. After World War I, the Western democracies preferred to play down their own role in the creation of the successor states. They distanced themselves in particular from the shortcomings of the new order. The tone was set by Charles Seymour, regional specialist for Austria-Hungary in the "Inquiry," renamed the "Territorial Section of the Peace Conference," which provided President Wilson personally, and the American government in general, with information on Central Europe's nationality affairs. In his account of what really happened, he wrote: "The United States and Great Britain would have been glad to create a federation of the Danubian nationalities," however, "by virtue of the principle of self-determination it was for the nationalities to determine their own destiny." Charles Seymour, "The End of an Empire: Remnants of Austria-Hungary, " in Edward Mandel House and Charles Seymour, eds., *What Really Happened at Paris* (New York, 1921), 89–90. The Bohemian-born British historian, Harry Hanak, saw the role of Western intervention during the birth of "New Europe" differently: "The help that [Henry Wickham] Steed, [Robert William] Seton-Watson, [Charles] Sarolea, [A. Frederick] White, [Ronald M.] Burrows, and others gave to the non-German and the non-Magyar nationalities of the Dual Monarchy and the similar help afforded by groups of like-minded men in France, Italy, and the United States was invaluable. The Monarchy might have collapsed in any case. Yet . . . without the help of these friends neither a Czechoslovak nor a Yugoslav state need have risen from the ruins." Harry Hanak, *Great Britain and Austria-Hungary,* 279.

26. Harold Nicolson, *Peacemaking 1919* (London, 1933), 34.

27. Since World War I, the Hungarians are often called "Magyars" in the English language without derogatory implications. During World War I, however, in addition to distinguishing Hungary's Magyars from non-Magyars, the

word was used intentionally as a derogatory reference to the Hungarians as "Asiatics." "New Europe" propagandists, including Masaryk, emphatically used it in that sense. Incidentally, Masaryk's low opinion of the "Magyars" predated World War I. Around the turn of the century he wrote: "The cultural standards of the Magyar people are lower than those of the Slovaks; even today the Magyars have no literature of any significance." His bias apart, Masaryk belies his ignorance; the late dualist era was the time of a golden age in modern Hungarian literature. T. G. Masaryk, *Česká otázka* (Prague, 1894 and 1908), 55. During World War I, he repeated the same allegation. See his wartime pamphlet written in 1918, *Nová Evropa,* (published in Prague 1920), maintaining that the Hungarians are "culturally weaker" than the Slovaks (p. 160). Also, he referred to Germany's allies, the Hungarians and the Turks, as "Asiatics," (p. 176).

✳ 2

Peacemaking after World War I: The Western Democracies and the Hungarian Question

Zsuzsa L. Nagy

Austria and Hungary, the two component states of the Habsburg Monarchy, laid down their arms together on November 3, 1918. But they signed their peace treaties as independent states separately on different dates: Austria on September 10, 1919, and Hungary not until June 4, 1920. From November 1918 to June 1920, Hungary had been without internationally defined and recognized borders. Certain territories of the new Hungarian state—some still in dispute—remained under foreign occupation until the ratification of the peace treaty, and in a few cases almost a year longer. Between November 1918 and November 1919, the Allied Powers (or "the Entente," as the Western democracies were known to the Hungarians) found none of the successive Hungarian governments qualified enough to come to Paris and sign a treaty of peace. The Hungarian situation was unusually complex and it took the Peace Conference a long time to resolve it.

During the war against the Central Powers, Hungary figured prominently in the anti-German secret wartime agreements which ushered in the creation of a string of independent nation-states stretching from the Baltic to the Adriatic and Black seas. The postwar reorganization of Central and Eastern Europe according to the nationality principle, as interpreted by the Western democracies, could not be achieved merely by dissolving the dualist union of the Austro-Hungarian Monarchy. To carry out the Entente Powers' peace plans, it was necessary to break up the historical unity of the Hungarian state as well. Furthermore, following the Bolshevik Revolution in Russia, the Entente-created nation-states in Central and Eastern Europe were to assume a twofold function: on the one hand, they were to isolate Germany, forming a bulwark against Germany's eastward expansion, and, on the other, they were to isolate Soviet Russia in order to prevent Communist revolutions from spreading westward into Europe.[1]

Thus, it was not the Hungarian question as such that engrossed the attention of the Peace Conference for almost two years, but, rather, the way it affected the general postwar objectives of the Allied Powers. In the spring of 1919, Béla Kun, head of the Hungarian Communist republic, pretty accurately described the situation when he said that in Hungary, "the battles of two world currents have clashed . . . [those of] imperialist capitalism and Bolshevik socialism."[2]

The Habsburg Monarchy's military defeat swept Hungary's ruling regime away, thus clearing the way, on one hand, for the non-Magyars to secede and, on the other, for Hungary to embark on a program of democratization. In the fall of 1918, a bourgeois democratic revolution took place in Budapest, just as it did in Vienna and Prague. Count Mihály Károlyi formed a new Hungarian government with the support of the progressive bourgeoisie and intelligentsia. Although of outstandingly high quality, this government proved of limited appeal to the nation as a whole. Elsewhere in the Danube region, the nationalist factors helped the consolidation of new regimes (as in Czechoslovakia) or the strengthening of old ones (as in Romania). In Hungary, however, they played an entirely different role. The hostile policy of the Entente Powers, combined with the shock of the ensuing collapse of the historic Hungary, had unique and most unfortunate consequences. National grievances had been generated which, in turn, became the decisive factors affecting both the fall of the Hungarian bourgeois democracy and everything that followed from that collapse.

When the Peace Conference in Paris opened on January 18, 1919, the main territorial issues concerning Hungary's partition were no longer a matter for debate, only the exact demarcation of the lands promised to Hungary's neighbors had to be decided. In the secret treaty of August 18, 1915, Britain, France, and Russia had promised

Serbia the territories of Bosnia, Herzegovina, part of Dalmatia, Slavonia, and Croatia, as well as parts of historical Hungary inhabited
by southern Slavs or of mixed population, including the Banat.[3] Romania, too, after two years of negotiations, concluded a secret treaty
on August 17, 1916. In that treaty Britain, France, Russia, and Italy
had promised the Romanians Transylvania and additional territories
to the west, formerly known as the Partium, as well as the acquisition
of Bukovina and Dobrudja. The Banat, too, was assigned to Romania, leading to a bitter conflict later with Yugoslavia, a rival con-
tender for the same province.[4] The Czechoslovak emigrés led by T. G.
Masaryk and Edvard Beneš could not rely on secret agreements. But
when the Entente Powers in the last months of the war acknowledged
the Czechoslovaks as their allies, they conceded the Czechoslovak
right to independence "within the historical borders of their territories." This phrasing was highly inaccurate: Bohemia and Moravia constituted the historic lands of the Czechs but the Slovaks never had a
state of their own and hence had no historical borders. Slovakia was
to be carved out of Upper Hungary with borders yet to be determined.[5]

At the end of the war, the Great Powers intended to fulfill their
wartime promises only insofar as they were in accord with their interests under postwar circumstances.[6] Furthermore, various governments held different opinions of what those interests were, in
particular with reference to the Danube region. The resolution of
these differences was far from simple.

The United States did not join the Allied Powers until 1917, and
thus it had not been a signatory to the secret agreements. Although
President Woodrow Wilson's team of experts, the so-called Inquiry
in charge of postwar plans, endorsed the basic principles of the secret
agreements, the United States had neither economic nor political interests in the Danube region. That lack of vested interest, along with
President Wilson's own views, caused the American standpoint on
several questions to be fairly favorable toward the Hungarians, for
the American peace planning stressed primarily the ethnic principle
and the traditional economic relations within the region.[7] The head
of the British delegation, Lloyd George, agreed with President Wilson
on many points. The Foreign Office, however, had followed the traditional British policy of balance of power, striving primarily to prevent France from increasing her influence on the European continent.[8]

Among the Entente Powers, France's policy was the least flexible: it aimed at weakening Germany and her allies as much as possible. Opposed by the United States, and often restrained by Britain, France supported every claim against Hungary to the full.[9] Italy, meanwhile, would have liked to draw the Danube region into her own sphere of influence, but Italy's position was weak within the alliance system of the Entente Powers and Italian policy was less consistent in the Danube region than that of the French.[10]

Not surprisingly in light of the foregoing, the postwar Károlyi government focused its foreign policy on Wilson and on the Wilsonian principles of national self-determination. It should also be noted that although Soviet Russia withdrew from the Entente following the October Revolution of 1917 and took no part in the Paris Peace Conference, the existence and influence of Russia had a significant effect on the conference's work.[11]

The armistice agreement of November 3, 1918, laid down a demarcation line for Hungary that mainly corresponded to Italian interests. Accordingly, the only change in the borders of historical Hungary spelled out by the armistice agreement was the loss of Croatia, which even in dualist Hungary had enjoyed a separate status.[12] This demarcation line, however, was not to last long. On November 13, 1918, the Károlyi government signed a military convention with General Louis Franchet d'Esperey, the French commander of the Allied forces in the Balkans. The new agreement modified the earlier demarcation line in the south and the southeast to the advantage of the Romanians and the Yugoslavs. In the north, it brought about no changes in the existing situation since that area was beyond the Entente's immediate military interests.[13] Among the countries affected, however, only Hungary was ready to respect the new agreement.

On November 8, 1918, the Czechoslovak government ordered its troops to advance into Upper Hungary in order to claim "Slovakia" as its own. On December 3, 1918, Stéphen Pichon, the French foreign minister, obtained the belated consent of the Entente Powers to that move.[14] After a few minor battles, the Hungarians withdrew, upon which General Ferdinand Foch assented to a further advance of the Czechoslovak troops in accordance with Czechoslovak territorial claims. In December 1918 Károlyi was informed of the Czechoslovak-

Hungarian demarcation line, which largely coincided with the frontiers later endorsed by the Peace Treaty of Trianon.[15]

The Romanian government was most unhappy with the demarcation line established by the November armistice agreement: Romanian claims, based on the 1916 secret agreements with the Entente, were far more far-reaching. If honored the border between the two countries would have been at the Tisza River, in the heart of today's Hungary. In addition to Entente promises, Romania was also in possession of a declaration of union with Transylvania issued by self-appointed representatives of Transylvanian Romanians in case territorial claims based on secret wartime treaties were declared null and void. Already in December the Romanian forces, encouraged by Franchet d'Esperey, crossed the demarcation line and by February reached a line running through Máramarossziget (Sighet), Nagybánya (Bania Mare), Zilah (Zilau), and Csucsa, well beyond the historic boundaries of Transylvania. The Allies were forced to send French troops to Arad after bloody encounters took place there between Romanians and Hungarians.[16] And, since both Yugoslavs and Romanians claimed the Banat, armed conflicts also broke out between them, stopped only by the French.[17]

Following their advance, the Romanian and Czechoslovak forces took over public administration and began to integrate the occupied areas into their respective countries despite the explicit stipulation of the armistice agreement that administration would remain in Hungarian hands until the final decisions over the fate of these territories were determined by the peace conference. Hundreds of thousands of Hungarians, mainly administrators, clerks, teachers, and their families, fled to Budapest from the occupied territories, leaving all their possessions behind.[18]

As a result of both the international and domestic situation, Hungarian bourgeois democracy found itself in a catastrophic situation. The popularity of Károlyi and his administration was shaken. The hopes that democracy and Károlyi's Entente orientation would ensure an equitable and just treatment for Hungary at the hands of the victors quickly vanished. Needless to say, there was no chance whatsoever to implement the Danubian peace plans for an "Eastern Switzerland" advocated by Oszkár Jászi, leader of the Bourgeois Radical party and minister in charge of nationality affairs in Károlyi's cabinet. Any compromise with Hungary's non-Magyar nationalities at that late date became unattainable. The Károlyi government's federal peace plans were no match for the attractiveness of territorial annexations proposed by the Entente to the non-Magyars of the Danube region.[19]

With the Romanian and Czechoslovak occupations, defeated Hungary lost much of her food and raw material supplies. A further blow was Hungary's exclusion from the aid programs of the Supreme Economic Council and the American Relief Administration. By contrast, defeated Austria received considerable food relief and other supplies.[20] All these factors, according even to Allied reports,[21] tended to strengthen the extreme left. The Communist opposition to bourgeois democracy was daily engaged in fanning the flames of hatred against the rich and the victorious Western democracies. An instructive account of public feeling was given by the Social Democratic leader Dezső Bokányi: "We realized that the whole appeal [of President Wilson's Fourteen Points] had been a disappointment; it was quite fruitless to make harangues in favor of the English and the French. By then only the light of the Russian star was left."[22]

The Entente's hostile actions against Hungary continued relentlessly. They culminated, on March 20, 1919, in the notorious Vyx note ordering the formation of a so-called Hungarian-Romanian neutral zone whose western line bore a suspicious resemblance to the promised border of the 1916 secret agreement between Romania and the Allies.[23] Károlyi, supported unanimously by his government, was not prepared to concede further territories. The Károlyi government resigned and the Hungarian bourgeois democratic regime collapsed.

The situation in the spring of 1919 had two contradictory results. In the short run, it paved the way for the establishment of the Hungarian Soviet Republic which, with Béla Kun as its head, came to power without encountering any resistance. Indeed, it enjoyed the support of the most varied strata of Hungarian society, since the change in regime in itself signified a protest against the brutal policy of the Entente Powers. In the long run, however, the events of 1919 deepened and reinforced Hungarian conservative and nationalist sentiments. The grievances aroused by Hungary's humiliation were so strong that, following the fall of the Soviet Republic, the counter-revolutionary Horthy regime was able to make use of them in support of its antidemocratic, right-wing nationalist policy.

By the time the peacemakers in Paris began to deal with the Hungarian question, a fait accompli had been created in the Danube region, allowing no essential modifications in the peace conditions dictated by the victors. The losers had no opportunity to participate in preparing the peace treaties. Hungary's delegates were not permitted to take part in the negotiations. The Czechoslovak, Romanian, and Yugoslav peace delegations, on the other hand, were allowed to submit their demands and argue in favor of their acceptance. The territorial decisions were made in subcommittees, then submitted to the Central Territorial Committee under André Tardieu, and finally ratified by the Supreme Council.[24]

The most heated and frequent discussions developed over the Romanian territorial claims demanding full implementation of the 1916 secret wartime agreements.[25] Italian Prime Minister Vittorio Orlando and British Prime Minister Lloyd George questioned whether the inhabitants of Transylvania, Bukovina, Bessarabia, and the Banat really desired union with Romania. Doubt was also cast on the data on the ethnic composition of these territories. However, when Lloyd George raised the idea of a possible referendum, Romanian Prime Minister Ion Brațianŭ countered by saying: "Roumania had fought in order to impose her national will on the Hungarian minority in Transylvania. It was certain, therefore, that if the Hungarians were asked to vote in favor of union with Roumania, they could hardly be expected to do so."[26] American experts continued to argue strongly, though in vain, against some of the Romanian claims and proposed to leave a number of Hungarian towns—such as Szatmárnémeti (Satu Mare), Nagyvárad (Oradea), and Arad—in Hungarian hands.[27]

The Czechoslovaks aimed at setting their border along the Danube and then, going even deeper into Hungarian ethnic territory, along a line as far as Vác, Miskolc, and the Ung River. They were supported by the French and the British who sympathized with the Czech politicians Masaryk and Beneš far more than with the Romanian Brațianŭ.[28] However, the American delegation—and, eventually, Britain's Lloyd George too—expressed reservations and were more successful in influencing the outcome than in the case of Romania. As a result, Vác, Salgótarján, with the surrounding coal mines, and Miskolc, one of the centers of Hungarian heavy industry, as well as Sárospatak, Sátoraljaújhely, Tokaj, and Csap, remained in Hungarian hands. But, despite American opposition, the Csallóköz (a purely Hungarian island located between the Little Danube and the main Danube) was annexed by Czechoslovakia; and so was mostly Ruthenian-populated Subcarpathia which figured on the list of Romanian claims as well.[29] The Czechoslovak territorial demands against Hungary formed part of Prague's aspiration to fill the power vacuum in the Danube region and assume a leading role there among the small allies of the victorious powers.[30] For that reason Czechoslovakia also sought access to the Adriatic Sea through a swath of Austrian and Hungarian territory. This so-called corridor plan[31] was opposed by the Great Powers, and also by Yugoslavia.[32] But Beneš and his supporters did not give up the corridor plan easily, despite being told by an exhausted Harold Nicolson, the British representative on the commission: "Je vous en prie, n'en parlez pas. C'est une bêtise."[33] When the Peace Conference was trying to prepare a military attack on the Hungarian Soviet Republic in July 1919, Prague again requested the corridor as a price for her intervention.[34] As the Czechs saw it, the corridor was to surround Hungary completely by a ring of hostile countries territorially linked by common borders. Since a common border had already been established between Czechoslovakia and Romania, the corridor would have closed the ring by creating a common Czechoslovak-Yugoslav border, and cutting Hungary off from Austria.[35]

In connection with her claim for a leading role in the Danube region, Czechoslovakia also wanted to obtain the Těšin (Teschen) coal basin, coveted by Poland, and the coal mines in northern Hungary (Salgótarján).[36] Masaryk, although generally more moderate, supported Beneš in that instance since he too believed that coal would help exert political influence, not only on defeated Austria and Hungary but on Germany as well.[37] In all these matters it is not hard to discern the outlines of the future Little Entente already taking shape in the spring of 1919.

The drawing of borders between Hungary and Yugoslavia was accompanied by far fewer conflicts, and quite understandably so. Neither the size nor the political weight of the territories involved were comparable to those of Transylvania or Upper Hungary. Also, Belgrade was in a more difficult position than the other claimants against Hungary. (Yugoslavia's aspirations clashed with those of both Romania and Italy, since the Banat had earlier been promised to both Romania and Serbia. The Paris peacemakers eventually decided to partition it between Romania and Yugoslavia.) Yugoslavia would have liked to obtain the city of Pécs and the valuable coal mines nearby from Hungary. Although not awarded to her, both remained under Yugoslav occupation through the summer of 1921.[38] The drawing of the border between Austria and Hungary concerned two vanquished countries. Despite conflicting claims, there were no heated debates.[39] The Austro-Hungarian border question concerned the so-called Burgenland. Austria was eager to get the whole of it, inhabited as it was, more or less, by a German-speaking population. The Peace Conference showed sympathy toward Austria, eager as the Entente Powers were to prevent Austria from slipping, in a state of frustration, from bourgeois democracy into a dictatorship of the proletariat as Hungary did. Nevertheless, the Austrian territorial demands were only partially fulfilled by the Peace Conference. Moreover, after the signing of the Austrian peace treaty, the city of Sopron and its surroundings, by virtue of a referendum, remained in Hungary—this being the only instance when old Hungary's new borders were decided by a popular vote.

A few further examples may illustrate the flimsy ways Hungarian territorial issues were handled by the Peace Conference. The decisions were all based on expediency, paying little or no attention to ethnic principles, let alone to the wishes of the populations involved. Thus, in western Transdanubia certain territories (Szentgotthárd, Csorna, and a few other towns and their surroundings), were awarded to Hungary as compensation in part for her territorial losses elsewhere such as the Csallóköz, and the city of Kassa (Košice) which had been awarded to Czechoslovakia. Since Pozsony (Pressburg), too, was annexed by Czechoslovakia (despite Italian opposition), Szeged in southern Hungary remained Hungarian (even though Romania also claimed it).

On May 8, 1919, with the peacemakers' work finished, Hungary's borders were fixed.[41] They were based on the unilateral decisions of the victors and were arrived at mainly in consideration of the victors' economic and strategic interests. States were thus created in a way that allowed territorial aggrandizements by overriding the ethnic principle entirely. The populations concerned were given no opportunity to exercise their right to national self-determination by voting in a referendum. In Hungary's case, the principles of President Wilson's Fourteen Points were wholly ignored.[42]

Among the countries formed in the Danube region as a result of the peace treaties, only two, Austria and Hungary, could be considered national states in the sense that they had no significant national minorities. The result of territorial gains by Czechoslovakia, Romania, and Yugoslavia, on the other hand, was the creation of large national minorities, which became the source of serious postwar problems and tensions in Central Europe.[43] To make matters worse, the various nationalities were at different levels of historical development, with different traditions, and belonging to different cultural and religious spheres—in some cases, the national minorities stood at a higher level of development than the majority nations now ruling over them. Thus, the main postwar concern of the new multinational states was to unify themselves economically, socially, and culturally—a process that was slow, and has still not ended.

The peacemakers were not entirely unaware of the dangers inherent in the new situation their decisions had created. Lloyd George pointed out as early as the end of March 1919 that the decisions they had taken laid the foundations for a German-Hungarian-Bulgarian-Turkish alliance to work for the revision of the peace treaties.[44] Also, President Wilson proposed that separate provisions aimed at protecting the national minorities be included in the peace treaties. Dubbed the Minority Treaty, these provisions were meant to ensure that the national minorities should enjoy equal citizenship rights with the ruling nations.[45]

In reality, the idea of the Minority Treaty was met with repugnance by the ruling majority nations. Among the Danubian states the most vehement opposition came from the Romanian government. Brǎtianǔ refused to sign it, claiming that it constituted interference in Romania's internal affairs. The Romanian government's opposition to any international protection of minority rights led to several months' delay in completing the work of the peacemakers. Efforts to induce Romania to sign the Minority Treaty prompted the Supreme Council to award Bessarabia to Romania.[46] (In deciding this territorial issue in Romania's favor, Romanian help in defeating the Hungarian Soviet Republic had also scored points in the eyes of the peacemakers.[47]) The storm over the Minority Treaty brought to the surface the problem of Romanian Jews. As late as 1919, they still did not enjoy equal citizenship rights, and the Romanian government remained reluctant to grant them those rights.[48]

Signing the Minority Treaty in itself was no guarantee that its provisions would be carried out. Once the treaties were ratified, the Great Powers showed no concern with the matter. For years, the complaints lodged by the Hungarian government at the League of Nations concerning the legitimate grievances of the Hungarian minorities in the neighboring countries were treated as if they were merely propaganda moves of irredentist Hungarian policy.

Between March and August of 1919, the Hungarian question had also figured on the Peace Conference's agenda in a different context from that of debates on boundaries. The establishment of the Hungarian Soviet Republic, in protest against the conditions of peace, had brought a Soviet-type regime into Central Europe. The Great Powers were worried lest the Hungarian example was to be followed by defeated Austria and Germany. Even victorious Czechoslovakia, Romania, and Yugoslavia might not escape the consequences of such a turn of events.[49] If proletarian revolutions were to sweep across Europe, as predicted by Lenin, the whole peace plan of the victors would be ruined.

It was this concern with spreading Bolshevism that singled out Hungary for the particular attention of the Great Powers. Actually, only after the Hungarian Communist success did the Entente begin to pay serious attention to the situation in Hungary. Some Entente diplomats and experts proposed instant armed intervention to overthrow Béla Kun's government. But the idea was discarded, mainly because of the adverse experience with a policy of intervention in Soviet Russia.[50] Instead, in the early days of April, the Entente sent the South African General Jan Christian Smuts to Budapest to study the Hungarian situation. The aim of the Smuts mission was to negotiate with Béla Kun in order to reach an agreement on a new demarcation line more favorable to Hungary than the one outlined in the Vyx note of March 20, 1919, which toppled the Károlyi government.[51]

This was a significant peace move, at a time when the French Balkan Army Command had planned a campaign against Hungary in concurrence with Prague and Bucharest and had even set a date for the attack. The Smuts mission in fact delayed Romania's and Czechoslovakia's troop movements against the Hungarian Soviet Republic.[52] The anti-Bolshevism of both countries was motivated mainly by their eagerness to obtain more Hungarian territory than had been awarded to them so far at the Peace Conference.

There are many facts that contradict the view, often advanced between the two world wars, that Hungary's becoming a Soviet republic led the Peace Conference to make decisions detrimental to Hungary's interests. Had that been the case, the victors would have satisfied all the claims of their small allies in Central Europe, then and there, in line with the promises of wartime agreements and other propositions. But the Peace Conference did not do that. Prague was not awarded the notorious corridor, nor the Salgótarján-Miskolc industrial area; Bucharest failed to obtain the area beyond the Tisza River as far as Debrecen; Belgrade was not allowed to have Pécs and the adjacent coalfields.

Nor was there any connection, as claimed, between the territorial decisions and the refusal of the Peace Conference to invite the Kun government. The issue of invitation had come up several times in the Supreme Council: April 25, April 30, and May 1. President Wilson, in particular, was in favor of it. The invitations to the German and Austrian governments had not been questioned, and Wilson believed that every defeated country should be treated equally. However, the French government thought of using the invitation issue as a means of hastening the collapse of the Communist Kun regime.

Contrary to expectations, in May 1919, when Czechoslovak and Romanian troops began military operations against the Hungarians, the Kun government did not collapse. Meanwhile, since the Peace Conference in Paris was busy with disagreements over Italian claims, and since the head of the French mission in Vienna, Henri Allizé, was in charge of delivering the invitation to the Hungarian government, the French were able to withhold the invitation without any difficulty.[53] The whole matter of inviting the Hungarians did not resurface on the agenda of the Peace Conference until the end of 1919. By that time, the Soviet Republic had indeed collapsed. In May, however, the Kun government not only survived the crisis precipitated by the Czechoslovak and Romanian attacks, but—after the Hungarian army had been reorganized—a counterattack was launched on the Czechoslovak front. In northeastern Slovakia, advancing through Kassa (Košice), Eperjes (Prešov), and Bártfa (Bardejov), the Hungarian Red Army reached Hungary's historic frontiers. The aim of the Hungarian counterattack was to establish contact with Soviet Russia and then turn against the Romanian army which had advanced deep into Hungary as far as the Tisza River.[54]

The Hungarian military successes caused considerable anxiety in Paris. The Great Powers had reckoned with a rapid defeat of the Soviet Republic following the Czechoslovak and Romanian attacks. In a heated debate and mutual recriminations over the Hungarian issue, the British and the Americans blamed French importunity, while the diplomats blamed the narrow-minded aggressiveness of the military. At this point, an ultimatum by French Prime Minister Georges Clémenceau concerning territorial decisions prompted the Hungarian Red Army to withdraw.[55] In fact, on June 13, 1919, all interested parties received a note from the Supreme Council of the Peace Conference defining Hungary's new boundaries and calling on the governments in Budapest, Prague, and Bucharest to withdraw their troops behind those borders.[56]

The impact and consequences of the Supreme Council note differed from country to country. Czechoslovakia received it with satisfaction, since it halted the Hungarian army's advance into Slovakia. In Hungary, the Kun government complied with the note and evacuated the territories seized in May and June,[57] but the note came as a catastrophic shock to the Hungarians for that was the moment when it became definitely known that Hungary was to lose not only territories inhabited by non-Magyar nationalities or mixed populations but also areas where the population was exclusively Magyar-speaking. Until then, Hungary's situation was seen to be in a state of postwar chaos. Now, it became clear that Hungary had to reckon with a radically reduced national territory which was considered insufficient even for the construction of an independent national economy.[58] (Among the economists holding this view was Jenő Varga, who later became an internationally respected economist as an exile in the Soviet Union.)

The withdrawal of its troops scuttled all the Hungarian efforts to consolidate the home front. Growing demoralization undermined the Soviet Republic and narrowed the basis of its initial popular support. To further aggravate the situation, the Romanian government and its peace delegation in Paris reacted to the Supreme Council's note with defiance. As if they were hearing of the Hungarian-Romanian border decision for the first time, the Romanians refused to accept it. In Paris, Brațianŭ protested dramatically and resigned as prime minister. The Romanian government crisis staged by Brațianŭ served to postpone Romanian fulfillment of the terms of the note. The Peace Conference was officially informed by Bucharest that Romania refused to withdraw her troops and would continue to occupy Hungarian territories east of the Tisza River.[59]

The Kun government decided to force Romania to comply with the decision of the Supreme Council, but the July Hungarian offensive collapsed in a matter of days.[60] Meanwhile, the Czechoslovak army advanced again to the Salgótarján-Miskolc line and kept the area under occupation for several months. The Romanian troops eventually occupied not only the entire area east of the Tisza River as far as Tokaj in the north but also Budapest, the Hungarian capital. These were the circumstances under which the Kun government resigned. The Soviet Republic collapsed while the counterrevolutionary forces were waiting in the wings. They managed to establish themselves in power with the help of the armed forces of Admiral Miklós Horthy, who later was elected head of the Hungarian state.

Only in January 1920 was the Hungarian peace delegation able to set out to present the Hungarian case at the Paris Peace Conference. The counterrevolutionary regime under Horthy's regency had been legalized by the Allied Powers, with the assistance of Sir George Clerk, the British head of the Allied mission to Budapest.[61] The Hungarian delegation was led by Count Albert Apponyi and one of its members was Count István Bethlen, who later, as prime minister, consolidated the Horthy regime[62] Of course, there was no way in which the Hungarian peace delegation could reject the borders, which had already been fixed, even though they found them unjust and would have liked to keep historical Hungary intact. Apponyi put forward ethnic, economic, and cultural arguments against the new borders and proposed that the status of certain territories should be decided by referendum, but the Peace Conference resorted to a referendum only in quite exceptional cases. A comprehensive referendum in Hungary's case was out of the question since it would certainly have challenged the Great Powers' decisions and upset the status quo.

By 1920, the main points of the territorial decisions taken a year earlier were fundamentally unalterable. Even minor changes made under the label of readjusting the frontiers were mostly at Hungary's expense. By this point the United States took no part in the dealings of the Peace Conference, having withdrawn its delegation following the completion of the Treaty of Versailles dealing with Germany.

One of the last items on the agenda of the Peace Conference was the Budapest government's response to the draft of the peace treaty. Lloyd George favored some readjustments in Hungary's favor. He believed that the inclusion of three million Hungarians within the territories of the new or enlarged countries surrounding Hungary was indefensible. Lloyd George was supported by the new Italian prime minister, Francesco S. Nitti.[63] However, Alexandre Millerand, the French prime minister, and his foreign minister, Philippe Berthelot, were firmly opposed to any change in Hungary's favor. Extremely heated debates ensued,[64] yet to renegotiate the Hungarian issue and hold referendums, as the Hungarian delegation requested, was entirely out of the question. In any case, the British Foreign Office, as it had done before, turned against its own prime minister concerning the Hungarian question. Meanwhile, Yugoslavia, Czechoslovakia, and, most vehemently of all, Romania protested in joint memorandum against any possible alterations and, in particular, against any referendum.[65]

On June 4, 1920, the Peace Treaty with Hungary was signed in the Trianon Palace at Versailles. Ágost Benárd, minister of welfare and labor relations, and Ambassador Alfréd Drasche-Lázár were the Hungarian signatories. On July 31, 1921, the Hungarian National Assembly enacted the Trianon Treaty as Act 1921:XXXIII of Hungary's historic Corpus Iuris. The so-called Millerand cover letter, attached to the Peace Treaty as a result of British insistence,[66] referred all further Hungarian complaints to the League of Nations. The Hungarian state had lost more than seventy percent of its former territory, while one-third of the Hungarian people were assigned to live outside Hungary's new borders as minorities.

Hungarian despair over the territorial decisions of the Peace Conference was boundless due to the harsh treatment meted out in Paris. Yet, some victors were still not satisfied. Despite achieving the dream of a Greater Romania, Bucharest gave the impression of being aggrieved and held the British responsible for not achieving more. Bratianŭ thought, as recorded by Sir Eyre Crowe, that the British delegation was moved by "the most intense hostility to Roumanian claims," and that British policy was mainly affected by "considerations of international and Jewish finance."[67] Czechoslovakia's Beneš had his own grievances. He felt that "too much" had to be conceded in fixing the southern borders of Slovakia.[68] Among the victors of the Danube region, only Yugoslavia voiced no official complaints about the borders with Hungary. But even Belgrade made several attempts at acquiring parts of Baranya county and the city of Pécs which the Yugoslav troops refused to evacuate until 1921.

The peacemakers, to be sure, did not create new states by force alone or out of thin air. Their creation reflected the meeting of two historical currents: emergence of modern nationalism among the intellectual elite of the minorities, on the one hand, and the wartime policy of the Western democracies, on the other. The Entente Powers thus gave their full support to the national aspirations of their small allies in the Danube region.[69]

Bourgeois capitalist development in the Danube region had been stepped up in the last third of the nineteenth century. Economic, social, and political modernization had taken place within the framework of the Habsburg Monarchy. Although the levels of development in various parts of the Empire prevented the various nationalities from enjoying the modernization in equal measure, each of them had shared in it to a greater or lesser extent. There had been a marked acceleration both in the social development of national minorities and in their awakening to national and political consciousness. But the general structure of the Austro-Hungarian Monarchy and, in particular, the dual system of government, were not capable of making the necessary adjustments to satisfy the demands for fundamental change. The Monarchy proved incapable of providing a flexible framework within which its people might assert their national aspirations.

In Western Europe, the process toward bourgeois nationalism and the formation of independent nation-states was an accomplished fact before World War I. By 1918 the nation-state became the objective of the majority of the nations in the Danube region. A force for internal disruption of such strength had arisen within the Habsburg Monarchy that it became a prime cause of Austria-Hungary's dissolution. A federalist reorganization of the Danube region, such as Oszkár Jászi and others had devised, was the program of a small opposition pitted against the ruling powers. It could only have been put into practice had the opposition in time won a victory over their adversaries. In the autumn of 1918, when the Habsburg Monarchy collapsed, events had outstripped the reform plans of the democratic federalists.

National tensions in the Habsburg Monarchy were accompanied by social tensions that were unavoidable concomitants of a fast and dynamic capitalist development. Social and class contradictions were bound up with national contradictions and could easily be interpreted and explained as part of the latter. At any rate, the transformation of the Danube region within the framework of the Versailles peace system could lead only to further tensions and conflicts. The new order not only worsened interstate relations, but spoiled the political and intellectual climate of the entire region, thus engendering all kinds of vicious forms of nationalism. Ultimately, it paved the way to a situation in which Hitler's Germany was able to set the successor states of the defunct Habsburg Empire against one another and subdue them all.

The post-World War I Danubian transformation was not the product of an organic internal development. It occurred through the intervention of vast external forces. Between the Austro-Hungarian Compromise of 1867 and the breakup of the Habsburg Empire in 1918, a peculiar cycle of history was completed. Neither the birth of Austria-Hungary in 1867 nor its demise in 1918 had been the work of internal forces alone. In 1867, the Dual Monarchy was born in the wake of a Central European explosion precipitated by the Hohenzollern Prussian triumph over Habsburg Austria. In 1918, the Habsburg Monarchy was shattered to pieces by forces of an all-European explosion. A violent transformation had taken place from which eventually no one emerged unscathed.

Notes

1. Arno J. Mayer, *Politics and Diplomacy of Peacemaking: Containment and Counterrevolution at Versailles, 1918–1919* (New York, 1969), 183, 286, 343, 596–97; United States, State Department, *Papers Relating to the Foreign Relations of the United States: The Paris Peace Conference* (henceforth cited as *FRUS PPC*), 13 vols. (Washington, D.C., 1942–47), 3:581–83.

2. "A Munkás és Katonatanács történelmi űlése," *Népszava*, April 20, 1919.

3. Ivo J. Lederer, *Yugoslavia at the Paris Peace Conference* (New Haven,

1963), 12ff.; David Lloyd George, *The Truth about the Peace Treaties* (London, 1938), 1:39.

4. H. W. V. Temperley, *A History of the Peace Conference of Paris* (London, 1921), 4:516–17; Sherman David Spector, *Rumania at the Paris Peace Conference: A Study of the Diplomacy of Ion I. C. Brațianŭ* (New York, 1962), 35–37.

5. Piotr S. Wandycz, *France and Her Eastern Allies 1919–1925* (Minneapolis, 1962), 10, 14–15; Felix John Vondracek, *The Foreign Policy of Czechoslovakia, 1918–1935* (New York, 1937), 24ff.

6. Wandycz, *France and Her Eastern Allies,* 22–23; Spector, *Rumania,* 37; *FRUS PPC,* 2:376–77.

7. *FRUS PPC,* 1:34, 41, 85; B. H. Williams, *The Economic Foreign Policy of the United States* (New York, 1929), 159; Victor S. Mamatey, *The United States and East Central Europe, 1914–1918: A Study in Wilsonian Diplomacy and Propaganda* (Princeton, 1957).

8. J. Hugh Edwards, *David Lloyd George* (London, 1930), 2:564; *Political and Strategic Interests of the United Kingdom: An Outline* (Oxford, 1939), 9, 24, 73; Jacques Chastenet, *Les années d'illusions 1918–1931* (Paris, 1960), 41.

9. André Tardieu, *La Paix* (Paris, 1921), 426–27; Chastenet, *Les années d'illusions,* 40–41; Wandycz, *France and Her Eastern Allies.*

10. M. H. Macartney and P. Cremona, *Italy's Foreign and Colonial Policy 1914–1937* (London, 1938), 121, 196, 198, 208–9; C. A. Macartney, *Hungary and Her Successors: The Treaty of Trianon and Its Consequences, 1917–1937* (London, 1937), 316.

11. See Louis Fischer, *The Soviets in World Affairs: A History of the Relations between the Soviet Union and the Rest of the World, 1917–1929* (Princeton, 1951), 1:157; Williams, *The Economic Foreign Policy of the United States,* 157.

12. Temperley, *A History of the Peace Conference,* 4:121ff.; Alfred D. Low, *The Soviet Hungarian Republic and the Paris Peace Conference* (Philadelphia, 1963), 13; Tibor Hajdu, *Az 1918-as magyarországi polgári demokratikus forradalom* (Budapest, 1968), 121–24.

13. Hajdu, *Az 1918-as magyarországi polgári demokratikus forradalom,* 125–28. Michael Károlyi, *Faith without Illusions* (London, 1956), 132–33; Low, *The Soviet Hungarian Republic,* 13–15.

14. Hungary, Külügyminisztérium, *The Hungarian Peace Negotiations* (Budapest, 1920–22), 1:383–84; Wandycz, *France and Her Eastern Allies,* 62.

15. *The Hungarian Peace Negotiations,* 1:384; Hajdu, *Az 1918-as magyarországi polgári demokratikus forradalom,* 133–34, 161–62.

16. József Breit, *A magyarországi 1918–1919. évi forradalmi mozgalmak és a vörös háború története* (Budapest, 1925), 1:133; Lederer, *Yugoslavia,* 97ff.

17. Hajdu, *Az 1918-as magyarországi polgári demokratikus forradalom*, 131, 161–63; Pál Schönwald, *A magyarországi 1918–1919-es polgári demokratikus forradalom állam és jogtörténeti kérdései* (Budapest, 1969), 62.

18. Oszkár Jászi, *Magyarország jövője és a Dunai Egyesült Államok* (Budapest, 1918); Oszkár Jászi, *Magyar kálvária, magyar feltámadás* (Vienna, 1920).

19. Zsuzsa L. Nagy, *A párizsi békekonferencia és Magyarország, 1918–1919* (Budapest, 1965), 43–46; Suda Lorena Bane and Ralph Haswell Lutz, eds., *Organization of American Relief in Europe 1918–1919* (Stanford, Calif., 1943), 12–13, 50–53, 177; Zsuzsa L. Nagy, "Az antant segélyprogramja és az 1918–1919. évi forradalmak," *Párttörténeti Közlemények* 9 (1963): 48ff.

20. *FRUS PPC*, 12:232–35, 373–74.

21. Nagy, *A párizsi békekonferencia*, 26.

22. Ibid., 74–77; *FRUS PPC*, 4:59–60, 145–47, 157–59.

23. Jules Laroche, (*Ambassadeur de France: Au Quai d'Orsay avec Briand et Poincaré 1913–1926* [Paris, 1967]) gives a full account about the activity of the territorial committee.

24. *FRUS PPC*, 3:840ff.

25. Ibid., 849.

26. Spector, *Rumania*, 103–8.

27. *FRUS PPC*, 3:877–83; Wandycz, *France and Her Eastern Allies*, 56–57.

28. *FRUS PPC*, 3:883–87; 9:748ff; Francis Deák and Dezső Újváry, eds., *Papers and Documents Relating to the Foreign Relations of Hungary* (Budapest, 1939), 1:165–66.

29. See Vondracek, *The Foreign Policy of Czechoslovakia*, 147–48, 181–82.

30. Ibid., 31ff.; Elisabeth de Weiss, "Dispute for the Burgenland in 1919," *Journal of Central European Affairs*, 2 (1943); *FRUS PPC*, 3:877; 12:275.

31. Lederer, *Yugoslavia*, 107; *FRUS PPC*, 12:275.

32. Harold Nicolson, *Peacemaking 1919* (London, 1933), 273.

33. Wandycz, *France and Her Eastern Allies*, 65, 69, 72.

34. *FRUS PPC*, 12:403–4.

35. *FRUS PPC*, 4:286–87.

36. Wandycz, *France and Her Eastern Allies*, 92–93.

37. *FRUS PPC*, 3:822ff; Lederer, *Yugoslavia*, 117ff.

38. Mrs. Sándor Gábor, *Ausztria és a Magyarországi Tanácsköztársaság* (Budapest, 1969), 46ff., 131ff.; Katalin G. Soós, *A nyugat-magyarországi kérdés, 1918–1919* (Budapest, 1959).

39. Deák and Újváry, eds., *Papers and Documents*, 1:165–66; Wandycz, *France and Her Eastern Allies*, 53.

40. *FRUS PPC,* 4:505–7, 814–17.

41. Gyula Juhász, *Magyarország külpolitikája, 1919–1945,* 2d ed. (Budapest, 1975),

C. A. Macartney and Allan Palmer, *Independent Eastern Europe: A History* (New York, 1966), 4; Hugh Seton-Watson, *Eastern Europe between the Wars 1918–1941* (Cambridge, 1946), chap. 7.

42. *FRUS PPC,* 4:363, 414–15; David Hunter Miller, *My Diary at the Conference of Paris* (New York, 1924–26), 15:367ff.

43. Lederer, *Yugoslavia,* 239; Spector, *Rumania,* 206; László Rehák, *A kisebbségek Jugoszláviában* (Novi Sad, 1967), part 1.

44. *FRUS PPC,* 3:391ff.; Spector, *Rumania,* 140ff.; Lederer, *Yugoslavia,* 242ff.; Great Britain, Foreign Office, *Documents on British Foreign Policy, 1910–1939,* 1st ser. (London, 1947–60), 6:74–75, 323.

45. *FRUS PPC,* 8:552; 9:330–31, 537–40, 915–17.

46. *FRUS PPC* 9:351ff., 537–40.

47. Mayer, *Politics and Diplomacy,* 566, 578, 584–86; Ellis A. Bartlett, *The Tragedy of Central Europe* (London, 1923), 65. Chastenet, *Les années d'illusions,* 13.

48. *FRUS PPC,* 12:282, 285, 287–88, 291; Low, *The Soviet Hungarian Republic,* 174; Mayer, *Politics and Diplomacy,* 577f.

49. Nagy, *A párizsi békekonferencia,* chap. 4; Mayer, *Politics and Diplomacy,* 726ff.; Low, *The Soviet Hungarian Republic,* 50–56.

50. Mayer, *Politics and Diplomacy,* 734–35; Tibor Hajdu, *A Magyarországi Tanácsköztársaság* (Budapest, 1969), 76–80, 144ff.

51. *FRUS PPC,* 5:368–69, 392–93, 406; 12:455–56, 494.

52. See Ervin Liptai, *A Magyar Vöröshadsereg harcai, 1919* (Budapest, 1960).

53. Nagy, *A párizsi békekonferencia,* chap. 7.

54. *FRUS PPC,* 6:284ff., 351–52, 399, 411–16.

55. *FRUS PPC,* 4:811.

56. See Kun's statement and the note of the Hungarian government to the Paris Peace Conference, in *A magyar munkásmozgalom történetének válogatott dokumentumai* (Budapest, 1959), 6/B:151, 246.

57. *FRUS PPC,* 4:804ff., 814–15; Spector, *Rumania,* 152; *Documents on British Foreign Policy,* 6:82.

58. Hajdu, *A Magyarországi Tanácsköztársaság,* 322ff.

59. György Ránki, "Adatok a Clerk-misszió történetéhez," *Történelmi Szemle* 10 (1967): 156–87.

60. Juhász, *Magyarország külpolitikája,* chaps. 1 and 3; *The Hungarian Peace Negotiations,* 1:165ff., *FRUS PPC,* 9:872–84.

61. *Documents on British Foreign Policy,* 7:284, 384, 387–89.

62. Ibid., 384–85.
63. Ibid., 440–44.
64. Ibid., 448–49.
65. Ibid., 6:371.
66. *FRUS PPC*, 3:105–6.
67. Documents on British Foreign Policy, 6:371.
68. *FRUS PPC*, 3:105-106.
69. Jászi's complaint of "the diplomatists of the Entente supporting Hungary's rivals was not unfounded. He wrote:"(had they) offered a tithe of this goodwill and support to the democratic and pacifist government of Károlyi, the disaster which befell our unfortunate country could have been avoided." Oscar Jászi, <u>Revolution and Counter-Revolution in Hungary</u> (London, 1924), 155. For the culmination of that "disaster", see Eva S. Balogh, "Romanian and Allied Involvement in the Hungarian coup d'état of 1919", <u>East European Quarterly</u>, IX, 3.

✳ 3

Hungarian Foreign Policy, 1918–1945

Eva S. Balogh

Whether one accepts or rejects the view that revision of the Treaty of Trianon was the *sine qua non* of the nation's "survival and independent existence,"[1] the fact remains that revisionism was the cornerstone of Hungary's interwar foreign policy. Successive governments preached the gospel of revisionism to anyone who would listen, repeating its message so often and with such fervor that many Westerners soon became convinced that "the Hungarian people were not quite sane on that subject."[2]

The zeal with which Hungary promoted the cause of revisionism was commensurate with the difficulty of the undertaking. István Bethlen, who as prime minister laid the foundation of Hungarian interwar foreign policy, did not exaggerate when he claimed that although "this nation had gone through many catastrophes, never in her history did she face such a formidable task as the question of revision."[3] The obstacles in the way of revising the Treaty of Trianon were enormous: the opposition of those who had benefited from the reorganization of Central Europe in 1919, the Great Powers' antagonism toward or lack of sympathy for the Hungarian demands, and Hungary's insignificance in economic, military, and diplomatic terms. Without a general territorial reshuffle of the whole region between Germany and Russia, Hungarian revisionism did not have the slightest chance of success.

As peace began to give way to war by the late 1930s, revisionism became a more realistic goal. The obstacles which had formerly blocked Hungary's revisionist path were no longer insurmountable, and the futile rhetoric of the past could now be replaced with diplomatic maneuvering. Hungarian policymakers took full advantage of the new situation. Spurred on by early diplomatic triumphs, they relentlessly pursued their revisionist aims. Nonetheless, the result was total failure; after World War II the victorious Allies reimposed the same borders (with one minor change, and that to Hungary's detriment) which had been so odious to her after World War I and which she had tried to change for more than two decades.

What were the diplomatic underpinnings of this revisionist foreign policy? A good summary of them appeared in the 1938 spring issue of the *Hungarian Quarterly,* the English-language publication of Bethlen and his circle. György Ottlik, a diplomat, writer on international relations, and a member of the periodical's editorial board, recalled in an article that "after the war, there existed in Hungary two political orientations. One desired to establish friendly relations with her neighbours endeavouring to strike a bargain with each of them in the hope of getting some territory back from one or other of the Successor States. The other theory tried to remove Hungary from her isolation and to get the backing of one of the Great Powers."[4] From the Károlyi regime to the different cabinets of Regent Miklós Horthy, Hungarian governments experimented with both.

It has been customary to date Hungarian revisionist policy either from the the actual signing of the Treaty of Trianon in June 1920[5] or from the post-Soviet period beginning in August 1919.[6] Prior to that time, the argument goes, the democratic regime of Mihály Károlyi was striving for peaceful coexistence with its new neighbors, while the pro-Soviet Kun regime put its faith in proletarian internationalism, paying little attention to national borders. It was only the reactionary, counterrevolutionary Horthy regime which first embarked on a sinister and eventually destructive revisionist course. Such an interpretation has been influenced by political considerations and a view of history which would like to draw a sharp division between the periods before and after the demise of the Hungarian Soviet Republic. But it is almost a commonplace to state that ideology concerning domestic matters has little to do with foreign policy which, in the final analysis, is determined by geopolitical considerations and national self-interest. In the case of Hungary the losses inflicted by the peacemakers on her were so enormous that Hungarian foreign policy became, more or less, predetermined from the moment the first foreign troops crossed the demarcation lines. From semi-fascists to Communists, all Hungarians were of the same mind: the Treaty of Trianon had to be revised. Some might have been satisfied with a less drastic revision of the borders than others, but the Hungarian population as a whole fully supported the policy of revision all through the interwar period.

Initially, Károlyi's foreign policy was enthusiastically pro-Entente; in fact, his popularity rested on his promise that an immediate change from a pro-German to a pro-Entente foreign policy accompanied by "domestic reform," as Károlyi called the "realization of the aspirations of the national minorities,"[7] would lead to an independent, democratic, and federated Hungarian republic, within the thousand-year-old borders of the Kingdom of Hungary.[8] However naive the Károlyi regime's trust in the country's former enemies appears today, at the time it seemed a promising course to follow. After all, who knew exactly what "self-determination of nations" meant? For Károlyi, one of the leaders of the Party of Independence, it could certainly mean the independence of Hungary from Austria, which the majority of Hungarians wanted. As for the country's nationalities, Károlyi and his followers hoped, Wilson's formula would mean recourse to plebiscites in order to ascertain the wishes of Hungary's non-Hungarian inhabitants. One ought not to fault Károlyi or Oszkár Jászi, his minister of nationalities, for trying this course, but one can be more critical in assessing the Károlyi regime's responses to the rapidly unfolding world of reality.

Following the armistice there were immediate signs that Károlyi's initial foreign policy assumptions were unrealistic. In his memoirs Károlyi spends several pages recalling the frustration of his government in the face of repeated violations of the Belgrade Military Convention duly signed by the representative of the Allied and Associated Powers. Ironically, the victorious small allies of the Entente in the Danube region seemed to have trusted the peacemakers a great deal less than the defeated Hungarians did. Although they were assured of a sympathetic hearing and they knew that they would receive sizeable territories at the expense of Hungary, they did not know to what extent their maximum demands would be met. To be on the safe side, all three neighbors, with or without Allied blessing, launched military action against Hungary in order to be in possession of territories they coveted by the time the peace conference began its deliberations. Most of these requests for military operation were received sympathetically by the Allied foreign ministries but, even if they had not been, it is hard to see what the peacemakers could have done to prevent this onslaught short of sending troops to protect the former enemy against their own allies.

The failure of Károlyi's initial policy formulations based on the benevolence of the Entente Powers became evident within a few weeks, but the Károlyi government was unable to resort to the only course which was open to it: military defense of the demarcation lines agreed upon by the two parties at the Belgrade Military Convention. However, one needs an army for defense and there was no Hungarian army to speak of by December 1918. While Hungary's neighbors were arming to the hilt, the Budapest government disarmed and sent the returning troops home, ostensibly for internal security reasons.[9] One also suspects that Károlyi, who had been the chief critic of the war since at least 1916, paid minimal attention to army affairs. At least the selection of his minister of military affairs indicates that much. Although the new prime minister had picked his future cabinet months before he took power, he had no one in mind for the post. And when the selection was made it was a most unfortunate one. It is hard to imagine a minister of military affairs and a soldier by training who would announce that he did "not want to see any more soldiers!" Although he departed in disgrace, his successors were no better in bringing order to the general chaos which reigned in the ministry throughout the period. Admittedly, an energetic organization of a new army would not have been an easy task, but as the improvised fighting units of Hungary's neighbors, and, following the Károlyi regime's collapse, the achievements of the Hungarian Red Army amply demonstrated, it would not have been an impossibility.[10] With an army behind it, Károlyi's government would have been able to do more than receive notes from the Allies. Under the circumstances, however, the Berinkey-Károlyi government had no choice but to resign in March.

As for the general thrust of the Károlyi government's ideas on foreign policy, later Károlyi claimed that, if he had been in power after the signing of the peace treaty, his foreign policy would have consisted of good relations with the Allies as well as with the successor states. Given the complexities of the postwar relationships among the Great Powers themselves, the delicate bonds between the successor states and the Great Powers, and the tangled antagonisms among the successor states, this utterance cannot be taken at face value. No one can say with certainty what would have happened had Károlyi stayed in power. One thing, however, is certain: no Hungarian government could survive without seeking "justice for Hungary." After Károlyi's fall, this was exactly what endeared Béla Kun's regime to the Hungarian people.

Fundamentally, Kun's frame of mind was not very different from that of Károlyi. Although by different means, both of them were committed to saving Hungary from its neighbors. Whereas Károlyi had abiding faith in the Entente, Kun believed just as ardently in the outbreak of a world revolution. If the world revolution Kun was hoping for had engulfed Central Europe, a federal reorganization of the former Habsburg Monarchy might have solved Hungary's nationality problems on the Soviet-Russian model. Lenin in fact urged Austria-Hungary's nationalities to unite in support of world revolution and transform the Danubian Empire into a peoples' union of soviets. This did not happen but Kun, as Lenin's disciple, tried to make it happen—and by doing so, he drew the Entente's serious attention to the Hungarian problem, something Károlyi was unable to do. Károlyi later complained bitterly that Kun had been treated better by the Entente than he had been. Indeed, while the pro-Entente Károlyi had met only with rebuffs, the Bolshevik Kun was to receive the Entente's emissary, General Jan Smuts. Of course, Kun had also shown a kind of strength which the Entente could not ignore. He demonstrated that a Hungarian army could be recruited to challenge the territorial transgressions of Hungary's rapacious neighbors, the allies of the Entente. Eventually, Kun lost his nerve and agreed to withdraw his hard-pressed Red Army from territories it had occupied in a spectacular offensive in Northern Hungary. He relied on the Entente promise of Romanian withdrawal from the Tisza River, which turned out to be empty. The Romanians overran the Hungarian Red Army and the Hungarian Soviet Republic collapsed under circumstances similar to those surrounding the fall of the Károlyi regime—in a vain effort to bring "justice to Hungary."

Following the fall of Kun's Soviet Republic, the Entente eventually recognized a government which was actually its own creation.[11] During this early phase of the post-Soviet period one cannot speak of a Hungarian foreign policy in the accepted sense of the term. In foreign affairs the regime returned to the Károlyi mold of impotence. The country signed the humiliating Treaty of Trianon in an utterly helpless state. This, however, did not prevent accusations that Hungary was a threat to the status quo. The protagonist of this allegation was Edvard Beneš, Czechoslovakia's foreign minister. Even before the signing of the peace treaty, he launched an encirclement policy against Hungary which eventually resulted in the formation of the Little Entente.

Beneš seemed to have acted more from weakness than from strength. During the summer of 1919 the Hungarian Red Army had torn Czechoslovakia apart. Entente military circles began to doubt the military viability of the new Czechoslovakia. Moreover, Entente diplomatic observers were certain that Slovakia was "ripe for revolution" as a result of the Slovaks' disenchantment with the new Czech order. It was reported that the Slovaks wanted to form an "autonomous state connected with Hungary."[12] In fact, one leading Slovak politician, Andrej Hlinka, was in jail while another, František Jedlička, was in Budapest negotiating with the Hungarians concerning Slovak autonomy.[13] Moreover, news leaked out that the French foreign ministry was conducting secret negotiations with the Hungarians indicating a change of heart in some French circles. All these sounded ominous to Beneš who felt more and more that Czechoslovakia could not rely solely on the Great Powers.

As early as September 1919, Beneš approached the Yugoslav foreign minister, Ante Trumbić, in Paris with the idea of a defensive alliance against Hungary.[14] After being turned down by the Yugoslavs, Beneš sold his idea to Austria's Socialist chancellor, Karl Renner. They signed an agreement in January 1920, and both of them urged the Romanians to adhere to it but were rebuffed.[15] Meanwhile, Hungary made diplomatic moves to counteract Beneš's endeavors. In December 1919, Budapest approached Prague with the idea of a commercial treaty, but the Czechs were not interested.[16] A Hungarian offer of alliance to Yugoslavia was also rejected.[17] Attempts for a political agreement between Romania and Hungary has also failed.[18]

From the Czechoslovak point of view the most upsetting among these unfavorable developments was the episode of an attempted rapprochement between France and Hungary in late 1919 and early 1920. This strange interlude in postwar French diplomacy was the work of Maurice Paléologue, secretary general of the French Ministry of Foreign Affairs. It was intertwined with the French *cordon sanitaire* plans against Soviet Russia in which Hungary might have served as a pivot.

The whole Hungarian foreign ministry was electrified by the Paléologue plan.[19] But, when Philippe Berthelot took over Paléologue's post, the plan was promptly dropped. The whole affair did more harm than good to Hungary. In the final analysis it only helped Beneš to bring his Little Entente system of alliances together. The Yugoslavs, upset by France's furtive negotiations with Hungary, accepted Beneš's second offer for an alliance. The following year, in 1921, the Habsburg restoration attempts in Hungary prompted Romania to join. Hungary's encirclement was complete, the Little Entente was born and France became a staunch supporter of the new alliance.

By the time the Horthy regime was consolidated, Hungarian diplomacy was confronted with the fait accompli of the Little Entente and a static international scene generally unfavorable to Hungarian interests. Postwar consolidation was the work of István Bethlen and it was under his premiership that Hungary's interwar foreign policy was formulated. Bethlen's ideas on strategy were well summarized by Gusztáv Gratz, one of postwar Hungary's foreign ministers before the Bethlen era: "On principle, Bethlen was not against an understanding with the neighboring states. But he held all steps in this direction to be premature so long as Hungary was not in the position to confront those states as an equal partner, or at least with powerful protectors at her back. The time for such efforts would come, he said, when Hungary also had some trump cards to play."[20]

The first opportunity to find a "powerful protector" of sorts came in 1926. At Italian urging, Hungary interrupted ongoing negotiations with Yugoslavia and ended up signing, in 1927, a treaty of eternal friendship and arbitration with Italy. One of the Hungarian requests was Italian help in rearming—illegally—the Hungarian army. Despite Mussolini's fascist blustering, Italy certainly was not the ideal "powerful protector" Bethlen was seeking. But he might have thought that Hungary had to seize the opportunity to end her isolation with the help of one of the European powers, even if it was not the most desirable one. When a truly "powerful protector" appeared on Hungary's revisionist horizon, it was an even less desirable one—Hitler's Nazi Germany. By that time, Bethlen was out of office, but he, too, believed that any territorial reorganization of Central Europe would most likely be carried out by Germany and Italy.[21] What he did not foresee was the Axis alliance between Nazi Germany and fascist Italy—let alone that revisionist Hungary would be confronted with a shift in the European balance of power which would enable Hitler to redraw virtually singlehandedly the map of Central Europe.

By 1938 the long-awaited opportunity for a territorial reorganization of the Danube region seemed to be on hand, but the danger of German eastward penetration was threateningly looming behind it. The revision of the Trianon Treaty, always a complex problem, now seemed to be even more intricate, given the nature of the Nazi regime and Hitler's ambitions for a German *Lebensraum*. The question was how long Hungary could, as C. A. Macartney put it, "pluck for herself the fruits which Germany's growing power brought within her reach, while escaping the danger."[22]

Between November 1938 and April 1941, Trianon Hungary took full advantage of German patronage and, in four different stages, doubled its size. Ethnically, these acquisitions were a mixed bag. Some were populated mostly by Hungarians. Others, such as Ruthenia, were almost wholly non-Hungarian in composition, while still others (for instance, Transylvania) had such a mixed population that any ethnic claim, on either side, was dubious at best. However, the ethnic composition of these territories, although important as far as world opinion at the time went, was not the determining factor in their final fate. As the second Paris Peace Conference proved, national self-determination could be ignored as easily in 1946 as it had been in 1919. A permanent revision of Trianon Hungary's borders depended on the success of rival nations in their wartime diplomacy and on the influence and intentions of the Great Powers in Central and Eastern Europe.

Hungary's revisionist drive began auspiciously enough. The First Vienna Award in 1938 was the result of Italian-German arbitration and, therefore, not subject to four-power guarantees as envisaged by the preceding Munich conference. Nevertheless, the British government tacitly recognized the Vienna settlement as binding. In fact, the Foreign Office "received the news of it with satisfaction and even relief."[23] The new Hungarian border with Slovakia as devised by Germany and Italy favored the Hungarians slightly, thanks to Mussolini's arguments against those of Hitler which favored the Slovaks. Strategic considerations which justified the border devised by the Entente Powers after World War I did not count anymore—and some areas, the island of Csallóköz in particular, even at that time were awarded to Czechoslovakia only against the better judgment of the Allied peacemakers.

With the outbreak of World War II, Hungary's prospects for retaining the territories acquired from Slovakia looked even brighter. The Slovak state created with Hitler's help became a vassal of Nazi Germany and took part in the war against Poland, while Hungary, to the West's satisfaction, resisted Hitler's pressure and remained neutral. Sympathy toward Budapest, conspicuously lacking earlier, began to grow both in Great Britain and France.[24]

Hungary's second territorial acquisition in March 1939, the annexation of Ruthenia by independent military action, was a different kettle of fish. Hungary had no valid ethnic claim to the area since the population was of Slavic stock. Nevertheless, at that time, the Hungarian move was greeted with some measure of sympathy in the West.[25] The reason was obvious. Following the German occupation of the Czech lands and the proclamation of Slovak independence in March 1939, a group of Ukrainian nationalists declared the independence of Ruthenia as a Carpatho-Ukrainian state. The Hungarian annexation—only grudgingly endorsed by Germany—prevented the Carpatho-Ukraine from becoming another Nazi satellite; moreover, it brought about a common border between Poland and Hungary, also not in German interests.

While the first two territorial revisions were justifiable in one way or another, the third border revision—between Hungary and Romania—carried out by another German-Italian arbitration in Vienna in August 1940, marked the beginning of "an impossible situation," as Hungary's Prime Minister Pál Teleki himself realized.[26] Cooler Hungarian heads, of those no longer in office, suggested a very different policy. In fact, they pressed for a rapprochement between Hungary and Romania.[28] What course wartime history would have taken had their advice been followed no one can know with certainty. It may, or may not, have helped Hungary in the long run.

Hungary's position was extremely precarious, and the possibility of an uninvited German march through her territory was quite likely. The situation was further complicated by Russian interests in the Balkans. Stalin was eager to work hand in hand with Hitler to draw further gains from the Nazi-Soviet pact of 1939, this time by redrawing the map of the Balkans and adjacent areas. The British maintained that if Hungary resisted a German move across her territory, even if this action were followed by the establishment of a Hungarian Quisling government in Budapest, Hungary would be placed in the same category as Nazi-occupied Denmark vis-à-vis the Allies. Moreover, if Regent Horthy and his government went into exile, Hungary's chances of receiving favorable treatment after the war would be good. On the other hand, Hungarian cooperation with Nazi Germany would have very serious repercussions.[28]

The revision of Romania's boundaries began in 1940 with the Soviet annexation of Bessarabia and northern Bukovina. At this point, Hungarian revisionist diplomacy committed the mistake of pressing Germany for help in fulfilling Hungarian territorial claims to Transylvania. In return for such a favor, the Hungarian government declared itself ready to grant Germany free traffic through Hungary.[29] The damaging effect of this move was not immediately discernible. In fact, Hungary's position, under the then prevailing circumstances, even seemed to improve. After Romania repudiated the British guarantee of her territorial integrity and moved into the Axis camp, Great Britain was no longer sensitive to territorial changes between Romania and Hungary. In addition, Moscow declared that Hungarian claims to Transylvania were justified and that the Soviet Union was prepared to support those claims at a possible future peace conference.[30]

The settlement of the territorial dispute between Romania and Hungary, seemingly approved by both London and Moscow, was meant to be achieved through direct Romanian-Hungarian negotiations. But these negotiations broke down and in August 1940 the issue was decided by another Axis "arbitration." Italy assisted at this Second Vienna Award, but it was little more than a German *Diktat*. Although the British did not mind a peaceful solution to the Romanian-Hungarian dispute, they very much minded a German-Italian arbitration. The Soviet leaders were also greatly annoyed by the obvious German determination to exclude them from the affairs of the Balkans.

The Second Vienna Award greatly indebted Hungary to Germany. Shortly thereafter, Berlin launched its request for the transportation of German troops via Hungary to Romania, and naturally the request had to be granted. A few months later Hungary adhered to the Tripartite Agreement which eventually committed her to war against the

United States. Hungary was rapidly drifting into the Nazi camp and was dangerously close to the point of no return by the spring of 1941 when Hitler decided to invade Yugoslavia. The Nazi war machine chose Hungary as one of its invasion routes. Yugoslavia's collapse set the stage for Hungary's fourth and last border revision. But Hungary's complicity in Hitler's war against Yugoslavia compromised all of Hungary's revisionist successes. The Yugoslav episode is usually interpreted as a watershed in Allied-Hungarian relations. Actually, it was a logical extension of the Hungarian diplomatic decision made during the previous summer at the time of the Romanian border revision.

Prime Minister Teleki's suicide as a protest against his country's role in the attack on Yugoslavia was a tragic symbol of Hungary's own predicament. Yet not all was lost. Hungary was still not a belligerent. Admittedly, her behavior in the Yugoslav events was particularly dishonorable in view of the recently signed friendship treaty with Yugoslavia. Great Britain broke diplomatic relations with Hungary. But still, by doing as little as possible, there was room for maneuvering. Germany was not forcefully pressing Hungary to participate in the war. The longer that fateful step was postponed the better it was for the country. Pressure there was, but less from Germany than from Hungary's own Nazis and the military, dazzled by the ease of German victories. Prudence dictated extreme caution. After all, the ultimate success of Hungarian revisionist foreign policy depended on Hungary's siding with the victors. And as the Romanian case amply demonstrated (both in the First and the Second World Wars) such volte face could be performed at the very last minute.

Since 1919 Hungarian foreign policymakers rarely showed decisiveness, and given the complexities of the country's situation between the two world wars, one ought not to be surprised by their hesitancy. The prime minister who was an exception to that rule was László Bárdossy, Teleki's successor. He prided himself on making bold decisions and he paid for his boldness with his life after the war. Under his premiership, Hungary declared war on the Soviet Union without Germany asking her to do so.

Bárdossy's decision to join the German war effort without being forced to do so by Hitler is one of those perplexing events in Hungary's recent history. Marxist historians claim that Hungary's attack on the Soviet Union was predetermined by the Horthy regime's "re-

visionist policy and its counterrevolutionary nature."[31] However, Bárdossy's personality and his faith in German victory had more to do
with it than anything else. If at that juncture Hungary had had a
different man with a different set of priorities at the helm, the outcome might have been different. Of course, sooner or later Hungary
would have had to show her real colors, but the question is when that
move should have been made and in what manner.

Hungary's active participation in Hitler's war radically reduced her
chances of keeping her territorial gains in case of German defeat.
After all, Czechoslovakia and Yugoslavia, represented by governments in exile, became cobelligerents of the Western powers and,
after the German attack on the Soviet Union, of their eastern ally.
The activities of the puppet governments in Slovakia, Croatia, and
Serbia could, in case of Allied victory, simply be repudiated without
the countries themselves losing their earlier gains or damaging their
reputations. These neighbors of Hungary had a cushion that Hungary
did not have. Hungary, like Romania, would have had to change sides
when the fortunes of war turned—a much more difficult undertaking
than that which faced the other two neighbors.

Hungary did make a half-hearted attempt at disentangling herself
from the embrace of Germany. It started with the replacement of
Bárdossy by a pro-Allied prime minister, Miklós Kállay. From the
autumn of 1942 a change in attitude became evident. By 1943, anticipating an Allied landing in the Balkans, Hungary began a series of
secret negotiations with the Western powers. But Hungarian resolve
was weakened by the very thought of a possible Russian occupation.
Yet it was impossible to ignore the fact that the Soviet Union was an
ally of the Western powers and a drastic reminder of that fact was
the British and American refusal to negotiate unilaterally with the
Hungarians. Ultimately, fear of the Soviet Union, fear of German
occupation and atrocities, and insistence on some political guarantees
concerning border revisions paralyzed the Hungarian government's
efforts at doing anything at all.

Allied recognition of Czechoslovakia and Yugoslavia as cobelligerents greatly diminished the possibility of favorable Hungarian border adjustments in the north and in the south at any future peace
treaty. Romania, on the other hand, was still in the German camp,
and if Hungary wanted to retain any of her gains in Transylvania it

was imperative for her to change sides as soon as possible. Timing was all important. Such an about-face would have had to occur before a similar Romanian move. Kállay, however, was unable to respond to Allied urgings. Even after the fall of Mussolini, the government in Budapest lacked the will to act, afraid of German military occupation and retribution.

The German occupation came anyway in March 1944. The secret negotiations with the Western Allies (not at all secret as far as German intelligence was concerned) had resulted in nothing tangible; they only heightened German suspicion of the Kállay government.

Hungary's German occupation offered another opportunity for Regent Horthy to denounce the German alliance. Instead, the weak-kneed Horthy, compounding the ineptness of recent Hungarian moves, remained in office and cooperated with the Germans. Already very low, Hungary's stock plummeted in the eyes of the future victors. Hungary's hopelessness reached its greatest depths in August 1944 when Romania changed sides and joined the Soviet army in its advance against Hungary. In October, at long last, Horthy announced over the radio his intention to cease hostilities against the Soviet armies. Yet the proclamation was so cautiously worded with regard to the German alliance that it was almost meaningless. And in any case, the pro-German officers refused to obey Horthy's orders. But even if they had obeyed, it would not have mattered in the long run because a few days later Horthy withdrew the document. Moreover, he gave his blessing to the formation of a Hungarian Nazi government headed by Ferenc Szálasi, the leader of the fascist Arrow Cross party. This was Horthy's last act as regent of Hungary. Although some of the Hungarian officers and troops, on an individual basis, did go over to the Soviet side, officially Hungary was the only country to remain with the German cause to the bitter end.

Given the disgraceful performance of Hungary after March 1944, it is not surprising that the Allies made no effort to settle the Hungarian question in a more equitable manner than had been done in 1919. For the peacemakers of 1946 the settlement was not a question of the "justice" Hungary had so often talked about. It was simply a matter of not taking territories from friends and giving them to the only foe in Central Europe. Whether this expected response was wise or not is another matter.

Notes

1. István Bethlen, "Előszó," *Bethlen István gróf beszédei és írásai,* 2 vols. (Budapest, 1933), 1:12.
2. John F. Montgomery, *Hungary the Unwilling Satellite* (New York, 1947), 54.
3. István Bethlen, "A békerevizió gyakorlati politikája: A Reviziós Liga Nagygyűlése, 1932. május 22," *Bethlen István gróf beszédei és írásai,* 2:375.
4. György Ottlik, "Hungary's Foreign Relations," *Hungarian Quarterly* 4 (1938)): 31.
5. For example, C. A. Macartney, *October Fifteenth: A History of Modern Hungary, 1929–1945,* 2 vols. (Edinburgh, 1957).
6. Marxist historians, on the whole, draw a sharp line separating the period before and after the fall of the Hungarian Soviet Republic. See, for example, Gyula Juhász, *Magyarország külpolitikája, 1919–1945* (Budapest, 1969), 7–33, where he merely summarizes the events of the pre-August 1919 period.
7. Cf. Mihály Károlyi,"Az egész világ ellen, II," *Az új Magyarországért: Válogatott írások és beszédek, 1908–1919* (Budapest, 1968), 367; and Zsuzsa L. Nagy, *A párizsi békekonferencia és Magyarország, 1918–1919* (Budapest, 1965), 60.
8. Károlyi, "Az egész világ ellen, II," 372–73.
9. Ibid., 372.
10. By December 1918, there were many volunteers who could not be used because of lack of funds. See Gyula Kádár, *A Ludovikától Sopronkőhídáig* (Budapest, 1978), 68–75. Kádár was a recruiting officer at that time.
11. I have dealt with this period extensively in two articles: "István Friedrich and the Hungarian *Coup d'État* of 1919: A Reevaluation," *Slavic Review* 35 (1976): 269–86; and "Power Struggle in Hungary: Analysis in Post-War Domestic Politics, August–November 1919," *Canadian-American Review of Hungarian Studies* 4 (1977): 3–21.
12. The quotation is from Richard Crane to Robert Lansing, October 7, 1919, National Archives, Record Group 59, M367/540/0812. For a similar gloomy prediction, see Great Britain, Foreign Office, *Documents on British Foreign Policy 1919–1939,* 45 vols. (London, 1946–73), 1:6. For a detailed discussion, see Eva S. Balogh, "The Road to Isolation: Hungary, the Great Powers, and the Successor States, 1919–1920" (Ph.D. diss., Yale University, 1974), 395–98.
13. For more details on the Hungarian government's endeavors in this direction, see Balogh, "The Road to Isolation," 416–48.
14. Stefan Osuský, "La genèse de La Petite Entente," *Revue d'histoire diplomatique* 46 (1932): 134. Support for Osuský's statement can be found

in a letter from Sir Alban Young, British minister to Belgrade, to Lord Curzon, dated March 2, 1920, according to which "six months ago the Government of this country was approached by the Czechs with proposals for a defensive agreement against Hungary," Great Britain, Foreign Office, 371, 3520.

15. See Gusztáv Gratz to Pál Somssich, January 26, 1920, Hungary, Külügyminisztérium, *Papers and Documents Relating to the Foreign Relations of Hungary*, eds. Francis Deák and Dezső Újváry, 3 vols. (Budapest, 1939–48), 1:122, and Edvard Beneš to Alexandru Vaida-Voevod, January 5, 1920, Czechoslovak Republic, Ministerstvo zahraničních věci, *Documents diplomatique relatifs aux conventions d'alliance conclue par la République Tchéchoslovaque avec le Royaume des Serbes, Croates et Slovènes et le Royaume de Roumanie: déc. 1919–août 1921* (Prague, 1921), 15–16.

16. Gratz to Somssich, December 15, 1919, *Papers and Documents*, 1:86–90.

17. Márton Lovászy to the Yugoslav Government, August 20, 1919, English translation of the German original, N.A., Record Group 59, M367/436/0104–0106.

18. On the long and intricate negotiations with the Romanians and the negative Entente attitude, the Hungarian National Archives, the Foreign Office, and the National Archives in Washington have a fair amount of material. Based on these unpublished sources, I have treated the negotiations in detail in my dissertation, "The Road to Isolation," 206–319.

19. These negotiations are amply documented at least on the Hungarian side in the volumes of English-language documents published by the Hungarian foreign ministry.

20. Quoted in Macartney, *October Fifteenth*, 1:83.

21. He was also certain that sooner or later Austria would join Germany. During his trip to Rome in April 1927, he learned that Mussolini shared his views concerning an *Anschluss* and, what is more important, saw "no instrument which could prevent such an outcome." See Bethlen's notes on his conversation with Mussolini, April 4, 1927, Hungary, Országos Levéltár, *Iratok az ellenforradalom történetéhez, 1919–45*, eds. Dezső Nemes and Elek Karsai, 5 vols. (Budapest, 1953–78), 4:51.

22. C. A. Macartney, *Hungary: A Short History* (Edinburgh, 1962), 226–27.

23. Barcza MS. quoted in Macartney, *October Fifteenth*, 1:303.

24. For the British and French atttitudes, see Hungary, Magyar Tudományos Akadémia, Történettudományi Intézet, *Diplomáciai iratok Magyarország külpolitikájához, 1936–1945*, (henceforth cited as *DIMK*) ed. László Zsigmond, 4 vols. (Budapest, 1962–), 4:491–92, 628, and 541.

25. Ibid., 3:614–16, 619, 684–86.

26. Richard V. Burks, "Two Teleki Letters," *Journal of Central European Affairs* 7 (1947): 69.

27. Memorandum by István Bethlen received March 23, 1940, *DIMK*, 4:743–61.

28. Barcza MS. quoted in Macartney, *October Fifteenth*, 1:400; see also Gyula Juhász, *A Teleki-kormány külpolitikája 1939–1941* (Budapest, 1964), 108–10.

29. For details on German-Hungarian exchanges on this matter, see Germany, Auswärtiges Amt, *Documents on German Foreign Policy, 1918–1945*, Series C and D, 18 vols. (Washington, D.C., 1949–66), D:10:38–39, 56–57, and 85–86.

30. See Juhász, *A Teleki-kormány*, 139 and 128.

31. Even Gyula Juhász, whose book on Hungary's foreign policy between the two world wars is justifiably considered a balanced treatment, claims this, in my opinion, erroneously. See his *Magyarország külpolitikája*, 237–38.

✳ 4

Peacemaking after World War II:
The End of the Myth of
National Self-Determination

Bennett Kovrig

“Who won this war, the United Nations or Hungary?”[1] That rhetorical question, asked by Czechoslovak Foreign Minister Jan Masaryk at the Paris Peace Conference of 1946, bore the obvious implication that the defeated have no rights. The Hungarians, finding themselves for the second time on the losing side as allies of Germany, clung to the myth of national self-determination and believed that, despite their fatal alliance, the injustice of the Treaty of Trianon would be weighed by their judges as a mitigating factor. They also hoped that the positive aspects of their wartime record would be appreciated.

During World War II, prior to the German occupation of Hungary in March 1944, Hungary's cooperation with Hitler was grudging, prompting Nazi complaints and unfavorable comparisons with more willing allies, notably Romania. The Germans knew about the Hungarians' "secret" negotiations with the Western Allies.[2] For years, a working group in the Hungarian Ministry of Foreign Affairs had made preparations for a separate peace and, under the Kállay government, contacts were established with the Allies in neutral capitals. These preparations were based on the assumption that for strategic reasons the Western powers would not countenance Soviet rule over southeast Europe and that the British and Americans would mount a Balkan thrust and occupy the Danubian plain ahead of the Russians. Moreover, recalls the Hungarian diplomat Stephen Kertesz, the Allied war aims expressed in the Atlantic Charter and the Four Freedoms "had a tremendous impact upon all social classes in Hungary. It was supposed that the Western powers, in addition to these general principles, had some concrete plans for the reorganization of Europe in general and the Danubian region in particular."[3] It was further assumed that an armistice agreement could be negotiated with the British and Americans, rather than with the hated Russians. With these relatively comforting assumptions the Hungarians proceeded to plan for democratic reforms, for Danubian cooperation or even federation, and for safeguarding the integrity of frontiers that bore a closer relation to the distribution of Magyar population than did the Trianon line. Regrettably for Hungary, the fortunes of war and Allied strategy conspired to disappoint these expectations.

The United States and Britain, conscious of their own prevarication in opposing Hitler in the late 1930s, reserved a certain understanding for the predicament of Germany's East European allies. The Soviet Union felt no such sympathy for the hostile Hungarians and Romanians whose armies fought alongside the Germans. Indeed, early in the life of the Grand Alliance it became clear that Stalin's designs for postwar Central and Eastern Europe might not be fully consistent with the professed ideals and interests of the Western allies. The Atlantic Charter, which antedated Pearl Harbor by four months, had proclaimed all peoples' rights to choose their governments freely and precluded territorial changes "that do not accord with the freely expressed wishes of the peoples concerned." The Soviet Union endorsed the Charter with reservations, as it did subsequent statements of intent of the Grand Alliance such as the United Nations Declaration and the Yalta Declaration on Liberated Europe.

To the extent that this noble rhetoric was designed for psychological warfare it reinforced the East Europeans' affinity with the West, but it failed to mitigate traditional hatred and fear of the Soviet Union. And the latter was looming ever more clearly as the dominant power in the area thanks to Allied military strategy and political compromises. Franklin D. Roosevelt adopted a posture of "no predetermination," preferring to leave contentious political issues for resolution in peacetime.[4] The British, like Stalin, were rather more conscious of the political stakes in Eastern Europe, but to little effect. Winston Churchill's proposal for a confederation in the Danube region was rejected by Vyacheslav Molotov in October 1943 as a faintly disguised anti-Soviet scheme. The prime minister's repeated advocacy of Anglo-American strikes at the "soft underbelly" of the Axis received short shrift from his allies, and Eastern Europe was left entirely to Stalin's sphere of military responsibility. Churchill's percentage deal with Stalin in October 1944 was an attempt to gain recognition of Britain's primacy of interest in Greece. Over Hungary, influence was to be divided equally, an illusory notion in light of the total absence of British or other Western military power in the area.

In these circumstances the Hungarian schemes for a separate peace were foredoomed. For tactical reasons the Western allies did talk to the Hungarian envoys, and an OSS team was parachuted into Hungary just in time for the German occupation. But the principle of unconditional surrender and the Soviet Union's primary military responsibility allowed neither for bargaining on terms nor for a Western-oriented armistice. When the Hungarian government finally resigned itself to plead for peace in Moscow, the Germans were ready. Horthy's armistice proclamation on October 15, 1944, coincided with his seizure by Otto Skorzeny's commandos and the installation of a Nazi puppet regime. It was left to a provisional government, established under Soviet auspices in eastern Hungary, to receive the armistice terms in January 1945.

With victory a mere question of time, the Allies began in 1944 to consider the conditions of the many eventual peace settlements. On the question of frontiers, there was agreement that the changes effected in Eastern Europe by the Axis powers were to be reversed. Hitler's exploitation of the real and alleged injustices of the Versailles settlements impeded an objective reevaluation of the territorial and ethnic complexities of the area. Nevertheless, the U.S. State Department in particular sought to transcend the simple formula of a return to the status quo ante and to plan equitable solutions conducive to stable and cooperative regional relations.

The case of Hungary was perhaps the thorniest, for it was an enemy state with territorial claims on both Allied and enemy states. The proposed terms of surrender for Hungary, prepared by the State Department in July 1944 for its representative on the European Advisory Commission, provided for the restoration of the Trianon frontiers with Yugoslavia and Czechoslovakia "subject to any rectifications which these two countries might agree to make as part of a general settlement of the issues in dispute between them and Hungary." With regard to Transylvania, "Hungary might be assured that an attempt will be made to establish a more just ethnic boundary between Hungary and Rumania, the territory in dispute to be controlled by the United Nations pending the final territorial settlement."[5] An earlier memorandum from the Division of Southern European Affairs advanced the view that "probably some form of autonomy for the entire Transylvanian area may prove to be the solution best suited to serve the interest of international security and of future collaboration and peaceful relations among the Danubian States."[6] The experts did anticipate that the Russian claim to Bessarabia and Northern Bukovina would further complicate the issue.

The department's briefing paper on Hungary, sent to Roosevelt on September 6, 1944, argued that while the starting point ought to be the pre-Munich status quo, changes in those boundaries might serve a stable settlement:

> Thus, in the case of the frontier with Czechoslovakia, if an opportunity arises for revision by agreement which would leave to Hungary certain overwhelmingly Magyar-inhabited districts, the United States would favor such a solution. In the case of the frontier with Yugoslavia, the United States sees some merit in a compromise solution which would leave to Hungary the northern part of the Voyvodina, although this Government should not, we feel, press for such a solution. In the case of the frontier with Rumania, the American position will be more or less frozen by our agreement to the armistice terms for Rumania which provide for the restoration to that country of "all or the major part of Transylvania, subject to confirmation at the peace settlement." In the final settlement the United States would favor, at the least, a revision of the pre-war frontier on ethnic grounds, transferring to Hungary a small strip of territory given to Rumania at the end of the last war.[7]

The American experts' view on the merits of Hungary's territorial interests was shared by some of their British counterparts, but the whole matter had very low political priority as the war in Europe ground to an end.

While a peace settlement could be delayed, interim conditions for the cessation of hostilities had to be determined, necessarily by the Soviet Union. When Ambassador W. Averell Harriman raised the matter of equal participation on the projected Allied Control Commission for Hungary, Molotov observed that the Soviet Union was already master of most of that country and therefore could, if it wished, forego the formality of an armistice.[8] The eventual document, signed by Hungary's representatives on January 20, 1945, declared the Vienna Awards null and void (article 19) and bound Hungary to evacuate all troops and officials from Czechoslovakia, Yugoslavia, and Romania back to the December 31, 1937 frontiers, and to repeal all legislative and administrative provisions relating to the annexation or incorporation of those three states' territory (article 2).[9] Back in October, Secretary of State Cordell Hull had reminded Harriman of his "firm view . . . that territorial settlements should not be embodied in the armistice document and that no final decisions on territorial disputes should be taken during the course of the war."[10] The U.S. Ambassador, supported by his British colleague, recommended therefore that Article 2 be prefaced with the phrase "without prejudice to ultimate settlement of disputed territorial claims." Molotov demurred, objecting that such a qualification would arouse concern in Czechoslovakia and Yugoslavia, and it was agreed simply that the territorial clauses could not be interpreted as definitive boundary settlements.[11]

The Romanian armistice, concluded the preceding September, determined the provisional disposition of Hungary's interest in Transylvania. The loss of northern Transylvania as a result of the Second Vienna Award had aroused a Romanian irredentism as passionate as that of the Hungarians of the post-Trianon era, and during the war the Antonescu regime courted Hitler in the hope of regaining the lost area. The ethnic mosaic of Transylvania made national self-determination difficult to apply. Magyar majorities did exist in Romania's northwest, along the Trianon border, as well as in the eastern (Székely) corner of Transylvania. The territory reannexed by Hungary encompassed these districts. But with the reannexed territory also a large Romanian minority came under Hungarian rule, while in southern Transylvania a smaller Magyar minority remained under Romanian rule. The Romanians, like the Hungarians, made peace overtures to the Western allies in early 1944 and were advised to deal with Moscow.[12] Recognizing that the loss of Bessarabia to the Russians was a foregone conclusion, they sought Stalin's support for their claim to all of Transylvania. Stalin had a pronounced dislike for Hungarians,[13] and Transylvania was handy compensation for Bessarabia and

Northern Bukovina and an incentive for Romanian participation in the final battle against Germany.

In the proposed armistice terms, the Soviet Union considered "unjust the decisions of the Vienna Award" and declared itself "ready to conduct operations in common with Rumania against the Hungarians and the Germans with the object of restoring to Rumania all Transylvania or the major part thereof."[14] The State Department's Southern European Division noted on April 11, 1944, that "the terms are essentially Russian, not allied nor tri-partite" and restated the basic U.S. position that the "whole complex Transylvanian problem should be left for postwar consideration."[15] Such reservations were, as usual, of little consequence. They were sidetracked by the Soviet Union's political and military interests and the adamant view of the U.S. Joint Chiefs of Staff that all political considerations be subordinated to the most expedient and earliest defeat of the Axis powers. If Romania could be brought over to the Allies, a compromise over Transylvania seemed a small price to pay.

Negotiations were still under way when, on August 23, King Michael proclaimed Romania's switch to the Allies and called on his people to "liberate our Transylvania from enemy occupation."[16] However, the original Soviet formulation about the restoration of all or the major part of Transylvania found its way into the final armistice document, with the qualifying phrase, "subject to confirmation at the peace settlement," which was added on Churchill's advice to preserve the appearance of no predetermination.[17]

While the Hungarian and Romanian armies, now on opposite sides, fought over Transylvania, Hungarian political factions in the region, including the underground Communists, began to prepare for an uncertain peace. Even some non-Communist leaders anticipated that the safety of the Transylvanian Hungarians lay more in a left-wing alliance with Romanian Communists than under the rule of the established, nationalist parties.[18] Indeed, as Transylvania came under Soviet-Romanian occupation in the autumn of 1944, the Hungarian population was subjected to more or less officially sanctioned reprisals—to mass murders and pillage—at the hands of the vengeful Romanians. The Communist-led Hungarian organization, MADOSZ, linked to the Romanian Communist Party, condemned Bucharest's anti-Hungarian incitement and called for peaceful collaboration in a new and "democratic" Romania.

Having secured Romania's military aid, the Soviet Union felt little need to accommodate the "bourgeois" government in Bucharest. On November 11, the Soviet-dominated Allied Control Commission ordered the removal of Romanian civil administration from northern Transylvania and the region was placed under direct Soviet military rule. Stalin's envoy, Andrei Vyshinskii, denounced the persecution of Hungarians in a move calculated to undermine the legitimacy of the Bucharest regime. A Minorities Law offering some protection to the Hungarians was passed on February 7 by the Radescu government, but the latter's days were numbered. Soviet pressure compelled King Michael in early March to appoint a Communist-dominated government led by Petru Groza. On March 9, Stalin acceded to Groza's request for the return of northern Transylvania to Romanian administration on condition that the equal rights of all nationalities be guaranteed. Although Groza was relatively well disposed toward Hungarians, the minority remained subject to harassment, one official measure being the dismissal and expropriation of Transylvanians who had chosen Hungarian citizenship after the Vienna Award.[19]

In the late spring of 1945, in devastated Budapest, the Hungarian Foreign Ministry began to prepare the country's case for the peace conference. The conditions could hardly have been less propitious. The provisional government, followed after the November elections by a coalition government, was constrained in both domestic and foreign policy by the Soviet-led Allied Control Commission and by the Soviet-sponsored Communist party. Peace aims had to have the support of these two, yet the non-Communist consensus held that Hungary's interests demanded a reasoned case for modification of the armistice's economic and territorial provisions. Even in the absence of clear policy guidelines, experts coordinated by the Foreign Ministry's Kertesz studied various options, notably models of Central European federation.[20]

On August 14, 1945, an introductory note on Hungary's peace aims was delivered to the three principal Allies.[21] The note stressed the need for Danubian economic cooperation and went on to observe that the prerequisite political stability would depend in part on a settlement of the outstanding territorial and nationality issues. Both the Trianon Treaty and the resulting nationalist excesses on all sides were deplored: "The most effective measure to counteract national antagonism . . . would be the delimitation of boundaries according to the freely expressed wish of the population and to the principles of nationality wherever the nationalities live on contiguous territories." The transfer of populations was justified "only when nationalities live in isolated fragmentary groups, that is to say, when it is impossible to reunite the national minorities with the mother country by redrawing the boundaries." For the remaining national minorities, international protection through the United Nations was "absolutely necessary." The note was a modest enough statement of Hungary's Danubian outlook, but its indirect suggestion of regional integration was criticized by the Soviet Union and the Hungarian Communist leader Mátyás Rákosi as premature—that is, as not serving the Soviet strategy of piecemeal absorption of Eastern Europe into its sphere of dominance. In January 1946 a note to the three powers requested the appointment of a committee of experts to conduct a proper appraisal of Hungarian-connected problems for the peace conference.[22]

The Transylvanian question was treated in some detail in a note drafted in February 1946, but the Communists and Social Democrats objected to its allegedly nationalist proposal for an equitable division of the region between the two countries, with the aid of international experts and plebiscite.[23] Prime Minister Ferenc Nagy and Foreign Minister János Gyöngyösi chose to avoid confrontation with the left-wing parties in the hope of gaining time until the eventual peace treaty and Soviet military withdrawal. Privately, Soviet representatives had encouraged the Hungarian leaders to address their territorial proposals to Romania and even hinted at support if Hungary acceded to the Czechoslovak demand for a population transfer.[24] Meanwhile, the U.S. Minister to Budapest, H. F. A. Schoenfeld, advised Washington that an adjustment of the Transylvanian frontier in favor of Hungary would correct past injustice. He observed that it was "more important for us to consider the effect of a frontier revision on Hungarian internal politics than on Rumanian internal politics inasmuch as Hungary is still a twilight zone in respect to Soviet expansion whereas the shadows falling on Rumania are already of deeper hue."[25] Playing a devious game, the Russians relayed Schoenfeld's recommendation to the Groza regime, whose public outrage served as useful anti-American propaganda.[26]

The Hungarians' hopes were kindled on the occasion of a top-level visit to Moscow in April. The delegation was armed with two alternate proposals regarding Transylvania. The first was for the reannexation of 22,000 square kilometers to Hungary. The area had a Romanian majority, but the idea was that the roughly comparable size of the Hungarian minority in Romania would result in decent treatment in both countries. The second scheme was for the return of 11,800 square kilometers, with a majority of Hungarian inhabitants.[27] The Hungarians were cordially received by Stalin. They won concessions on reparations, and with respect to Transylvania Stalin ostensibly agreed that according to the Romanian armistice terms Hungary was entitled to advance claims for Transylvania. Molotov thereupon urged the Hungarians to negotiate directly with Bucharest before approaching the Allies. Prime Minister Nagy voiced doubts about the Romanians' willingness to negotiate, and asked Molotov to intercede, but to no avail.[28]

As Nagy expected, the Groza government refused to negotiate, and on April 27 Hungary addressed a note to the three allies advancing the larger of the two claims to parts of Transylvania.[29] The future of Transylvania, however, was already in the process of being settled and with scant regard for Hungary. In September 1945, at the London session of the Council of Foreign Ministers (which had been created at the Potsdam Conference to prepare peace treaties), Molotov had recommended the award of all Transylvania to Romania. Secretary of State James F. Byrnes argued in favor of minor changes in the Trianon line to return some predominantly Hungarian-inhabited border areas to Hungary, all in the interest of facilitating better Hungarian-Romanian relations. At the Council's session in Paris the following May, the die was cast. In the interval, the British had decided that on balance their interests would not be served by an obviously token concession to Hungary that would nevertheless alienate the Romanians. Encouragement of the Hungarians at Moscow had been a diplomatic charade, for Molotov also rejected any concession. The Americans thereupon abandoned what was for them a very minor issue, and proposed that the treaty provide at least for recognition of any future rectification of boundaries agreed to by Hungary and Romania "which would substantially reduce the number of persons living under alien rule." Even this failed to win support, and on May 7 Byrnes agreed to support the original Soviet recommendation.[30]

The non-Communist members of the Nagy government were appalled at this ruling. Hungary had not even been given an opportunity to present its case. Later in May, Nagy took a delegation to Washington in a display of political independence that was unique in Eastern Europe. With regard to Transylvania, Byrnes offered to consider Hungary's claims sympathetically if the Russians chose to bring up the issue at the forthcoming peace conference. On his way home, Nagy learned from Molotov in Paris that the matter was closed.[31]

The Hungarians nevertheless submitted a brief to the Peace Conference that convened in Paris that summer. It painted a grim picture of the sufferings of the Hungarian minority and advanced the larger claim. The two countries' cases were heard at a joint meeting of the Romanian and Hungarian Political and Territorial Commissions. On that occasion Hungary also introduced the lesser claim (encompassing the cities of Szatmár, Nagyvárad, and Arad), whose ethnic merits were countered on the Romanian side by economic arguments. Finally, the Hungarians requested that Romania grant extensive autonomy to the 600,000-strong Székely-Magyar enclave in eastern Transylvania. An Australian proposal for a thorough study of the area's ethnic distribution to find the fairest boundary pleased the Americans, but there was to be no alteration at this stage in a decision that had its origin in the Kremlin.[32]

With all its flaws, the Trianon dictate was thus reconfirmed. As in 1919, the decision owed little to the facts and merits of the Transylvanian tangle and much to the remote priorities of great power strategy. The closest and most interested great power, the Soviet Union, had found it convenient to strengthen the friendly Groza regime and ease its own territorial acquisitions from Romania by the gift of Transylvania. The less tractable Hungarians were thus punished, and the Western Allies were not prepared to champion the interests of a former enemy state even if its government was relatively representative and pro-Western.

Hungary's territorial and ethnic interests were difficult enough to advance against another former enemy state. The other Hungarian reannexations with Axis help, cancelled by the armistice, involved two members of the United Nations, Yugoslavia and Czechoslovakia.

Most of the half million Hungarians in Yugoslavia lived in the Vojvodina, which was made in 1945 into an autonomous region within the Serbian Republic. Hungary's interest in their fate was reduced to urgings that they receive no worse treatment than Yugoslavia's other nationalities. A bilateral agreement was concluded in September 1946, providing for the voluntary exchange of up to 40,000 Hungarians and Yugoslavs, but it was never implemented. Czechoslovakia's Ruthenia, renamed Carpatho-Ukraine, had a Ukrainian majority (formerly called Ruthenians) as well as other nationalities, including over 150,000 Hungarians representing some seventeen percent of the population. Hungary recovered part of the district from Czechoslovakia through the First Vienna Award, the rest by occupation in 1939. Its disposition after World War II did not involve Hungary directly. Fearing that the dogma of integral restoration of Czechoslovak sovereignty would be undermined, Beneš agreed to cede Ruthenia to the Soviet Union only with great reluctance and in the hope of retaining Stalin's goodwill. The treaty, which gave the Soviet Union a common border with Hungary, was signed on June 19, 1945.[33] The eventual Hungarian Peace Treaty simply recorded these losses.

The recreation of the sovereign state of Czechoslovakia was an Allied objective from the start of World War II. The legitimacy of the Munich Pact and of the First Vienna Award had been erased by Hitler's subsequent annihilation of the Czechoslovak state and by the war itself. Beneš's government-in-exile was a recognized ally and actively prepared for the restoration of the pre-Munich status quo. For Beneš, the moral of his country's dismemberment was that the disloyal German and Hungarian minorities had to be expelled or assimilated. As early as 1943 he secured American approval in principle for the expulsion of the Germans. The British, for their part, acquiesced to the eventual transfer of minority populations including the Hungarians to make Czechoslovakia ethnically more homogeneous.[34] The United States did not extend its approval of punitive transfers beyond the Germans and, as noted above, the State Department even saw some merit in a territorial adjustment in favor of Hungary.

The Hungarian minority in prewar Czechoslovakia had indeed been disloyal to that state in its resentment of the Trianon settlement. It was too large a minority, too close to the mother country, to be satisfied with even generous legal protection. A millennium of Hungarian history, they felt, represented a greater legitimacy than twenty years of Trianon. Many Czechs and Slovaks would, however, charge that the German and Hungarian minorities had stabbed their young and relatively enlightened state in the back, and therefore deserved to be branded with collective guilt. The government's Košice program, proclaimed on April 5, 1945, provided for the confiscation of property of Germans and Hungarians who had "actively helped" the enemy. The decree of June 22 imposed the confiscation of movable and real property of *all* Germans and Hungarians. On August 2, a presidential decree deprived all members of the two minorities (except those who had assisted in the Allied war effort) of their citizenship. In practice this meant loss of employment and all social benefits and services, including education. Hungarians were summarily expelled to Hungary. Large numbers were deported to the newly depopulated Sudetenland.[35]

The initial inclination of the Hungarian government, and notably of Foreign Minister Gyöngyösi, was to seek good relations with Czechoslovakia.[36] However, the discriminatory measures against the Hungarian minority soon set off a stream of diplomatic protests to the three members of the Allied Control Commission. Washington advised both Prague and Budapest of its opposition to collective punishment and unilateral transfers of population.[37] In October, Secretary of State Byrnes reminded the Czechoslovak government that the Potsdam Agreement did not provide for the expulsion of Hungarians.[38] When the persecution did not abate, the Budapest regime requested in September and again in November that the United States, the Soviet Union, Great Britain, and France set up an international commission to investigate the problem. The U.S. ambassador in Prague, Laurence Steinhardt, deplored what was "in effect a request that an international body be created at the instance of a defeated nation to investigate the conduct of one of the victorious nations" and noted that this would "create deep resentment throughout Czechoslovakia and might well raise the cry that Czechoslovakia was again 'being sold down the river by the Western democracies.'"[39] The United States, which among the Allies remained the most sympathetic to Hungary, ruled out such a commission along with another Hungarian proposal for international control of the disputed area. Instead, it joined its partners on the Allied Control Commission in urging Hungary to resolve the problem bilaterally.

Finally, on December 2 negotiations were begun between the Czechoslovaks and Hungarians in Prague. Inauspiciously, Beneš told Gyöngyösi that good relations depended on the elimination of minorities.[40] The Czech proposals, presented by the Communist deputy foreign minister, Vladimir Clementis, envisaged an organized and balanced exchange of Hungarians for Slovaks who wished to leave Hungary and the eviction of the remaining Hungarians. Budapest's delegation, in turn, pressed for the abolition of discriminatory measures and would only consider an equal exchange. The remaining minority, they argued, could only be transferred along with its territory (a theoretically defensible proposition given the solid Hungarian majorities in certain areas along the border). Three days of negotiations ended in deadlock.[41]

The Hungarian government thereupon came under strong pressure from the Soviet Union. Ambassador Georgii M. Pushkin made it clear that Czechoslovakia enjoyed Moscow's full support, and even observed to Gyöngyösi that the Czechs would have been smarter to expel all Hungarians promptly.[42] Public opinion in Hungary was much aroused by the trials of the Hungarian minority in Czechoslovakia. Even the Communist leaders felt impelled to intercede with their Czech and Slovak counterparts, only to be rebuffed with the report of Stalin's support.[43] The Western powers urged further negotiations, and talks were resumed on February 6, 1946. An agreement was finally signed on February 27 providing for a limited (up to 100,000 persons) and balanced exchange, voluntary as far as Slovaks in Hungary were concerned, compulsory for the selected Hungarians of Slovakia. In a separate provision, major war criminals and up to one thousand minor criminals were also to be transferred to Hungary. In a protocol to the agreement the Czechoslovaks promised to suspend temporarily the discriminatory measures.

Notwithstanding this agreement, the Czechoslovak government reserved the right to discuss the "total liquidation" of the Hungarian minority, and the ink had hardly dried on the document when Clementis proposed the transfer of an additional 150,000 to 200,000 Hungarians over and above the numbers to be exchanged.[44] There would remain, he claimed, only Hungarians of Slovak ancestry, and these would be "re-Slovakized." Behind the Population Exchange Agreement there lay inflated Czechoslovak estimates of the Slovak minority in Hungary.[45] As for Clementis's proposal for "re-Slovakization," it affected anywhere from 200,000 to 350,000 people. A Czechoslovak Resettlement Commission was dispatched to Hungary to urge Slovaks to volunteer, but the number of valid applications (and therefore the equal number of Hungarians to be transferred from Czechoslovakia to Hungary) fell woefully short of the Czechoslovak target and became the subject of a protracted dispute between the two governments. Initially Prague also claimed to have identified 23,192 Hungarian war criminals, proposing in effect to expel, without their property, as many as 100,000 men, women, and children.[46] The Hungarian government, meanwhile, rejected Clementis's proposals and called for full minority rights while suggesting the cession by Czechoslovakia of territory amounting to 8,000 square kilometers and inhabited largely by Hungarians.

On the occasion of the Nagy visit to Moscow, Stalin was as deceitful on this issue as on the Transylvanian question, for he professed to support equal rights for the Hungarians of Czechoslovakia.[47] When it counted, however, the Soviet Union consistently supported Prague's proposals,[48] whereas the Americans and the British avoided the appearance of favoring Hungary or endorsing Hungarian initiatives. Not surprisingly, in these circumstances the Czechs were not disposed to make concessions in bilateral negotiations with the Hungarians.

As with the Transylvanian case, the two protagonists came to Paris armed with historical grievances and irreconcilable demands. The Czechs charged that the Hungarians had been disloyal and revisionist and therefore the Czechoslovak delegation proposed an amendment to the Hungarian Peace Treaty which would provide for the expulsion of 200,000 Hungarians from Czechoslovakia. The Hungarian minority was being persecuted, retorted the Hungarians. If Czechoslovakia wished to keep the ancestral land of Hungarian peasants, said Gyöngyösi in an impassioned address before the plenary session on August 14, let her keep the inhabitants and give them full rights; if the people were undesirable, Hungary would receive them but with their land.[49] The United States opposed the proposed population transfer, and at the concurrent meetings of deputies of the Big Four tried without success to win support for a token territorial concession in favor of Hungary.[50] In addition to the expulsion of the Hungarian minority Czechoslovakia also demanded five Hungarian villages situated on the right bank of the Danube across from Bratislava which were allegedly of vital importance to that city's economic life. The Americans joined the Hungarians in noting the strange juxtaposition of proposals for transferring Hungarians both from and to Czechoslovakia.

At New Zealand's suggestion, the Czechoslovak amendments were referred to a subcommittee. New Zealand also proposed the two final compromises. The "Bratislava bridgehead" to be awarded to Czechoslovakia was reduced to three villages from the five originally demanded. As for the population transfer, the two countries were instructed by way of the treaty to enter into bilateral negotiations on the fate of those Hungarians left after implementation of the earlier exchange agreement. If agreement was not reached within six months, Czechoslovakia had the right to request the assistance of the Council of Foreign Ministers. The American delegate on the Political and Territorial Commission for Hungary, General Bedell Smith, offered the penultimate wish that "voluntary transfer should be stressed to the utmost and every effort including minor territorial adjustments made to the end that a minimum number of people be uprooted."[51]

As John Campbell, the secretary of the U.S. delegation, conceded, it had been an evasion of responsibility to "turn over the tough problems to the parties least likely to agree on solutions." The Americans recognized that Hungary's government, not yet Communist-dominated, desperately needed some satisfaction on the territorial and minority issues, but they were unwilling to challenge Allied nations in seeking fair terms. Many of the Hungarians' arguments were valid, but coming from a defeated nation they carried little weight.[52] Not surprisingly, Stephen Kertesz judged Allied attitudes toward the mistreatment of the Hungarian minority to be the "greatest disappointment of Hungarian foreign policy in the armistice period."[53] A State Department postmortem (dated January 30, 1947) found that "the attitude of the Czechoslovak Government and certain actions of a unilateral nature which it has taken in regard to the Hungarian minority in Czechoslovakia have contributed materially to the difficulties being encountered."[54] As the non-Communist majority in the Nagy government was being progressively decimated and incapacitated by Communist and Soviet harassment in the early months of 1947, vague expressions of Western sympathy brought only cold comfort.

The deadlock over the implementation of the Population Exchange Agreement lasted a few months longer, until in March 1947 the two sides reached an understanding. Under the agreement, over 60,000 of each nationality were actually exchanged. With the seizure of power by the Communists in Hungary in the summer of 1947 and the Prague coup of February 1948, the complexion of the minority problem changed. The exchange program was terminated, the expulsion and assimilation threats were dropped and the discriminatory legislation rescinded.[55] The officially cordial relations between the two Communist states suppressed the dispute and alleviated the worst hardships of the minority while introducing new ones.

In the interwar period, Hungary had based its claims for revision of the Trianon territorial settlement on the very Wilsonian principles of national self-determination which ostensibly inspired the peacemakers at Versailles. The peacemakers cynically misapplied the principles, wholly to the detriment of Hungarians, but the latter nevertheless seized on Wilsonianism to seek redress. The two Vienna awards were justified by Hungary in terms of national self-determination. Although the awards were invalidated by the war, the Allies gave the Hungarians cause for hope that Wilsonianism would guide postwar peacemaking.

That the Atlantic Charter and the Yalta Declaration turned out to be inoperative was a function more of the distribution of power in Europe in 1945 than of deals among the victorious Allies. The Soviet Union resorted to the time-tested divide-and-rule tactic to entrench its influence in Eastern Europe. Thus it favored Romania's territorial claim and Czechoslovakia's expulsion policy against Hungary—in the first case to strengthen the Groza regime, in the second because Czechoslovakia was a friendly ally. Stalin could of course have lent his weight to an Allied-inspired compromise settlement, particularly in the second case, but evidently he preferred to incite the still largely non-Communist Prague and Budapest regimes to self-defeating, nationalistic excess. The western allies, and particularly the United States, recognized the imperfections in the frontiers drawn in 1919, but the decisive voice, at least in the Hungarian case, was that of Moscow. As John Campbell observed, "east of the dividing line the United States showed little inclination to tilt at windmills by pressing for 'ethnic lines' and 'fair solutions.'"[56] The division of Europe into spheres of influence had left Hungary at the mercy of the least sympathetic judge.

Hungary's postwar leaders may have been a more democratic and progressive lot than their predecessors of the Horthy era, but they found no better grounds on which to defend territorial and minority interests than the principle of national self-determination expounded by Wilson. Beneš's argument that national minorities materially contributed to the collapse of the interwar order and deserved to be extirpated aroused more sympathy than agreement among the Allies. Thus the impassioned but ultimately sterile debates regarding historical legitimacy were played out once again: Was a thousand years of Hungarian settlement and rule in Slovakia outweighed by the alleged injustices of that rule, by the legal sanctity of the Versailles settlement, and by the persistence of Hungarian nationalism? Did Romanians or Hungarians have first historical claim to Transylvania; which nationality oppressed the other more brutally; which could offer the better guarantee of tolerance and prosperity?

Meanwhile, the balance of power among the increasingly divided and hostile Allies determined a peace settlement that owed little to Wilsonian or any other principles of justice. It is only too easy to speculate in retrospect on alternative policies and actions that could have had a less dismal outcome. A politically more calculated military strategy on the part of the western allies might have forestalled the Soviet occupation of some of Central and Eastern Europe. A less precipitous withdrawal of American power from the continent might have helped western interests in peacemaking. Western insistence on settling the Austrian case at the same time as those of the other enemy states might have ended that country's occupation, and therefore the presence of Soviet troops in Hungary, before the Communists, with Soviet assistance, seized power in Budapest. The reality was Soviet will and power unmatched on the part of the West. In these circumstances, reflects Kertesz, the best Hungarian foreign policy was doomed to failure.[57] The idealism that suffused Wilson's principles and the aims of the United States in World War II had aroused the hopes of the small and the weak. Once again, for many the hopes would remain unfulfilled.

Notes

1. Quoted in John C. Campbell, "The European Territorial Settlement," *Foreign Affairs* 26/1 (October 1947): 213–14.

2. Stephen D. Kertesz, *Diplomacy in a Whirlpool* (Notre Dame, Ind., 1953), 67–69.

3. Ibid., 74.

4. See Bennett Kovrig, *The Myth of Liberation* (Baltimore, 1973), chap. 1.

5. United States, Department of State, *Foreign Relations of the United States* (henceforth cited as *FRUS*) *1944* (Washington, D.C., 1965), 3:886.

6. Ibid., 851.

7. *FRUS, The Conference at Quebec, 1944* (Washington, D.C., 1972), 215.

8. Herbert Feis, *Churchill, Roosevelt, Stalin* (Princeton, 1957), 548.

9. World Peace Foundation, *Documents on American Foreign Relations, 1944–1945* (Princeton, 1957), 244–50.

10. *FRUS 1944*, 3:907.

11. Ibid., 946, 951, 953–54.

12. See Alexander Cretzianu, "The Rumanian Armistice Negotiations: Cairo 1944," *Journal of Central European Affairs* 11/3 (October 1951): 243–58.

13. See Robert E. Sherwood, *Roosevelt and Hopkins* (New York, 1948), 711.

14. *FRUS 1944* (Washington, D.C., 1966), 4:170.

15. Ibid., 172–73.

16. Robert R. King, *Minorities under Communism* (Cambridge, Mass., 1973), 36.

17. Campbell, "The European Territorial Settlement," 200.

18. See Daniel Csatári, *Dans la tourmente* (Budapest, 1974), 349–51.

19. See ibid., 366–75.

20. Kertesz, *Diplomacy in a Whirlpool*, 164–67.

21. Ibid., 262–66.

22. Ibid., 177.

23. Ibid., 178–79. Cf. Sándor Balogh, *A népi demokratikus Magyarország külpolitikája, 1945–1947* (Budapest, 1982), 144, 318.

24. Ibid., 175–76, 178.

25. *FRUS 1946* (Washington, D.C., 1969), 6:272–73. Cf. Balogh, *Magyarország külpolitikája*, 149–50.

26. *FRUS 1946*, 6:579–80.

27. Kertesz, *Diplomacy in a Whirlpool*, 181.

28. See Ferenc Nagy, *The Struggle behind the Iron Curtain* (New York, 1948), 208–10. Cf. Balogh, *Magyarország külpolitikája*, 167–69.

29. Hungary, Külügyminisztérium, *Le Hongrie et la Conférence de Paris* (Budapest, 1947), 1:108–11.

30. See Campbell, "The European Territorial Settlement," 211–12; Amelia C. Leiss and Raymond Dennett, eds., *European Peace Treaties after World War II* (Boston, 1954), 102; and *FRUS 1946*, 6:301–2.

31. Nagy, *The Struggle*, 225–37, and *FRUS 1946*, 6:316.

32. Leiss and Dennett, *European Peace Treaties*, 102–3; Campbell, "The European Territorial Settlement," 212–13.

33. King, *Minorities under Communism*, 27–31.

34. Edvard Beneš, *Memoirs* (London, 1954), 206–7. Cf. Balogh, *Magyarország külpolitikája*, 18, 103–6, 311.

35. See Hungary, Külügyminisztérium, *Hungary and the Conference of Paris* (Budapest, 1947), 2:150–52, and 4:178–86; and Joseph B. Schechtman, *Postwar Population Transfers in Europe, 1945–1955* (Philadelphia, 1962), 131–32. Cf. Balogh, *Magyarország külpolitikája*, 107–8.

36. Stephen D. Kertesz, "Peacemaking on the Dark Side of the Moon: Hungary 1943–1947," *Review of Politics* 40/4 (October 1978): 490–91.

37. See *FRUS 1945* (Washington, D.C., 1968), 4:928–52, and *FRUS 1946*, 6:361–73.

38. *FRUS 1945*, 4:937. The Potsdam Agreement provided for the transfer of German minorities to Germany from several Central and East European countries, including Hungary. The Hungarian government made no request for the expulsion of Germans. However, the Czechoslovak government submitted a plea for the expulsion of Hungary's German minority in order to make room for the Hungarians it was eager to expel from Czechoslovakia. With Soviet support, Hungary's Germans were thus included in the transfer provisions of Potsdam. The expulsion of Germans from Hungary proceeded at a desultory pace until the Communist Minister of Interior László Rajk accelerated the process. Ultimately, about two-thirds of the German minority in Hungary was expelled. See Stephen Borsody, "Potsdam and the Expulsion of Germans from Hungary" (in Hungarian), *Új Látóhatár* 32/1 (1981): 103–6; Stephen D. Kertesz, "The Expulsion of the Germans from Hungary: A Study in Postwar Diplomacy," *Review of Politics* 15/2 (April 1953): 179–208; and Bennett Kovrig, *Communism in Hungary* (Stanford, 1979), 202. Cf. Balogh, *Magyarország külpolitikája*, 77–102.

39. *FRUS 1945*, 4:947.

40. Ibid., 945.

41. Kertesz, *Diplomacy in a Whirlpool*, 123–25; Schechtman, *Postwar Population Transfers*, 134–35.

42. Kertesz, *Diplomacy in a Whirlpool*, 124.

43. Kovrig, *Communism in Hungary*, 200; King, *Minorities under Communism*, 54–55.

44. Schechtman, *Postwar Population Transfers*, 135.

45. Hugh Seton-Watson, *The East European Revolution* (New York, 1951), 344. See also the Editor's Note at the end of Chapter 5, below.

46. Schechtman, *Postwar Population Transfers*, 137–38. See also Balogh, *Magyarország külpolitikája*, 120–21.

47. Nagy, *The Struggle*, 208.

48. See Annex II in chapter 5, below.

49. *FRUS 1946: The Paris Peace Conference* (Washington, D.C., 1970), 3:217.

50. Campbell, "The European Territorial Settlement," 213.

51. Quoted in Leiss and Dennett, *European Peace Treaties,* 96. The full text of the Hungarian Peace Treaty can be found in ibid., 273–97.

52. Campbell, "The European Territorial Settlement," 214.

53. Kertesz, *Diplomacy in a Whirlpool,* 122.

54. *FRUS 1947* (Washington, D.C., 1947), 4:266. In the autumn of 1946, the Prague government forcibly resettled over 40,000 Hungarians in formerly German-inhabited Czech districts. This action precipitated the flight of many Hungarians from Slovakia across the border to Hungary, and Budapest resorted to the usual futile protest. See Balogh, *Magyarország külpolitikája,* 126–28.

55. Schechtman, *Postwar Population Transfer,* 146–47.

56. Campbell, "The European Territorial Settlement," 201.

57. Kertesz, *Diplomacy in a Whirlpool,* 184.

✳ 5

The Soviet Union and the Hungarian Question

François Fejtő

Several different periods can be distinguished in the Soviet Union's attitude toward Hungary and the Hungarian question in general. It evolved within the framework of Soviet external politics, beginning with revolutionary internationalism and ending up in naked realpolitik of imperialism. The factors shaping these changes are intertwined with four stages of Soviet policy.

I

At the beginning, there was the ideological tradition of socialism. Lenin, too, embraced among his doctrines the "right of nations to self-determination," as it emerged from the passionate discussions on the "national question" in 1908–9 among the contemporary Socialists, particularly Rosa Luxemburg, Otto Bauer, and Karl Kautsky. Lenin took Kautsky's side without hesitation when he warned his comrades against "underestimation of the tendency of all nations to form a state of their own."

In his treatise, *The Right of Nations to Self-Determination,* written just before World War I, Lenin contrasted Austria-Hungary with tsarist Russia, viewing the former more favorably than the latter. The Habsburg Empire, he wrote, could transform itself from a dual monarchy into a "trialist" state with three centers: a German, a Hungarian, and a Slav. In his view, the nations of the Habsburg Empire had a common interest in federating themselves, particularly in order to defend their independence against "more rapacious and stronger neighbors." In tsarist Russia, on the other hand, the non-Russian peoples (57 percent of the population), as long as they remained forcibly united with the Great Russians, could look only, in Lenin's view, to ever greater oppression.[1]

By championing, during World War I, self-determination and a federal system (somewhat in spite of himself, given his temperament favoring centralization, indeed étatism), Lenin had no doubt that he might save the Russian empire from dissolution. Meanwhile, he also saw quite clearly that, thanks to wartime French diplomacy and to the subversive activities and intrigues of exiles, the Austro-Hungarian Monarchy might be broken up and its successor states might become, as they indeed did, easy victims of "more rapacious and stronger neighbors."

In any case, Hungary's dismemberment envisaged by the separatist nationalities of the Habsburg Monarchy was very far from the thinking of Lenin and his circle.[2] No doubt the latter also had in mind the judgment of Marx and Engels which was favorable to the Hungarians in view of their war against Austria in 1848–49 which placed them among the "advanced great nations." At the same time, Lenin and his circle thought that the Czechs, Slovaks, and others might just as well stay where they were, within Austria-Hungary, that is, once the empire evolved into a fully democratic federated regime.

II

The Soviet Union's favorable predisposition toward Hungary was reinforced by the events of 1917–19. It should not be forgotten that a large number of Hungarian prisoners-of-war in Russia played an important role in the revolutionary struggles on the side of the Bolsheviks, in sharp contrast to the Czech Legion. Furthermore, under the leadership of Béla Kun—a disciple and, indeed, a friend of Lenin—the young Hungarian Communist party succeeded in establishing, in 1919, the first Soviet republic outside of Russia.

Thus, the enemies of Béla Kun's republic—the Romanians, Czecho-Slovaks, Yugoslavs, all allied with the Entente powers—became enemies of Soviet Russia itself. In fact, they offered themselves, in line with French design, to be part of a *cordon sanitaire* against the Russian Soviet republic. All this contributed to turning the Soviet

Union into a sworn enemy of the Versailles settlements and into a bitter critic of the unitary, centralizing nature of the successor states. The Comintern and the Soviet press never ceased to emphasize the artificial, annexationist character of these countries and their oppressive behavior toward their minorities (including Hungarian minorities). Hence the support the Comintern gave to the struggle of the minority peoples against national oppression, in conjunction with the struggle against "the imperialistic bourgeoisie, victorious in the war." This thesis was then developed in the Comintern resolution of 1924 on the "National Question in Central Europe and the Balkans." (See pertinent excerpts below.)

This internationalist, antichauvinistic stance of the Comintern also explains the large proportion of minority elements in Central and Eastern European Communist parties (Hungarians, Jews, Ukrainians, and others), especially in leadership capacity.

III

A new phase of Soviet policy toward Central and Eastern Europe (this time rather unfavorable to Hungarians) began with the ascendancy of Hitler, which placed Europe's reorganization on the agenda of international affairs. In view of the new situation, the Soviet Union, in an about-face, came to the defense of the Versailles settlement. To stand up against Nazi expansionism appeared to the Soviet leaders to be more important than opposition to the nationalism of the successor states. In Moscow's judgment, the collapse of Czechoslovakia and Yugoslavia—which would have profited the Soviet Union in the 1920s—would have now benefited Germany. Consequently, Soviet foreign policy was completely reversed. The non-aggression pact concluded with France in 1935 opened the way to a series of agreements, signaling attempts at rapprochement with France's allies.

The few tentative Soviet gestures toward Hungary received no response, however. The Hungarians persisted in their alliance with the Italians and later with the Germans. Thus, the Czech, Yugoslav, and Romanian Communist parties were instructed, from 1935 onward, to drop their internationalist, antichauvinist party line—until then hostile to the centralizing, unitary "bourgeois" regimes—and to work toward an alliance with the bourgeois nationalist parties, in order to defend national independence. At the same time, in the Soviet Union itself, a shift occurred toward realpolitik, virtually a renewal of the nationalistic traditions of tsarism, with a view to taking advantage of the destabilization of Europe and ensuring Soviet participation in the reshaping of spheres of influence following the expected collapse of the Versailles system. The recasting of Soviet foreign policy coincided with the purge of "cosmopolitan" leading personalities from the Communist party. There were many Hungarians among them, well established in the Soviet party apparatus following the civil war. This was coupled with an equally severe purge of the Communist parties in exile; the Hungarian Béla Kun was one of the victims.

The oppressed nationalities were now forgotten. Their cause was taken into account only if it corresponded with the interests of the Soviet Union at any given moment. The principles of sovereignty, of self-determination, came to be subordinated to the selfish interests of the Soviet empire.

IV

After the interlude of the Soviet-German pact (which allowed the Russians to take part in the dismemberment of Poland, but also obliged them to accept the breaking up of Czechoslovakia and the destruction of Yugoslavia), the 1935 party line was reinstated. Henceforward the Soviet Union supported the Allied objective of restoring the successor states, with the explicit or implicit reservation that the Soviet Union was striving for the annexation of eastern Poland, the Carpatho-Ukraine, and Bessarabia.

The Hungarians, as Nazi Germany's allies, fought the Soviet forces and attempted to join the victors only after it was too late. The Soviet Union had no reason to look on Hungarian requests for frontier revisions with favor, although the Russians admitted now and then that—in theory—the Hungarian claims were not without foundation. Yet, it was not only Hungary's alliance with Germany, pure and simple, which made the Soviet leaders consistently anti-Hungarian at the Peace Conference. One can ask, for example, why did the Soviet Union support with such persistence the inhuman plan of Czechoslovakia to expel all Hungarians living within its frontiers? (See extracts from Andrei Vyshinskii's speech at the Paris Peace Conference in 1946, below). And why did the Soviet Union favor the Romanians—

another erstwhile ally of Hitler—against the Hungarians in the dispute over Transylvania?

As to the first question, Khrushchev gave the key answer in his conversation with Tito in 1956: "The Soviet Union cannot but be ill-disposed toward the Hungarians; after all, Hungary fought in two world wars against Russia, in alliance with the West."[3] Indeed, public opinion in Hungary had been traditionally Western-oriented. The Czechs, on the other hand, panting with revenge, were more pro-Russian than ever. Moreover, the Hungarian Communist party was weak. The Communist party received only 16 percent of the votes at a relatively free election in 1945. The Communist party in Czechoslovakia, on the other hand, gained considerable strength following the end of the war. Hungary's new government was certainly not pro-Soviet while Beneš founded his foreign policy on unquestioning loyalty to Moscow.

Under these conditions, it was in the interest of the Soviet Union to appear as the protector of Czech nationalism and to support the Czechs and the Slovaks in their determination to humiliate the Hungarians, the ruling ethnic group of yesteryear. And, besides, it was in the Soviet interest to egg on the Czechs to do things that could not but displease Western public opinion. The brutal treatment meted out to the German and Hungarian minorities was a sad disavowal of the humanism of Tomáš G. Masaryk.

As to the question of support of Romania there were several reasons for Soviet action. The incorporation of Transylvania in its entirety into the Romanian state was a kind of compensation for the Russian annexation of Bessarabia. After the war, it seems, Stalin did not immediately make a final decision on the fate of Hungary. Hungary may have appeared to him as a useful object of bargaining in any future haggles with the Western powers. However, Romania was already considered by him to belong definitively to the Soviet sphere of influence. Thus, the Soviet Union had good reason to flatter Romanian nationalism and, at the same time, also slip a few aces in the power game to the tiny Communist party in Romania, led by Ana Pauker and Gheorghiu Dej.

Finally, an intriguing question remains: why did the Red Army initially render a conspicuous, albeit temporary, protection to the Hungarian minority against atrocities committed by Romanian nationalists in Transylvania after it was reconquered by the Romanians?

The answer, if we exclude humanitarian considerations, as we must, lies probably in the Soviet aim of weakening Romanian resistance over the question of Bessarabia by waving the "Hungarian card" and, at the same time, reinforcing Romanian dependence on Soviet goodwill concerning the reintegration of Transylvania into "Greater Romania."

Notes

1. *Lenin's Selected Works* (Moscow, French edition), 6:476.
2. On the issue of the peoples of the Habsburg Monarchy, Lenin's thinking was duly reflected in the Soviet manifesto "To the Workers, Peasants, and Soldiers of the Former Austro-Hungarian Empire," November 3, 1918, which appealed for "an alliance of the proletariat of all nations" and lashed out against "an alliance with the national bourgeoisie" carving out from the defunct Monarchy nation-states. The manifesto stated: "We are deeply convinced that when the German, Czech, Croat, Hungarian, Slovene workers, soldiers, and peasants take power into their hands and complete the work of the entire national liberation, they will conclude a brotherly alliance of free peoples and with united forces they will defeat the capitalists." And it concluded: "Long live the freedom of the peoples of Austria; the Hungarians, Czechs, Slovenes, Ruthenians. Long live the Councils of the Workers', Soldiers', Peasants' Deputies of Austria-Hungary! Long live the alliance between them and the Soviets of Russia for the common struggle!" For the full text of the manifesto, see Jane Degras, ed., *Soviet Documents on Foreign Policy* (London, 1951–53), 1:120–23.
3. V. Micunovic, *Journées de Moscou, 1956–1958,* ed. Robert Laffont (Paris, 1979), 72–78, passim.

Annex I
Excerpts from a Resolution of the Fifth Comintern Congress, 1924, in Support of National Self-Determination*

The imperialist war, into which the bourgeoisie drew the workers by hypocritical slogans about the defense of small nationalities, and the

*Excerpts from the "Resolution on the National Question in Central Europe & Balkans," *Communist International* 7 (December 1924–January 1925): 93–99.

right to self-determination, actually led to the intensification of national antagonism as a result of the victory of one of the groups of capitalist powers and national oppression in Central Europe and in the Balkans.

The Saint-Germain, Versailles and subsequent treaties dictated by the victorious Entente powers, created a number of new small imperialist states—Poland, Czecho-Slovakia, Yugoslavia, Rumania, Greece—as a means of fighting against proletarian revolution. These states were formed by the annexation of large territories with foreign populations and have become centres of national oppression and social reaction. . . .

The national question has thus attained new importance since the war, and has become at the present time one of the essential political questions of Central Europe and the Balkans. At the same time the struggle of the oppressed peoples against national oppression has become a struggle against the power of the imperialistic bourgeoisie who were victorious in the World War, since the strengthening of these new imperialist powers means the strengthening of the forces of world imperialism.

The importance of the struggle against national oppression is still further augmented by the fact that the nationalities oppressed by Poland, Czecho-Slovakia, Yugoslavia, Rumania, and Greece, in their social composition, are largely peasants, and the struggle for their national liberation is at the same time the struggle of the peasant masses against foreign landlords and capitalists.

In view of these facts, the Communist Parties of Central Europe and the Balkans are confronted with the task of giving full support to the national revolutionary movement among the oppressed nationalities.

The slogan "the right of every nation to self-determination, even to the extent of separation" in the present pre-revolutionary period must be expressed in the case of these newly arisen imperialist states in the more definite slogan, "the political separation of the oppressed peoples from Poland, Rumania, Czecho-Slovakia, Yugoslavia, and Greece. . . ."

The Congress charges all the Communist Parties of Central Europe and the Balkans with the task of giving complete support to the national revolutionary movements of the oppressed peoples against the power of the ruling bourgeoisie, and of organising Communist nuclei in the national revolutionary organisations, in order to win the leadership of the national revolutionary movement of the oppressed peoples, and to direct it along the clear and definite path of revolutionary struggle against the power of the bourgeoisie, on the basis of the close solidarity of all workers and their common struggle for a workers' and peasants' government in every country.

Only by a union of the Communist elements within the national revolutionary organisations can the former secure priority for the toiling masses in the latter, as a counter-poise to the bourgeois landowning and adventurous elements, which frequently used these organisations for their own class aims, or converted them into tools for imperialist aims in the various capitalist States.

The Congress imposes on all the Communist Parties the obligation of carrying on an energetic struggle against the provocation of national hatred and chauvinism by the bourgeois and the social-traitor parties, and of explaining to the working masses of both the oppressed and oppressing nationalities, the social character of national oppression and the national revolutionary struggle and the dependence of this struggle on the struggle of the world proletariat for the complete social and national emancipation of the workers. . . .

The Congress notes the counter-revolutionary significance of the colonising of these small imperialist powers carried on by the ruling classes, leading to an aggravation of the national differences. The Congress charges the Communist Parties of Poland, Rumania, Yugoslavia, Czecho-Slovakia, and Greece, with the obligation of conducting a vigorous campaign against this colonising policy.

The Congress approves of the slogan launched by the Communist Parties of the Balkan countries advocating a Balkan Federation of equal and independent Workers' and Peasants' Republics. . . .

As regards the particular national questions of the different countries of Central Europe and the Balkans, the Congress considers the position to be as follows: . . .

VIII
The Magyar Question

The Congress considers it essential to intensify the Communist work among the Magyar population of those territories annexed by Czecho-Slovakia, Rumania, and Yugoslavia, and that the Communist Parties of these countries should launch the slogan of the right of these Magyars to self-determination, even to separation from the States that annexed them.

IX
The Transylvanian and Dobrudja Questions

The Congress approves of the slogans advanced by the Communist Party of Rumania for the separation of Transylvania and Dobrudja from Rumania and forming independent regions of them.

Annex II
*Excerpts from Andrei Vyshinskii's Speech at the Paris Peace Conference, 1946, in Support of Population Transfers**

The Soviet Government has wide experience in the solution of problems of nationality, as well as of questions of national minorities. The settlement of these questions is assured in the Soviet Union, by the soundness of the radical policy which is applied in the Soviet Union and which is based on the high principles of the teachings of Lenin-Stalin. In turn, inspired by high ideals of equality and fraternity, in the full meaning of the word, the Soviet foreign policy, as well as its internal radical policy, are guided by the principle of respect of equality of races, and on the principle of self-determination of nations. The Lenin-Stalin radical policy guarantees the successful development of the economic life of the innumerable nationalities which populate our country, and the bright dawn of radical culture, in the broad sense of the word, the dawn, thanks to which creative forces which were slumbering in the depths of the sixteen Soviet Socialist Republics and the peoples who populate these Republics, have developed with brilliance and wealth, which have turned out to be a worthy recompense for

---

*Excerpts from a speech by the delegate of the USSR, Andrei Vyshinskii, at the session of the Political and Territorial Commission for Hungary, Conference of Paris, September 20, 1946, as published in *Hungary and the Conference of Paris* (Budapest, 1947), 4:72–78. Official English version, C.P. (H/P) Doc. 16.

the leaders of the Soviet State, for their practical participation in the Socialist construction. It is on the basis of respect for the principles of national self-determination, the principle of respect for the equality of races, that the Soviet foreign policy is based. And it enables the Soviet Union to consider itself competent to participate in the questions which are at present occupying the attention of this distinguished gathering. This is the basis upon which internal treaties of the Soviet Union and agreements with other nations are founded. It is on this foundation that the Soviet Union bases its economic agreements, political and other agreements, signed by the Soviet Union, and which are analogous with the problems which our Commission is considering. I am referring to agreements which concern the question of the transfer of populations, repatriation, option and of all questions relating to the solution of these difficult problems, because the questions of option, nationality, repatriation, and the transfer of populations, is not an easy problem. As an example, I would like to cite a document such as the Soviet-Polish agreement of 6 July, 1945 as a result of which over a million people were transferred from the Soviet Union to Poland, over a period of 18 months; and hundreds of thousands of Ukrainians, Byelorussians, Russians and people of many other nationalities were transferred from Poland to the USSR. This agreement was based on the principles I have just referred to, and it is therefore natural that the Soviet Government should welcome, on the part of governments of other nations, any efforts which would lead to the realisation or accomplishment of the same principles of mutual respect and an effort at fraternal co-operation. . . .

The Soviet Government considers that one of the possible solutions of the national problem when faced with conflicting national interests is to free one of the countries of persons of the nationality of the other country and to settle these persons at home, that is in their own country. This is the way the question stands before us and no one can deny that it is well founded. I think that it is hardly possible to approve the stand of the Government of any country which far from doing all in its power to bring back its children from abroad, tries to turn the children of its race into step-children, marooning them abroad. . . .

The right is on the side of Czechoslovakia. . . . Our commission decided to include in Article 4 of the Draft Peace Treaty with Hungary an addition forbidding revisionist propaganda. . . . This means that the revisionist tendencies in Hungary and amidst the Hungarian population are still alive, that we here have a menace to peace, to peaceful relations. . . . These revisionist tendencies and trends, this constant revanche-like smouldering of public opinion is a cause of danger and cannot be tolerated. . . .

The transfer is called 'forced.' . . . It is certainly a serious measure, but it has become unavoidable, it is brought about by the development of events. . . . We are told that this measure spells catastrophe for Hungary. . . . The Hungarian Government contends that there is no place for them in Hungary. Is there room for them or not? . . . 500,000 Germans from Hungary must be transferred to the American zone in Germany. . . . This is the plan approved by the Control Council for Germany. . . . If these 500,000 people are transferred from Hungary to Germany, will there be room enough left in Hungary for 200,000 Hungarians, transferred from Czechoslovakia? I think there will be. . . . These measures are described as an 'inhumane' act! . . . It is clear that there is nothing 'inhumane' in this plan.

The Story of the "200,000 Hungarians"

EDITOR'S NOTE. In the speech quoted above, Andrei Vyshinskii was arguing in support of the Czechoslovak demand to transfer the remaining "200,000 Hungarians" from Czechoslovakia to Hungary. This was a misleading figure. The story behind it has never been pieced together with all of its ramifications although it is one of the most intriguing maneuvers of Beneš's diplomacy.

President Beneš, originator of the expulsion policy of the national minorities, had been successful during the war in gaining East-West approval, confirmed at Potsdam, for the expulsion of Germans from Czechoslovakia but had met with Western opposition to the expulsion of the Hungarians. In the spirit of the then flourishing Pan-Slav brotherhood, only the Russians supported, in principle, Beneš's attempt to transfer the Hungarians (see excerpts from the Jaromír Smutný documents in Annex I of Chapter 11, below). Undaunted, Beneš resorted to intricate moves to maneuver the Western powers into approving his plan.

In 1945, in a memorandum on the problems of national minorities submitted to the Potsdam Conference, Czechoslovakia requested the "transfer" of Hungary's Germans, as well as "population exchange" as means of solving remaining national minority problems. Both demands were approved at Potsdam, presumably with Soviet support. (For additional references on the Potsdam expulsion clauses, see note 38 in Chapter 4, above.) The connection between the two demands was revealed at the Paris Peace Conference. The Czechoslovaks argued—supported by Vyshinskii's speech quoted above—that, since the expulsion of the Germans from Hungary had already been approved at Potsdam, there would be room for the "remaining" 200,000 Hungarians from Czechoslovakia.

The figure of 200,000 "remaining" Hungarians, earmarked for that particular transfer, had been arrived at by the following calculations:

(1) Czechoslovakia claimed that 200,000 of its Hungarians would be transferred in exchange for the same number of Slovaks from Hungary in the course of the "population exchange" between Hungary and Czechoslovakia already approved at Potsdam.

(2) Another 200,000 Hungarians living in Czechoslovakia would "re-Slovakize," the assumption being that they were actually "Magyarized" Slovaks.

(3) Thus, there would be only 200,000 Hungarians left, and they should be transferred since there would be plenty of room for them after the Potsdam-approved transfer of Germans from Hungary.

Actually, despite Czechoslovak propaganda efforts promising free land and furnished houses, only 59,774 Slovaks were willing to take advantage of the population exchange and leave Hungary for Slovakia. As for the "re-Slovakized" Hungarians, almost all of them renounced their newly-found Slovak nationality as soon as the postwar anti-Hungarian terror subsided. And at the Peace Conference, the American-led opposition foiled the Soviet-backed Czechoslovak plan to expel the "remaining" 200,000 Hungarians from Slovakia.

✳ 6

International Minority Protection from the League of Nations to the United Nations

Ferenc A. Váli

The system of international protection of national minorities, launched by World War I and destroyed by World War II, was ill-fated in Central Europe from the very beginning. The Treaty of Trianon created massive Hungarian minorities in Czechoslovakia, Romania, and Yugoslavia. But, paradoxically, the peace treaty obliged Hungary alone, not its neighbors, to assume commitments for the protection of national minorities, although few remained in Hungary. Nor did the Covenant of the League of Nations, signed simultaneously with the peace treaties, contain any provisions for the safeguarding of minority rights. Furthermore, at that time it was considered incompatible with the status of great powers to be subjected to such restrictions of their sovereignty, even if defeated. Thus, in the otherwise harsh Treaty of Versailles, defeated Germany, in her capacity as a great power, escaped such international obligations, a circumstance which later served well Hitler's purpose in providing warrant for his claim that the persecution of Jews was strictly a domestic matter.

The international system of minority protection itself was of considerable interest to Jews, being a persecuted minority for centuries. In fact, the first international initiative for such a protection came from Jewish interest groups, mainly in the United States. However, the principal powers of the Paris Peace Conference of 1919–21 may themselves have realized the need for minority protection in view of some of the unfair ethnic situations created by the territorial settlements. Thus, Czechoslovakia, Romania, and Yugoslavia (and also Poland and the Baltic states) were persuaded or forced, as a condition of their extensive territorial acquisitions in violation of the ethnic principle, to enter into special treaties for the protection of ethnic groups annexed against their will. These treaties were concluded not with the mother countries of the minorities, but with the Principal Allied and Associated Powers: Great Britain, France, Italy, and Japan. The United States, becoming increasingly critical of the whole process of peacemaking, refused to participate in any of these transactions.

The separate treaties, dubbed "minority treaties," between the Principal Allied and Associated Powers on the one hand, and Czechoslovakia, Romania, and Yugoslavia on the other, were signed on September 10, 1919, at Saint-Germaine-en-Laye, a Paris suburb. The purpose of the minority treaties was the preservation and protection of the ethnic, religious, and linguistic identity of those groups which had come under alien regimes against their will and as a result of the new frontiers. In other words, the ethnocultural status of these minorities was not to be endangered or adversely affected by the changes of territorial sovereignty imposed on them. Also, it was believed by the sponsors of the minority treaties that internationally guaranteed protection would prevent the minorities from opposing the new regimes and help to convert them into loyal citizens of their new fatherlands. On the other hand, Czechoslovakia, Romania, and Yugoslavia (soon allied against Hungary in the Little Entente) believed that in return for their minority obligations, the great powers should guarantee their territorial integrity. The intention of tying the two issues to one another was evidently specious.[1] Threats to territorial integrity stemming from the creation of large national minorities could have been in many cases eliminated by boundary changes. However, beneficiaries of the post-World War I distribution of territorial spoils adamantly refused such an option.

While the need for protection of national minorities appeared obvious, any contrary views were eagerly embraced by the Little Entente states. One such view was that of Afranio Mello-Franco, foreign minister and representative of Brazil in the Council of the League of

Nations. His thesis on "minority protection," pronounced in February 1926, was the following:

> It seems to me obvious that those who conceived this system of protection did not dream of creating within certain states a group of inhabitants who would regard themselves as permanently foreign in the general organization of the country. On the contrary, they enjoy a status of legal protection which might ensure respect for the inviolability of the person in all its aspects and which might *gradually prepare the way for the conditions necessary for the establishment of a complete national unity.*[2]

The Mello-Franco thesis was enthusiastically acclaimed by the Little Entente countries forgetting that, if applied before World War I, the Slovak, Romanian, or Serb minorities could have hardly survived in historic Hungary.

Mello-Franco's assumptions may have been compatible with conditions of immigrants in Brazil, or elsewhere in the world, but were completely incompatible with the state of affairs in Central Europe. Old, established populations in the Old World could not be compared to immigrants who voluntarily chose to settle in new lands overseas or even closer to their former homes. The Mello-Franco doctrine clearly contradicted the purpose of the minority treaties and it was never officially endorsed by the European powers.

The minority treaties intended to protect "language, race, and religion" of all people without distinction as to their origins. They generally contained identical provisions, but also included some special clauses to meet individual national conditions. In particular, no restrictions were to be imposed on the use of any minority language—in private or public, in commerce, in the realm of religion, in the press or other publications, as well as in public meetings. Use of the minority language was also to be assured in public offices and before the courts. The minority treaties also sought to ensure public education of the children of minorities in their mother tongues, at least on the levels of primary instruction. However, the official (majority) languages could be made a compulsory subject on all levels of instruction in minority schools. The minorities were also assured of the right to maintain their own private schools and other social institutions with the right to use their own languages. Furthermore, the treaty with Czechoslovakia, unlike those with Romania and Yugoslavia, guaranteed the right to education in minority tongue beyond primary instruction. It also provided an autonomous regime for Carpatho-Ruthenia. The treaty with Romania, on the other hand, included special commitments to grant limited autonomy in cultural and religious matters to the Hungarian-speaking Székelys and the German-speaking Saxons of Transylvania.

The minority treaties were placed under the guarantee of the League of Nations and they were not to be modified without the consent of the League. Czechoslovakia, Romania, and Yugoslavia agreed that any member state represented in the Council of the League had the right to draw the attention of the Council to any breach or violation of the minority treaties. The Council was also authorized to take action or give direction in minority matters.

Hungary had never been elected to membership on the Council, thus it never had the opportunity to submit a minority complaint directly to the Council. A most circuitous procedure was thus the only resort available to the Hungarians for lodging a complaint. This channel was open both to a complaining state and to a member of the complaining minority. The complaint had to be filed with a special bureau of the League Secretariat, called the Minorities Question Section, where it was first examined.

When the petition was submitted by a government, it was passed directly to that government against which the complaint was directed. After an exchange of comments and counter-comments, the case was forwarded to a Committee of Three (consisting of three Council members). The Committee could freely act as it pleased; it could summarily dismiss the complaint, or suggest negotiations between the Minorities Question Section of the League Secretariat and the governments concerned. Members of the Minorities Question Section could also report the complaint to the Council. Only the final actions were conducted in public; all prior procedures were confidential. Only twice did Hungary's numerous complaints reach the Council of the League of Nations.[3]

When a petition was filed by a member or organization of a national or religious minority, the Minorities Question Section was authorized to examine it first to determine whether it fulfilled the requirements of "receivability." In practice, this meant that the Minorities Question Section could reject the petition outright. It could also discuss the complaint with the petitioners and reach a solution in private. Very few of these complaints ever reached the Committee of Three. Furthermore, a minority organization or members of a minority were running considerable risks by bringing cases against their own governments before an international forum. And even if they dared to do so, they had little chance of passing the gauntlet of bureaucratic obstacles.

The attitudes of the Little Entente states toward their Hungarian minorities varied greatly, and thus their respect for the provisions of the minority treaties also varied. Czechoslovakia, burdened by its enormous German minority but living under a democratic regime, proved relatively more law-abiding than Romania or Yugoslavia. It was in Romania that Hungarian deputies most often intervened on behalf of their people, while in Yugoslavia, under royal dictatorship, the situation for such actions was rather delicate.

There were also charges other than the routine minority-language complaints lodged against the Little Entente governments. These were mostly complaints of a financial nature which could be brought before the Mixed Arbitral Tribunals established by the peace treaties. Best known among them were the claims of the Hungarian "optants," so called because these Hungarians opted to retain Hungarian citizenship under the provisions of the peace treaties, although their original places of residence were in the territories annexed by Hungary's neighbors. These plaintiffs owned real estate in the three Little Entente countries, often expropriated under the guise of "agrarian reforms" even if they were not large estates. "Agrarian claims" might have been a more appropriate name for these cases.[4] It was Article 250 of the Peace Treaty of Trianon that said that properties of former enemy citizens in the territory of the former Austro-Hungarian Monarchy were not to be seized and, if they had been seized, they should be returned to their owners.

In the early 1920s, Czechoslovakia, Romania, and Yugoslavia introduced large-scale agrarian reforms which were implemented in a discriminatory manner against Hungarian owners. When Hungarian citizens started proceedings against the Little Entente governments, these governments insisted that the Mixed Arbitral Tribunals had no jurisdiction over such claims because the expropriations had not been implemented under the terms of Article 250, but under domestic agrarian reform legislations. When the Mixed Arbitral Tribunals rejected the plea of non-competence, the defendant governments withdrew their arbitrators and prevented the tribunals from functioning. The Hungarian government forthwith asked the Council of the League of Nations to appoint the missing members of the tribunals as provided by the peace treaty. Lengthy discussions followed. Eventually a compromise was agreed upon. By the Hague-Paris Agreement of 1930 (which also settled Hungary's reparation debts) an Agrarian Fund was set up, financed partly by indemnity payments by the defendant states, partly by the war reparation payments of Hungary, and partly by the contributions of the great powers. Thereafter, based on judgments of the Mixed Arbitral Tribunals, and in proportion to the availability of funds, the Agrarian Fund indemnified the owners of the confiscated lands.[5]

Much attention was also drawn to another case. The Péter Pázmány University of Budapest owned large landholdings in Slovakia, estates which had been donated by the Hungarian kings in the seventeenth and eighteenth centuries. After Slovakia's annexation, the Czechoslovak government had seized these properties, whereupon the university initiated a lawsuit before the Tribunal. The confiscation was based on the thesis that the university was a state institution, therefore the Czechoslovak state duly inherited it. The Tribunal, however, held that the university's landholdings constituted private property, and ordered, in 1933, the Prague government to return it. The Permanent Court of International Justice at The Hague rejected the Czechoslovak appeal and confirmed the decision of the Mixed Arbitral Tribunal. Subsequently, the claim was settled by a lump-sum payment by the Czechoslovak government.[6]

In the latter part of the 1930s, Hungary's and the world's attention was diverted from arguments over minority problems to Nazi Germany's actions. Minority treaties were no longer invoked when revision of frontiers became the topic of discussion by the Great Powers.

The inhumanities committed before and during World War II, especially by Nazi Germany and Japan, induced the Allied governments and those represented at the San Francisco Conference of 1944, which founded the United Nations Organization, to enact provisions for the respect and protection of "human rights and fundamental freedoms." The safeguard of such rights had already been pledged during the war by the Atlantic Charter (1941), the Declaration of the United Nations

(1942), and by the Teheran Declaration (1943). In 1947, the peace treaties with Hungary, Bulgaria, Romania, Finland, and Italy contained clauses for the protection of human rights and individual freedoms. But none of them provided for special guarantees to ethnic minorities, as was the case with the treaties concluded after World War I. At the same time, in 1947, interwar treaties for the protection of national minorities were declared terminated "through basic changes in conditions."[7]

The Charter of the United Nations Organization contained several specific references to human rights and fundamental freedoms. Article 1 listed one of the purposes of the United Nations as "promoting and encouraging" respect for human rights "without distinction as to race, sex, language, or religion." By Article 62, the Economic and Social Council was empowered to make recommendations "for the purpose of promoting respect and observance of human rights and fundamental freedoms for all." But the Charter mentioned nowhere specifically the safeguarding of the rights of minorities, whether ethnic, racial, or religious. And it seemed especially uncertain whether protection of ethnicity was included under the term "human rights."

With the introduction of the concept of "human rights" and "fundamental freedoms" in the Charter, as well as in other conventions, the protection of ethnic minorities had been, in fact, obscured and largely ignored. As a United Nations study on ethnic, religious, and linguistic minorities, published as late as 1979, admitted: "For quite a long time (at least 20 years) after the end of the Second World War, it was thought—and stated in writing—that the question of international protection of minorities was no longer topical."[8] There were several reasons for this manifest disregard:

(a) The extermination of six million Jews in Europe must have appeared to the public as an event which in its enormity overshadowed violations of minority rights.

(b) Accordingly, the protection of human rights—that is, of life, liberty, and the pursuit of happiness—must have appeared more important to the drafters of the charter than the safeguarding of ethnic cultures.

(c) Many people believed that the guarantees for national minorities had been used by Hitler as a pretext to threaten Germany's neighbors.

(d) It might have been believed that with the wholesale and indiscriminate expulsion of German minorities from Poland and Czechoslovakia, as well as the attempt by Czechoslovakia "to exchange" its Hungarian minority, national minority protection had become both anomalous and superfluous.

(e) Since the United States and Latin American states had been instrumental in drafting the new international legal statutes, the impact of the alleged principle of "American Public Law" (as already foreshadowed by the Mello-Franco thesis), that is, that immigrants should have no claim for status and protection as an ethnic minority, also contributed to the neglect and disregard of national minority rights.[9]

The charter drafters were eager to emphasize the need for the protection of human rights. But Article 2 (par. 7) prohibited the United Nations from intervening "in matters which are essentially within the domestic jurisdiction" of any state. The inherent contradiction between these two postulates has plagued the proceedings of the world organization ever since. Theoretically, it had been agreed that, with the adoption of the charter and subsequent instruments providing protection of human rights, the violation of such rights had ceased to be a matter "essentially within the domestic jurisdiction" of states and had become a question of international concern. But, in practice, many violators of such rights, headed by the Soviet Union, refused even to discuss such complaints in the United Nations and elsewhere on the grounds that such action would constitute illegal interference in their internal affairs.

The United Nations Economic and Social Council, at its first session (January–February 1946), set up the Commission of Human Rights with the task of preparing the following international enactments:

(a) The Universal Bill of Rights;

(b) International declarations or conventions on civil liberties, the status of women, freedom of information and similar matters;

(c) Arrangements for the protection of minorities (this may be a clear indication that minorities were not meant to be covered under the "human rights" protection);

(d) Arrangements for the prevention of discrimination on grounds of race, sex, language, or religion.

The commission first prepared the Universal Declaration of Human Rights; it was adopted by the General Assembly on December 10, 1948. The declaration listed such rights as the right to life, to security, and to equality, the right to marry and to own property, freedom of thought and religion, the right to assembly, the right to work as well as to education and participation in the cultural life of the community. However, the declaration did not specifically state that members of a national minority have the right to education in their own language, to use their language before authorities and the courts, to speak in assemblies in their own language, or to enjoy their own special ethnic cultural life.

The International Covenant on Civil and Political Rights, adopted by the Human Rights Commission in 1962, provided in its Article 1 that: "All peoples have the right to self-determination. By virtue of this right they freely determine their political status and freely pursue their economic, social, and cultural development."

However, in the interpretation of the United Nations organs, especially the General Assembly, this right to self-determination only applied to colonial or ex-colonial peoples.

Article 27 of the covenant seemed to recall the existence of national minorities by providing that: "In those states in which ethnic, religious, or linguistic minorities exist, persons belonging to such minorities shall not be deprived of the right, in community with other members of their group, to enjoy their own culture, to profess and practice their own religion, or to use their own language."

Besides such a general pronouncement, there was no provision in the covenant for schooling in a minority language, for use of a minority language before public offices and in courts of law or assemblies, nor for the right to use such language in the press or other publications. Because Article 27 was to have universal application, it is—unlike the specific post-World War I minority treaties—less elaborate and extremely cautious. In fact, its meaning is unclear and obscure.[10] Incidentally, the Covenant on Civil and Political Rights also failed to mention the protection of the right to own property. Facing the opposition of the Communist governments, the drafting commission dropped any reference to property.

The United Nations Economic and Social Council also set up the Subcommittee on Prevention of Discrimination and Protection of Minorities. This Subcommittee, unlike the Human Rights Commission (which consisted of government representatives), was composed of twelve persons in individual capacities. Its program was to study discrimination in certain fields, such as education, employment, political rights, and religious practices. The main activity of the subcommittee was devoted to these topics rather than to the question of national or other minorities. Nevertheless, at its first session in 1947, the subcommittee passed a decision on the protection of minorities, reaching an agreement on the following convoluted phrasing:

> The protection of non-dominant groups which, while wishing in general for equality of treatment with the majority, wish for a measure of *differentiated treatment* in order to preserve basic characteristics which they possess and which distinguish them from the majority of the population. The protection applies equally to individuals belonging to such groups and wishing the same protection.[11]

This convoluted but laudable pronouncement was, however, never followed up by legislative or other actions. In fact, for years the subcommittee debated the question of defining a "minority," but there was no agreement reached, not even on this preliminary point.[12]

The rules of implementation introduced for the protection of minorities by the treaties of the post-World War II era are far less complete and practical than those of the interwar treaties which themselves were less than satisfactory.

The Covenant on Civil and Political Rights provides for the establishment of a Human Rights Committee (to be distinguished from the Human Rights Commission), consisting of eighteen members, elected for a term of four years by the states which were parties to the covenant. This body is to be the guardian of implementation. The actual measures of implementation were divided into three gradual stages. First stage: The signatories submit reports on compliance with the provisions of the treaty and these reports are examined by the committee. Second stage: Complaints by governments for violations of the provisions of the covenant may be submitted to the committee; but only if the states which are parties to the treaty have made a special declaration recognizing the competence of the committee to examine such complaints is the body authorized to propose a solution to the dispute. Third stage: If the solution proposed is not acceptable to either party, the committee, again only with the consent of the interested states, may appoint an ad hoc Conciliation Commission of five persons which undertakes the task of reaching a settlement. But, in any case, the parties to the dispute are free to accept or reject the report of either the Human Rights Committee or that of the Conciliation Commission.

The covenant primarily deals only with complaints submitted by governments. Individual petitions are only admissible if the parties have signed and ratified the Optional Protocol. In such a case, the Committee would examine the complaint in a closed meeting and eventually "forward its views to the State Party concerned and to the individual." There is no provision under any of these cases for any enforcement measures. It seems clear that the procedure of implementation is essentially based on the willingness of the parties to cooperate. There is no possibility of achieving even a quasi-judicial binding decision.[13]

The Covenant of Civil and Political Rights entered into force on March 23, 1976. Hungary, Czechoslovakia, Romania, and Yugoslavia, and also the Soviet Union, are among its signatories. But none of these states had made any special declaration recognizing the competence of the committee, nor did they sign the Optional Protocol.

By way of comparison, it should be pointed out that under the United Nations Declaration on Granting Independence to Colonial Countries, and under the provisions of the Special Committee on Apartheid Policy, individual complaints and petitions are freely admitted without any conditions whatsoever. Such a preferential treatment reflects the desire of the Afro-Asian majority in the United Nations to press for a change of policy in some countries, especially in South Africa.[14] On the other hand, national sovereignty is vigorously defended by Soviet bloc states of Central and Eastern Europe against interference in domestic affairs. Within the bloc, however, Moscow regards such an interference as justifiable according to the so-called Brezhnev doctrine.

The Helsinki Accord of August 1, 1975, attempted to pierce the Iron Curtain and establish a quasi-right to influence developments in the sphere of human rights. In that sense, the Final Act of the Helsinki Accord is a unique document. While it is not a formal treaty, it did establish the right to question any infringement of human rights (including minority rights) without committing an "interference" into the domestic jurisdiction of the states in question.[15]

The so-called Basket III of the Helsinki Accord deals with all the aspects of human rights, including those relating to national minorities. Principle VII of the Final Act dealt with this matter by declaring:

> The participating States on whose territory national minorities exist will respect the right of persons belonging to such minorities to equality before the law, will afford them the full opportunity for the actual enjoyment of human rights and fundamental freedoms and will, in this manner, protect their legitimate interests in this sphere.

Similar to various other enactments of post-World War II vintage, the Helsinki Accord seeks to safeguard respect for human rights for minorities, as well as for the majority population. But, nowhere is it clearly stated that national minorities should be allowed to enjoy their ethnic culture in order to prevent their involuntary merger into the ethnic majority of the states in which they happen to exist.

Principle VIII of the Helsinki Final Act handles the question of self-determination of people. Here we find the following rather ambiguous provisions:

> The participating States will respect the equal rights of peoples and their right to self-determination, acting at all times in conformity with the purposes and principles of the Charter of the United Nations and with the relevant norms of international law, including those relating to territorial integrity of States.
>
> By virtue of the principle of equal rights and self-determination of peoples, all peoples have the right, in full freedom, to determine, when and as they wish, their internal and external political status, without external interference, and to pursue as they wish their political, economic, social and cultural development.

In the above context, "internal" self-determination implies the right of a people to become independent, whereas "external" self-determination could mean the right to secede from the state to which they belong. During the Helsinki negotiations it was, however, emphasized by the Soviet Union and other socialist countries that "national minorities" differ from "peoples" in so far that only the latter have the right of "external" self-determination, that is, the right to secede, whereas such a right was not to be granted to national minorities.[16] If this interpretation is correct, one may ask: What is precisely the sense of Principle VIII within the framework of the Helsinki Final Act?

The Helsinki Final Act was signed by all thirty-three European states (except Albania), as well as the United States of America and Canada. It does not appear that it has, in any significant manner, changed the attitudes of Hungary's neighbors toward their national minorities.

The minority treaties concluded after World War I contained fairly satisfactory legal provisions for the protection of national minorities, although the rules of implementation and the practice by which these rules were applied were manifestly inadequate.

In the era following World War II, enactments for the protection of human rights and fundamental freedoms, because of their generalizing character, failed to provide legal safeguards for the national minorities, especially with respect to their language and other aspects of their cultural heritage. Human rights protection is supposed to prevent discrimination against ethnic groups. In reality, it remains blind to the special protection which national minorities need in order to avoid submergence in the majority and loss of their national-ethnic identity, including their language. It must be further emphasized that, despite the impressive rhetoric of the human rights treaties and declarations, even the general protection of human rights and individual freedoms has remained, by and large, deficient or nonexistent.

The global ideological cleavage prevents Hungary from raising the question of Hungarian national minorities before the United Nations and its associated agencies. Hungary, being a member of the Soviet-led bloc of Communist states, could not think of bringing a complaint against another member of the bloc before an international agency. Such legal proceedings are absolutely out of the question. Only inter-Communist party channels could be used for such purposes and they could be used only with the approval and support of Moscow.[17]

In the interwar period, Hungary never had influential allies who would or could help her in the complicated maze of procedures before the League of Nations. Today, to protect Hungarian national minorities against violations of their human rights, complaints could only be brought directly to the United Nations Security Council by a member state on the grounds that such violations endanger peace. So far, no Western government has shown any inclination to undertake such actions.

Accordingly, the Hungarian minorities in Czechoslovakia, Romania, Yugoslavia, and the Soviet Union are at the mercy of those totalitarian regimes irrespective of human rights provisions in the charter and elsewhere and of the ambiguous and deficient enactments in favor of national minorities in some treaties, including the Helsinki Final Act. And such totalitarian regimes are able to exercise very efficient discriminatory measures against their ethnic minorities.

The territorial reshaping of Central Europe after World War I resulted in the separation of millions of Hungarians from their fatherland. Boundary changes were carried out under the implied condition that the cultural survival of national minorities would be assured. Now such survival is even less assured.

Notes

1. See C. A. Macartney's article in Evan Luard, ed., *The International Protection of Human Rights* (London, 1967), 36.

2. C. A. Macartney, *National States and National Minorities* (London, 1934), 277 (italics added).

3. The Hungarian Settlers (Farmers) case was discussed at the Council of the League of Nations in its sessions in June, September, and December 1925. Agreement was reached when the Romanian government promised to pay compensation. The second case concerned a petition by székely residents of Transylvania which was also against Romania; the council handled this case at its sessions of May and September 1931, as well as January and May 1932, and finally in September 1932 when a report was adopted. See Macartney, *National States and National Minorities,* 335, 346, 352, 356.

4. See Francis Deak, *The Hungarian-Rumanian Land Dispute: A Study of Hungarian Property Rights in Transylvania under the Treaty of Trianon* (New York, 1928).

5. For The Hague-Paris Agreement, see *Agreements Relating to the Obligations Resulting from the Treaty of Trianon,* signed at Paris, April 28, 1930, *League of Nations Treaty Series* 121, no. 2785: 69–90.

6. For the judgment of the World Court, see Permanent Court of International Justice at The Hague, *Appeal from the Judgment of the Czechoslovak-Hungarian Mixed Arbitral Tribunal* (Péter Pázmány University v. Czechoslovakia), Judgment of December 15, 1933, series A/B, no. 61. See also, Manley O. Hudson, ed., *World Court Reports, 1932–35* (Washington, D.C., 1938), 3:311–67. The author served as one of the representatives of the university and negotiated the final settlement of the case.

7. Gerhard von Glahn, *Law among Nations* (New York, 1976), 448–49.

The decision was published in United Nations Document, E/CN, 4/367, pp. 36–38.

8. *Study on the Rights of Persons Belonging to Ethnic, Religious and Linguistic Minorities.* By Francesco Capotorti, Special Rapporteur of the Sub-Commission on Prevention of Discrimination and Protection of Minorities. United Nations Document, E/CN, 4/Sub.2/384/Rev.1, p. iii.

9. At the Lima Conference of American States in 1938 a special declaration announced that immigrant aliens should not be allowed to claim in their new homes the status of national minorities. This principle was reaffirmed in 1942 as a "Principle of American Public Law" at Rio de Janeiro and again in Mexico City in 1945. Charles G. Fenwick, *International Law,* 4th ed. (New York, 1965), 317–18.

10. See Egon Schwelb's article in Asbjorn Eide and August Schon, eds., *International Protection of Human Rights* (New York, 1968), 121–22.

11. Economic and Social Council, Official Records, 6th Session, Supplement no. 11, E/CN, 4/52, December 6, 1947.

12. See Sir Samuel Hoare's article in Luard, ed., *The International Protection of Human Rights,* pp. 75–76.

13. See Francesco Capotorti's article in Eide and Schon, eds., *International Protection of Human Rights,* 131–48.

14. Ibid., 147.

15. See Thomas Buergenthal, ed., *Human Rights, International Law and the Helsinki Accord* (Montclair, N.J., 1977).

16. Ibid., 101.

17. See Ferenc A. Váli, "Transylvania and the Hungarian Minority," *Journal of International Affairs* 20, no. 1 (1966): 32–44.

✳ *PART TWO*

*The Hungarians of
Hungary's Neighbors*

"Perhaps there is still time to halt the process threatening our very
existence as a nationality."
>   Memorandum of Transylvanian Hungarians to the Madrid
>   Conference, 1980–83, reviewing adherence to the provisions
>   of the Helsinki Final Act.

✳ 7

Transylvania:
Hungarians under Romanian Rule*

George Schöpflin

The relationship between Romania and Hungary has proved to be one of the most troubled and uneasy in the Danube region. Despite the enforced adoption of a Marxist-Leninist ruling ideology and Communist political system after World War II in both states, the relationship between the two countries did not improve; indeed, in some respects it has actually deteriorated.

It has been generally assumed that the differences between Hungary and Romania can be reduced to a territorial dispute over Transylvania.[1] In reality, however, the Romanian-Hungarian conflict encompasses a broader set of problems which ultimately derive from the different historical and political experiences of the two national communities, and the different political cultures evolved by them.

Transylvania has been invested with a mythic significance by the political cultures of the two nations. It is regarded as having made crucial contributions to the autonomous survival of both nations. The distinction between Transylvania as myth and Transylvania as current political problem is thus being blurred by assumptions which seem to make a rational resolution of the conflict impossible.

Today, this complex problem is further exacerbated by the nature and interests of the ruling Communist regimes. They sustain their claim to legitimacy by references to a Marxist utopia, and they impose

*This text represents an abbreviated version of the author's original.

a myth of unanimity on their national polities. Furthermore, contrary to doctrinal Marxism, self-interest prompted the ruling elites of the Communist regimes to use nationalism as an instrument of legitimacy. In that respect, Romania has definitely been far more strident than Hungary.[2] Indeed, the Romanian leadership went so far as to discard the orthodox Leninist position and, in effect, proclaim a new doctrine of Communist nationalism.

This, then, is the background against which the deeper factors of the Romanian-Hungarian conflict are to be discussed before turning to the current problems of Transylvania's Hungarians under Communist Romanian rule.

I The Conflict of Two Political Cultures

The first factor to notice in any interpretation of Romania's political culture is the surprisingly weak concept of the state and the relatively low level of civic consciousness among its people. This has gone hand-in-hand with major discontinuities in the Romanian cultural tradition and a corresponding disorientation of values. Furthermore, there is a serious gap between high culture, as represented by the intelligentsia, and mass culture.

The weakness of the concept of the state can be attributed to repeated ceasuras in Romanian history. Also, it has something to do with the inability of the Romanian political elite to construct a strong state prior to the mid-nineteenth century, or even to 1918. Historically, the modern Romanian state was territorially limited to and divided between two state formations, Moldavia and Wallachia. Moreover, both provinces were, for centuries, under a peculiar semiautonomous system of subordination to the Ottoman Empire. The relationship between the Porte and its satellite rulers in the Romanian provinces was essentially tributary. By the sixteenth century, the traditional nobility of boyars was transformed, under the weight of Ottoman power, from landholders to officeholders in the service of the sultan. This situation encouraged the Romanian elite to concentrate on the economic exploitation of the peasantry, while at the same time destroying earlier bonds of loyalty between the two classes. This major shift in relations between ruler and ruled was accompanied by a destruction or weakening of existing moral codes and values. Inevitably, as far as Romanian society was concerned, the political elite and the state which it controlled came to be seen as alien and parasitical. The new political rituals adopted by the elite intensified this alienation. In both Romanian provinces, particularly in Moldavia, the rulers established a neo-Byzantine court incorporating both Ottoman and Hellenic elements as well as conscious archaisms and anachronisms. The style of rule, therefore, was more and more divorced from political reality.[3]

Another set of discontinuities arose from the fate of organized religion, generally a repository and guarantor of both popular and elite values. In the seventeenth century, Orthodoxy in the Romanian lands was affected by outside influences from Roman Catholic Poland and Protestant Transylvania, as well as reformist movements in Orthodox Constantinople. When the conservative faction achieved dominance in Constantinople, the Romanians followed, at the cost of intellectual stultification, an empty ritual in the practice of religion. One result was externalization in political culture. External conformity, as distinct from internalized loyalty, came to be regarded as sufficient in political behavior.[4] A further cause of erosion of traditional loyalties was the relative independence of the elite underpinned by the prosperity of the grain trade. Different factions among the boyars looked for different foreign protectors—Poland, Transylvania, Constantinople, or Vienna. Loyalties were unstable, offices were bought and sold. The process culminated in the emergence of Phanariot rule, a system that was corrupt and inefficient, causing backwardness and encouraging dependence on foreign protectors.

With the decline of Ottoman power in the late eighteenth century, changes of a different kind began to affect the Romanian provinces. The most significant of these was the new cultural shift away from neo-Byzantine patterns to Western, particularly French styles. The Romanian political class thenceforward aspired to achieve modernization on Western models of enlightenment and absolutism, which they sought to implant in the very different political soil of the Balkans. No other European political community underwent two such major changes in its cultural aspirations in such a short period of time. These changes resulted in dislocations and discontinuities in Romania's political culture.[5]

The nineteenth century, despite the founding of an independent Romanian state at mid-century, did little to promote stronger loyalties between ruler and ruled. The peasantry remained subject to the exactions of a state which did little or nothing for the great bulk of the population. Indeed, the degree of peasant dissatisfaction was shown by the 1907 uprising, the last jacquerie in Europe.

The territorial enlargement of the Romanian state after World War I, including the annexation of Transylvania from Hungary, was primarily of benefit to the elite. Moreover, the Regatean elite of prewar Romania was not particularly welcoming toward the Transylvanian Romanians with their rather different, legalistic political culture imbibed in Hungary. The interwar state failed to promote either social or national integration. The political gap between elite bureaucrats and the people remained as pronounced as before, while the ethnically non-Romanian population, making up approximately thirty percent of Greater Romania, was given little incentive to develop a sense of loyalty to its new state.[6]

The post-World War II period has, of course, seen far-reaching improvements in the ability of the Romanian state to exercise control over the entire country. The rulers have at their disposal administrative instruments and means of communication undreamed of by King Carol and his regime. Yet, even in the Communist period, identification with the state, as distinct from the party or the nation, has tended to be weaker than in other East European countries. For many Romanians, the state remains a parasitical body and the power of the state is seen to be exploited for personal advantage.

Corruption in Communist systems is not, of course, confined to Romania. Nevertheless, Romania in the 1980s presents a unique spectacle of personalized rule by Nicolae Ceauşescu and his extended family.

The innovations introduced by the Romanian party constitute a major divergence from orthodox Communist concepts of the state. According to classical Marxism-Leninism the party and the state should be kept separate and the party should exercise powers through an appointed "nomenklatura" (the ruling elite). The Romanians adopted a doctrine of intertwining the party and the state, even to the extent of occasionally subordinating the party to the state. This is unique in the Communist world.[7]

Romanian Features

Seen against this background of a fractured historical development, the Romanian political culture has tended toward the construction of systems of myths, symbols, and abstractions. One of the most persistent of these has been the concept of "national soul" and the "national specificity of the Romanian people."[8] These abstractions tend to be put forward as axiomatic and incapable of empirical verification. It is particularly striking that these myth values are apparently freely accepted by the bulk of the Romanian intelligentsia and little attempt is made to question them, at any rate in public.[9]

In the context of Romanian-Hungarian relations, this mythicizing has had two major consequences. In the first place, it makes political communication complex and fraught with the danger of constant misunderstanding, a danger which is made all the greater because of the existence of parallel Hungarian myths.

The web of myths woven around this relationship on the Romanian side is such that all Hungarian utterances concerning Transylvania are interpreted as de facto irredentism. For Romanians, it is difficult to separate questions of historical or personal or sentimental interest in Transylvania from concrete expressions of Hungarian irredentism. Transylvania has become a mystical, abstract concept having little or nothing to do with the concrete reality of the situation. It is seen as the embodiment of everything that is good and worthy in the Romanian national soul, the cradle of the Romanian nation and the symbol of harmony which Romanians have always regarded as central to their own image of themselves. Transylvania is the mystical guarantor of Romanian-ness—"Romanity," that is—which in itself is a potentially mystical notion. To some extent, it may play even a different role for Transylvanian Romanians whose experiences at times set them apart from the Regateans. At any rate, non-Romanians are not welcome in Romanian Transylvania. And Romanian-Hungarian relations are further bedevilled by Romanian fear that the presence of a Hungarian population in Transylvania might once again provide a pretext for detaching part of it from Romania, as happened in 1940. By intensifying this fear, the Soviet Union has used the Romanian-Hungarian territorial conflict as a means of manipulating both countries to the advantage of Soviet imperialism.

In Romanian nationalist perceptions, since World War II the Soviet Union has triggered anxieties similar to those caused by Hungary. Again, the issues concern both territory and "Romanity." The Romanian territorial dispute with the Soviet Union over Bessarabia has similarities to its dispute with Hungary over Transylvania. And, while the Hungarians of Transylvania were seen as denationalizers, their institutions seen as an offense to Romanian uniformity, the Soviet Union has been detested as the source of Slavicization, the continuing impediment to Romania's national self-realization. In addition, the Soviet Union is disliked as the source of an alien modernizing ideology, one which is completely at variance with Romanian populism, a significant current in the country's intellectual life.

Romanian nationalism as a dominant component of the ideology of that country's Communist party can be dated from the early 1960s. It had its positive and negative aspects. Under Communist rule, the Romanian state was an effective instrument for enforcing national integration, more so than its prewar predecessor had been. On the other hand, conformity with an ideology equating Romanian nationhood with Romanian citizenship as the sole criterion of true loyalty to the state, had a negative effect on the non-Romanian minorities. Inevitably, it exacerbated relations with Hungary, where these developments were viewed according to an entirely different set of criteria.[10]

From the early 1960s onward, Romanian nationalism was expressed by means of the traditional abstract and symbolic language. Great stress was placed on national sovereignty as a fundamental value, ensuring the harmonious development of the Romanian nation. Even rapid industrialization acquired an abstract quality. It became a yardstick by which a variety of errors or injustices were justified, most notably the catastrophic neglect of agriculture. Slogans replaced substance. Ad hoc political considerations prevailed over technical rationality. Grandiose developments, like a large petrochemical industry, acted as a facade of modernity, behind which political relations remained authoritarian and arbitrary. The frustrations resulting from the Ceauşescu strategy of rapid industrialization were channeled into the mysticism of official nationalism, encouraging propaganda campaigns, such as the *Cântece România* (A Song for Romania).

The clearest expression of mysticism in Romanian culture and its application to politics can be found in the so-called "traditionalist" school of thought. It dates back to the late nineteenth century and it constitutes a far-from-negligible source of values in Romania today. Traditionalism denied the possibility of applying rational criteria to the decoding of political, economic, and social phenomena, but argued that the glorification of nationhood, mysticism and contemplation transcended reason.[11] The clearest expression of this is to be found in the poem *Miorița,* a hymn to self-sacrifice and communion with nature, which exalts passivity, spirituality, and irrationalism.[12] The philosopher Lucian Blaga defined the "mioritic" space as the Romanian dimension of existence, "a mystical existence of reunion with nature," with its stress on "contemplation, disregarding and ignoring history's temporal dimensions."[13] For the protagonists of traditionalism, there was no room in the Romanian way of life for democracy or parliamentarianism. The introduction of Western institutions was pointless, because they constituted only "forms" which ignored the Romanian "content." Individual or group action, social autonomy, and the existence of intermediate institutions between state and society could have no room in that scheme of things.

Today, neo-traditionalism coexists comfortably with Communist party rule, indeed, in some respects, it offers a highly satisfactory ideology for conformist intellectuals who can thereby justify their passivity and cooptation. Also, one of its central components is xenophobia. In current practice, this emerges as covert anti-Russian sentiment and overt anti-Hungarianism, as well as anti-Semitism. It argues that because Transylvania has always been a Romanian land—indeed, the quintessential Romanian land—the other national groups that live there are there only by the good grace of the majority. They are intrinsically strangers and always will be. Any assertion of minority rights or demands that the minority be accorded powers of autonomy, even those which can be reconciled with the dictates of Marxist "democratic centralism," are at best treated with incomprehension and at worst as irredentism.

A recent work by Ion Lăncrănjan illustrates this tendency very clearly. He takes issue, for example, with a Transylvanian Hungarian writer who had claimed that he had been brought up in Transylvania "in the spirit of Hungarian culture" in a community that was 99 percent Hungarian. To Lăncrănjan, this was an impossibility, for that spirit of Hungarian culture never existed in Transylvania.[14] The implications are illuminating. Hungarian-ness cannot and should not exist as an autonomous value system in a Romanian land, and insofar as the rights of the Hungarian minority should be respected, these must always be subordinated to Romanian political and cultural interests. Another member of the neo-traditionalist current, Adrian Păunescu, who has distinguished himself by his performance as Ceauşescu's court poet, went so far as to extend the argument over Transylvania into outright irredentism. Păunescu rhetorically complained: "Why does Romania have truncated rivers?"[15] To Romanian ears this is an allusion to the unfulfilled promise of the secret Treaty of Bucharest of 1916, in which, as a price for Romanian participation on the Entente side in World War I, the great powers promised Romania a western frontier all the way to the Tisza River. Păunescu's complaint expresses a lingering Romanian resentment at the failure of the Entente powers to keep their promise.

Hungarian Features

Although there are some features of the Hungarian political culture that resemble its Romanian counterpart, there are others which are very different. Among the latter, the most significant has been the different development of the Hungarian concept of the state.

The Hungarian state, too, was alienated from the population socially, yet it retained or recovered its native quality. The unbroken tradition of the Hungarian nobility (both the aristocracy and the gentry) ensured a continuity in perceptions of the state from medieval to modern times. The conservatism of the gentry stood in the way of modernization in the nineteenth century, yet at the same time it was the bedrock of continuity and contributed to the survival of the concept of a native state. During the lengthy periods when Hungary was divided and ruled by foreigners, the perception of Transylvania was particularly significant. Having played a crucial role in the survival of the Hungarian national community, Transylvania came to be regarded as the repository of many authentic Hungarian values.

After the Austro-Hungarian Compromise of 1867, Hungary became for all practical purposes autonomous. This meant that a much stronger native political class could emerge to rule the state and to begin the process of modernization. Hungarian society—the peasantry in particular—certainly regarded the activities of this elite as exploitative and parasitical, but it did not consider the state as alien and illegitimate. The state was accepted as a native Hungarian institution. Furthermore, more successfully than the Romanians, the Hungarian elite did create middle social strata. Albeit never as important as in the West, they did serve as bridges between the elite and the people below.

The Hungarian elite, unlike the Romanian, based its residual power, before the Compromise, on an authentic native institution, the county (*megye*) system. Despite repeated attempts by the Habsburgs to break down this bastion of gentry power, the conservative nobiliary class successfully defended it. A somewhat analogous, though probably vaguer, role was played by the Hungarian Diet, representing the elite's "ancient liberties." These factors contributed to the emergence of a key feature of Hungarian political culture—litigousness and legalism. That, in turn, implied the existence of tribunals which were at least partially autonomous and therefore not the creatures of the rulers. All these features were absent from Romanian development.

Religion, too, played different roles in the history of the two nations. Unlike Orthodoxy in Romania, neither Roman Catholicism nor Protestantism in Hungary was subjected to the state and therefore neither could be readily transformed into value systems of the state. Both religions offered political refuge for those threatened by the Habsburgs. But since the Habsburgs stood for the extension of Roman Catholicism, Calvinism assumed functions of a semi-national religion, especially in Transylvania and eastern Hungary. The different role played by religion, coupled with differences in the development of feudalism, lay behind another distinctive aspect of Hungarian culture, namely the traditional notion of peasant autonomy, which relied ultimately on the protection of the Hungarian crown. Here the contrast with Romanian traditional passivity, only occasionally punctuated by spasmodic uprisings, is very striking.

The challenge of modernization beginning in the nineteenth century pulled Hungary toward a corporatist state controlled by a native elite. While much of Hungarian society was excluded from political participation, the native elite, including elements of the intelligentsia, succeeded in developing an ethos of self-determination, a claim to control their destiny as a nation. During the period of Austro-Hungarian Dualism, this self-image went even further and Hungarians saw themselves as carriers of a civilizing mission in the central Danubian region.

That particular myth, which was expressed in the concept of the Crownlands of St. Stephen and the thousand years of Hungarian imperium, was shattered by Hungary's partition after World War I. Nevertheless, it was kept alive by the revisionist ideology of the postwar Horthy regime. The collapse of the Horthy system in World War II destroyed the stratum that had kept this ideology alive and thereafter the concept of the Crownlands disappeared from Hungarian political thinking. However, this did not mean the abandonment of interest in those Hungarians now beyond the frontiers, it merely evoked a reformulation of the problem. If integral revisionism was discredited, the concept of a single cultural community of Hungarians, with no political *arrière-pensées* involved, arose to take its place.[16]

The argument, propagated since Hungary's partition, that all Hungarians of the Danube region were an organic part of a broader community of language and culture always found ready echo in Hungary itself. It was not, in the same way, quite so acceptable in Transylvania, where autonomist currents of Transylvanianism existed as long as the Romanian state did not require a total identification of loyalty to the state with loyalty to the Romanian nation. Obviously, there were Hungarians who wished for the reattachment of Transylvania to Hungary. Influential Hungarian elements sought, however, safeguards of Hungarian cultural life in Romania as an end in itself. Such a separation of *cultural* and *political* loyalties was not just unacceptable but incomprehensible to Romanians. Hungarians could make a distinction between state and nation because of their confidence in their state and nation. Romanians, on the other hand, feeling insecure and blending as they did the two concepts of state and nation, automatically assumed that the Hungarians were only dissimulating their irredentist aims, just as the Romanians were disguising their intentions toward Bessarabia in the various pseudo-historical debates of the 1960s and 1970s.

Today, the concept of the Hungarian nation is based on the assumption of one community of Hungarians transcending boundaries of states. Occasionally, expressions of nationalism promoting this community of all Hungarians may seem to justify Romanian fears of Hungarian intentions. Such fears were triggered, for instance, by the Hungarian celebrations on the occasion of the return of the Crown of St. Stephen to Hungary in 1978 from its place of safekeeping in the United States. And, in 1982 an article in the Budapest daily *Magyar Nemzet* on St. Stephen's Day (August 20) had the same effect. The article spoke of the community of Hungarians, wherever they may live throughout the world. Unmistakably, the author was less than enthusiastic about the fact that the Hungarian state founded by St. Stephen did not encompass today the entire community of the Hungarian people.[17]

On the other hand, Hungarian fears of Romanian intentions are kept alive by the policy of the Romanian state. As Romanian state policy became increasingly oppressive even toward its own people in the 1970s, the Hungarian minority suffered under the dual hardship of national as well as socioeconomic persecution.

The Hungarians of Transylvania are doubly unacceptable to the Romanian majority. They are rejected as not belonging to the dominant cultural-political community of a state in which the ruling ethos places great stress on loyalty to a transcendental concept of nationhood overshadowing civic duties. And, at the same time, they are rejected because they constitute a potential or actual source of competing values which are readily branded alien to the majority. The very demand for cultural autonomy—the chance of being allowed to live a Hungarian life—is unacceptable from this perspective.

Thus, from the Romanian viewpoint, the only long-term solution that makes sense is the disappearance of the Hungarian minority. This is unacceptable to the Hungarian minority and is equally intolerable to the Hungarians of Hungary. Hence, the Romanian-Hungarian conflict will persist, with all its risks of regional destabilization—including external intervention—and subordination of democratic goals to nationalistic manipulations.

II Transylvania's Hungarians in Communist Romania

On paper, the legal provisions made by Communist Romania for the minorities look generous and sensible. Article 17 of the Romanian Constitution states:

> The citizens of the Socialist Republic of Romania, irrespective of their nationality, race, sex or religion shall have equal rights in all fields of economic, political, juridical, social and cultural life. . . . Any attempt at establishing restrictions [on the rights of minorities], at nationalist-chauvinist propaganda and at fomentation of racial or national hatred shall be punished by law.

To that, Article 22 adds:

In the Socialist Republic of Romania the coinhabiting nationalities shall be assured the free use of their mother tongue, as well as books, newspapers, periodicals, theatres, and education at all levels in their own languages. In territorial-administrative units also inhabited by population of non-Romanian nationality, all the bodies and institutions shall use in speech and in writing the language of the nationality concerned and shall appoint officials from its ranks or from among other citizens who know the language and way of life of the local population.

These constitutional provisions are reinforced by a battery of other laws and decrees. Formal statements of official policy on the rights of minorities are further supplemented by Communist party documents and by high level statements today deriving exclusively from the party leader and head of state, Nicolae Ceauşescu.

Transylvania's principal non-Romanian ethnic group whose existence as a nationality depends on the observance of the constitutional provisions for the minorities is the Hungarians. The population pattern in Transylvania is extremely complex. Its total population numbers around 7 million, the majority of which—around three-fifths— is Romanian. The bulk of the rest is Hungarian (around 2 million); there is a German minority of perhaps 400,000, and there are smaller minorities of Serbs and Ukrainians, and other much smaller groups of Slovaks, Czechs, Bulgarians, and until relatively recently there were thought to be several thousand Armenians. There is also an unspecified number of Gypsies. Many of the settlements are nationally mixed and there are comparatively few communes which do not contain a minority population of at least one nationality. All urban settlements are mixed and the dynamic urbanization has ensured that the composition of several towns has undergone changes favoring the Romanians over the last thirty years. Bilingualism is thought not to be uncommon and this includes many members of the Romanian majority as well. In the Banat, individuals sometimes grow up speaking all three major languages—Romanian, Hungarian, and German.[18]

While the primary badge of loyalty and national self-identification is linguistic and cultural, religion does play an important reinforcing role in Transylvania. The overwhelming majority of Romanians are Orthodox, while Hungarians and Germans are Catholic and Protestant. Religious adherence has come to be identified with national and cultural loyalties. Churches have tended to be regarded as national institutions which have helped to underpin national cultures, and attacks on religious life—whether before or after the Communist take-over—have always been interpreted in national as much as religious terms.

The General Trend

The general principle according to which Communist states are supposed to treat their national minorities is derived from the Marxist-Leninist doctrine of primacy of class over that of nation. In Romania's case, this doctrine was initially interpreted as a call for providing the Hungarian minority with extensive cultural facilities of their own. On the other hand, from the outset, it was made evident that the Hungarian-language educational network was to teach a Romanian Communist culture in Hungarian. As early as 1948, history textbooks were being revised to stress the Romanian as against the Hungarian version of the history of Transylvania.

Today, despite the large number of Marxist-Leninist legal regulations providing for minority rights, it appears that the Romanian policy to satisfy the minorities, to the extent that such a policy exists, is shaped by industrialization. The basic thrust of the country's policy of modernization is in industrialization, and the rights of the minorities are emphatically subordinated to it. Another factor of relevance, which is common to all Communist societies, is the existence of internal regulations, usually kept secret, which may directly contradict the formal rights entrenched in the Constitution.

The general trend of Romanian policy toward the Hungarians is perhaps best illustrated by the fate of the Hungarian Autonomous Region. Comprising the Székely population of Transylvania, it was established on Soviet prodding in 1952. In 1960, its area was reorganized in such a way that, while its Hungarian-speaking population fell, its Romanian-speaking population rose. At the end of 1967 the region was abolished altogether.

From the mid-1970s onward, a growing number of Hungarian intellectuals came to feel that the situation was less and less tenable. In particular, they were forced to the conclusion that, whatever the declared or undeclared aim of the Romanian leadership was, the possibility of leading a Hungarian life in Romania was shrinking. It is this conclusion that characterizes the present state of relations between the Hungarians and the Romanian state.

Hungarian intellectuals took stock of the potential international action, notably in the framework of the Helsinki Final Act, which specifically safeguarded nationality rights. Other international developments, like the U.N. sponsored Ljubljana and Ohrid seminars on national minorities, and the upsurge of minority actions in Western Europe, were also taken into consideration. Contacts with Hungary no doubt also played a part in persuading members of the Hungarian minority to put pressure on the Romanian state by publicity in the West. This coincided with the favorable reception of the concept of "human rights" in the West and with the recognition of samizdat as a legitimate and reliable means of communication. The Hungarians of Romania must also have been aware of the leverage provided by unfavorable publicity for a state that, overtly at any rate, makes its independent foreign policy contingent on Western approval. The result of all this was the rising amount of information made available about the Hungarian minority in Transylvania—such as the 1977 memorandum by Professor Lajos Takács[19]—and consequent pressure on the Romanian leadership to account for its treatment of the minority.

Cultural Pauperization

For a while after the war, under Petru Groza's premiership, unprecedented Romanian tolerance prevailed toward the Hungarian minority. Hungarian-language schools were opened on all levels throughout Transylvania wherever there was a substantial Hungarian population, and even in the Regat—in the Hungarian-inhabited areas of Moldavia. The pinnacle of the educational system was the Hungarian-language university network, consisting of the Bolyai University at Cluj (Kolozsvár), the Medical and Pharmaceutical Faculty at Tîrgu Mureş (Marosvásárhely) and also an agriculture college in Cluj. In other words, despite the authoritarian pressure that weighed on all the inhabitants of Romania, until the 1950s, it was perfectly possible in Transylvania to receive a full Hungarian education. The period of Communist tolerance, however, was of short duration. Intolerance began under the Gheorghe Gheorghiu-Dej regime, to escalate into an undisguised policy of repression under Nicolae Ceauşescu.

The turning point occurred in the aftermath of the Hungarian Revolution of 1956. To usher in the policy of repression, a decision was taken to dismantle the Hungarian educational system. As a general principle, the dismantling was to take place in two stages. First, Hungarian schools were merged with Romanian institutions and allowed to function as parallel "sections." In the second stage, the two sections were fully merged. In practical terms this meant that receiving education in Hungarian became a privilege granted by the Romanian-run institutions.

The merging in 1959 of the Bolyai University in Cluj with the Romanian Babeş University was the first action in this process. As a result of the merger, university education in Hungarian shrank drastically. According to the memorandum prepared by Lajos Takács—a former pro-rector of the university, one time nationalities minister, and an old Communist—in the academic year of 1957–58 (the last one before the merger of the two universities), the total number of the country's Hungarian full-time undergraduates was about 5,500, and most of them were studying in the Hungarian language. They represented about 10.75 percent of all undergraduates in Romania, which corresponded favorably to the percentage of Hungarians in the country's total population. By 1974–75, the number of undergraduates throughout Romania had more than doubled, but the number of Hungarian undergraduates had risen only to 6,188. Thus, the latter declined proportionately from 10.75 to 5.7 percent of the total undergraduate population, and appears to have remained at that low level, according to calculations based on the figures given in the official booklet *Full Harmony and Equality*. [20]

A generally similar policy has been followed with regard to primary and secondary education. Here the nub of the matter appears to be Law No. 278/1973, which stipulates that at the primary level there must be a minimum of 25 applicants every year before a class giving instruction in the minority language is opened for that year; at the secondary level, the minimum number of applicants is 36. Thus, under the 1973 law, if there are only 24 Hungarian (or, for that matter, German) applicants, no class will be opened. By contrast, there is no such restriction on Romanian pupils: "Romanian language sections or classes shall be organized regardless of the number of pupils," states the 1973 law. The significance of this is that when 25 Hungarian schoolchildren fail to turn up any one year even in purely Hungarian villages, they must be educated in Romanian. For a while, parents attempted to resolve the problem by busing children to the nearest large village where a Hungarian school still existed. But the authorities banned this effort on the pretext that there was an insufficient amount of gasoline—a curious pretext indeed in light of the fact that Romania was the largest oil producer in Europe. Of course, the dismissal of Hungarian teachers has gone hand-in-hand with the closing down of Hungarian-language classes.

Thus, a substantial proportion of Hungarian schoolchildren in Romania are no longer educated in their mother tongue. According to Árpád Debreczi, head of the nationalities department of the Ministry of Education, in the year 1971–72 about one-fifth of Hungarian schoolchildren were not receiving their education in their mother tongue.[21] (Calculations based on other official statements indicate that this proportion has remained constant in more recent years.) Even in Hungarian schools a large proportion of what is taught is in Romanian: history, geography, literature, as well as technical subjects. Furthermore, great emphasis is placed on the learning of the Romanian language—indeed, one article in the Romanian press described it as "a patriotic duty." Extracurricular activities, such as literary circles, excursions, artistic programs, and reunions are organized jointly with the Romanian section of each school and are regarded as instruments for teaching Romanian.[22]

Hungarian cultural complaints concentrate on two points: shortages of materials and control of Hungarian institutions by non-Hungarian speaking Romanians. For example, after the merger of the Hungarian theatre at Tîrgu Mureş, a new Romanian director was appointed and he knew no Hungarian. Meetings of the Hungarian section of the Cluj branch of the Romanian Writers' Union have to be held in Romanian, because of the presence of Romanian writers.[23] Shortages are regularly used as a pretext to curtail Hungarian activities. After expansion of Hungarian-language newspaper publishing in the late 1960s, there was a cutback in 1973. Some daily newspapers were converted to thrice-weekly papers or the number of their pages was reduced. The pretext was paper shortage. The same fate befell local Romanian papers, but soon the Romanian papers were returned to their original size, while Hungarian papers were not. There is a persistent shortage of books in libraries; local libraries have often found it extremely difficult to stock up with Hungarian-language books, and their stocks may include a large proportion of Romanian-language material which no one wants to read. In one small village in the Székely country, a farmer complained that the only agricultural text in the local library in Hungarian was about buffalo breeding— in an area where no one has seen a buffalo for generations.[24]

Takács argued in his memorandum that while the activities of three publishing houses with a Hungarian output were satisfactory (these were Kriterion, Politika, and Dácia), the activities of the others were not. There were particular shortcomings in scientific and technical literature and in children's and juvenile literature. Takács also put in a plea for a special Transylvanian radio and television station which would be able to devote more time to Hungarian programs. He made a particular point of arguing for the founding of a scientific journal which would deal at a high level with the natural and social sciences.

Another area which gives rise to complaints is that of the archives and museum collections. The Law on National Cultural Patrimony (63/1974) and the Decree on National Archives (207/1974) summarily nationalized all materials over thirty years old in private or institutional possession. The pretext was the protection of the "national cultural patrimony," but the legislation was used against the Hungarian churches in a confiscatory manner.[25]

One of the most harmful features of Romanian policy from the standpoint of the Hungarians is the rewriting of the history of Transylvania in such a way as to exclude them completely. In effect, Romanian history writing virtually denies the Hungarian presence in the history of Transylvania.[26]

In an analogous fashion, bilingual signs have all but disappeared with the exception of a few places in the Székely country. (Recent reports speak of the reinstallation of some Hungarian-language inscriptions.) Hungarians have also complained (perhaps this is an example of oversensitivity) that whenever urban renewal takes place, it is buildings with Hungarian associations that are demolished and replaced by modern blocks. Certainly, the physical aspect of Transylvanian towns is very different from the Regat. The center of Braşov (Brassó) and the old town of Sighişoara (Segesvár) suggest the medieval Germany (which is, of course, their origin). The center of Cluj (Kolozsvár) is similar to other late nineteenth-century Hungarian towns; the same is true of Oradea (Nagyvárad). Romanians are conscious of this and evidently do not mind if traces of the Hungarian presence disappear during rebuilding. There have even been reports that this attitude has been extended to cemeteries, in that sometimes when tombstones are given a facelift, their deceased Hungarian occupants are turned into Romanians—a practice that recalls Mussolini's Italy.[27]

Economic and Political Aspects

Hungarians are also highly suspicious of one of the main planks of official economic policy, that of increasing investment in the nationality areas as a way of evening out different levels of development. The Székely country has traditionally been an underdeveloped area—this was so even when the region was part of Hungary—and the Romanian state has invested considerable sums there. A fair number of factories have been built (twenty-two in Covasna [Kovászna] and Harghita [Hargita] between 1966 and 1975), but the managerial and skilled positions too often go to Romanians, even when qualified Hungarians are available. Romanians from the Regat are offered special incentives (e.g., housing) to take up jobs in the new factories. It is a matter of policy that in all plants, including those in areas where the population is overwhelmingly Hungarian, the language of the plant is exclusively Romanian.

In fact, the problem of language in factories is a genuine one. Bilingualism in administration or education is relatively straightforward to implement, it is much more difficult to run an enterprise on that basis. It adds considerably to costs, it confuses chains of command, it makes for problems in contacts with the planners and ministries at the center, as well as laterally with other enterprises, and it can give rise to potentially dangerous situations, as, say, in an emergency. The Romanian state feels that it cannot afford the luxury of making certain enterprises predominantly Hungarian in character. Any such solution would gravely damage the unitary quality of Romanian society. From a nationalist standpoint, the creation of islands of employment reserved for Hungarians would be an intolerable provocation. On the other hand, there is force in the Hungarian argument that all educated Hungarians today speak Romanian and that this places them in a favorable position to mediate between the Romanian state and the Hungarian community. The employment of Hungarian engineers in factories with large numbers of Hungarians on the shop-floor would be of advantage to society as a whole, in that it would ease the communication problem, it could be the basis for a measure of de facto bilingualism, and it would remove a serious grievance.[28]

The political representation of the Hungarian community is made extremely difficult by the interlocking principles of centralism and nationalism professed by the Romanian state. According to Communist Hungarian argument, it is perfectly possible to be a good Communist citizen of Romania without being a member of the Romanian nation. For example, Takács argues that the Hungarians are a community with their own history and their own perspective for the future, but this does not make them in any way disloyal—and that should be the basis of policy toward them. This means that the Romanian state should recognize the collective existence of Hungarians and make provision for it as a "separately identifiable social category." Communist Hungarian and Romanian views are as far apart in these matters as are the non-Communist ones.

There seems to be general agreement that among the Communist party officials the number of Hungarians is kept at a level equivalent to the official proportion of Hungarians in the population. Hungarian representation is also proportionate in the higher party organs like the Central Committee, in the local party committees, and in the Grand National Assembly and the People's Councils. However, these are largely facade institutions with no real powers, and Hungarians are often excluded from the real policymaking organs, like the local party bureaus. The Council of Workers of Hungarian Nationality, which is paralleled by a similar body for the Germans, is a typical facade institution. It is supposed to be an organ for the minority, but its existence is largely confined to occasional plenary sessions at which various figurehead individuals sing the praises of Romania's nationality policy. The Council has no headquarters, no office hours, its deliberations are censored, and its resolutions are empty formalities.

At the national level there are comparatively few Hungarians. They appear to be excluded completely from employment in a number of important ministries, notably the Ministry of Foreign Affairs, Ministry of Defense, and the Ministry of the Interior. Consequently, there are few if any Hungarians in the Romanian diplomatic service, in the officers corps and, above all, the police. There are no figures available, but it is clear from reports that the number of Hungarian policemen in Transylvania is minimal. As the policeman is frequently the first point of contact between individual and state, this has serious consequences for that relationship, especially when Romanian police-men resent being addressed in Hungarian.[29]

International Ramifications

The Transylvanian question has been enormously complicated by its international ramifications. It is probably no exaggeration that the absence of good will, which is so characteristic of the situation, derives above all from a persistent Romanian fear that the question has not been irrevocably settled and that one day, using the existence of the minority as the pretext, the Hungarian state will again lay claim to the province. No amount of disclaiming from Budapest can dispel this sense of insecurity. Hungarian leaders, János Kádár included, have repeatedly insisted that the Hungarian state has no claims to Roma-nian territory. Yet, concern from Budapest about the minority is au-tomatically interpreted in Romania as covert irredentism.

This fear has been exacerbated by the invisible role that Transyl-vania has played in the triangular relationship between Romania, Hungary, and the Soviet Union. On a number of occasions in the past, the Soviet Union has tacitly encouraged the Hungarian party to express criticism of the Romanian party in international Communist terms—criticism that was automatically translated by public opinion in both states as criticism in national terms, focused on Transylvania.

In May 1977, presumably after Soviet pressure, the Romanian gov-ernment agreed to hold bilateral discussions with Hungary on, inter alia, the problem of the Hungarian minority in Romania. After what was reported as a fairly chilly meeting between Ceauşescu and Kádár, the two sides issued a joint communiqué, in which the Hungarian minority in Romania (ca. 2 million) and the Romanian minority in Hungary (ca. 25,000) were declared to be bridges between the two nations. In political terms, this declaration was seen as giving Hungary its much coveted status vis-à-vis the Hungarians of Transylvania. The two sides agreed to promote cultural contacts and that a Hungarian consulate would be reopened in Cluj, while a Romanian consulate was to be set up in Debrecen. In the year that followed, no movement of any significance took place on either front and when Ceauşescu's personal representative, Ştefan Andrei, visited Budapest in February 1978, he was told by his Hungarian hosts that matters had dragged on for long enough.[30]

The entire question of cultural links between the Hungarian minority and the Hungarian state is a highly sensitive one from the Romanian standpoint. It arouses precisely those fears of Hungarian irredentism that the Hungarian authorities are so anxious to dispel. The results have been absurd. For years, Hungarians complained that it was virtually impossible to buy newspapers from Hungary, largely due to Bucharest's decision to limit their numbers in their import quotas from Hungary. When under pressure the quantities of Hungarian dailies became greater, the authorities made sure that they were put on sale in the Regat, where there were hardly any Hungarians living. Subscriptions by Transylvanians to journals from Hungary are frowned upon and the Romanian authorities make difficulties with deliveries and payments. At one stage in the 1960s, it was reported that whenever the Romanian authorities screened films from Hungary, they showed them either dubbed into Romanian or with Romanian subtitles and with the volume of the Hungarian soundtrack turned down to make it unintelligible. Listening to Hungarian radio or watching Hungarian television is disapproved of by the authorities. The Communist regime in Hungary is incomparably more liberal than the one in Romania and the Romanian authorities are afraid of the comparisons with Hungary, where—quite apart from anything else—the standard of living is much higher. This problem also extends to Romanian intellectuals, many of whom know Hungarian and use Hungary as their window on the West. In this sense, publications from Hungary are seen as subversive.

The raising of the Transylvanian issue in the West, particularly in the United States where various bodies have been campaigning energetically on behalf of the Hungarian minority with the object of revoking Romania's most-favored-nation status in trade with the United States, has forced the Romanian leadership to respond. This response has varied from bland denials of discrimination to abuse of the Hungarian minority's case. Ceauşescu personally denounced traitors to the fatherland, "weak elements or morally decadent persons who, for two gold or silver coins, for a bowl of lentils or goulash, sell their services to foreign circles." This was interpreted as a reference to the letters protesting Romanian minority policies, written by Károly Király, a prominent Transylvanian Hungarian Communist. Though addressed privately to the party leadership, the letters have received wide publicity both at home and abroad.[31] Annoyed by the

Király affair's international repercussions, Romanian officials in the West sought to give assurances that the Hungarian minority has never been better treated in its entire existence. To support their contention, however, they could quote only official documents and statistics.

As far as non-official viewpoints go, a case could be made for a position I have heard from a number of thoughtful Romanians. They agree that it is counterproductive to dismiss the Hungarian complaints as the work of malcontents fuelled by irredentism. According to them, the problem would be better approached through regional concern for Transylvania. They would argue, however, that the Transylvanian Hungarians have not been alone in being swamped by a kind of know-nothing Romanian nationalism. Transylvanian Romanians suffer, too, along with Transylvanian Hungarians and Germans, from the Ceau-şescu line which pays no attention to the specific character of the region. Thus, for instance, the Romanians have also been at the receiving end of the unthinking "mobilizatory policy." They, too, are ordered to go to any part of the country. In turn, large numbers of Regatean Romanians are relocated to Transylvania. The Regatean newcomers lack sensitivity toward local Transylvanian preferences and habits; and they are not at all sympathetic to Hungarians.

There appears to be a genuine spirit of Transylvanianism in this view. Essentially, it looks at the Transylvanian way of life as a fusion of all three main national cultures (Romanian, Hungarian, German). It recognizes that all three owe a great deal to one another. This line of thinking appeals strongly to Hungarian intellectuals, especially those on the left, who are by no means committed to the idea of irredentism—indeed, they often reject interference from Hungary as suspect and possibly counterproductive. But Transylvanianism, however attractive it may seem and however workable it is at the grass-roots level where relations between the nationalities are often very good, founders on the rock of Romanian state nationalism, for which Transylvanianism is a dangerous concept in that it questions the unity and integrity of the Romanian nation.

Actions of the Hungarian Minority

After the Király-letters affair and the consequent international attention focused on the Hungarians in Romania, there was a brief lull in the antiminority campaign. Some ad hoc concessions were made by the Romanian authorities, notably in education by permitting the temporary opening of Hungarian-language sections in primary and secondary schools. However, once Romania was struck by a major economic and financial crisis in 1980–81, the minority problem was brought back onto the central government agenda. The government realized that, due to poor planning and the bunching of debt repayments to the West, the country was close to bankruptcy. The authorities were constrained to squeeze consumption. Not unnaturally, the squeeze was highly unpopular with Romanian public opinion. The authorities sought to ease the resultant tensions by making the Hungarian minority a target of hostility.

The renewed anti-Hungarian campaign was fostered through hints and whispers, by tangential allusions to "aliens" and "incomers," and by renewed emphasis on Daco-Roman continuity which effectively served as clear notice to the public that the authorities regarded the Hungarians as a hostile element in the body of the national territory. In a situation where the regime had run out of the possibilities of making its rule acceptable on economic grounds—the promise of a prosperous Romania—or on the grounds of international prestige, traditional nationalism was the sole option left open. Attention was to be diverted from Romania's economic ills with the suggestion that, if only the country could be nationally homogeneous, the Romanian people would not suffer the difficulties they were experiencing. Discontent was inevitably focused on the Hungarian minority, for the other acceptable target, the Soviet Union, was too dangerous.

Irrational though this may seem, the Hungarian scapegoat propaganda was an attractive way to please the Romanians. The response from the Hungarian minority, on the other hand, was one of near despair. It too had largely run out of options. It obviously lacked the political power to take on the ruling regime—backed as it was by the Communist party and the security forces—and could turn only to international opinion for whatever support it could muster. To reach international opinion, the minority—or more properly a small number of Hungarian intellectuals—launched in December 1981 an underground (samizdat) journal, entitled *Ellenpontok* (Counterpoints). By January 1983, nine issues had been published. Samizdat, as an instrument of political action, had two basic objectives: to arouse international opinion, and to strengthen minority consciousness by demonstrating to the minority that they were not as isolated and atomized by Romanian state power as they thought.

The content of *Ellenpontok* offered some guide to the attitudes of at least a section of the Transylvanian Hungarian intelligentsia. They were concerned with the preservation of their culture. But, whereas an earlier generation had sought to create a concept of "Romanianity"—an idea that the Hungarians were loyal citizens of the Romanian state while conserving their separate Hungarian cultural identity—the new current represented by *Ellenpontok* was different. The editors of *Ellenpontok* were concerned primarily with showing what they perceived as the long historical roots of Romanian intolerance and xenophobia and, by implication, the impossibility of coming to terms with the existing nationalist current.

The longer term prospects of the Hungarian minority had deteriorated in tandem with the worsening of Romania's economic situation and the concurrent decay of the Ceauşescu system. It was a logical supposition that the Romanian regime was least likely to make concessions to the minority when it felt itself under severe pressure from external and internal circumstances. This exacerbation of the position of the Hungarian minority in Romania was not without its impact on the Communist regime in Hungary as well. The latter found itself under pressure from Hungarian opinion to do something. Since bilateral discussions with the Romanian government produced no results, the Hungarian regime allowed a semiofficial polemic against Láncrănjan's book on Transylvania, using his tacit attack on Kádár as the pretext.[32] This polemic was not unwelcome in Budapest, for it too could manipulate opinion in a nationalist direction at a time of some economic dislocation. But this had little or no impact on the prospects of the Hungarian minority, which were regarded as uniformly gloomy.

The thinking of the Hungarian minority was also shown by the two documents submitted by the editors of *Ellenpontok* in September 1982 to the conference held in Madrid as a follow-up to the Helsinki Accord (both are reproduced in the Annexes, below). The first of these, the *Memorandum*, stresses the importance of internationally recognized collective rights for minorities as a means of interest protection. It calls for the right of the Hungarians of Romania to be regarded as an inseparable part of a broader cultural community of Hungarians, including Hungary and other Hungarian minorities; for the right to safeguard this community's individuality and collective values; for the right to establish an independent body for the protection of minority interests; and to have these rights secured by an international commission. The second document, the *Program Proposal* for a nationalities policy, emphasizes the gravely endangered situation of the Hungarian community in Romania and puts forward a series of demands aimed at finding a remedy. These are mostly of a cultural and educational nature, but in some respects they come close to proposing the establishment of an autonomous political corporation to represent the interests of the minority.

The proposed solution would give the Hungarians a good deal of independence vis-à-vis the state. It has certain affinities with the Austro-Marxist approach to the minority question adopted in interwar Estonia (with some success). However, it should be added that its chances of realization are nil. The Romanian regime has no interest whatsoever in giving its Hungarians a "privileged" position of this kind, nor would the Romanian majority stand for it, and there is no chance that international opinion would be capable of persuading the Ceauşescu regime to introduce such reforms. Furthermore, the damaging precedent a move of this nature would create for Communist political practice in the whole of Eastern Europe makes such a solution unattainable. The fact of the matter is that as things stand today, no one has a particular interest in defending the rights of the Hungarians in Romania, apart from the Hungarian community itself. And the Hungarian community, as the record shows, lacks the political strength to defend its interests effectively.

"Hungarian Life" in Romania

Hungarian minority aims may be summarized as the aspiration to live a "Hungarian life" in Romania. The problem with this aim is that a "Hungarian life" has its own imperatives which are simply incompatible with Communist policy in Romania. If the Hungarians are anxious to transform the Hungarian Nationality Council into a genuine body, the Romanian people would be only too glad to achieve this for their own national organs. But this is an impossibility in a system where every institution is by and large a facade and where the whole society, the Communist party included, is run undemocratically in the interests of an authoritarian clique.

Thus, the Hungarians are really asking for the introduction of liberalization, perhaps akin to the dispensation that prevails in Hungary today. This is something that no one enjoys in Romania. Yet, there can be no doubt that the Romanian state treats the Hungarian minority as an alien body, considers it a potential danger to the territorial integrity of the Romanian state, and therefore subjects it to greater pressure and discrimination than the Romanian majority has to accept.

The Romanian leadership may as a result find itself in the grip of a self-fulfilling prophecy. By permitting the Hungarians to feel themselves second-class citizens in their own country, they may actually be creating the disloyalty toward the Romanian state on the part of the Hungarians that they fear. The developments of the last few years have unquestionably aroused public opinion in Hungary to the point where it is acting as a major source of pressure on the Budapest government to do something about Transylvania; and it is inevitable that the Soviet Union should be drawn into this dispute.

The irony of the situation is that the Hungarians of Transylvania have traditionally had a strong identity and consciousness of their own which did not automatically identify them with the Hungarian state. Until the early 1970s, the Romanian state had a good opportunity to create an autonomous Hungarian nationality consciousness, in which political loyalty was owed to Romania and Hungarian aspirations would have been restricted to culture. There are numerous indications that this opportunity has been missed and that the Hungarians of Transylvania are less and less likely to feel loyalty toward a state that denies them what they see as their basic rights as a national minority.

Notes

1. The Latin word "Transilvania" means the land beyond the forest; that is, beyond the forests between the Hungarian Plains and Transylvania. The Hungarian name, "Erdély," has the same meaning (derived from the ancient Magyar word "erdóelve"). Transylvania's original Romanian name, "Ardeal," borrowed from the Hungarian, has been pretty well abandoned in this century for the Latino-Romanian "Transilvania." The German name, "Sie-

benbürgen," originally referred only to the seven towns founded by German settlers invited by Hungary's kings in medieval times.

2. George Schöpflin, "The Ideology of Rumanian Nationalism," *Survey* 20, nos. 2–3: 77–104.

3. William H. McNeill, *Europe's Steppe Frontier* (Chicago, 1964), 101–8.

4. Ibid., 108–10.

5. Ibid, 105. Daniel Chirot (*Social Change in a Peripheral Society: The Creation of a Balkan Colony* [New York, 1976]) attributes greater significance to economic factors and emphasizes different aspects of the process of development in Wallachia.

6. On the weakness of the Romanian state, see Emmanuel Turczynski, "The Background of Romanian Fascism," in Peter Sugar, ed., *Native Fascism in the Successor States 1918–1945* (Santa Barbara, 1971), 101–11.

7. Robert R. King, *History of the Romanian Communist Party* (Stanford, 1980), 106–9.

8. Radu Florian, in "A román társadalom marxista vizsgálata Lucreţiu Pătrăscanu műveiben" (*Korunk* 40/4: 250–55) discusses irrationalism and the writings of Nae Ionescu.

9. Attila Kővári, "The Romanian National Mystery: Myth-makers under the Microscope," *Crossroads* 3 (Spring 1979): 201–41.

10. The emergence of Romanian nationalism, as well as the Slavicization that preceded it, is discussed by George Schöpflin in "The Ideology of Rumanian Nationalism"; see also Attila Kővári, "The Romanian National Mystery."

11. Michael Shafir, *Political Culture, Intellectual Dissent and Intellectual Consent: The Case of Romania* (Jerusalem, 1978), 12ff. See also Ernő Gáll, "A népiesség gondolata a román művelődésben," in *Nemzetiség, erkölcs, értelmiség* (Bucharest, 1978).

12. Mioriţa is also discussed by Ion Ratiu in *Contemporary Romania: Her Place in World Affairs* (Richmond, England, 1975), 123.

13. Shafir, *Political Culture*, p. 22.

14. Ion Lăncrănjan, *Cuvînt despre Transilvania* (Bucharest, 1982), 175. See also George Cioranescu, "Romania: An Escalation of Polemics on Transylvania," *Radio Free Europe Research*, August 11, 1982.

15. Păunescu is quoted by Ferenc Kunszabó, "Modern Genocide and Its Remedy," in *Witnesses to Cultural Genocide* (New York, 1979), 34.

16. This discussion of the Hungarian tradition is based on C. A. Macartney, *The Habsburg Empire 1790–1918* (London, 1968); Andrew C. Janos, *The Politics of Backwardness in Hungary 1825–1945* (Princeton, 1982), and P. Toma and I. Volgyes, eds., *Politics in Hungary* (San Francisco, 1977). My own views are set out at greater length in "Hungary: An Uneasy Stability,"

in Archie Brown and Jack Gray, eds., *Political Culture and Political Change in Communist States* (New York, 1977). On this theme, see also Chapter 16, below.

17. Péter Ruffy, "Az államalapító," *Magyar Nemzet*, August 20, 1982.

18. A more detailed account of the state of the Hungarian minority is in George Schöpflin, *The Hungarians of Romania* (London, 1978), which served as a principal source material in preparing this report.

19. Lajos Takács, a professor of international law at Cluj (Kolozsvár) University; all references below on the state of the Hungarians are taken from his memorandum. Excerpts have been issued in English translation by the Committee for Human Rights in Rumania in *Witnesses to Cultural Genocide*, 145–61.

20. *A Living Reality in Romania Today: Full Harmony and Equality between the Romanian People and the Coinhabiting Nationalities* (N.p., n.d.), 18 pp. and 22 photographs; distributed by Romanian diplomatic missions in the spring of 1978, in various languages.

21. This statement appeared in the official Hungarian-language daily of the Romanian Communist party, *Előre*, March 31, 1972.

22. "Patriotic duty" is from Albert Szigeti's article in *Învătămîntul liceal şi technic profesional* (November 1976): 4–5. The minutes of the joint plenum of the Hungarian and German Nationality Councils were printed in Romanian and published by Editura Politică, Bucharest; the speaker referred to was Herman Schmidt of the Ministry of Education.

23. Committee for Human Rights in Romania, *Romania's Violations of the Helsinki Final Act Provisions* (New York, 1977) (mimeographed), 22.

24. Complaints about libraries have been appearing regularly in the Hungarian press in Romania, eg., *Előre*, March 19, 1972; *Igaz Szó*, no. 9 (1971): 345; and *Könyvtári Szemle*, passim. The dissatisfied farmer was at the village of Bodoc (Bódok), *Megyei Tükör*, May 18, 1972. *Könyvtári Szemle* was a specialized journal for librarians; it ceased publication in 1974, at the time of the paper shortage.

25. Text of the law in *Scînteia*, November 2, 1974; details of its enforcement in *Neue Zürcher Zeitung*, February 1–2, 1975, and *Frankfurter Allgemeine Zeitung*, December 9, 1977. The latter makes it clear that the German religious communities were just as adversely affected as the Hungarian ones.

26. Z. Michael Szaz, "Contemporary Educational Policies in Transylvania," *East European Quarterly* 11/4 (Winter 1977): 499. For more on this subject, see Chapter 15, below.

27. *Financial Times*, April 2, 1975.

28. The entire problem of official policy with regard to the language and its use in factories is a very complex one. The following quotations from various speeches by Ceauşescu illustrate uncertainties and oscillations in the

policy. They should be read in conjunction with Decrees No. 24 and 25/1976, which in effect gave the authorities the powers to direct labor, to order Romanian citizens to take up employment wheresoever the authorities choose; this is in contravention of every human rights and labor convention signed by Romania. Ceauşescu had this to say on October 24–25, 1968, to the Central Committee of the party: "While taking steps for the expansion and protection of training in the mother tongue, the state is facilitating to young people of other nationalities the assimilation of the Romanian language, this being an objective necessity for the full and effective implementation of the principle of equal rights . . . so that young people . . . may hold jobs in keeping with their capacities, at any economic, administrative, scientific or cultural unit, *in any locality*" (from Nicolae Ceauşescu, *Romania on the Way of Completing Socialist Construction* [Bucharest, 1969], 3:586; italics added. From volume 4 onward, this collection of Ceauşescu's speeches was entitled *Romania on the Way of Building Up the Multilaterally Developed Society*; twelve volumes had appeared by 1977). Two-and-a-half years later, in a speech to the German Nationality Council, Ceauşescu had this to say (February 17, 1971): "We have to concern ourselves less with the language we are writing in, but with what we are writing, for whom and how we are writing and if what we are writing serves socialism" (ibid., 5:531). A few weeks later, speaking to the Hungarian Council, Ceauşescu stated (March 12, 1971): "That means that the problem of assimilating the Romanian language should not be looked upon as an obligation to learn one more language; it is linked, in the last analysis, to ensuring equality in fact. If, on leaving his or her locality or country as a youth is unable to communicate with others, he or she will fail to feel truly equal or free" (ibid., 686). Finally, in a speech to the Cluj party *aktif*, Ceauşescu stated (October 31, 1973): "We must further ensure conditions for learning in the mother tongue and for a corresponding cultural activity. We must have in view that all the cadres we are training have to work as well as possible in factories, agriculture—everywhere where this is required by the general interests of society" (ibid., 9:463). It clearly never occurred to Ceauşescu that in certain cases equality of rights might have been served by Romanians learning Hungarian.

29. Viktor Meier, the highly esteemed Eastern Europe correspondent of the *Frankfurter Allgemeine Zeitung (FAZ)*, reported after a visit to a small Hungarian village near Cluj that only 10 of the approximately three hundred families there were Romanian and they were almost all families of policemen; on being asked whether the policemen spoke Hungarian, the villagers told him that they might know some, but it was better to speak to them in Romanian. *FAZ*, September 11, 1976.

30. "After the Andrei Visit to Budapest," *Radio Free Europe Research*, February 28, 1978.

31. For the text of the Király letters, see *Witnesses to Cultural Genocide,* 162–78.

32. Cf. György Száraz, "Debating an Odd Book on Transylvania," *The New Hungarian Quarterly* 24, no. 89 (Spring 1983): 96–104.

Annex I
The Madrid Memorandum
Memorandum to the participants of the Madrid
Conference reviewing adherence to the provisions of the
Helsinki Final Act*

In the interest of the survival of the approximately two million Hungarians in Rumania, we appeal to the peoples of the states represented at the Madrid Conference. Perhaps there is still time to halt the process, induced by the policies of the Rumanian government, which is threatening our very existence as a nationality.

The forced Rumanianization of Transylvania and the suppression of our culture are being carried out with unprecedented vehemence. Masses of Rumanians from beyond the Carpathian Mountains are being resettled into regions with a predominantly Hungarian population and into purely Hungarian communities, mainly cities. At the same time, according to official nationwide population statistics, the number of Hungarians remains stagnant. The Hungarian-language school system is gradually being destroyed. More and more obstacles are created to hinder the publication of Hungarian books and periodicals. Our language, in truth, has been forced out of public life entirely. The effort to seclude us from Hungarians living elsewhere is being carried out with increasing vigor. (Relations between Hungary and Rumania are at a sub-minimum level in all respects.)

All conceivable means are employed to thwart the natural development of our identity. Successive Hungarian generations are brought up in an atmosphere of chauvinism which denigrates our heritage and preaches the superiority of Rumanian history and culture, without allowing those Hungarians an opportunity to learn about their own ethnic background, or even the true history of Transylvania. The state

*English text, translated from the Hungarian, as submitted to the Madrid Conference.

powers treat us, especially intellectuals and workers, as if we were the enemies within. Terror on the part of the security forces is the order of the day. If we speak out in defense of our heritage, it is we who are called chauvinistic. We live as second-class citizens in Rumania, whose possibilities for career advancement are also limited by the fact that we are Hungarian.

We lack any means of self-protection. The individual is defenseless in the face of the tyranny of the state, and since 1949—when the Hungarian People's Alliance was liquidated—there has been no organization to safeguard our collective interests. Thus, our situation is characterized by the denial of not only our individual rights, but our collective rights as well, two sets of rights which are inseparable in our case.

The fact that existing international agreements do not deal with the collective rights of minorities bears profoundly upon the possibilities for bringing about a change in our situation. The focus on individual human rights, which constitutes the prevalent approach to this problem in the international arena, fails to take into consideration the shared values critical to a national minority as a collective entity—values which evolved through tradition and are carried on through a national minority's unique culture and the group identity of its members. These values would require special legal protection. While for the majority—due to its larger size and dominant position—the medium for the expression of its unique values exists as a natural given, for the minority to achieve the same purpose would require a means of collective self-protection. For this reason, regardless of the underlying motive, the effort to secure human rights for minorities, without taking into account their nature as collective entities, can actually place them at the mercy of the majority.

Having taken the above into consideration, we believe that in order to alter our present deprived condition, it would be of fundamental importance that the international agreements reached in Madrid establish on the record our right to survive, and in doing so, define those human rights which would insure the preservation of our culture:

1. Allow us to regard ourselves as bound by unbreakable bonds to the entire Hungarian people, and grant the same right to all national minorities.

2. Grant us the right to preserve our ethnic identity and collective values.

3. Allow us to establish an independent organization to protect our interests.

4. These rights—in our view—could acquire real validity only if an *independent, unbiased international commission were formed* which would examine our situation, act as arbitrator and also have supervisory authority.

*

Attached to this memorandum is a *Program Proposal* in which we endeavored to formulate the most important of our demands of the Rumanian government in the interest of ameliorating our situation.

Transylvania, September 1982

> By the editors of the samizdat periodical *Ellenpontok* (Counterpoints), whose continued anonymity in present-day Rumania—where critics of the regime disappear without a trace or become "accident" victims—unfortunately need not be explained.

Annex II
A Program Proposal
Presented by the editors of the periodical Ellenpontok
(Counterpoints) *in the interest of improving the deprived condition of the Hungarians in Rumania**

The Hungarians of Transylvania, and of Rumania in general, are presently experiencing a more critical period of threat to their existence than perhaps ever before. Legal provisions protecting their survival exist only for the sake of appearances; they serve only to veil practices and realities which are diametrically opposed to the formulations contained in ceremonial speeches and official declarations.

To the practitioners of this system of thought, the mere idea of

*English text, translated from the Hungarian, as submitted to the Madrid Conference.

someone actually *demanding* a right is a complete absurdity. Even the simplest petition in Rumania must take the form of a more or less humble entreaty, clad in official phraseology and supported by the "principles" which happen to be in style. It is unthinkable for any request to be fulfilled without the support of an influential member of some central body of authority, and the granting of a request is always akin to the benevolent gesture of a feudal lord, awarding a well-behaved subject. (The dispenser of awards to the citizen is the state; to the minorities, the dominant Rumanian nation.) The graceful gesture has nothing to do with the rights of the petitioner, merely with the merits of the gift-giver.

Numerous minority representatives, having accepted the conditions outlined above as given and believing themselves pragmatic, chose to force themselves to adapt, attempting through subservience and a defensive manner to protect the interests of their ethnic group.

From our point of view, though we commend the good intentions underlying such behavior, the facts convince us that a minority deprived of its resources cannot hope to defend its interests, except to the extent of gaining the minimal concessions absolutely necessary for the state to maintain outward appearances. In addition, behavior of this sort is alien to our nature.

As it is our conviction that two ethnic groups can live next to, and indeed together with, each other only if they regard one another as equal partners, *we demand that the Hungarians of Rumania be granted the fundamental freedom to voice demands regarding the protection of their rights and opportunities.*

We know all too well that a demand of this kind may appear ill-timed in present-day Rumania, where any expressed desires pertaining to Hungarian culture are openly labeled irredentist and revisionist, even when they are couched in the required phraseology. In our opinion however, this attitude is characteristic of the relationship a feudal lord maintains with his subjects.

We are also aware that, given present conditions in Eastern Europe, it is unrealistic to expect that a demand of this kind will be met. But since our situation is growing worse each day, we feel obligated to take action because we cannot afford the luxury of waiting for a miracle to change these conditions.

For these reasons:

I. *We demand that we be considered an inseparable part of the entire*

Hungarian people, and that as such, and as citizens of Rumania, we be permitted to maintain unhindered contacts with the Hungarian People's Republic, on both the institutional and the individual levels!

1. Allow every citizen of Rumania to travel to the Hungarian People's Republic without restrictions.

2. Repeal the regulation which forbids the accommodation of friends from abroad in our homes. (This regulation affects us, Hungarians, most of all.)

3. Permit our cultural institutions, as well as Hungarian cultural groups operating as sections of other institutions, to freely invite Hungarian ensembles and individuals from the neighboring countries.

4. Until the Transylvanian Hungarian universities are restored, permit Hungarian students from Rumania to study in Hungary. Upon their return, allow them to function according to the qualifications they have obtained.

5. Stop the practice by Rumanian customs officials of arbitrarily confiscating Hungarian-language publications.

6. With the help of relay-stations, make Hungarian (Budapest) television programming available in all parts of Transylvania.

7. Insure that Hungarian-language books published in countries inhabited by Hungarians (Hungary, Czechoslovakia, Yugoslavia and the Soviet Union) can be obtained in Rumania as well.

8. Allow us to subscribe to any and all newspapers and periodicals published in Hungary. See to it that such publications are, in fact, delivered to the subscribers by the postal service.

9. Stop treating the natural interest and justified concern of cultural and political figures in Hungary toward the fate of Hungarians in Rumania as interference in Rumania's internal affairs.

II. *We demand that cultural autonomy and institutionalized forms of self-protection be guaranteed to the Hungarians of Rumania, as an ethnic community!*

1. Expand paragraph 22 of the Constitution to grant minorities the right to form an organization to protect their interests, the officers of which are democratically elected.

2. Allow this organization the right to direct Hungarian cultural activity and education policy, to supervise cadre-policies affecting Hungarians, to maintain Hungarian historical monuments and to seek legal redress for minority grievances.

3. Allow Hungarians in all parts of Rumania (not just Transylvania) to be members of this organization.

4. Permit this organization to have its own official publication.

5. Publish the history of the Hungarian People's Alliance, and make known the true circumstances of its termination in 1949.

6. Publicly rehabilitate all formerly imprisoned leaders of the Hungarian People's Alliance, as well as all others who have been sentenced during the past 35 years for defending the interests of Hungarians, and declare their sentences null and void.

7. Officially acknowledge the fact that our culture is an organic part of Hungarian culture and not some kind of offshoot of Rumanian culture.

8. Create departments for the education of nationalities within the Ministry of Education and the county school boards, and treat these departments as equal to their Rumanian counterparts.

9. Re-open the Hungarian-language kindergartens and schools, granting every Hungarian child the opportunity to attend a Hungarian-language kindergarten or school. In all Hungarian-inhabited countries, make high school education in the humanities and the various trades available in Hungarian.

10. Establish Hungarian-language orphanages and schools for the handicapped, putting an end to the practice of placing Hungarian-speaking orphans and handicapped children in the respective Rumanian institutions—a practice used as a tool of Rumanianization.

11. Enforce regulation number 6/1969 relating to teaching staff qualifications, which provides that teachers whose command of the Hungarian language is inadequate or nonexistent may not teach Hungarian-language classes.

12. Reduce the minimum quota of children required to form a class, in order to prevent the elimination of Hungarian village schools. Enact legislation in Rumania similar to the exemplary nationality statute in Yugoslavia which requires a minimum of nine children in order to establish a school. In this regard, any quotas should apply to Rumanian and Hungarian children equally.

13. In Hungarian-language secondary schools, teach the history and geography of Rumania in the Hungarian language.

14. Reestablish the Hungarian universities, and establish Hungarian-language institutions of higher education in all trades.

15. Expand the sphere of activity of the minority language pub-

lishing house "Kriterion," and increase its financial base, to enable "Kriterion" to fulfill those minority-language publishing requirements which the other publishing houses are unable to satisfy at this time.

16. Allow the Hungarian-language press, and the Hungarian-language radio and television programs, to discuss the actual and real problems of the Hungarians in Rumania.

17. The Rumanian authorities should, once and for all, stop the practice of treating Hungarian intellectuals as suspicious elements, and of subjecting them to constant police surveillance and harassment solely because they are Hungarian.

18. Insure true freedom of worship, and grant the Hungarian churches real internal autonomy.

III. *For regions inhabited predominantly by Hungarians, we demand self-administration and an equitable share in the country's government!*

1. Restore autonomy to the Székely land—this time real autonomy, extended to the entire region.

2. In the villages inhabited predominantly or exclusively by Hungarians, stop the practice of appointing ethnic Rumanians to leadership positions (Chairman of the Village Council, Chairman of the Farm Collective, Party Secretary, policeman).

3. Allow Hungarians to be represented according to their percentage of the total population not only as Party members and representatives to the Grand National Assembly, but also among the managers of the economy, in the Party leadership at all levels, and in the government.

IV. *We demand an immediate end to measures aimed at artificially altering the ethnic composition of Transylvania (including historic Transylvania, the territories west of it, and the Banat region)!*

1. Terminate the massive and forced resettling of peoples from Moldavia and Wallachia into Transylvania.

2. Stop experimenting with the ethnic composition of purely Hungarian villages, trying to create a mixed population in those villages.

3. Stop the practice of assigning recent Hungarian graduates (especially physicians and engineers) to Moldavia and Wallachia, against their will.

V. *We demand the opportunity for the Hungarians in Rumania to develop and cultivate their identity!*

1. With regard to the past:

a. Allow the Hungarian pupils studying in their native tongue to learn the true history of their own ethnic group, and allow Rumanian pupils as well to become acquainted with that history, at least in broad outline.

b. Discuss the history of Transylvania objectively in historical publications. Stop using materials placed on museum display to conceal or trivialize the significance of Hungarians in the past, or their presence in Rumania today.

c. Discontinue the ideological function of the theory of Daco-Rumanian continuity. (Let this theory remain what it is, in fact: a working hypothesis of historians.)

d. Stop treating those who take an interest in the history and cultural heritage of Transylvania as exhibiting revisionist tendencies. Stop forbidding experts specializing in the history of Transylvania to research subjects.

2. With regard to the present:

a. Make public, and accessible to all, detailed statistical data regarding the present situation of the national minorities.

b. Allow anyone who so desires, to engage in sociological research pertaining to the national minorities, without police harassment against those who express an interest in this line of research.

c. Let schools, regardless of their language of instruction, teach their pupils an awareness of the country's national minorities and their culture.

d. Publish books in the Rumanian language as well which deal with the life, national customs, art, etc., of the national minorities who live here.

e. Expand the existing injunctions against manifestations of chauvinism to apply to those manifestations which are directed against Hungarians. (Thus, apply the same standard to such [anti-Hungarian] epithets as "bozgor" and "hazátlan" as to the [anti-Rumanian] "oláh".)

VI. *We demand that in all areas of greater Transylvania inhabited by Hungarians, the Hungarian language be treated as equal to the Rumanian language in official as well as everyday use!*

1. Grant, in practice, the right provided for in paragraph 22 of the Constitution to use the Hungarian language in administrative offices and before the various authorities, and to submit to those

offices documents written in that language. Make identification cards, passports, official form letters, etc., bilingual.

2. Within the regions described, require workers employed in the field of health care, commerce and public services to be familiar with the Hungarian language.

3. In the areas inhabited by Hungarians, make the Hungarian language a required subject in Rumanian schools as well. (During the Horthy regime in Northern Transylvania, it was compulsory for Hungarian children to learn Rumanian!)

4. In these areas, make the inscription of place-names and street-names, the signs on shops, factories, museums and public institutions, and the inscriptions on consumer products, etc., bilingual.

VII. *We demand the same career opportunities for the Hungarians of Rumania as the Rumanians have!*

Terminate the practice whereby job hiring and professional advancement are determined primarily according to ethnic background rather than professional expertise. Discontinue the practice of applying the proportion of Hungarians nationally to determine the number of Hungarians hired locally, even in firms located in overwhelmingly Hungarian areas.

VIII. *We demand the preservation of the environment which reflects our historic and cultural past!*

1. Preserve the traditional townscape of Transylvanian cities.

2. Stop tearing down the buildings which are significant for cultural or historical reasons.

3. Register as protected cultural properties all items deserving that title.

4. Stop altering the surroundings of Hungarian cultural landmarks, to show the landmarks at a disadvantage.

5. Establish a source of funds for the preservation of perishing historical and cultural monuments.

IX. *We demand that the Hungarian-speaking natives of Moldavia, the Csángós—whom official statistics have declared to be Rumanian, without exception—be permitted to declare themselves Hungarians again, and to participate in Hungarian cultural life!*

1. Permit them to join the organization representing Hungarian nationalities interests.

2. Permit them free use of their native Hungarian language.

3. Reopen their Hungarian-language schools.

4. Grant them the right to conduct religious services in the language of their choice.

5. Put an end to the forced isolation of the Csángós, the obstruction of their contacts with Hungarians from elsewhere and the persecution of visitors to Csángó villages.

X. *We demand that an impartial international commission (whose members would also include Hungarians and Rumanians) examine our situation and make decisions in the issues which bear upon our fate!*

*

The foregoing, which was written on behalf of two million Hungarians, provides only a partial cross-section of the country's problems: those affecting the Hungarians (and even those only in a summary and incomplete fashion). We are quite aware that the solution to these problems cannot be isolated from the more general set of questions. Our primary purpose, however, is to identify these problems, since if we do not do so, no one will do it for us. As far as calling attention to the general issues affecting all of us, this is not our responsibility alone, and perhaps not even ours primarily; it would first and foremost be the responsibility of the Rumanian people.

Nevertheless, we do not consider this act of ours premature. The wall of silence must at last be broken from somewhere on the *inside,* as must that enormous, motionless and seemingly immovable block of tyranny and deprivation of rights which weighs nightmarishly on every inhabitant of Rumania (except for those who profit from it) and which is ultimately responsible for the totally catastrophic condition in which the country finds itself. In this regard, it is our conviction that our program proposal, which may be considered by "some" to be directed against the Rumanian people, actually supports their interests, because any increase in the respect for human rights would necessarily lead to an increase in their rights as well.

SUPPLEMENTARY NOTE. The Romanian police tracked down and dispersed the group of Hungarians responsible for the Madrid Memorandum. *Ellenpontok* ceased publication. The three identified authors of the Memorandum were arrested, interrogated, beaten, and subsequently expelled from Romania to Hungary: Attila Ara-Kovács in May 1983, Károly Tóth in July 1984, and Géza Szőcs in August 1986. However, Géza Szőcs, before his expulsion, submitted in September 1985 a petition to the Central Committee of the Romanian Communist party for consideration at the forthcoming Thirteenth Party Congress. The principal demands of the petition are:

1. Revision of the country's constitution to include a guarantee of collective nationality rights in order to recognize Romania's Hungarians and Germans as "independent ethnic-historical entities."

2. Restitution of the Ministry of Nationalities disbanded in 1953.

3. Drafting of a Nationality Law based on the Nationality Statute of 1945, on the draft law proposed by the Hungarian People's Alliance in 1946, and on the "Program Proposal" submitted by the editors of *Ellenpontok* to the Madrid Conference in 1982.

Among other demands (most of them spelled out in the "Program Proposal"), the petition proposes that, since the government of Hungary proffers no support for the Hungarian minority, Romania should take the international initiative on behalf of the proposition at the United Nations to add to the Universal Declaration on Human Rights the explicit protection of minority rights and to the Convention on Genocide the explicit ban on cultural genocide and ethnocide.

For the text of the petition in Hungarian, see Magyar Füzetek, no. 16 (1985): 104–120.

✳ 8

The Hungarians of Slovakia: From Czechoslovak to Slovak Rule

Kálmán Janics

EDITOR'S NOTE: *This chapter is composed from several writings by Kálmán Janics both published and unpublished, both in Hungarian and English, as specified in the editor's "Acknowledgments." To arrive at a coherent presentation of the topic from several sources, textual modifications were necessary. The editor alone is responsible for both the textual adjustments and the structure of the chapter as a whole.*

Czechoslovakia is a federated socialist republic, consisting of two nation-states of equal rights: the Czech Socialist Republic with a population of over 10 million, and the Slovak Socialist Republic with a population of about 5 million. The census of 1980 found 579,000 Hungarians in Czechoslovakia; all of them are either living in Slovakia or have their ethnic roots there. While the Hungarians make up only 3.8 percent of Czechoslovakia's total population, in Slovakia they amount to a more substantial 12 percent—which is about the same percentage the Slovaks themselves once held (before World War I) in the multinational Kingdom of Hungary.

The Czech lands of Czechoslovakia are largely identical with the territories of the historic kingdom of Bohemia-Moravia. Slovakia, on the other hand, took shape only after World War I with Czech assistance, when Hungary's northern territories were transferred to the newly-founded state of Czechoslovakia. The boundaries of Slovakia—drawn for the first time in history—placed at that time almost one million Hungarians, living mostly in Slovakia's southern border areas adjacent to Trianon Hungary, under Czechoslovak rule. Czechoslovak sources estimate that, following a drop to 580,000 according to the census of 1930, the Hungarian population in the late 1930s before World War II rose to 630,000.[1] At any rate, statistically, the size of the Hungarian minority during the last fifty years or so has not increased, while the Slovak majority population during the same period has more than doubled. Today, of the Danube region's total Hungarian minority of over three million, about one-fifth belongs to Czechoslovakia.

Following the Munich Diktat of 1938, Czechoslovakia's Hungarian-populated territories—as well as some ethnically mixed ones—were returned to Hungary by the Vienna Award. After World War II, with the pre-Munich frontiers restored, some 600,000 Hungarians affected by these boundary changes became again citizens of Czechoslovakia—or, rather, they would have become citizens had the postwar rule of terror against the national minorities under Edvard Beneš's restored presidency not deprived them of their citizenship rights.

The Hungarian minority was declared collectively guilty on the grounds of betraying the Czechoslovak state in 1938. In order to justify this charge against the Hungarians, the prewar treatment of minorities in Czechoslovakia was described in glowing terms and considerably embellished. It is true that the minority policy of Czechoslovakia was far more democratic than that of Hungary, Romania, Poland, or Yugoslavia. Yet, the Hungarian minority in Czechoslovakia could never feel entirely free of discrimination. It was primarily in the economic field that the status of second-class citizenship was felt at every step. This discrimination was admitted even by those so-called "activist" minority politicians who supported the Czechoslovak Republic and defended it against hostile attacks from both inside and outside. For instance, in Piešťany, on September 7, 1936, István Csomor, a Hungarian member of the Czechoslovak Agrarian party, presented to Prime Minister Milan Hodža a memorandum detailing the grievances of the Hungarian minority. It read in part:

> We have wounds and we are waiting for the curing balm. Grievances have accumulated and these have to be redressed. The Hungarian minority has

a new home, but that home has no roof yet. A lot remains to be done for the benefit of the Hungarian minority. . . . Let's see to it that every Hungarian of Czechoslovakia feels at home in his new homeland, that they are free citizens of a free state, the Republic of Czechoslovakia. We have put into writing the grievances of the Hungarian minority, its cultural and economic demands. We request that these be given serious consideration. Listen to the words and fulfill our wishes.[2]

Despite grounds for such grievances, during World War II, and even more so after 1945, the principal charge against the Hungarian minority was its lack of appreciation of its privileges. It was said that, despite "complete" equality in the bourgeois republic, they almost unanimously betrayed the "common fatherland" during the crisis of 1938.

In a nutshell, the interwar story of Czechoslovakia's Hungarian minority is this: The Trianon frontier confronted the Hungarians in Czechoslovakia with two painful realities. They had ceased belonging to a nation whose undisputed authority over other peoples lasted for one thousand years. Suddenly, the former assimilators became an insecure minority in fear of their ethnic survival. The other unpleasant reality was that the Hungarian minority lost some 100,000 of its most valuable members. Voluntary exodus and forced settlement to Hungary deprived the Hungarians of Slovakia of a sizable part of their intelligentsia. The Hungarians never accepted the new order, and the flames of Hungarian nationalism flickered beneath the surface of enforced submission throughout the interwar period. In 1938, the Hungarians' thin veneer of loyalty to Czechoslovak rule cracked, and they readily participated in the destruction of the Czechoslovak state.

The political climate in the aftermath of World War II was unfavorable to revealing the facts about the prewar minority situation. And ever since, Czechoslovak historiography has failed to evaluate the facts with professional objectivity. On the other hand, several works of progressive Hungarians have pointed out the homeless feelings in prewar Czechoslovakia. For instance, Edgár Balogh, a well-known Hungarian Communist in interwar Czechoslovakia, now living in Transylvania, wrote: "The crux of the problem was that this state [Czechoslovakia] was unable to become our fatherland. . . . We were facing chauvinistic ambitions of the same kind with which, in former times, the Hungarian imperialists have persecuted their minorities."[3] Imre Forbáth, another Hungarian writer of the same leftist background, bids goodbye to Czechoslovakia with the same bitter sincerity:

Even the minority policy of a most democratic bourgeois system [such as prewar Czechoslovakia's] is not free of the ruling class ambition to maintain the hegemony of the ruling nation, to hide the social antagonism of classes behind artificially nurtured racial, national, and other conflicts. The tragic disintegration of the Czechoslovak Republic—albeit its principal cause was certainly the attack of Fascism and the surrender of the bourgeoisie—was also the consequence of its minority policies. . . . After decades of neglect, not even in the moment of extreme danger, could a greedy and shortsighted ruling clique bring itself to correcting the situation by a rapid and earnest reform. Thus, not even honest efforts of the best people were able to save the fatherland from the consequences of a mass of crimes. . . . In the decisive moment, the large majority of Czechoslovakia's minorities had left the country in the lurch.[4]

From Postwar Terror to Socialist Revolution

The present status of Slovakia's Hungarian minority, too, requires a brief historical elucidation. After World War II, there were two important ethnic minorities in Slovakia: the Hungarians and the Germans. The Germans (mostly descendents of medieval settlers) together with their Sudeten German cousins (with whom before Czechoslovakia's foundation they had nothing in common) were singled out as the primary culprits of prewar Czechoslovakia's collapse and punished accordingly. But, in the eyes of the architects of postwar Czechoslovakia's expulsion policy, the Hungarians were not far behind the Germans.

The rule of terror unleashed against the Hungarians was perceived by the Hungarian minority as an unexpected disaster. As the Hungarians saw it, Hungary may have been, as charged, Hitler's "last satellite," but fascist Slovakia under Jozef Tiso's presidency was Hitler's first satellite. Slovakia joined in the war against Poland and preceded Hungary in participating in the Nazi "final solution" of the Jews. In general, Slovakia's record in repressing fundamental freedoms certainly was worse than Hungary's. Also, Slovaks often made life miserable for the small community of Hungarians left in Slovakia after the Vienna Award of 1938, denouncing them as enemies of National Socialism. Remembering Slovakia's dubious wartime record, the Hungarians were surprised at suddenly finding the Slovaks sitting in judgment over them during the postwar period. The Hungarians seemed to have forgotten one of the basic lessons of history: losers cannot argue against victors, let alone against the interests of great powers and the accomplished facts of diplomacy.

Thanks to President Beneš's wartime diplomacy, the principle of Czechoslovakia's legal continuity absolved the Slovaks as a nation of any guilt for fascist crimes. The Hungarians who returned under Czechoslovak rule learned to their astonishment that Nazi-allied Slovakia was treated just like the Nazi-occupied Czech lands. President Beneš's postwar regime treated with equal hostility the Sudeten Germans and Slovakia's Hungarians. Branded as "fascist," Slovakia's centuries-old Hungarian community was to be liquidated. By virtue of the so-called Košice Program, the Hungarians (along with the Germans) lost their citizenship rights in liberated Czechoslovakia. A series of decrees issued by President Beneš deprived the Hungarians of their cultural rights and made their properties liable to expropriation without compensation. In everyday life, the Hungarians of Slovakia were subjected to humiliations without precedence in Slovak-Hungarian relations.

The ultimate aim of postwar Czechoslovak policy against the Hungarian minority, their expulsion from their homelands, has failed. But during four years of a postwar rule of terror, the Hungarians totally lost their cultural institutions. Their schools were closed, their children coming of school-age remained illiterate. The educated elite either fled or were expelled to Hungary.[5]

Following the Communist takeover in February 1948, beginning with the spring of 1949, Slovakia's Hungarians slowly recovered from the blows of the rule of terror. But it was an arduous process, never successfully completed. They had to reconstruct their cultural base from scratch. It took years for the minority school system to reach even remotely acceptable standards. Also, forced population transfers had wrought irreparable havoc. In the winter of 1946–47, some 45,000 Hungarians were forcibly resettled to the depopulated German Sudetenland in Bohemia as farmhands. After the Communist takeover, many of these deported Hungarians were permitted to return, though not always to their homes which, in the meantime, had been confiscated and allocated to Slovak settlers. Even more harmful was the Hungarian-Czechoslovak population exchange treaty of 1946, forced upon Hungary as a part of the Beneš plan to liquidate the Hungarian minority. According to that plan, promoted at the Paris Peace Conference, 200,000 Slovaks were to be transferred from Hungary to Slovakia in exchange for the transfer of the same number of Hungarians from Slovakia to Hungary. However, of Hungary's 170,000 Slovaks only about 60,000 opted for resettlement, despite promises of free land and furnished houses. Slovakia's Hungarians were even less willing to leave their homes—only about 6,000 signed up. About 68,000 more were forcibly deported.[6] This large exodus shook the Hungarian community to its foundation. Many formerly purely Hungarian villages became mixed communities. Ironically though, in a very few instances, but to the great annoyance of the authorities, Slovak settlers in Hungarian villages soon became assimilated into the Hungarian minority.

The post-World War II settlement policy actually continued the discriminatory trend already apparent in the post-World War I agrarian policy, only more radically. The First Czechoslovak Republic, too, had settled Slovak peasants on formerly Hungarian-owned land in order to push the Slavic ethnic boundary line ever more southward toward Hungary. In general, of course, conditions under the first democratic republic were incomparably better than after World War II. About 90 percent of the Hungarian children attended primary schools in their mother tongue.[7] The Hungarian historical establishment collapsed, but culturally the Hungarians continued to maintain a highly developed organization of their own in all fields. There were justifiable grievances, the lack of a Hungarian university foremost among them. Only a gesture had been made to fill that gap: the founding of the Masaryk Academy in the 1930s by a personal gift from President T. G. Masaryk. In general, however, economically the discrimination was more glaring and affected many more people. In economic terms, the Hungarians were definitely treated as second-class citizens. Official statistics reveal the facts. For instance, according to the 1930 census, among a thousand employed people there were 181.8 poor Slovak laborers who belonged to the truly proletarian segment of the working class. The Hungarian ratio was 245.5 out of a thouand. The corresponding figures for the more desirable class of white-collar workers are no less revealing: 67.9 Slovaks as against 40.3 Hungarians.

Since World War II, following the coup of 1948, the trend has been reversed. Economically, Slovaks and Hungarians are now treated as equals, more or less. It is mainly culturally that the Hungarian conditions are inferior. The most devastating blows were suffered during the terror of postwar persecution before 1948. What was left of the Hungarian intelligentsia after 1948 was weak both in numbers and in levels of education. Under such poor leadership the reconstruction of culture posed immense problems. The four-year ban on Hungarian cultural activities, with the illiteracy it forced upon the school-age children, has left its mark even after decades—not to speak of the psychological effects of persecution. For four years, the Hungarians suffered under a barrage of crude denunciation as members of a 'fascist nation' and a 'guilty nation.' They had been charged with crimes they never committed against the Slovak nation during southern Slovakia's post-1938 Hungarian reannexation. The humiliation and intimidation, the inferiority complex feeding on memories of persecution, the debilitating moral and spiritual effects of postwar terror are still affecting generations of Slovakia's Hungarians.

Some aspects of Hungarian hardships in Czechoslovakia are related to the postwar problems of national minorities in general. The post-World War II era created an unsympathetic milieu for a fair consideration of minority rights in Central and Eastern Europe. Both East and West condemned European minorities as the principal cause of World War II. At the 1946 Peace Conference hostile world public opinion prevented the revival of international minority protection as it existed in the inter-war period.

The post-World War II antipathy against Europe's national minorities—shared by East and West alike—was neither just nor justifiable. After all, sooner or later Hitler would have launched his war machine even if no German minorities had existed in Central and Eastern Europe. Moreover, the national minorities were a byproduct of the Versailles peace settlement. Their dissatisfaction with their lot, which Hitler exploited, stemmed from the shortcomings of that settlement. Peacemaking after World War II disregarded all these circumstances in accepting the proposition (advanced mainly by President Beneš) that national minorities are a threat to peace and a cause of war, therefore, they should be liquidated.

In Central and Eastern Europe, in particular, no distinction was made between ethnic diasporas of immigrants and long-established autochthonous populations who had become ethnic minorities only as a consequence of changed national boundaries. The Hungarian ethnic minorities in the Carpathian Basin are a classic example of this latter category. Most of them live in compact settlements in four countries adjacent to Hungary; they possess a strongly developed sense of collective national consciousness and attachment to Hungarian historical traditions—also a strong desire to preserve their Hungarian language and culture. To expect that such national minorities should behave like the immigrants in the American "melting pot" is both unfair and foolish.

No less unrealistic is the theory of "automatism" which was applied to problems of national minorities by some Marxist theoreticians in the postwar socialist states of Eastern Europe. According to this approach, national minority problems disappear automatically with the successful revolutionary transformation of class society into a classless one. Classical Marxism in fact plays into the hands of ruling majorities, and some Marxists do not hide this fact. They maintain that the proletarian revolution will inevitably establish unilingualism in each nation for the sake of convenience. Moreover, minorities are supposed to expedite this process by voluntarily facilitating their assimilation into the majority on pain of being labelled reactionary class enemies. In the 1960s, the Marxist writer Jan Šindelka elaborated this theme in Czechoslovakia.[8]

According to Šindelka assimilatory processes evolve through three phases. First, mutual antagonism disappears through mutual understanding. Second, ethnic groups become better acquainted. Third, they fuse—with the smaller group adopting the cultural standards of the larger one. As far as Czechoslovakia's Hungarian minority is concerned, Šindelka's paradigm has fundamental flaws. It assumes a cultural reciprocity and parity which is lacking between Slovaks and Hungarians. Whereas most Hungarians by now know the Slovak language and culture, very few Slovaks know the Hungarian language and culture. Slovak is a compulsory subject in every Hungarian minority school, but few Slovaks are taught Hungarian. Even Slovak historians are no longer familiar with the Hungarian language, though a common history of a thousand years would certainly warrant such familiarity, if for no other than professional reasons. In short, "mutual knowledge," which is at the bottom of Šindelka's theory, is missing.

Šindelka reproves minorities for wishing to defend themselves against assimilation. He deems it reactionary bourgeois nationalism if a minority wishes to maintain its ethnic isolation, conserve its national distinctions, and support its own national development at all costs, without exercising due regard for a process of "international rapprochement."[9] He does not seem to understand that national minorities see no reason why they should sacrifice their national identity in the service of the ruling majority nation's utopian assimilatory objectives. Nor does Šindelka seem to realize that ruling majorities are in a far better position to advance the cause of "mutual understanding" than the national minorities relegated to the status of inferiority. The fact of the matter is that it is the ruling Slovak establishment that systematically keeps ethnic hatred at fever pitch. A recent example is the book by the Slovak historian, Samuel Cambel, which approves all the worst excesses perpetrated by Slovaks against the Hungarians during the post-World War II persecutions, despite the fact that the Slovak Communist party has repeatedly condemned these outrages.[10]

Advocates of the Šindelka-type assimilation dogma have been forced to admit in due course that there is more to solving national minority problems than trusting the economically determined "automatism" of Marxist "revolutionary transformation."

In Slovakia, the struggle of the Hungarian minority is chiefly centered on restoring the quality and quantity of minority schools—in general, on rescuing Hungarian culture from declining standards. The assimilatory Slovak ethnic majority collides with the endangered but determined Hungarian ethnic minority. Both justify their position by citing various Marxist nostrums. The Hungarians seek to achieve cultural autonomy by invoking the Soviet principle of Marxist-Leninist nationality policy. The Slovaks counter such propositions by quoting Lenin's turn-of-the-century dictum spurning cultural self-determination for ethnic minorities. More pragmatic factors must be taken into consideration in order to understand the minority problem and evaluate the status of the Hungarian minority in Slovakia.

In the fall of 1948, when the Hungarians were once again recognized as Czechoslovak citizens, a slow improvement began; substantial results could not be discerned until ten years later. The gradual improvement was mirrored in official ethnic statistics. At the 1950 census, only 350,000 respondents dared to declare themselves Hungarian. By 1961, they approached the half million mark. This accretion certainly did not result from greatly augmented Hungarian fertility rates, but from having fears of persecution allayed.

In constitutional legal terms the turning point came in 1956. For the first time, a constitutional law made mention of the Hungarian nationality. Article 2 of the 1956 Constitution guaranteed "favorable conditions for the economic and cultural life of the population of Hungarian and Ukrainian nationality." Article 20 of the 1960 Constitution marked further progress by guaranteeing "equal rights of all citizens irrespective of nationality or race," while Article 25 explicitly secured the right of "citizens of Hungarian, Ukrainian and Polish nationality to education in their mother tongues and all possibilities and means of their cultural development."

Actual improvement of conditions, however, did not keep pace with the progressively improved language of the law. Slightly more than one out of five Hungarian children still attended Slovak schools. And even in the relatively more evenhanded struggle for economic equality the Hungarians were left behind. At war's end, about 60 percent of the Hungarian population was employed in agriculture. Despite the countrywide rapid progress of industrialization, by 1961 still 40 percent of the Hungarians were engaged in agricultural pursuits. And the 1970 census confirmed a continued discrepancy: 34.7 percent of the Hungarian population was engaged in rural occupations as compared with only 18.6 percent of the Slovaks; and, while 35.2 percent of the Slovaks were industrially employed, only 22.8 percent of the Hungarians were listed in that category.[11] One of the main reasons for their relatively slower economic progress is that far fewer Hungarians continued to be educated past the age of fourteen than their Slovak counterparts.

Not until the year of the "Prague Spring" were the Hungarians of Slovakia given the chance to voice their grievances publicly. CSEMADOK, the official Hungarian cultural organization, took the political initiative with a declaration on March 14, 1968, summing up the Hungarian minority grievances and proposing ways to redress them. On behalf of "Czechoslovakia's citizens of Hungarian nationality, workers, peasants, the intelligentsia, [Communist] party members and non-members," the declaration expressed agreement with the reform program of the Central Committee of the Czechoslovak Communist party and with the changes that had already taken place. On the subject of the party's program to regulate the nationality problem on a "new foundation," the CSEMADOK declaration stressed the necessity of "complete equality of rights," within a "federative reorganization" which would also grant a new constitutional status to the Hungarians and other nationalities according to the principle of self-administration." Furthermore, the new constitution must spell out "unequivocally and concretely" the equality of "nations" and "nationalities." Equality must be guaranteed not merely "individually," but also "collectively."

Following the Warsaw Pact intervention in August 1968, events took a very different course from the one anticipated by the March declaration of the Hungarian minority.

Hungarian Survival under Slovak Rule

The new constitution, promulgated October 28, 1968, on the fiftieth anniversary of Czechoslovakia's founding, carried out the promise of a federative reform. Since 1968, Czechoslovakia has been a dualist federation of two equal nations: the Czech and the Slovak. The Hungarians are now under Slovak rule in the Slovak Socialist Republic. Since 1968, the constitutional laws regulating the status of nationalities have fallen woefully short of the anticipated reforms. Not only has autonomy not been granted to the Hungarians, but even their constitutionally guaranteed language and cultural rights, including the right to "cultural-social association," have been curtailed or unfulfilled in Slovak practice, making Hungarian survival under Slovak rule in dualist Czechoslovakia even more precarious than before 1968. The 1970s in fact turned out to be, as Kálmán Janics calls them, a "decade of deterioriation."[12]

Slovak ascendancy in Czechoslovakia's national power structure is noteworthy also. Viliam Široký's long tenure in the post of prime minister (1953–64) was followed by that of another Slovak, Jozef Lenárt. The liberal episode of the Prague Spring in 1968, essentially a Czech affair, came to be identified with Alexander Dubček, at that time the Communist party head of Slovak origin. And post-invasion Czechoslovakia since 1968 came under the leadership of another Slovak Communist, Gustav Husák. The "decade of deterioration" of Slovakia's Hungarians, analyzed here by Kálmán Janics, coincides with the Husák era in Czechoslovakia's history. S.B.

Paradoxically, it was during the height of the cold-war years—from the fall of 1948 to 1958—that the situation of Slovakia's Hungarian national minority was the most favorable. The détente years of the 1960s then witnessed a certain deterioration, which increased during the 1970s following the brief flare-up of great hopes in the spring of 1968.

The so-called "Action Program of the Communist Party of Czechoslovakia," adopted at the plenary session of the Central Committee on April 5, 1968, recognized the collective rights of the national minorities. This was a decision of great significance not merely within the framework of events known as the "Prague Spring," but in the history of Central and Eastern Europe as well. It is worth saving from oblivion the passages concerning the national minorities contained in this remarkable document. The Action Program recognized the "national individuality" of all nationalities in Czechoslovakia—of Hungarians, Poles, Ukrainians, and Germans. To that end, the Action Program declared the necessity "to stipulate constitutional and legal guarantees of a complete and real political, economic, and cultural equality," and "to ensure an active participation of the nationalities in public life, in the spirit of equality of rights according to the principle that the nationalities have the right to independence and self-administration in provinces that concern them."[13] In brief, this was a promise of autonomy for the nationalities.

The draft-constitution of 1968 retained the essential parts of the Action Program concerning the rights of the nationalities. At the last moment, however, all the passages that smacked of autonomy were crossed out, including words such as "independence and self-administration" or "economic and cultural equality." And, although the preamble of the constitution still retained the reference to *collective* recognition, the subsequent articles reduced the rights of the nationalities to the old unsatisfactory *individual* citizen level.

Despite the mutilated 1968 Constitution, there was no abrupt end to the hopes of a new era in Czechoslovakia's nationality policy. It took three years or so for the new anti-minority trend to assert itself fully. When the new Constitution took force on January 1, 1969, along with the Slovak government of the Slovak Socialist Republic, a Nationality Council was set up, composed of 28 members of which 9 were Hungarians and 4 Ukrainians. Before long, however, it became evident that the Slovak nationality policy was not merely bent on destroying the reformist spirit of 1968 but was even curtailing the constitutionally guaranteed rights of the Hungarian minority. Such was the case with the revision of the role which CSEMADOK had assumed since 1968. In 1971, CSEMADOK was deprived of its constitutionally guaranteed functions as a "cultural-social organization" and was ordered to limit its activities to bureaucratic cultural affairs. Thus were dashed the hopes that CSEMADOK might serve as a representative of collective minority interests, as it did in the spring of 1968. Also killed was the hope that it might become the initiator of minority studies, filling the gap in Hungarian cultural life left by the lack of institutions of higher learning. It is one of the axioms of minority existence that if there is no articulated self-knowledge there is no collective self-awareness either, no cultural base for defending minority self-interests.

The defense of minority self-interest is a long-debated issue. Ushering in the decade of deterioration, in the spring of 1970, a press campaign was launched against minority self-administration, arguing that in a socialist society only the international working class is entitled to defense of its self-interest. The ideological salvo was fired by the Slovak historian Juraj Zvara with an essay in the Hungarian-language paper *Új Szó*.[14] Zvara built his thesis around Lenin's turn-of-the-century censure of the Czechs' seeking cultural autonomy in the Austro-Hungarian Monarchy. Without clarifying why Lenin's particular anti-Austromarxist view should be valid in Slovakia today, Zvara branded as "anti-Leninism" any demand for cultural autonomy in the Slovak Socialist Republic. Publicly, only a former Czechoslovak Hungarian Communist, living in Budapest, begged politely to differ with the Zvara thesis.[15] Thus ended the Marxist theoretical debate on Hungarian autonomy in Slovakia, while in practice the policy of Slovakization took over the field. Since then an air of intimidation has been rising ever more menacingly in the Hungarian communities, reminiscent of the anti-Hungarian climate of the immediate postwar era.

Statistically, the results of this "decade of deterioriation" have been registered on two fronts: in the census of 1980 and in the field of education. In addition to Slovakization pressures, Hungarian losses on both fronts are explainable by fear spreading among the Hungarians. In 1980, based on population growth estimates, a 6.4 percent increase of the Hungarian population was expected; it was only 1.5 percent. Many Hungarians did not dare to declare their nationality. The drop in the number of Hungarian children attending Hungarian primary schools is due partly to fear, too. That figure dropped from 71,000 in 1970 to 50,000 in 1980. Besides fear there are several other factors that account for these statistical losses. School reforms of the 1970s reduced, in many cases, the geographic accessibility of Hungarian schools. Partly due to lack of facilities, 35 percent of Hungarian minority children of kindergarten age start their education in a Slovak environment.

In the long run, the most serious factor seems to be the growing conviction among parents that it is in the interests of the children to be educated in the language of the majority. Relentless persuasion to this effect is going on under the auspices of the well organized Slovakization campaign. But the higher quality of the Slovak institutions, alone, is an effective temptation in convincing the parents to shun even the available Hungarian schools. This lowering of standards of Hungarian culture in general is no doubt the most alarming phenomenon from the point of view of Hungarian survival.

Historian Zvara declared not long ago: "Under socialism the nationality problem is being solved not by assimilation but through evolution and rapprochement between nations and nationalities."[16] This sounds very much like the Šindelka thesis of the 1960s, but Šindelka at least admitted that what he was talking about was the ultimate merger of the minority into the majority. Zvara scolds the Hungarians for opposing the trend of "rapprochement": "They [the Hungarian minority] would—if we would allow them—make use of nationalism in the battle against socialism."[17] Attaching labels of "anti-Leninism," "anti-socialism"—as well as the greatest of anti-Marxist crimes, that of "nationalism"—is old hat. This is the usual way the majority nations in Communist countries denigrate the minority nationalities' struggle for survival.

In conclusion, let's face the charge of minority nationalism. Undoubtedly, past persecution and continuing discrimination have provided the psychological breeding ground for defensive nationalism among Slovakia's Hungarians. But they harbor no nationalism which would hurt the interests or rights of the Slovak majority. Apart from current grievances, interpretations of the past also contribute to pitting Hungarian and Slovak nationalist feelings against each other. Common Hungarian-Slovak historical experiences are interpreted differently and create competing, even hostile, systems of thinking. The Hungarians have often been made to appear by the Slovaks as history's culprits. Slovak historians have overemphasized past oppression of the Slovaks under Hungarian rule, whereas Hungarian contributions in the past millenium for the common good have been totally ignored. All this antagonizes the Hungarians and stokes the fires of separatist nationalism on the one hand but, on the other, also adds to Hungarian feelings of inferiority, of minority helplessness and isolation.

Inferiority feelings have crept into the Hungarian minority consciousness in Slovakia and are increasing because minority problems have been relegated to limbo and suspended there. Socialist literature is forbidden to discuss minority problems in concrete terms. At best, it does so only in the nature of philosophical or ideological abstractions. There are no mutually agreed pragmatic guidelines to govern the behavior of either the minority or the majority. Should a minority possess special constitutional privileges? If so, what criteria should be used? Should all minorities have similar rights, regardless of numbers or distribution patterns, whether they live scattered throughout the country or in compact ethnic blocs? Should minorities be permitted to organize along ethnic lines? Are they a corporate body, or merely a collection of individual citizens speaking a different tongue? It has caused great harm that all these grave issues, which were raised in 1968, have since then been suppressed as nonexistent. The assumption today seems to be that national minorities are mere relics from the bourgeois past, which industrialization and urbanization will ultimately extinguish and thereby eliminate as a point of friction.

Indeed, it is chimerical to suppose that any force might eradicate so many centuries of ethnic and national traditions within mere decades. On the contrary, the scientific-technological revolution, which many have hoped would eliminate minorities, has certain characteristics which actually help preserve their peculiarities. For example, radio and television broadcasts from Hungary play a significant role in preserving the language and cultural traditions of the Hungarian minorities in the Danube region. Assimilation may win battles, but the minorities' struggle for national survival goes on.

Notes

1. *Demografická příručka* (Prague, 1966), 46.
2. József Sebestyén, *Hodža Milán útja* (Bratislava, 1938), 170.
3. Edgár Balogh, *Hétpróba* (Budapest, 1975), 158, 234.
4. Imre Forbáth's reminiscences in *Irodalmi Szemle* (September 1967): 835.
5. A detailed account of these four years of lawlessness can be found in my book: Kálmán Janics, *A hontalanság évei,* with an introduction by Gyula Illyés, published by the European Protestant Hungarian Free University in Bern (Munich, 1979). An English version adapted from the Hungarian by Stephen Borsody was published by Brooklyn College Studies on Society in Change: *Czechoslovak Policy and the Hungarian Minority, 1945–1948* (New York, 1982). On President Beneš's diplomatic moves to expel the Hungarians, see the Editor's Note at the end of Chapter 5, above.
6. Cf. Juraj Zvara, *A magyar nemzetiségi kérdés megoldása Szlovákiában* (Bratislava, 1965).
7. Cf. Zdenka Holotiková, "Niektoré problémy slovenskej politiky v rokoch 1921–1925," *Historický Časopis* (1966): 3.
8. Jan Šindelka, *Národnostní otázka a socializmus* (Prague, 1966). See Juraj Zvara's ideas on this subject below; also see Annex I in Chapter 9, below, for a Yugoslav-Hungarian Marxist interpretation by László Rehák.
9. Šindelka, *Národnostní otázka,* 287.
10. Samuel Cambel, *Slovenská agrárna otázka 1944–1948* (Bratislava, 1972).
11. Figures from the official publication, *Demografia* (1971): 4.
12. Kálmán Janics, "A romlás évtizede," *Új Látóhatár* 34/3 (1983): 330–41.
13. Quoted from the English translation of the Action Program as published in Robin Alison Remington, ed., *Winter in Prague: Documents on Czechoslovak Communism in Crisis* (Cambridge, Mass., 1969), 108–9.
14. *Új Szó,* April 19, 1970.
15. Endre Arató in *Kortárs* 11 (1970): 1810.
16. *Sociologia* 5 (1981): 513.
17. *Sociologia* 3 (1976): 227.

Annex I:
The Duray Affair

EDITOR'S NOTE. Deteriorating conditions in the 1970s convinced a handful of concerned Hungarian intellectuals that public defense of

Hungarian minority rights in Slovakia by legal means had become impossible. In 1978, they agreed to act anonymously as an informal group under the name of "Committee for the Defense of the Rights of the Hungarian Minority in Czechoslovakia." The aim of the committee was to collect data on the violations of the constitutionally guaranteed rights of the Hungarian minority. At home, they established contact with the Czech Charter 77 civil rights movement, while abroad they tried to get international publicity for their cause.

The committee's first memorandum, addressed to top government and party officials in the fall of 1978, protested against recent Slovak school reforms which were undermining the very structure of Hungarian education. The next memorandum, in the spring of 1979, summed up the violations of Hungarian minority rights in light of the Czechoslovak Constitution and demanded redress of grievances in all areas of minority life. Truly, it was a "Petition of Rights," an outstanding document of the Hungarian struggle for survival under Slovak rule. (See Annex III, below.) This document, with a cover letter stressing the committee's conviction that "nationality oppression is a violation of human rights," was sent to the spokesmen of Charter 77, the Czech civil rights movement. Later that year, another communication was sent to Charter 77, a general statement on minority problems in the framework of Hungarian-Czechoslovak relations (Annex II). In 1980, a study by the Committee discussed Slovakia's minority oppression in light of the provisions of the United Nations human rights resolutions and the Helsinki agreements. Also, the committee's letter of protest concerning Hungarian-language education was sent to Hungarian schoolteachers and parents throughout Slovakia. Two of the committee's statements (Annex II and III, below) were circulated among participants of the Helsinki follow-up conference in Madrid (1980–83). Finally, in 1980–81, a comprehensive memorandum on the situation of the Hungarian minority was prepared for the Minority Rights Group in London (Annex IV).

The moving spirit behind the committee's activities was Miklós Duray, a geologist and writer, who is one of the leading Hungarian intellectuals of the postwar generation in Slovakia. Born in 1944 into a working class family, Duray's first public appearance dates back to the Prague Spring of 1968, as a leader of the Hungarian minority youth movement. Since then, he has written several studies on minority problems, and one of his writings appeared in an important

Budapest underground publication, *In Memoriam István Bibó*. He has also authored most of the memoranda issued in the name of the Committee for the Defense of the Rights of the Hungarian Minority in Czechoslovakia. Suspecting him of involvement in the committee's activities, the Slovak police interrogated and warned Duray against such activities several times since 1979. In June 1982, the Slovak political police searched his apartment in Bratislava and confiscated some of his papers, notes, and books, as well as his mimeographing machine, which is an illegal possession in Czechoslovakia. On November 10, 1982, he was arrested.

On December 28, 1982, the State Prosecutor in Bratislava charged Duray with "bourgeois nationalist" activities undermining the socialist social order and slandering the republic at home and abroad. He was charged with disseminating documents which "deliberately distort the facts, are anti-socialist, prone to arouse nationalist sentiments, and play into the hands of institutions abroad because they create the impression as if Czechoslovakia had not solved its nationality problem." Duray's arrest has aroused considerable attention abroad. Protests against his prosecution have been voiced in both Western Europe and in the United States. In an open letter, addressed to the prime minister of Hungary, the American writers Irving Howe, Susan Sontag, and Kurt Vonnegut have urged intervention on Duray's behalf.

The Duray trial began on January 31, 1983. Among western observers who attended the trial was a representative of Amnesty International. But most conspicuous was the presence of a three-member delegation from Hungary's Writers' Union. Duray, in his defense, reminded the court that thirty years ago President Husák himself was tried under the same charges of "bourgeois nationalism." Duray admitted authorship of the memoranda issued in the name of the Committee for the Defense of the Rights of the Hungarian Minority in Czechoslovakia but insisted that the threats to Hungarian survival as described in those documents correspond to facts.

The verdict in the trial was to be pronounced on February 11, but was postponed. Unexpectedly, on February 24, 1983, Duray was set free without a verdict, but under the condition that he refrain from any future seditious activities. Rumor had it that, behind the scenes, the Hungarian government intervened.

Undaunted, Duray led successful public protest against a draft bill aimed at liquidating, for all practical purposes, education in the mother tongues of national minorities in Slovakia. Under pressure of a massive Hungarian protest, the Slovak government was forced to withdraw the most objectionable (in fact, unconstitutional) passages of the proposed legislation. However, in reprisal for his role in the campaign against the draft bill, Duray was rearrested in May 1984 and faced old and new charges of "activities contrary to the interests of the state" and "distributing inciting material." In May 1985, after a year in detention without a trial, Duray was set free with all charges dropped under the provisions of a general amnesty issued on the fortieth anniversary of VE-day.

Shortly before Duray's release, Béla Köpeczi, Hungary's minister of culture, had paid an official visit to Czechoslovakia. His negotiations in Prague and Bratislava, he said, have been held "in a creative atmosphere of mutual search for new avenues in cultural ties and with a decisive resolve to strengthen results already achieved." S.B.

Annex II
Petition of Rights

EDITOR'S NOTE: In May 1979, the Committee for the Defense of Rights of the Hungarian Minority in Czechoslovakia sent a petition to top government and party leaders. Listing in detail instances of discrimination against the Hungarian nationality, the petition proposed measures to stop violations of constitutional rights. This petition was among the memoranda which were brought to the attention of the participants of the Helsinki follow-up conference in Madrid. In addition to the full text of proposed measures, the excerpts that follow are from a summary which introduces the petition.

The full text of the petition was published in Hungarian by *Irodalmi Újság*, (Paris), September–October 1979.

Ten years ago Constitutional Law 143/1968 amending Constitutional Law 100/1960 of the CSSR [Czechoslovak Socialist Republic] took effect. This law pertains to the federal structure of the state [consisting of two Socialist Republics, those of the Czech and Slovak nations]. Simultaneously, Constitutional Law 144/1968, pertaining to nationality [i.e., national minority] affairs, was also passed. It should be noted, however, that the implementation of Constitutional Law 144/1968 did not fulfill the expectations of the nationalities for the following reasons:

1. It failed to secure the social, economic, and cultural development of the nationalities aiming at the reduction of differences that developed since 1945 in their relationship to the two [Czech and Slovak] nations.

2. It failed to secure collective participation of the nationalities in the political life of the state.

3. It failed to secure for the nationalities proportionate development on all levels of education.

4. It failed to stop the forcible assimilation of the nationalities.

The above failures are the results of nonimplementation [of the constitutional law] by supportive legislation either by the National Assembly or by the Slovak National Council.

During the past ten years the degrading of constitutionally guaranteed rights of the nationalities to institutional independence affected most seriously the Hungarian nationality [living in the Slovak Socialist Republic].

This unconstitutional discrimination clearly manifests itself . . . [in the field of education, culture, economic life, political life, and legal rights].

[To end discrimination and violations of law,] . . . we urge enactment of the following measures in accordance with the constitutional principle of national equality.

A. Education

In accordance with Constitutional Law 100/1960, Chapter II, Art. 19,. Par. 2, Art. 20, Par. 2, Art. 24, Par. 3, and Art. 26, as well as Constitutional Law 144/1968, Art. 3, Par. 1/a:

—The education of Hungarian youth in its native language should be unconditionally guaranteed, beginning with establishment of Hungarian nursery schools and expansion of the network of Hungarian kindergartens, continuing to all levels of primary and secondary schooling, including gymnasia, specialized technical high schools, as well as secondary vocational schools for apprentices, to satisfy the needs of all regions inhabited by citizens of Hungarian nationality.

—Concrete steps should be taken to increase the total number of Hungarian students (by approximately 250%) in colleges and universities: in medicine (by approximately 500%), law (approximately 400%) and economics (approximately 500%), to a level proportionate to the number of citizens of Hungarian nationality living in the country.

—Hungarian-language instruction should be guaranteed at the College of Agriculture of Nitra (Nyitra) and the College of Veterinary Medicine of Košice (Kassa) by increasing the Hungarian student enrollment at these institutions by 300%.

—The right to Hungarian-language practicum and the right to examinations in the native tongue should be guaranteed at the Komenský University of Bratislava (Pozsony), at the department of chemical technology of the J. P. Šafařik University of Košice (Kassa), at the departments of chemical, mechanical, architectural/structural, and electrical engineering of the Slovak College of Technology of Bratislava (Pozsony), as well as at the department of mechanical engineering of the College of Technology of Košice (Kassa).

—The department of Hungarian language at the philosophical faculty of the Bratislava (Pozsony) Komenský University should be expanded into a full-fledged department of Hungarian Studies.

—A Hungarian College of Education should be created in Bratislava (Pozsony) to train Hungarian educators for primary and secondary schools.

—We are asking for guarantees against all attempts to change the language of instruction in Hungarian schools from Hungarian to Slovak.

—Study opportunities at colleges and universities in the People's Republic of Hungary for [Czechoslovak] citizens of Hungarian nationality should be expanded, especially in the social sciences, and disciplines of special relevance to the needs of Hungarian-inhabited regions [in Czechoslovakia].

B. Culture

In accordance with Constitutional Law 100/1960, Chapter II, Art. 24, Par. 2, and Art. 28, as well as Constitutional Law 144/1968, Art. 3, Par. 1/b/c.

—The cultural offerings for citizens of Hungarian nationality should neither be reduced to belles lettres, nor degraded to amateurism, but kept on high level of competence and professionalism.

—By creating a permanent Hungarian theater in Bratislava (Pozsony) Hungarian stage culture should be further developed.

—Professionalism in Hungarian mass culture should be developed to ensure a progressive evolution of Hungarian popular culture. Within the framework of the Institute of Popular Culture in Bratislava (Pozsony) the nationalities section should be strengthened, and nationality sections should be created at district houses of culture.

—A central Hungarian library should be established with regional branches.

—A Hungarian cultural center should be established to assist professional regional development of the arts in fields of folk and local art.

—The print and paper capacity of Hungarian publishing should be increased. At the Madách Publishing House, the scope of publications should be expanded and the professionalism of the editorial staff improved.

—In addition to the [existing] literary periodicals, professionally staffed periodicals in the fields of natural and social sciences should be founded to ensure wide dissemination of scientific/technical knowledge.

—An independently edited Hungarian weekly devoted primarily to social problems should be established.

—Instead of the scattered and sporadically appearing local papers of low standards, regional bi-weeklies should be published. Western Slovakia needs two such bi-weeklies, while the central and eastern Slovak regions need one each.

—Hungarian-language programs should be introduced at Channel One of the Bratislava (Pozsony) television.

—An independent research institute with a social studies division for the study of the development of the Hungarian nationality should be established. The majority of the professional staff should be of Hungarian nationality.

—To stop "brain drain" through emigration under duress, appropriate employment opportunities for Hungarian individuals with higher education should be secured.

—The deliberate oppression of Hungarian culture by depriving it of financial resources should be stopped.

C. Economic Life

In accordance with Constitutional Law 143/1968, Chapter I, Art. 5, Par. 2 and Par. 5:

—The continuing economic decline of Hungarian-inhabited areas must be stopped. The industrialization of the areas should proceed in conformity with given social and natural conditions. Emphasis should be placed on agriculturally based and food processing industries. Lingering unemployment caused by reduced labor power following agricultural modernization should be corrected by the creation of new job opportunities in processing, light, and heavy industry. This will cut down the undesirable outmigration from the most seriously affected Hungarian-populated areas.

—The professional staff and technical experts of new industries should be recruited mainly from the ranks of the local inhabitants.

—Prior to industrialization the youth should be steered by adequate means of information into the appropriate Hungarian technical schools. The capacity of regional secondary technical and vocational schools should be adjusted to the industrial needs of the region.

—The development of agricultural and industrial production should take human and social factors into consideration. Specifically:

(a) The forced unification of agricultural collectives and villages in Hungarian-Slovak border areas should be discontinued.

(b) Reckless intensification of large-scale agricultural production, causing chemical pollution of the environment especially in the [Hungarian populated] Csallóköz and the East Slovak basin should be stopped.

(c) The massive chemical pollution in general of southern Slovakia [in the mostly Hungarian-populated regions] should be stopped.

—[In these regions] . . . small enterprises and light industry should be developed to tie down the inhabitants and to prevent outmigration and a demographic catastrophe due to deteriorating living conditions.

—Industrialization, urbanization, or economic development should not serve as pretexts for forced assimilation of Hungarians.

—The hydraulic and hydroelectric works being constructed on the

Czechoslovak section of the Danube should not be to the economic and ethnic detriment of the inhabitants of those regions whose majority is Hungarian.

D. Political Life

In accordance with Constitutional Law 100/1960, Chapter I, Art. 6, as well as Constitutional Law 143/1968, Chapter II, Art. 37, Par. 3:

—The participation of CSEMADOK [cultural association of the Hungarian minority] in the National Front should be renewed.

—The ministerial functions in charge of nationality affairs in the government of the SSR [Slovak Socialist Republic] should be renewed. The minister and deputy minister heading such department should be selected from the ranks of the nationalities.

—From the ranks of the nationalities deputy ministers and state secretaries should be appointed to the departments concerned with education, culture, public health, agriculture, food processing, development and technology, industry and construction. These officials should be concerned with nationality problems and their solutions in regions populated by nationalities.

—The practice of nominating Hungarian delegates to elective organs only to improve the proportionate representation of lower social strata should be discontinued.

—Interventions of nationality delegates on behalf of their own nationalities should not be regarded as seditious acts.

—Nationality representatives should be allowed to unite in nationality clubs.

—Nationality representatives should be allowed to consult independent experts in matters pertaining to nationality affairs.

—Nationality councils on district levels composed of nationality experts (Hungarian and Ukrainian) should be created.

—In districts with mixed populations, nationality councils, attached to the national district committees, should be created for overseeing of nationality affairs especially in education, culture, labor, social and health matters.

—In districts with mixed populations, nationality sections should be created in the local and municipal committees, charged mainly with matters of education, culture, and public health.

—Citizens of nationality origin should be able to use their native tongue effectively in written and oral official communications, including in districts with mixed population, and with the regional and central organs of state and party. In the Slovak Socialist Republic this means the use of Hungarian and Ukrainian.

—In areas of mixed population, on local as well as on the district level, bilingualism should be made obligatory in affairs of administration, telecommunication, and transportation.

E. Rights

In accordance with Constitutional Law 143/1968, Chapter V, Art. 76, Par. 2, as well as Chapter VI, Art. 87/b, Art. 89, Par. 9, and Art. 93:
—The non-implementation and neglect of the provisions of Constitutional Law 144/1968, Articles 1, 3, 4 and 5 should be investigated.

We submit this memorandum in accordance with Constitutional Law 100/1960, Chapter II, Article 29.

Annex III
Charter 77 and the Hungarian Minority

EDITOR'S NOTE. One of the objectives of the Committee for the Defense of the Rights of the Hungarian Minority in Czechoslovakia has been to establish contact with the Czech Charter 77 civil rights movement. The first communication took place in May 1979. Through a personal envoy, the committee sent its memorandum on the violation of Hungarian nationality rights (Annex II) with a cover letter expressing the hope for cooperation between the two human rights movements. Unlike on another occasion during the postwar terror—when an appeal by the Hungarian anti-fascist writer Zoltán Fábry to the Czech Writers' Union was ignored—the Czech reaction this time was sympathetic. Encouraged, the Hungarian Committee sent another document in October 1979, specifically prepared for the participants of the Charter 77 movement. The excerpts below are from that document and from its cover letter addressed to the Charter 77 movement as "Esteemed Fellow Citizens! Friends!" It was also included in the information material circulated among the participants of the Helsinki follow-up conference in Madrid (1982).

Incidentally, following his release in 1983 from detention, Miklós Duray issued a letter of thanks addressed to all those "Hungarians and non-Hungarians" from Hungary, Western Europe, and the United States who expressed their solidarity with him, as well as to "Hungarians, Slovaks and Czechs" in Czechoslovakia. And, calling the Charter 77 declaration on his behalf "particularly precious," Duray asked to be included among the Charter 77 signatories. Miklós Duray's letter, composed after his release from detention in 1983, was written in Hungarian and Slovak. It appeared in its original versions in the émigré periodicals, *Magyar Füzetek,* no. 13, and *Svědectví,* nos. 70–71, both published in Paris. The full text of the memorandum and cover letter to participants of Charter 77 was published in Hungarian by *Magyar Füzetek,* no. 6.

Information and thoughts are traveling only with great difficulty from Czechoslovakia's eastern parts to its western borders—and this is due not only to the country's elongated shape but also to lack of common historical traditions. Very few people in central Bohemia know what is happening in southwestern and southern Slovakia, and hardly anyone knows the problems of that region. Extending for over 500 kilometers, the south Slovak region of roughly ten thousand square kilometers is the home of the Hungarian minority. It has belonged to the Republic since 1918 with the exception of six years during World War II [when it was returned to Hungary]. Administratively, the [Czechoslovak] state has tried from the very beginning by rigorous measures to fuse this region with the rest of the country. Yet, even during that democratic era [after World War I], the integration met with little success. And today, the desperate cries of the Hungarians, who make up 12 percent of Slovakia's population, are drowned in the labyrinth of an oppressive political system. . . .

In 1968, during the four months of a budding new democracy, the Hungarian minority stepped forward—judiciously but resolutely—and demanded the solution of the nationality problem. The result of this action was the Constitutional Law No. 144 of 1968. However, during the past decade, the almost unpenetrable wall preventing the solution of the nationality problem has been rising ever higher. The issue of Hungarian nationality has passed from nationwide [Czechoslovak] jurisdiction under the ever more willful authority of Slovakia.

Recently, under the veil of phoney measures which conceal the true situation, reckless elements—with official support—have been rampaging in order to annihilate the nationality rights [of the Hungarian minority]. Past experience proves that solution of the nationality problem can be approached only on a nationwide level. The right of action cannot be transferred to the leadership of a narrow region, if for no other reason, because this problem was born with the Czechoslovak Republic itself.

Since 1968, during the period of so-called consolidation, the leaders of the Hungarian minority dedicated to democracy and human rights for the national minorities have been sidetracked and branded anti-Socialist and right-wing nationalist. . . .

In the attached report we have summed up our opinion of the country's domestic policies and nationality policies, as well as some of the salient facts concerning the past and present situation of the Hungarian minority in Czechoslovakia. We would like you to get acquainted with our position and discuss it. The results of such a debate would be most instructive for us. Nor do we deny our distant hope that, after getting acquainted with our situation, you will support our cause in the spirit of our shared principles. . . .

It so happened that often in the history of Central European nations Hungarian successes entailed Czech defeats, or Czech aspirations have succeeded in defiance of Hungarian interests. Yet, we also like to remember instances when Czechs and Hungarians have met on the field of solidarity. Unfortunately, friendly handshakes have never influenced the official policies of our nations. In the course of the last hundred years, Hungarian and Czech—or, later, Czechoslovak—interests have clashed in fatal conflicts. . . .

During the last sixty years, it was the existence of the Hungarian minority in Czechoslovakia that caused friction and conflicts in Czechoslovak-Hungarian relations. This is true today, too. . . . As a result of conditions that have developed since 1968, the situation of the Hungarian minority in Czechoslovakia has reached an unprecedented low point. This is part and parcel of the total deformation of Czechoslovak society, it reflects the general disintegration of legal and constitutional safeguards, the catastrophic retreat from European ideals. . . .

The Committee for the Defense of the Rights of the Hungarian Minority in Czechoslovakia is a more recent independent branch of the civil rights movement in Czechoslovakia. Its fate is bound up with that of other similar movements, and it assumes solidarity with them on that account. Its coming into existence is due partly to general political conditions, and partly to the specific anti-minority measures in Slovakia. The Committee believes that redress of Hungarian grievances is achievable primarily through realization of the principles of democracy, because democracy and minority rights are inseparable. Other aberrations of Czechoslovak society, too, are curable only by democratic means. Therefore, the struggle for democracy is the common cause of all citizens and of all nationalities in the Republic. The principles of democracy are the same in Prague and in Komárom [in southern Slovakia], and it is our common interest, too, that democracy should prevail.

Annex IV
The London Memorandum

EDITOR'S NOTE. In 1980–81, the Committee for the Defense of the Rights of the Hungarian Minority in Czechoslovakia prepared a lengthy memorandum entitled "The Hungarian Minority in Czechoslovakia" for the London-based Minority Rights Group. Its intended English translation from the Hungarian has so far not materialized. However, the Paris-based *Dialogues Européens,* an informal group of progressive Hungarian exiles and dissidents, published the original Hungarian text under the sponsorship of its periodical, *Magyar Füzetek.* The following excerpt, entitled "Summary," is translated from that publication. See the original "Report from Slovakia on the State of the Hungarian Minority," in *Magyar Füzetek Books,* no. 4 (Paris, 1982), 66–70.

One million Hungarians were severed from their mother country and transferred to Czechoslovakia by the frontiers drawn in the wake of World War I. Three quarters of these Hungarians are still living in Czechoslovakia while one quarter became Soviet subjects when the Soviet Union seized Carpatho-Ruthenia and incorporated it into the Ukraine after World War II. The frontier after World War I was drawn with disregard for ethnic and historical factors, without consulting the local populace—it was to satisfy the strategic claims of the newborn Czechoslovak state, then an ally of the victorious powers.

The Hungarians did suffer discrimination in Czechoslovakia between the two world wars, but international minority protection and the democratic constitution of the new state made their situation, in general, tolerable. Yet, it is only natural that they never lost their sense of belonging to the mother country and, following Munich, they greeted with enthusiasm the First Vienna Award in 1938, which returned the bulk of the contiguous Hungarian population to Hungary.

Since Hungary again landed on the losing side in World War II, boundaries were restored to the prewar status quo. However, this was not enough for the Czechoslovak politicians returning from exile. They put the blame for the collapse of the first republic on the national minorities—among them, the Hungarians. Their aim was the "final solution" of the minority problem.

All Hungarians of restored Czechoslovakia were stripped of their citizenship rights; nearly 100,000 were forcibly expelled to Hungary; about 50,000 were deported inside the republic; and more than 300,000 Hungarians were forced to declare themselves "Magyarized" Slovaks. Nevertheless, the complete liquidation of the Hungarian minority did not succeed. At first it was the western powers that raised objections, then—following the Communist takeover in 1948—the Soviet Union opposed open hostility between peoples under their rule; and, last but not least, the tenacious attachment of Hungarians to their national identity made things less than easy for their Czechoslovak oppressors.

Thus, the state of total lawlessness ceased in 1948; Czechoslovak citizenship of Hungarians was restored. The deported Hungarian peasants were allowed to return to their villages. The "Magyarized Slovaks" gradually became Hungarians again. In due course, the Hungarian minority made good even the demographic losses suffered by forcible expulsions.

1948, however, also meant the inauguration of a new, more subtle, less open and more underhanded policy aiming at the liquidation of the Hungarian minority. Up to 1968, this policy had not reached its full pitch. The centralist regime of President Novotný was largely occupied by conflicts between Czechs and Slovaks; therefore, manifestations of Slovak nationalism were curbed. Only following the Soviet intervention in 1968, and the destruction of the reformist movement, did the Moscow-oriented Slovak nationalism receive a shot in the arm and gain decisive weight in the political life of the country. The "cold" liquidation of the Hungarian minority has now become a government program of the Slovak Socialist Republic in federally reorganized Czechoslovakia. As a result, the demographic, economic, and cultural development of the Hungarian minority in Czechoslovakia has considerably slowed down. . . . [The no-growth demographic situation is also due to assimilation.]

The main causes of assimilation are: internal migration and mixed marriages. Young people quite often cannot find any kind of job near enough to their birthplace. Mixed marriages are a comparatively new phenomenon, but they are on the increase, especially as far as women are concerned. Yet, on the whole, the Hungarian minority seems to resist the pressures of assimilation, their loyalty to their nationality is unbroken.

The total development of the social structure offers, however, a less favorable picture. The changes in political power, the open persecution of Hungarians going on for years, and the radical transformation of the social composition, ensuing from a Soviet-style regime, have all worked toward the elimination of the Hungarian intelligentsia and educated middle class. The preponderance of industrial and agricultural workers contrasts unfavorably with the overall social composition in Slovakia as a whole, let alone with that of the more developed Czech lands. The bulk of Hungarians in industry is made up of unskilled laborers—particularly in the building trades—who, as a rule, only find work far away from home. It is true that the fast rate of industrialization in Slovakia following 1968 has affected the social and economic development of the Hungarian minority, too. But key investments are deliberately directed toward the Slovak-speaking areas. Furthermore, the demand for skilled workers for factories built in Hungarian areas cannot be met by Hungarians, because of lack of training. Thus, Slovak-speaking craftsmen and engineers are transferred to these areas. In this manner, industrial development is becoming another tool of dispersion and intermingling, thereby weakening the social cohesion of the Hungarian minority.

Proper participation in social and industrial expansion depends largely on acquiring higher education. In this respect open discrimination against the Hungarians is the rule. In the primary schools, attended by the six- to fifteen-year-olds, one-fifth of Hungarian children are compelled to study in Slovak. The authorities are untiring in their efforts to grind down Hungarian as a language of instruction. . . . The decisive setback the Hungarian young suffer is in quality of secondary education. Pupils of Hungarian schools who qualify for entrance examinations in institutions of higher learning make up only 22 percent of their age group. Even if one adds the Hungarians studying in Slovak, a total of only 30 percent stay for further education, while about 40 percent of the Slovaks do. In the age group of nineteen-year-olds and above the ratio is even worse, six percent for Hungarians compared to eighteen percent for the Slovaks. The Slovaks have the advantage, too, of studying in their mother tongue, while the number of Hungarians who may carry on their higher studies in their mother tongue is an insignificant percentage.

The use of the Hungarian language is discouraged not only in the field of education. In practice, no Hungarian may be used in offices or in administration. Hungarian notices and signposts have been eliminated everywhere. Even the use of Hungarian personal names—and of names of villages—is being discouraged. In industry, Hungarian workers are forbidden to speak their language, even among themselves. Those Hungarians who dare to stick up for the use of their language are the target of constant abuse. They are told to speak "the language of the state." Spontaneous manifestations of chauvinistic hostility are not only officially tolerated; they are actually fueled by an insidious propaganda directed from above.

In the ruling political system of Czechoslovakia today, minorities in general, and the Hungarians in particular, have no means to organize themselves in order to defend their interests. Even the high clergy of the Slovak Roman Catholic Church manage to be openly anti-Hungarian despite their own grievances against the state. Unlike the Catholic Church, the Calvinist Church is overwhelmingly Hungarian. But this does not make it any easier for them to stand up for minority rights.

Earlier on—particularly during the process of democratization in 1968—CSEMADOK (Cultural Association of Hungarian Workers in Czechoslovakia) succeeded in acquiring a measure of political influence. However, following the Soviet occupation of the country, CSEMADOK was expelled from the National Front and thus, for all practical purposes, the Hungarian minority was left without representation. Therefore, the Hungarians of Czechoslovakia have been recently compelled to turn to forms of defense of their rights which are officially proscribed.

The policy of discrimination systematically pursued against the Hungarian population affects not only its immediate victims. At a sensitive meeting point of East and West, conflicts over minorities provided the cause, or pretext, for several conflagrations—among them two world wars. In this region problems of oppressed minorities have been festering for two centuries, poisoning the relationships among countries and peoples thrown together, for better or worse, by geography and history. Their mutual enmity has always given opportunities to great powers for aggressive interventions, for playing off one small nation against the other. Last but not least, the oppression of minorities violates fundamental human rights and frustrates any truly democratic development in the countries of the region.

Annex V
The Bratislava Incident

EDITOR'S NOTE. Buildings and offices of Hungarian cultural institutions were vandalized in Bratislava, capital of the Slovak Socialist republic, during the night of March 8, 1987.

On this occasion, Charter 77 issued a statement addressed to the Federal Government and the Federal Assembly of Czechoslovakia. Following is an excerpt from this document. (Charter 77, No. 23/87.)

We regard the said acts of violence as alarming because they are the culmination of various regrettable expressions of nationalist intolerance, such as provocative slogans and the damaging of Hungarian property, insulting and belittling remarks against citizens speaking Hungarian in the streets and even the defiling of the statue of the world-renowned Hungarian poet Sándor Petőfi.

We are convinced that relations among nationalities of the state can be influenced by its citizens and that the constitutional organs have a special responsibility to keep the peace. We demand, therefore, that you devote maximum effort to the investigation of these terrorist acts.

✳ 9

The Hungarians of Vojvodina under Yugoslav Rule

Andrew Ludanyi

After World War II, Tito's leadership and the ideological commitment of the Yugoslav Communist party to Marxism-Leninism set the stage for an integrationist and tolerant ethnic policy. But before such policies could be enacted, deportations, transfers, emigration, and executions had drastically altered Vojvodina's ethnic composition. An estimated 150,000 Germans (Volksdeutsche) and 30,000 Hungarians were imprisoned or executed as war criminals and collaborators. Ultimately, about 450,000 Germans and 40,000 Hungarians were deported or, as a group, transferred to their mother countries.[1]

With Slav settlers replacing the Germans and Hungarians, Vojvodina's population today is over one-half Serb, nearly one-fifth other Southern Slavs, and less than one-fourth Hungarian. For a while, the size of the Hungarian population only stagnated, but beginning in the 1960s it started declining. Between 1961 and 1971, it dropped from 504,000 to 477,000, and there was a further drop to 420,000 according to the 1981 census. The Albanians, by contrast, Yugoslavia's next largest non-Slav nationality, are rapidly growing in numbers. The Hungarians' statistical decline may be a result of their more effective integration into the Slav majority, or it could be also due to their lower birthrate and continuing emigration.[2]

Yugoslavia is one of Europe's ethnically and linguistically most diverse states. Besides Serbs, Croats, and Slovenes (the founders of

Yugoslavia in 1918), there are Albanians, Hungarians, Germans, Romanians, Turks, Macedonians, Bulgarians, and some other ethnic groups in smaller numbers living in the country. Most of Yugoslavia's Hungarians live in a fairly compact area of the Vojvodina, today an autonomous province within the Socialist Republic of Serbia, one of the six republics of the Socialist Federal Republic of Yugoslavia. Once predominantly Hungarian, the region became ethnically mixed as a result of Turkish wars as well as Slav migration and German colonization following Habsburg liberation from Turkish rule.[3] At the time of Hungary's partition after World War I, the population of Vojvodina was roughly one-third South Slavic, one third German, and one-third Hungarian.[4]

In the interwar period Yugoslavia resorted to a two-pronged policy to weaken the country's Hungarian minority: outright repression on the one hand and divide-and-rule tactics of Habsburg times on the other. Beset by nationality problems, the government backed loyal ethnic groups against the irredentist Hungarians.[5] As elsewhere in the successor states, land reform served as a pretext for bringing in colonists from the ranks of the ruling nationality. The Serbian settlers, acting as "border guards," diluted the Hungarian areas to some extent but it was mainly the attempt to "Serbianize" the Hungarians linguistically and culturally that stirred up Hungarian resentment against Yugoslav rule. The cultural life of the Hungarians was linked to their churches, schools, and folklore. All three became targets of Yugoslav government policy to reduce the region's Hungarian character.[6]

Most Hungarians of the Vojvodina are Roman Catholics as opposed to the Orthodox Serbs. A postwar Concordat with the Vatican redrew the boundaries of the dioceses so as to make them correspond to the new state boundaries. The clergy of the Vojvodina became subject to the Croatian prelates in Zagreb. All church schools were transformed into state schools under the Ministry of Education in Belgrade. Instruction in the Hungarian language was limited to four elementary grades, but the allowed number of such schools was well below the Hungarian ethnic percentage.[7] Furthermore, education in Hungarian schools stressed indoctrination in Yugoslav nationalism by a teaching staff at least one third of which was of South Slavic origin.[8]

There was a perceptible easing of repressive measures against the Hungarians following the assassination of King Alexander in 1934. Under Regent Prince Paul—although Yugoslavia was a member state of the anti-Hungarian Little Entente—there were signs of a rapprochement with Hungary.[9] Subsequent events, however, foiled the rising hopes of a genuine Yugoslav-Hungarian reconciliation. In 1941 Hungary joined the Axis powers and took part in the dismemberment of Yugoslavia.

In light of two decades of adverse interwar experiences, it was no surprise that most Hungarians in the Vojvodina welcomed their return to Hungary. However, the Hungarian reacquisition of the Vojvodina was short-lived, with gruesome consequences. The Hungarian occupying forces committed atrocities, the worst among them the Novi Sad (Újvidék) massacre, but the local Hungarian population, rather than the actual perpetrators of the crimes, suffered under postwar retaliation.[10]

The Theory and Practice of Nationality Policy

The trauma of internecine ethnic strife, both prewar and wartime, convinced the Communist party of Yugoslavia that a new approach was needed to solve the country's nationality problems. The wartime ethnic solidarity of the partisan experience ushered in the new policy. The Communists led by Tito have created a partisan movement which has overcome the petty nationalism of the past. Partisan groups have been organized in all parts of the multiethnic country—even among Hungarians of the Vojvodina.[11] Struggle against the Germans demanded unity transcending ethnic divisions. As Milovan Djilas pointed out:

> It is incontestable that in the massacres going on between Serbs and Croats [during the war] the Yugoslav state would have disappeared had not the Communists appeared on the scene. They had all the conditions for such a role: vision, organization and leadership. The Communists were impervious not only to the demoralization of the ruling classes, but also to the chauvinistic excesses. They were the only party that was *Yugoslav* [emphasis in original] in the composition of its membership, in its political practice and—interpreted narrowly—in its internationalism.[12]

The postwar momentum of Titoist Yugoslav internationalism drew its force from the partisan mystique.[13] The partisan experience projected a sense of mission; it had a supranational appeal. The partisans were fighting not just against Nazi Germany but also against reaction and racism; they were fighting for progressive ideals, for a brighter future of mankind. Internationalism was the legacy of the partisan experience, although, until early 1943, the partisans were mostly Serbs and Montenegrins. In due course, however, Croats, Slovenes, Macedonians, and other nationalities joined the partisan movement. The partisans became thus a genuinely all-Yugoslav antifascist alliance. Even though most Hungarians were not sympathetic to the partisans, during the last few months of the war a Hungarian "Petőfi brigade" had been formed which actually saw action against the Germans in the Battle of Bolman—and a great deal has been made of it by Yugoslav historians.[14]

True to the partisan mystique, the first of the "basic principles" of Yugoslavia's postwar constitution proclaimed the right of every nation to self-determination. The principle, after undergoing several rephrasings, reads in the preamble of the 1974 Constitution as follows:

> The nations of Yugoslavia, proceeding from the right of every nation to self-determination, including the right to secession, on the basis of their will freely expressed in the common struggle of all nations and nationalities in the National Liberation War and Socialist Revolution, and in conformity with their historic aspiration, aware that further consolidation of their brotherhood and unity is in the common interest, have, together with the nationalities with which they live, united in a federal republic of free and equal nations and nationalities and founded a socialist federal community of working people—the Socialist Federal Republic of Yugoslavia.[15]

This declaration of principle goes far beyond what other East European Communist constitutions say about the subject of self-determination, in fact, beyond anything that the Yugoslavs themselves consider feasible or desirable. Actually, in the earlier constitutions, the right of secession and the right to self-determination were mentioned only in the preambles.[16] The articles of the 1974 Constitution, however, draw a line between those who have those rights and those who do not.

The earlier constitutions spoke rather loosely of "peoples" and "nationalities" of multiethnic Yugoslavia. The 1974 Constitution distinguishes between "nations" and "nationalities." While both nations and nationalities are guaranteed "equality" and "freedom" within the "socialist federal community of working people," only nations have the right to self-determination and secession.[17] By "nations" the

Constitution means the South Slav founders of Yugoslavia: Serbs, Croats, and Slovenes. By "nationalities" the Constitution means the other, mostly non-Slav nationalities: Albanians, Hungarians, Romanians, and so on, that is, the minorities.

As officially interpreted, by suppressing the old distinction between "majority" and "minority," equality has been established by the new constitution between "nations" and "nationalities." But, constitutional definitions and interpretations notwithstanding, the actual status of the non-Slav Hungarians (and of other "nationalities" as well) is that of a minority—and their lot is affected, as before, by both international and domestic developments.

The major postwar events that stand out in the context of the majority-minority relations in general are the following: the Tito-Stalin split in 1948, the Hungarian Revolution of 1956, the purge of Aleksandar Ranković in 1966, the Warsaw Pact invasion of Czechoslovakia in 1968, the Croatian unrest of 1970–71, and the Albanian stirrings of 1968 and 1981–82.

The Tito-Stalin confrontation had negative repercussions in the short run, but positive consequences in the long run. When the Yugoslav Communist party was expelled from the Cominform, Stalin expected Tito's demise and the reincorporation of Yugoslavia into the Soviet bloc. The Cominform unleashed a campaign of vilification against Tito and the Yugoslav "revisionists" in general. One aspect of this campaign was to discredit Yugoslav nationality policies and to foment unrest, particularly among the national minorities. Each one of the neighboring Soviet bloc states was given the assignment to stir up discontent among fellow nationals in Yugoslavia. Thus, the Bulgarians focused on the Bulgarian and Macedonian populations, the Albanians appealed to the Albanians, the Hungarians criticized the treatment of the Hungarians, while the Romanians took issue with the alleged persecution of their nationals and other minorities in the Banat part of the Vojvodina.

All Cominform criticism equated the Titoist policies with "chauvinist pan-Serbian" aspirations. Interestingly, the Cominform campaign was limited to arousing the national minorities and did not exploit the traditional rivalry between Croats and Serbs. The objective was not to destroy Yugoslavia, but to topple Tito and to bring the country back into the Soviet bloc intact.[18] Some tension was generated, but not enough to coax any of the minority nationalities into rioting or rebellion. Only a few desertions from the armed forces and illegal border crossings occurred.[19] In any case, the Yugoslav military presence in critical areas acted as a deterrent to serious unrest.

The events of 1948 made Yugoslav policymakers aware of the vulnerability of a multinational country. A sense of insecurity was the likely reason for seeking in the 1950s centralized handling of nationality problems. The Constitution of 1953 as well as the policy statements of that period stood for the centralist idea of "Yugoslavism" ("jugoslovenstvo").[20] The government emphasized Slav loyalty to the state in an effort to counter the potentially disruptive forces of non-Slav nationalities. Great stress was laid on the Slav self-consciousness and the role of the Serbs, Croats, and Slovenes as statemakers of the Yugoslav state. But the stress on the central powers of the state also tended to deemphasize the autonomy of the individual federal republics of the three Slavic nations. Consequently, central control over the autonomy of the Vojvodina and Kosovo-Metohia within the Serbian Republic (the home of Hungarians and Albanians, respectively) was also tightened.

Yet the Hungarian nationality within Vojvodina actually benefited from this centrally controlled restriction of the region's autonomy. The region's government was forced to conform with federal laws, and protection was thereby provided against local chauvinist abuses under "Yugoslavism."

Of all the Hungarian minorities in Eastern Europe, the Hungarians of the Vojvodina remained most passive during the Hungarian Revolution of 1956.[21] One of the explanations offered for this fact is that the Yugoslav treatment of Hungarians was improving at that time.[22] Another explanation could be that due to the brief but cruel period of postwar retribution the Hungarians were too intimidated. Also, initially, the Yugoslav government did not condemn the Hungarian uprising. In fact, Tito sympathized with Imre Nagy and with the Hungarian objective to free the country of Soviet interference in domestic affairs. Tito turned against the Hungarian Revolution only when it threatened the hegemony of the Communist party.[23]

The internationally calmer 1960s have served as a beneficial background to domestic reforms in Yugoslavia. The constitutional revision of 1963 ushered in a period of controlled decentralization. While providing more self-government on local levels, it strengthened the country's federal structure. It was a unifying instrument without imposing uniformity.[24] In 1966, Aleksandar Ranković, defender of Yugoslav centralism, was forced to resign. With his fall from power, the ethnic assertiveness could again more freely manifest itself, particularly among the individual Slavic nations. But the non-Slavic nationalities also registered gains—not as much though as they expected from the decentralizing reforms.

Decentralization heightened the expectations for greater ethnic freedom among the minority nationalities. Constitutionally, decentralization bestowed upon the autonomous provinces of Vojvodina and Kosovo within the Serbian Federal Republic virtual equality with the Republic itself. In reality, however, the longed-for self-government has not been achieved either by the Republic's Albanians or Hungarians. Frustration reached a particularly high point among the Albanians. In 1968, the year of the dramatic events in Czechoslovakia, the first massive postwar Albanian unrest broke out in both Kosovo and Macedonia.

In the Vojvodina, dissatisfaction erupted on two occasions. One, in the late 1960s, was the Rehák affair, involving the foremost Hungarian Communist scholar of the nationality question. (See Annex I, below.) As a representative in the Assembly of the Serbian Republic, László Rehák questioned the footdragging of the University of Novi Sad in setting up a Hungarian Studies Institute. The Serbian press attacked him as a nationalist and whipped up enough opposition to block his expected election to the vice presidential post of the Executive Committee of the Serbian Republic.[25]

The other incident was the so-called *Symposion* affair, involving Sándor Rózsa, a student at the University of Novi Sad. In 1971, the year of Croatian unrest, Rózsa described the Hungarians as the "niggers" of Yugoslavia in an article in the Hungarian periodical *Új Symposion*. Those who dare to speak Hungarian in public places, he wrote, are treated as second-class citizens.[26] Punished for his outburst of widely felt frustration, Rózsa was denounced as a nationalist troublemaker. He lost his university scholarship and was stripped of his responsibilities as Hungarian-language program coordinator at the Novi Sad Youth Council. The periodical itself had to make a public apology for publishing the article.[27]

It should be pointed out that these types of "affairs" are the exception rather than the rule of Hungarian life in Vojvodina. However, until the issue of bilingualism in matters of street signs, official forms and blanks, and public services in general, is solved to satisfaction, the social atmosphere surrounding the minority will remain stifling and often intimidating. (For another "affair," see Annex II)

The Future of Yugoslav Multinationalism

The present Belgrade government has tried to improve the atmosphere surrounding majority-minority relations. However, even the best intentions cannot remove the discriminatory legacy of the past. Ingrained biases and modes of behavior inherited from the interwar years still survive. Only through reforms on all levels—republic, autonomous province, cities, communes, and workers' councils—could the situation be radically improved.

But even under the present circumstances, the Hungarians of Yugoslavia have incomparably greater cultural and educational opportunities than during the interwar years. In general, they are better off as a nationality than the Hungarians in Romania, Slovakia, or the Carpatho-Ukraine. Under Tito, and under his successors since his death in 1980, the Yugoslav state has respected the Hungarians' right to be Hungarians. They do not have autonomy—not yet, Marxist theoreticians, like László Rehák, may say. The Hungarians of the Vojvodina are a minority in an autonomous province with a Serb majority. But the Yugoslav regime has provided the Hungarians with educational institutions, cultural facilities, and publishing opportunities which are doing a credible job in serving the Hungarian cultural interest of the Vojvodina.[28]

Yugoslavia's self-image and the image it wants to project to the outside world tends to reinforce the commitment to multinationalism. The Yugoslavs have been the hosts to international conferences and symposia dealing with the needs of national minorities. The most significant such conclaves have been the United Nations sponsored meetings at Ljubljana (1965), Ohrid (1974), and Novi Sad (1976). Also, at the Helsinki follow-up conference in Belgrade (1977) the Yugoslavs presented their nationality policies as a model to the rest of the world.[29] For Yugoslav self-image the role of a model for multi-ethnic societies is at least as important as the stand on non-alignment. In their international relations, these two aspirations are frequently presented as complementary.[30] National minorities are viewed as bridge builders between nations, both on the domestic and international scene.[31]

For the Hungarians of the Vojvodina the role of bridge builders between Yugoslavia and Hungary is a most welcome one. In fact, Hungary has eagerly reciprocated Yugoslav overtures to this effect. Cultural exchange programs of various kinds have been arranged. Dance groups, exhibits, films, books, periodicals, and other cultural products have crossed the border in both directions on a regular basis. Sister cities in the two countries have enhanced exchange opportunities. Also, a program assisting the Serbs of Hungary and the Hungarians of Yugoslavia provides for exchange of textbooks and even educational opportunities for teacher training on university levels.[32] This reciprocity is threatened only when relations between the USSR and Yugoslavia deteriorate.

Some tentative conclusions can be drawn from the present situation about future prospects. On the positive side, the treatment of Hungarians—aside from the immediate postwar years and during the Cominform conflict—has been much better after than before World War II. Also, it is tolerant and pluralistic in comparison to conditions that prevail in Romania, Czechoslovakia, and the Carpatho-Ukraine. On the negative side, the Hungarian minority in Yugoslavia is exposed to the whims of changing power constellations in a one-party autocratic political order. Within this system, Communist "democratic centralism" can override the interests, needs, and rights of any national group unless the leaders of the country are committed to ethnocultural pluralism. The delicate balance in both the domestic and international situations should caution us against confidently assuming that conditions will always favor tolerance. But should change bring intolerance in nationality policies, it is not likely that the Yugoslav state itself would survive. The very existence of the state, and the legitimacy of its present order, depends on the viability of pluralism that can secure the rights of all the peoples of multinational Yugoslavia.

Notes

1. For an overview of population changes in Eastern Europe, see Leszek Antoni Kosinski, "Population Censuses in East-Central Europe in the Twen-

tieth Century," *East European Quarterly* 5 (1971): 274–301. Also, Theodore Schieder, ed., *Das Schicksal der Deutschen in Jugoslawien in Dokumentation der Vertreibung der Deutschen aus Ost-Mittel-Europa* (Bonn, 1961), 5:11A; Elemér Hommonnay, *Atrocities Committed by Tito's Communist Partisans in the Occupied Southern-Hungary* (Cleveland, 1957); Zoltán Dávid, "A magyar nemzetiségi statisztika multja és jelene," *Valóság* 23/8 (August 1980): 92.

2. For speculations about the Hungarian demographic picture in Yugoslavia, see articles in *Új Symposion* by Károly Mirnics (February 1971): 112, and Csaba Utasi (May 1971): 216–17.

3. The repopulation of this war-ravaged area by Serbian and German "soldier-colonists" receives extensive treatment in Gunther E. Rothenberg, *The Military Border of Croatia, 1740–1881* (Chicago, 1966).

4. C. A. Macartney, *Hungary and Her Successors* (London, 1937), 381.

5. Ibid., 409, 433–34.

6. Robert Lee Wolff, *The Balkans in Our Time* (Cambridge, Mass., 1956), 156.

7. Macartney, *Hungary*, 418; Wolff, *The Balkans in Our Times*, 156.

8. Macartney, *Hungary*, 420–21.

9. For a discussion of change in Yugoslav foreign policy at that time, see Hamilton Fish Armstrong, "After the Assassination of King Alexander," *Foreign Affairs* 13/2 (January 1935): 224–25; J. B. Hoptner, "Yugoslavia as Neutralist: 1937," *Journal of Central European Affairs* 16:4 (July 1956): 156–76.

10. The most detailed study of the Novi Sad events is János Buzási's *Az újvidéki "razzia"* (Budapest, 1963).

11. Danilo Kečić, "'Figyelő': A JKP Vajdaságban a felkelés előkészítésének és megindításának napjaiban," trans. Józef Kollin, *Híd* 25 (September 1961): 784–94; Josip Broz Tito, "The Fascist or any Other Similar Threat Must Never Again be Allowed to Appear," *Socialist Thought and Practice* 15 (1975): 3–29.

12. Milovan Djilas, "The Roots of Nationalism in Yugoslavia," in Michael and Deborah Milenkovitch, eds., *Parts of a Lifetime* (New York, 1975), 397. Also, see Chapter 12, below, "The Tito Thesis."

13. Andrew Ludanyi, "Titoist Integration of Yugoslavia: The Partisan Myth and the Hungarians of the Vojvodina, 1945–1975," *Polity* 12 (Winter 1979): 225–52. Yugoslav nationality policies since World War II are discussed in J. Frankel, "Communism and the National Question in Yugoslavia," *Journal of Central European Affairs* 15 (April 1955): 49–65; Evangelos Kofos, "Balkan Minorities under Communist Regimes," *Balkan Studies* 2 (1961): 42–46; Paul Shoup, "Yugoslavia's National Minorities under Communism," *Slavic Review* 22 (March 1963): 64–81; George Schöpflin, "Nationality in the

Fabric of Yugoslav Politics," *Survey* 25 (Summer 1980): 1–19. On this subject, see also Chapter 12, below.

14. Bogdan Smiljević and Dorde Knezevic, *A legújabb kor története,* trans. Kálmán Csehák (Subotica, 1965), 146–224.

15. Dragolub Durović et al., eds., and Marko Pavičić, trans., *The Constitution of the Socialist Federal Republic of Yugoslavia* (Belgrade, 1974), 53.

16. Compare the 1974 Constitution with the 1946 Constitution (Annex I in Chapter 12, below) and with the Fundamental Law Pertaining to the Bases of the Social and Political Organization of the Federal Organs of State Authority (January 13, 1953), Amos J. Peaslee, ed., *Constitutions of Nations* (The Hague, 1956), 3: 766. See also Annex II in Chapter 12 for excerpts from the Statute of the Autonomous Province of Vojvodina.

17. Durović, et al., eds., *The Constitution,* 53.

18. Robert R. King, *Minorities under Communism: Nationalities as a Source of Tension among Balkan Communist States* (Cambridge, Mass., 1973), 68–69, 71.

19. Schöpflin, "Nationality in the Fabric of Yugoslav Politics," 4.

20. Ibid., 2.

21. King, *Minorities under Communism,* 86.

22. George Klein, "Yugoslavia," in Béla K. Király and Paul Jonás, eds., *The Hungarian Revolution of 1956 in Retrospect* (Boulder, Colo., 1978), 104–5.

23. Bennett Kovrig, *Communism in Hungary: From Kun to Kádár* (Stanford, 1979), 313–14.

24. Frederik W. Hondius, *The Yugoslav Community of Nations* (The Hague, 1968), 336; George W. Hoffman and Fred Warner Neal, *Yugoslavia and the New Communism* (New York, 1962), 213.

25. On the Rehák Affair, see articles by Csaba Utasi and István Bosnyák in *Új Symposion* (April–May 1967): 40–45.

26. *Új Symposion* (August 1971), 344–45.

Új Symposium (December 1971): 441–42.

27. See my "Hungarians in Rumania and Yugoslavia: A Comparative Study of Communist Nationality Policies") (Ph.D. diss., Louisiana State University, 1971), 277–87.

28. Dušan Popovski, "Respect for the Rights of Ethnic Minorities," *Socialist Thought and Practice* 16/12 (December 1976): 63–64; István Fehér, "Egyenjogúság és az oktatás," *Híd* 40/10 (October 1976): 1253–54.

29. Popovski, "Respect for the Rights of Ethnic Minorities," 58–59.

30. Atif Purivatra, "Tito's Contribution to the Theory and Practice of the National Question," *Socialist Thought and Practice* 19/2 (February 1979): 69–73.

31. László Kővágó, *Nemzetiségek a mai Magyarországon* (Budapest, 1981), 88–89, 135–42, 182–88.

Annex I
From Minority to Nationality
Summary of a Marxist Analysis by László Rehák

EDITOR'S NOTE. László Rehák is the foremost Yugoslav-Hungarian Marxist authority on nationality questions. One of his studies, prepared for a conference sponsored by the United Nations on nationality rights at Ohrid in 1974, was published in English, *Nations and Nationalities of Yugoslavia* (Belgrade, 1974). The summary of the argument and the selections below are from his book, *Kisebbségtől a nemzetiségig* (Belgrade, 1978).

In his books, Rehák presents the theoretical foundations of contemporary Yugoslav nationality policy. As usual, reality often contradicts theory. These theories are ideals. As far as practice goes, they are, at best, aspirations. This is obvious in Rehák's analysis, particularly in his discussion of territorial autonomy. As far as the Socialist Autonomous Province of Vojvodina is concerned, the introduction of autonomy actually amounts to a name change from "statute" to "constitution." Essentially, the switch from so-called bourgeois "minority" to socialist "nationality," is also a name change.

Rehák is interested primarily in Vojvodina's Hungarians of the Serbian Republic. The conditions of the Hungarians in the Croatian and Slovenian republics differ somewhat from those in the Vojvodina. Few in number, ca. 20,000, the Hungarians in Slovenia have the most far-reaching cultural and social opportunities as a minority community. The ca. 60,000 Hungarians in Croatia, despite relatively acceptable treatment, are threatened most by assimilation because of their geographical dispersal. Of course, the future of the ca. 420,000 Hungarians in the Vojvodina is of the greatest concern.

The excerpts that follow are from László Rehák, *Kisebbségtől a nemzetiségig* (Belgrade, 1978), 33–41, 107–115. For further excerpts from the Rehák analysis, see Annex III in Chapter 12, below.

The Leninist Legacy

While reviewing the Leninist theoretical legacy, László Rehák focuses on Lenin's criticism of the pre-World War I Austro-Marxist views. He expresses agreement with one of the leading Yugoslav Marxist ideologues, Edvard Kardelj, who observed:

> Lenin's polemics with the Austro-Marxists and other similar orientations within the international labor movement was based on the premise that the national question was basically an economic and political question and that it cannot be reduced simply to the question of cultural autonomy or some such issue. It is just on such premises that Lenin developed his position on the right of nations to self-determination.

Lenin's position, and that of the revolution which he headed, opened a new era for the solution of the minority question. Lenin rejected the liberal bourgeois solution, which claims equality as an abstract ideal but is divorced from the "social inequalities created by an economic order based on exploitation."

On numerous occasions Lenin raised the need for territorial autonomy in multinational states:

> Local autonomy is not precluded by the practice of democratic centralism. In territories with autonomy based on special economic and ecological conditions or the unique nationality composition of the inhabitants, it is imperative that autonomy and democratic centralism supplement each other. Too frequently we tend to confuse centralism with arbitrariness and bureaucratic despotism. Of course, the confusion of the two is not surprising in the context of Russian history; however, for a Marxist it is still unforgivable.

Lenin presented the need for territorial autonomy in a realistic and flexible fashion: "Why should territorial autonomy be granted only to nationalities numbering at least half a million, why shouldn't even an area with only 50,000 members of a nationality enjoy such autonomy—why not unite these areas with neighboring subdivisions of various jurisdictions within a unified autonomous region of the country, if this is advantageous or necessary from the standpoint of commercial or economic integration." Then Lenin observes: "While the national composition is one of the most important factors, it is only one of the factors and not the most important of all the factors. . . . To separate cities from the towns and countryside for nationality reasons is a foolish and impossible solution." In other words, Rehák concludes, the Austro-Marxist position is not acceptable because it stresses the importance of national criteria while ignoring the more significant factors of economic rationality and other factors relative to living conditions. As opposed to the "personal autonomy" of the Austro-Marxists, which would guarantee ethnic cultural rights by separating nationalities from each other, the Leninist approach was "territorial autonomy" which integrated different nationalities on the basis of their mutual economic interests within a federal framework.

The Question of Territorial Autonomy

Two basic assumptions of socialist society in Yugoslavia are the ruling power of the working class and the equality and fraternal interdependence of nations and nationalities. The autonomous provinces are a significant component of Yugoslavia's federal constitution. They have a significant role in the realization of Yugoslavia's nationality policies. However, the justification of territorial autonomy is not based solely on nationality considerations. Nationality considerations are only one of the factors—together with historical, economic and general social considerations.

Territorial autonomy in the socialist sense overcomes the isolation of one nationality from the other by consciously fostering the interdependence of the various nationalities. This is the only true socialist way to regulate a minority society for the sake of equality. However, to achieve this objective the constitutional institutionalization of territorial autonomy by itself is not enough, it must be supported by the revolutionary forces and policies of society. Socialist self-management facilitates the linking together of workers from various nationalities through their common territorial or regional interests. At the same time, this may also satisfy certain particular nationality interests.

The federal constitution of 1967 and the constitutional amendment of 1968 defined the role of autonomous provinces as social-political elements of federalism, with independent rights and responsibilities. On this basis, on February 21, 1969, the Socialist Autonomous Province of Vojvodina adopted a "Constitutional Law" to replace its "Statute." The changes provide the opportunity for a greater role in our general economic and social-political development as well as for the continuing development of nationality relations within a socialist context.

The Bridge Role of the Nationalities

Yugoslavia has consistently rejected the view that a multinational society is a hindrance or a disadvantage. Yugoslavia's Communists believe that it is the balance of social forces rather than the multinational makeup of society that determines cooperation or conflict. The League of Communists of Yugoslavia, as well as other organized socialist forces, turned with confidence toward the national minorities. . . . This is a primary consideration in determining the so-called "bridge role" of the nationalities on the domestic scene.

However, this "bridge role" also has international ramifications. Edvard Kardelj wrote about this in the following way:

> As long as state boundaries separate members of one and the same nation, we cannot claim that the problems of national minorities have been solved, that their conditions of existence are ideal. The final resolution of the problems of national minorities will be a consequence only of those historical and social developments which will lead, in general, to the elimination of state boundaries, without regard to the communities of which the minorities are now a part. . . . In principle we must fight for the right of minorities to maintain unhindered contact with their conationals beyond the state frontiers. Along some borders for political reasons these contacts are thwarted or at least restricted. As a socialist country, however, we must clearly state that we favor open borders with the countries that are our neighbors and that we favor a system whereby people have freedom of movement. . . . However, this kind of arrangement can be achieved only among friendly states and nations, which mutually accept the responsibility not to interfere in each other's domestic affairs.

These thoughts were cast into a resolution at the Eighth Congress of the League of Communists of Yugoslavia in 1964:

> We must expand and nurture our friendly good neighbor policies, and many-sided cooperation between states with mixed populations. Such cooperation will guarantee that state boundaries will not become walls of separation between nationalities and the people whom they regard as their mother-nation. The free and many-sided contacts between nationalities will not become a source of tension and conflict, as in the past, but rather that they will become the reason for closer ties and cooperation.

National minorities play a significant role in transmitting the cultural values of neighboring nations. In this way, they enrich another nation's material and intellectual culture, or at any rate they contribute to the understanding of it. In this way, the common interests and the forms of international cooperation are strengthened and enriched.

The role of nationalities as bridges remains an aspiration. In the actual world we cannot realize it yet. For this role to become a reality, more time is needed. It is more likely to be achieved in a socialist society than under a capitalist social order. At least, this is the case in theory. Yet, despite the fact that basic to socialist conditions is the abolition of every privilege and the elimination of class and nationality advantage, there are examples in our age where socialist states utilize the worn-out intolerant assimilationist policies of capitalist societies, either openly or in disguised fashion. Also, in today's world, examples abound where states misuse national minority contacts to interfere in the internal affairs of others. This is the reason why Edvard Kardelj stresses that national minorities can fulfill their linkage, bridging role "only among friendly states and nations."

Building bridges among nations and countries is not a simple task. Still, the future peaceful development and social progress of mankind depends on it.

Annex II
The Limits of Yugoslav Tolerance:
Reverberations of a Remark by Gyula Illyés
and the "Új Symposion Affair"

EDITOR'S NOTE. Gyula Illyés, the internationally known Hungarian poet and writer, died in April 1983. Revered as the "grand old man" of Hungarian letters, he has been considered by many as the voice of Hungarian national conscience, especially because of his outspoken concern for the Hungarian minorities (see Chapter 14, below).

A few months before his death, Illyés gave an interview to Harry Schleicher of the *Frankfurter Rundschau* (December 21, 1982). Speaking of the minority Hungarians, Illyés expressed the view that "even those in Yugoslavia are threatened," mentioning specifically the "de-Hungarianization" taking place in "urban centers." He also termed Hungary's Trianon frontiers "unjust," indirectly urging greater Western interest in the fate of the Hungarian minorities because, as he put it, the "political responsibility" for the territorial settlement that created these minorities lies originally with France and Great Britain.

Two months after the Illyés interview, the Hungarian-language daily of the Yugoslav Communist party, *Magyar Szó,* published a reply (February 20, 1983) by a highly respected member of the Vojvodina Hungarian community, Imre Bori, a professor at the University of Novi Sad (Újvidék). Bori paid tribute to Illyés's literary greatness but criticized the "unreality" of his ideas bearing upon the realm of politics—such as his "Swiss model" for solving the Danube region's nationality problems, or his poetic metaphor comparing the literature of the dismembered Hungarian people to "five reeds" of a shepherd's pipe. Condemning his *Frankfurter Rundschau* interview for "releasing the genies of irredentism from the bottle of the past," Bori charged Illyés with "revisionist views." Furthermore, he rejected Illyés's interference in Yugoslavia's domestic affairs, calling him a "self-appointed spokesman" for Yugoslavia's Hungarians. Translated into Serbian, the Bori article was simultaneously published in the Belgrade *Borba* (February 20, 1983), while the Zagreb *Večernji list* (February 25, 1983), approving Bori's reply to Illyés in an article of its own, condemned Illyés's "rude interference" in Yugoslavia's national and international affairs.

The Illyés affair came to be entangled in another affair, indicating the limits of Yugoslav tolerance. That other "affair" concerns the avant-garde Hungarian periodical *Új Symposion,* a literary forum of some of Vojvodina's most original and talented Hungarian writers and poets of the postwar generation. Controversial ever since 1965 (when out of a supplement to an official youth publication it became an independent magazine), *Új Symposion* had more recently been accused by the authorities of politically inadmissible transgressions against Yugoslav interests. In particular, it was resented that in 1982 the magazine published a poem expressing feelings of solidarity with the Serb poet Gojko Djogo, imprisoned for defaming Tito's memory.

In December 1982, on the occasion of Gyula Illyés's eightieth birthday, *Új Symposion* republished his famous 1956 poem, "A Sentence on Tyranny." Although it happened before the *Frankfurter*

Rundschau interview which triggered the Illyés affair, it is believed that the two almost simultaneous occurrences provided the last straw as far as the Yugoslav authorities' tolerance toward the controversial magazine was concerned. Charging *Új Symposion* with "ideological insensitivity and political immaturity," the Presidium of the Regional Council of the Vojvodina Socialist Youth Association, by its decision on May 9, 1983, dismissed the magazine's editor-in-chief and its entire editorial staff. Elaborating on the charges, the decision expressed objections to the magazine's policy of publishing poems "containing ideologically inadmissible messages," as well as writings "of the same kind" by foreign authors. In general, *Új Symposion* was found guilty of spreading views which are "alien to us" and permeated with "a certain degree of oppositionism" (*Magyar Szó,* May 12, 1983).

The dismissed editors protested publicly, charging that the decision violated the rules of "self-management" guaranteed by law. The effects of the *Új Symposion* affair have also spilled over into Hungary. Eighty members of the Hungarian Writers' Association requested that the issue be discussed by the association because it affects not merely the Hungarians of Vojvodina but Hungarian cultural life as a whole. The presidium of the association rejected the request.

For a detailed account of the affair see *Irodalmi Újság,* Supplement on the "Új Symposion Affair," 34/4 (1983): 11–14.

✳ 10

The Hungarians of the Carpatho-Ukraine: From Czechoslovak to Soviet Rule

Steven Bela Vardy

The land that since World War I has been variously known as "Ruthenia," "Sub-Carpathia," "Carpatho-Ruthenia," and since World War II as the "Carpatho-Ukraine" and "Trans-Carpathia," had neither a name nor boundaries prior to Hungary's partition in 1918–19. It was part of the Hungarian state and treasured by Hungarians of modern times for romantic nationalistic reasons. The Verecke Pass in the northeastern corner of the Carpathians has been thought of as the glorious route of the Hungarian conquerors who founded the Hungarian state. The Ruthenian people living on the southern slopes of the Carpathians have been known as "gens fidelissima," because of their loyal support of Ferenc Rákóczi II, hero of a Hungarian uprising and war against the Habsburgs in the early eighteenth century. And the Polish-Hungarian frontier in the Carpathians has been traditionally regarded by both Poles and Hungarians as a source of their national strength.[1]

After World War I, this multiethnic land of less than five thousand square miles was given the name "Subcarpathian Rus" (*Podkarpatská Rus*) and incorporated as an autonomous province into the newly founded Czechoslovak state. In March 1939, following Hitler's dismemberment of Czechoslovakia, local right-wing nationalists calling themselves Carpatho-Ukrainians proclaimed their independence in the expectation of receiving the same German support toward forming a separate state as had been given to the Slovaks. However, this two-day Carpatho-Ukrainian independence was smashed by Hungarian armed intervention aimed at restoring the historic Polish-Hungarian frontier along the Carpathians. Thus, on the grounds of historic claims, Subcarpathian Ruthenia was reincorporated into the Hungarian state and remained with Hungary for the next five years.

At the end of World War II, this land of conflicting national loyalties and national interests was annexed by the victorious Soviet Union. The Soviet-Czechoslovak agreement of June 29, 1945, dictated by the Soviet Union and supported by Carpatho-Ukrainian nationalists of various political persuasions, sanctioned the annexation in the then flourishing spirit of Pan-Slav brotherhood. The annexation was hailed as a "reunion" of an "ancient Slavic homeland" with the Ukrainian "mother country," and, ever since, the former Czechoslovak *Sub*-Carpathia has been named *Trans*-Carpathia from the Kievan Ukrainian perspective.[2]

The fact of the matter is that, prior to 1918, Ruthenia never had any specific association with any Slavic state. The great majority of the Ruthenes, or Rusyns, migrated to Hungarian Sub-Carpathia between the fourteenth and seventeenth centuries. This influx, as well as the subsequent undisturbed population growth in the isolated valleys of the northeastern Carpathians, gradually made the Ruthenes into the majority population of this region. According to the Hungarian census of 1910, the region's population of 571,488 was composed of 319,361 Rusyns (55.8 percent), 169,434 Hungarians (29.7 percent), 62,182 Germans (10.9 percent), 15,382 Romanians (2.7 percent), 4,067 Slovaks (0.7 percent), and 1,062 others (0.2 percent).[3] Following its annexation by Czechoslovakia in 1918, political and administrative power fell mostly into Czech hands. Czech modernization of this backward region introduced, among other changes, land reform. The landless Hungarian peasants, however, were denied the full benefits of this long overdue reform. They received only 27,000 acres of the 372,000 acres expropriated mostly from large Hungarian landowners.[4] On the other hand, Czech, Ruthene, and Slovak colonists settled in Hungarian villages, where they were given land and funds for building homes and churches. Hungarian villages were also compelled to open schools for the children of the colonists.

We know little about the years immediately following the Soviet annexation of 1945. The Soviet authorities were particularly harsh with the Greek Catholic (i.e., Uniate) clergy, who supported the Ruthenian claims to nationhood and resisted being categorized as Ukrainians. But, of all the peoples of this multiethnic region, the Hungarians suffered the most. According to spotty reports that appeared in the Western press, all manifestations of Hungarian nationality were suppressed, including speaking Hungarian in public. A sizable portion of the Hungarian male population was deported to the Soviet Ukraine on the other side of the Carpathians. Reports also spoke of a massacre in the Hungarian village of Nagydobrony (Velikaia Dobron) on July 8, 1945.[5]

Events concerning the fate of the Subcarpathian Hungarians during the transitional period from Czechoslovak to Soviet rule are largely unknown. The Hungarian witnesses are passing away—among them the noted poet, Vilmos Kovács, coauthor of an article in the Hungarian periodical *Tiszatáj,* who recalled:

> The pseudo-state Zakapartska Ukraina [Transcarpathian Ukraine] which came into being on the territory of Sub-Carpathia, existed from November 1944 to January 1946. It was sustained by the twin forces of Ukrainian nationalism and the [Stalinist] personality cult, both of them intensified by wartime conditions. The unlawful and discriminatory measures [of this period] brought irreparable damage and dealt a paralyzing blow to the Hungarians of Sub-Carpathia. At the end of 1944 the whole Hungarian adult male population was temporarily deported into the inner regions of the Ukraine, from where they were able to return only after several years. Hungarian secondary schools were abolished. This policy of discrimination [against the Hungarians] continued to a certain degree even after January 1946 when Sub-Carpathia received a new status [that of a district of the Ukraine]. Only very slowly and only in certain areas did it gradually begin to approach the norms of Leninist nationality policy. Not until 1954–55 did the initial signs of relaxation appear, when Hungarian secondary schools were gradually reopened, first in the cities and then also in the villages.[6]

The Hungarians under Soviet Ukrainian Rule

According to the Soviet census of 1979, there were 171,000 Hungarians in the Soviet Union, of whom 164,000 lived in the Trans-Carpathian *oblast* (district) of the Ukrainian Soviet Socialist Republic.[7]

Because it is safer, most of them claim Hungarian as their "mother tongue" rather than as their "nationality."[8] The actual number of Hungarians in the Carpatho-Ukraine today is probably closer to 200,000. Most of them live in the lowlands bordering on Hungary and Slovakia, on the southern and western fringes of this Carpathian region. The district of Beregszász (Berehovo) is 95 percent Hungarian. There are also significant compact Hungarian ethnic islands in the districts of Munkács (Mukachevo), Nagyszöllős (Sevliush), and Ungvár (Uzhgorod).

The Hungarians keep close to one another and do not mix with the Slav majority. This fact is acknowledged by a Soviet ethnographic report published in a 1970 issue of the *Sovetskaia etnografiia*:

> The largest national minority with the longest history of settlement here are the Hungarians (ca. 160,000), who live in well-defined settlements on the southern and western lowlands. During the two months of our expedition we have visited twenty-seven Hungarian villages of between 500 and 7,000 inhabitants. The population of the great majority of these villages is almost exclusively Hungarian. In these villages the Hungarians are strongly attached to their national traditions. Even today only a few of them speak Russian or Ukrainian, notwithstanding the fact that these languages are taught in the Hungarian schools. Hungarian-Ukrainian marriages are rare. There are also villages of mixed nationality in the region, but in those villages the nationalities are locally segregated.[9]

Great Russians are newcomers to the area; they were settled as part of the Soviet policy of Russification of Carpatho-Ukrainian cities. Some Ruthenes who have remained loyal to their separate nationality sympathize with the Hungarians. They do so not only because of common traditions, but also because of their mutual dislike of the intolerant Ukrainian nationalists. However, under the Soviet system, the transformation of the former Subcarpathian Ruthenes into Transcarpathian Ukrainians is progressing rapidly. And the Ukrainians are more intolerant toward the Hungarians than are the Great Russians. In fact, the newly settled Russians, reportedly, show no anti-Hungarian sentiments.[10]

The future of a national minority depends to a large degree on its ability to cultivate its language—hence the significance of education in the minority language. It is in this area that the Hungarians of the

Carpatho-Ukraine are most endangered. Today, there are about seventy Hungarian schools which are divided into three categories: (1) Hungarian schools where the language of instruction is Hungarian, but often one day per week is a "Russian Day" when only Russian is used; (2) bi-lingual schools that have parallel Hungarian and Russian or Hungarian and Ukrainian classes; (3) modified Hungarian schools where Russian or Ukrainian classes have been set up for Hungarian children.[11] Of these three types, the third type is the most dangerous. The parents are usually pressured into enrolling their children in such classes so that the few newly-settled Russians and Ukrainians should have eventually legal title to a school of their own language. In Nagydobrony, for example, of the 6,550 inhabitants only 270 are either Ukrainians or Russians (4 percent of the population), yet the Hungarian school now has parallel Russian classes. Actually, 99 percent of the students in these Russian classes are Hungarians.[12] On the other hand, Hungarians in mixed villages are given few chances to study in their own language, in violation of Soviet law. There are many towns and villages where half of the population is Hungarian, yet they either have no Hungarian schools, or Hungarian children can study in their mother tongue only in the first three grades.[13]

The number of the Hungarian schools has been on the decline, particularly since the late 1960s. In 1968–69, there were 93 purely Hungarian schools and only 6 mixed schools. By 1969–70, the former had declined to 68, while the latter increased to 29. This drastic one-year change resulted in an almost 10 percent decline in the number of students enrolled in Hungarian schools, from 22,800 to 20,873.[14] Today, only 31 of the Hungarian schools are ten-year schools, a combination of primary and secondary schools typical of the Soviet educational system.[15] There are, however, no Hungarian kindergartens, the foundation of education in the mother tongue. Hungarian children are unable to familiarize themselves with the basic concepts of education in their own language. Many parents give in to pressure from kindergarten teachers or local administrators and enroll their children in Ukrainian- or Russian-language schools. Such pressures are often successful because parents are given to understand that enrolling their children in Hungarian schools puts the children at a disadvantage compared to those who study in the Ukrainian or Russian languages.[16]

Furthermore, as there are no Hungarian technical high schools in the whole province, all children who wish to study technical fields have to enroll in a Russian or Ukrainian school.

Entrance examinations at the Uzhgorod State University are given only in Russian and Ukrainian.[17] The result is that Hungarians enter the province's only university in far fewer numbers than do the Ukrainians and the Russians. In 1970, only 9.4 percent of the students at Uzhgorod State University were Hungarian, which is barely half their share in the region's population.[18] Of the nearly 1,000 Hungarians studying at the university only a small fraction can study a few subjects in their native tongue by taking courses in the Department of Hungarian Studies, established in 1963 for the purpose of training Hungarian teachers. After an initial annual enrollment of twenty, today the department admits only ten students per year. But, since even this number have difficulty finding appropriate positions upon graduation, in 1979 the department actually enrolled only two students.[19] Today, the faculty of the Department of Hungarian Studies consists of three linguists and three literary scholars. It is chaired, however, by the Rusyn-Ukrainian linguist Petro Lizanec, who is also the Dean of the Faculty of Arts. Characteristic of the Department's ideological orientation, the bulk of its literary offerings consists of such courses as "Lenin's Image in Hungarian Literature," "Shevchenko and Hungary," "The Problem of Internationalism and the Critique of Hungarian Bourgeois Nationalism in Hungarian Literature," and "Anti-Religious Motifs in Hungarian Literature."[20]

Other topics are limited to Hungarian folklore, ethnography, and linguistics of the Carpatho-Ukraine. The study of history is conducted in the spirit of the "prize winning" history text under the title suggestive of its contents: "Toward Happiness: The Outline History of Trans-Carpathia."[21] It is made up of half truths and conscious misinterpretation of facts, and it is passed off as the first scientific history of the Carpatho-Ukraine which is to replace all earlier works produced by "bourgeois falsificators of history." (See excerpts from this "scientific history" in Annex II, below.)

The Hungarians of the Carpatho-Ukraine have several Hungarian newspapers. These include the four-page daily *Kárpáti Igaz Szó* (Carpathian Word of Truth), as well as several other periodical publications, such as *Kárpátontúli Ifjúság,* (Trans-Carpathian Youth) which is the Hungarian translation of the province's official Komsomol paper, *Vörös Zászló* (Red Flag) of Beregszász, *Kommunizmus Fényei* (Lights of Communism) of Ungvár, and *Kommunizmus Zászlaja* (The Communist Flag) of Nagyszöllős. The very titles of these papers indicate their contents.

Originally, the daily *Kárpáti Igaz Szó* was simply a verbatim translation of the Ukrainian *Zakarpatska pravda*. Only in 1965 did it become an independent paper under the editorship of László Balla, who is one of two Hungarian members of the Soviet Writers' Union (the other one is Borbála Szalai). However, *Kárpáti Igaz Szó* and its sister papers have no real independence. They are Soviet Ukrainian papers in the Hungarian language, with only a small percentage of their space devoted to Hungarian matters. They do not serve the interests of the Hungarian minority against the Soviet and Ukrainian nationalism that dominates all aspects of social and intellectual life in the province. It is hard for a Hungarian, even one reared in the atmosphere of this Soviet-dominated province, to endure these papers.[22] Of greatest interest to Hungarians are the daily programs of Hungarian radio and television printed in the *Kárpáti Igaz Szó*. These programs are the only regular link between the Hungarians of the Carpatho-Ukraine and Hungary.

Not unlike the state of Hungarian journalism, bleak, too, is the situation in Hungarian book publishing. The Carpathian Publishing House of the Carpatho-Ukraine, founded in 1945 and reorganized in 1964, now publishes close to a hundred titles per year. In 1981, 36 of these were in the Hungarian language: 12 were indigenous works, while the others were joint publications with various publishing houses in Hungary. The number of books sounds rather impressive until we examine their contents. The director of the publishing house, Boris Gvaradinov, summed up their character in a recent interview:

> Our main goal is to make available in sufficient number of copies the necessary political, ideological, and sociological works . . . such as those of Vladimir Ilyich Lenin and Leonid Ilyich Brezhnev, the constitutions of our republic and of the Soviet Union, their election laws, the documents of the five-year plans and of the party congresses, atheist brochures, as well as other works needed for the ideological struggle. In addition, we also publish works in three broad areas: specialized works on industry and agriculture . . . , touristic works . . . , and works of belles lettres.[23]

Even in the category of belles lettres, it should be noted, a goodly number are works translated from the Russian or Ukrainian.

The first Hungarian work published by the Carpathian Publishing House (called *Kárpáti Könyvkiadó* in Hungarian) was in 1951. Today, there are about a dozen writers publishing works on the life and problems of that most forgotten Hungarian minority in the Danube region. Most of their works consist of poetry or short stories. Books in Hungarian are usually published in 1,000 to 2,000 copies. The bulk of the printer's sheets alloted to Hungarian works per year is reserved for the *Kárpáti kalendárium* (Carpathian Almanac), published annually since 1957 in about 15,000 to 19,000 copies. It is filled with the usual political and ideological propaganda, yet it is called a "kind of anthology."[24] Another "kind of anthology" is the slender volume published every five years by the *József Attila Irodalmi Stúdió* (on the origins of this organization, see Annex I, below). The most recent volume, entitled *Lendület,* appeared in 1982 on the occasion of the sixtieth anniversary of the foundation of the Soviet Union.[25] The goal of this politically streamlined literary circle and its publications is to advance the cause of a "subjectively partisan socialist-realist literature that is imbued with revolutionary romanticism."[26] Although *Lendület* contains some valuable poetical contributions, it also indulges in political sloganism, such as an ode to Lenin and a crude anti-American description of an American arms manufacturer's "visit" to his workers.[27]

Occasionally, Kárpáti Könyvkiadó publishes Hungarian works in the so-called "scholarly" category. The most recent work in this category was *Századok öröksége,* published in 1981 jointly with a publishing house in Budapest (Gondolat). It deals with various aspects of Russian-Hungarian and Ukrainian-Hungarian historical relations, demonstrating the beneficial influence of those "great Slavic neighbors" on Hungary and the Hungarians. All historical works follow the official line to such a degree that they have little credibility with the professional historian—either in Hungary or in the West. This is even more true of the textbooks, most of which are translations of Ukrainian originals published in Kiev. A few exceptions are those that deal with Hungarian literature, which are usually prepared by local Hungarian authors, with due attention of course to official guidelines.[28]

The Resources of Resistance to Denationalization

Although the Hungarians of the Carpatho-Ukraine are constantly subjected to a demeaning interpretation of their national history and traditions, so far their attachment to their Hungarian nationality appears to be unbroken. They can manifest their national attachment only in limited ways, mainly by stressing the role of Hungarian historical personalities who qualify as "forerunners of socialism." These include some of the heroes of Hungary's struggles against the Habsburgs, such as Ferenc Rákóczi II and Lajos Kossuth, as well as such local heroes as Rákóczi's peasant-general, Tamás Esze. To make them "acceptable" these Hungarian heroes are placed next to the heroes of Soviet communism. The Hungarian spirit of resistance is also evident in the lively interest in Hungarian folk traditions of the region.[29] However, the Institute of Ethnography of the Soviet Academy of Sciences, which also deals with the folklore and folk habits of the Carpatho-Ukraine, employs no Hungarian ethnographer.

Despite widespread anti-religious propaganda, religion remains a significant force of resistance against the official Soviet-Ukrainian cultural policy. Ever since the Union of Ungvár of 1646, the dominant religion of the region has been Greek Catholicism. There is also a Roman Catholic minority, as well as a small Calvinist (Reformed) religious community, both of which are almost exclusively Hungarian. Since the early nineteenth century, the immigrant Jews became Magyarized and when Carpatho-Ruthenia was part of Czechoslovakia they were among the most nationally conscious Hungarians of the region.[30] During World War II, however, when the province became again part of Hungary, the Nazi holocaust, engulfing German-occupied Hungary in 1944, wiped out this Magyarized Jewish population along with much of the rest of the Jewish community.

Following the Soviet takeover, the Greek Catholic majority (most of whom were Rusyns) was forced into union with the Ukrainian-Russian Orthodox Church. This compelled the Greek Catholic Hungarians, and even many Rusyns, to make a choice between Orthodoxy and Roman Catholicism. Virtually all of the Hungarians chose the latter, and so did a number of Rusyns. Thus the Rusyns who opted for Roman Catholicism actually joined Hungarian Catholic parishes and are attending Catholic mass in Hungarian.[31] However, the number of these Rusyns is very small.

Little is known about the fate of the Calvinists, although a recent report in the official bulletin of the Hungarian Reformed Church, *Reformátusok Lapja,* speaks of about 80 congregations.[32] In 1979, their bishop, Pál Forgon, was awarded an honorary doctorate by the Reformed Theological Seminary of Budapest—significantly though, Forgon received this degree in the company of the Ukrainian Patriarch of Kiev.

The life of the churches, whether Catholic or Calvinist, is difficult. Religious life is frowned upon and both churches suffer from a shortage of clergymen. According to a 1976 report, a single Catholic priest or Reformed minister is often obliged to take care of as many as five congregations. But at least they are tolerated, which is not true on the other side of the Carpathians in Soviet Ukraine proper.

Life for the Hungarians in the Carpatho-Ukraine is grim—to the Hungarian intellectuals, it is virtually hopeless. Resettling in Hungary is their ultimate, but mostly unattainable, goal. To them, Hungary represents the envied world of Western civilization. An almost impenetrable wall—according to one of the resettled Hungarian intellectuals—"locks them into a culturally and psychologically alien world that gradually suffocates them."[33] This wall is penetrated regularly only by the Hungarian radio and television and by some Hungarian books and newspapers. Occasionally Hungarian intellectuals give vent to their resentments. Such was the case in the early 1970s when a group of young writers, members of *Forrás Stúdió,* drew up a protest against the official Ukrainianization of the Hungarian schools in violation of the terms and spirit of the Soviet Constitution. They were silenced. Some of them were able to resettle in Hungary. *Forrás Stúdió* itself was banned and was replaced by the officially sponsored *József Attila Irodalmi Stúdió.*[34]

How do Hungarians in Hungary view the plight of the Hungarians in the Carpatho-Ukraine? The average Hungarian knows little about the minority problems in general. The nationally conscious Hungarian intellectuals, however, are ever more aware of the plight of the Hungarian minorities in the neighboring states. But while it is now permissible to talk, and occasionally even to write, about the problems of the Hungarians in Transylvania and Slovakia, no one dares to raise openly the problems of the Hungarians in the Carpatho-Ukraine. The weight of the powerful Soviet neighbor is too great; all attempts at demanding intercession are silenced.

The rare reports that do appear in the Hungarian press about life in the Carpatho-Ukraine paint a rosy picture.[35] But few Hungarians believe in these reports. Some intellectuals occasionally protest these unrealistic portrayals.[36] However, the Hungarian Communist party leadership does not dare to challenge the great Soviet neighbor.

The future of the Hungarians in the Carpatho-Ukraine appears to be no less difficult than their present condition. Though slowly rising, their number is small. They are cut off from the motherland, and they are subjected to a relentless pressure of denationalization. The resources that have saved their self-identity so far stem mainly from their rural existence, their lack of mobility, and their resistance to intermarriage. The process of industrialization and urbanization, however desirable in itself, would only further imperil their survival as a distinct nationality. Yet the situation is not hopeless, for there are inscrutable factors at work, not the least of which is the resistance of the human spirit to the forced transformation of one's identity.

Notes

1. Stephen Borsody, *The Tragedy of Central Europe,* rev. ed. (New Haven, 1980), 79.

2. Quoted from Vyacheslav Molotov's speech at the signing of the Czechoslovak-Soviet Treaty of June 29, 1945, as cited by Frantisek Nemec and Vladimir Moudry, *The Soviet Seizure of Subcarpathian Ruthenia* (Toronto, 1955; reprint, Westport, 1981), 170. Cf. Eduard Táborský, "Beneš and Stalin—Moscow, 1943–1945," *Journal of Central European Affairs* 13/2 (1953): 167–75.

3. Statistics quoted from Oscar Jászi, "The Problem of Sub-Carpathian Ruthenia," in Robert J. Kerner, ed., *Czechoslovakia* (Berkeley and Los Angeles, 1949), 193–215.

4. Statistics quoted from János Ölvedi, "A magyarság helyzete Kárpátalján," *Katolikus Szemle* 30/2–3 (1978): 159.

5. While some reports on the Nagydobrony (Velikaia Dobron) massacre appear to be exaggerated, there is no doubt that atrocities did take place. On the extreme claims see László Árkay, "Helye a térképen üres: Rekviem Nagydobronyért," in János Nádas and Ferenc Somogyi, eds., *A XVI. magyar találkozó krónikája* (Cleveland, 1978): 67–70; and György Stirling, "Nagydobrony, a magyar szuper-Lidice," in *Katolikus Magyarok Vasárnapja* (Youngstown), October 1, 1978.

6. Vilmos Kovács and András Benedek, "Magyar irodalom Kárpát-

Ukrajnában," *Tiszatáj* 24/10 and 12 (October and December 1970): 961–66, 1144–50. See also, Miklós Beládi, ed., *A határon túli magyar irodalom* (Budapest, 1982), 162.

7. These statistics are cited by Csaba Skultéty, "A kárpátaljai magyarság szellemi élete," in Éva Saáry, ed. *Magyar mérleg* 3 (1980): 123–24.

8. *United Nations Demographic Handbook* (New York, 1964), 319. On the question of "mother tongue" versus "nationality," see Alfred Bohmann, "Russians and Russification in the Soviet Union," *Aussenpolitik* (English edition) 32/3 (1981): 252–62.

9. *Sovetskaia etnografiia* (1970), as quoted by Ölvedi, "A magyarság helyzete," 162.

10. Skultéty, "A kárpátaljai magyarság szellemi élete," 126–27.

11. Miklós Zelei, "Magyar művelődési élet Kárpát-Ukrajnában. Interjú Fodó Sándorral, az Ungvári Állami Egyetem tanárával," *Magyar Hírlap*, September 29, 1979.

12. Information taken from the 1971 appeal of *Forrás Stúdió,* as published in the émigré monthly *Nemzetőr* (Munich), September–November 1983. Henceforth cited as *Forrás Stúdió* appeal. See also Annex I, below.

13. Ibid.

14. Ibid.

15. A recent official source refers to the unrealistically high figure of 100 Hungarian schools, among them 20 high schools: Péter Lizanec, "A magyar nyelv és irodalom oktatása az Uzsgorodi Állami Egyetemen," in Judit M. Róna, ed., *Hungarológiai oktatás régen és ma* (Budapest, 1983), 36–40. One of my informers, most knowledgeable in Carpatho-Ruthenian affairs, claims that today there is only one Hungarian high school in the whole province, at Péterfalva.

16. *Forrás Stúdió* appeal.

17. Ibid.

18. Ibid.

19. On the Department of Hungarian Studies, see Lizanec, "A magyar nyelv," 36–40. Concerning the lack of applicants, see Zelei, "Magyar művelődési élet."

20. Lizanec, "A magyar nyelv," 37.

21. *A boldogság felé: Kárpátontúl vázlatos története* (Uzhgorod, 1975), 296. For excerpts, see Annex II, below.

22. Concerning Hungarian journals, book publishing, and literary activities in the Carpatho-Ukraine, see Kovács and Benedek, "Magyar irodalom," 961–66, 1144–50; Ölvedi, "A magyarság helyzete," 344–47; Skultéty, "A kárpátaljai magyarság szellemi élete," 128, 130, 133–36; József Máriás, "Sorok Kárpátontúl magyar irodalmáról," *Korunk* 39/4 (April 1980): 312–14; András Görömbei, "Kárpát-ukrajnai magyar írók," *Alföld* 32/11 (November

1981): 18–26; and the recent summary in Beládi, ed., *A határon túli magyar irodalom*, 159–74, which is based to a large extent on the above-cited article by Kovács and Benedek.

23. "Testvérkiadók: Pozsony, Ungvár, Újvidék, Bukarest," *Kritika* 5 (May 1981): 4–5.

24. Ibid., 5.

25. *Lendület: Ifjúsági almanach* (Uzhgorod, 1982). The earlier volumes include: *A várakozás legszebb reggelén* (Uzhgorod, 1972), and *Szivárványszínben* (Uzhgorod, 1977).

26. *Lendület*, 3.

27. Ibid., 5–6.

28. See, for example, the following textbooks: Gizella Drávai, *Magyar irodalom az Ukrán SZSZK magyar tanítási nyelvű középiskoláinak 9. osztálya számára*, 4th rev. ed. (Kiev-Uzhgorod, 1971); László Balla, *Irodalom az Ukrán SZSZK magyar tanítási nyelvű középiskoláinak 10. osztálya számára* (Kiev-Uzhgorod, 1975). Almost one-third of these texts is devoted to Ukrainian literature. All selections and interpretations are geared to class struggle.

29. Skultéty, "A kárpátaljai magyarság szellemi élete," 137–38. See also "Magyar néprajzi kutatás a szomszédos országokban," *Valóság* 18/6 (June 1975): 29–44, especially 39–40.

30. Concerning religious life in Carpatho-Ruthenia, see Walter C. Warzeski, *Byzantine Rite Rusins in Carpatho-Ruthenia and America* (Pittsburgh, 1971); Paul Robert Magocsi, *The Shaping of a National Identity: Subcarpathian Rus', 1848–1948* (Cambridge, Mass., 1978); and some of the studies in Basil Shereghy, ed., *The United Societies of the U.S.A.: A Historical Album* (McKeesport, Penn., 1978).

31. Skultéty, "A kárpátaljai magyarság szellemi élete," 138–39.

32. "A Kárpátontúli Református Egyház életéből," *Reformátusok Lapja* 24/50 (December 14, 1980).

33. In the 1970s and early 1980s, I spoke with several Hungarian intellectuals from the Carpatho-Ukraine. The view presented here is based on these conversations.

34. For excerpts from *Forrás Stúdió* appeal, see Annex I, below. On *József Attila Irodalmi Stúdió* (JAIS), see György Dupka, "Visszatekintés alkotó közösségünk tíz esztendejére," in *Lendület*, 60–62.

35. See, for example, articles by János Siklós: "Barangolás a Kárpátok alatt," *Népszava*, February 6, 1972; "Nézelődés a világban," *Délmagyarország*, July 4, 1972.

36. In Budapest, I had the opportunity to examine several of these protests (including a 160 page memorandum) submitted in the late 1970s by prominent Hungarian intellectuals to the leadership of the Hungarian Communist Party. Glowing reports about the life of the Hungarian minority in

Carpatho-Ukraine, such as those of Janos Siklós (see note 35 above), was singled out for criticism.

Annex I
The "Forrás Stúdió" Affair
Excerpts from an Appeal by Hungarian Writers

EDITOR'S NOTE. The Soviet Ukraine is more intolerant of criticism of its nationality policy than the other Communist countries with Hungarian populations. Thus, it takes greater courage to air grievances in the Soviet Ukraine than elsewhere. One of the few known public protests is an appeal by *Forrás Stúdió*, a group of young poets and writers founded in 1967. In 1971, the appeal excerpted below was prompted by an attack in the Hungarian-language daily, *Kárpáti Igaz Szó*, denouncing the *Forrás Stúdió* group as "alienated" from society.

In addition to the editorial committee of *Kárpáti Igaz Szó*, the appeal was sent to the Secretary of the Transcarpathian Territorial Committee of the Ukrainian Communist party and to the secretary in charge of the Transcarpathian Organization of the Ukrainian Union of Writers. The appeal has never been made public in the Soviet Ukraine, but the official response was quick. *Forrás Stúdió* was disbanded.

The excerpts that follow are from the introductory passages; the rest of the appeal deals with grievances discussed in Chapter 10, above, which is partly based on this document. The critical view, as expressed in this excerpt, is no less valid of general conditions today than it was in 1971.

The full text of the *Forrás Stúdió* appeal appeared in *Nemzetőr* (Munich), September–November 1983.

An article entitled "Alienation" was published in *Kárpáti Igaz Szó* on August 20, 1971. . . . The anonymous author of this article [it was László Balla] indulged in insults, libel, falsification of facts, and political accusations.

We, members of the *Forrás Stúdió*—against whom these accusations were directed—could be content with the moral satisfaction of seeing the widespread indignation elicited by this article and the undivided support shown toward us by Hungarian public opinion [in the Carpatho-Ukraine], contrary to the intentions of the author.

However, since this anonymous article is part of a brutal campaign whose purpose is not spelled out but whose consequences have now affected even people beyond our group, and since we have no other means of public expression, we are forced to state our views in this appeal. . . .

The pretext for this campaign [against us] was a literary essay, written by Vilmos Kovács and András Benedek [at the time on the staff of *Kárpáti Igaz Szó*] under the title, "Hungarian Literature in the Carpatho-Ukraine," published in the October and December 1970 issues of the periodical *Tiszatáj* of Szeged [Hungary].

We would like to make it crystal clear that, in our opinion, this essay is the first serious attempt to give a realistic picture of our [Hungarian] literature [in the Carpatho-Ukraine] from its beginnings to the present day. In line with the facts, the essay tries to explain our achievements and our problems, through an analysis of historical facts and of cultural policies. In doing so, it shows deep understanding and a sense of responsibility.

We cannot understand, therefore, the reasons for the official hostile reactions to this essay here in the Carpatho-Ukraine. The very people who should have taken note of our problems [set out in this essay], indeed, whose official duty it should have been to deal with them, instead of acknowledging the existence of these problems and trying to do something about them, have started a campaign of persecution against the authors and, when they protested, have taken reprisals against them. Their right to publish was revoked, disciplinary proceedings were started against them, they were demoted in their jobs and were officially slandered. Furthermore, an unofficial smear campaign was started at meetings and other forums throughout the territory [of the Carpatho-Ukraine]. This poisoned atmosphere left no other choice to the two authors [of the essay] but to leave the editorial office of the *Kárpáti Igaz Szó*.

This, however, was far from being the end of the "affair." The next step was an attack against those who had been named in the essay: members of *Forrás Stúdió,* and the *Stúdió* itself, which had to be destroyed as an organization. This task—like many other character-assassinations—was performed by László Balla [editor of *Kárpáti Igaz*

Szó]. It was with this intention that he brought into being under the auspices of the *Kárpáti Igaz Szó,* the *József Attila Stúdió.* Some members of the *Forrás Stúdió* were actually invited to join. His purpose was clear: to destroy us through the principle of "divide and conquer." When his plans did not succeed, the anonymous article [referred to above by László Balla] appeared. It was directed against those whom László Balla tried to transplant—unsuccessfully—to the *József Attila Stúdió.*

The motives and purposes of this article are self-evident. Its followup has been the constant harassment of the "stigmatized ones"—mostly university students.

In order to clear away any misunderstanding, we must declare that we are not against the principles of the *József Attila Stúdió,* nor against those of socialist literature. We simply reject László Balla's underhanded maneuvers and the hopeless dilettantism he tries to create around himself, pretending that it is literature. He not only pretends, he also protects it under the slogan of "socialist realism." . . .

Closely linked to this "affair" is an article by László Balla that appeared in the April 28, 1971, issue of the *Kárpáti Igaz Szó* under the title, "The Small Hungarian Community in the Great Soviet Family."

What does this article say? It lists our social and cultural achievements, our bemedalled shock workers. Then comes the reproach: ". . . there are still some phenomena, some scattered manifestations amidst our fellow Hungarians . . . that may, among others, imperil the development and prosperity of our small national community." . . . Then comes the promise that "the few remaining problems we are still confronted with today" will gradually find their solutions. And then the warning: ". . . we must not forget, however, that the primary precondition and guarantee of this success is the careful cultivation, protection, and continued development of our links with the Ukrainian people, and the other peoples of the Soviet Union."

The whole article betrays a despicable inferiority complex. . . . In order to prove our insignificance, it tries to befoul and to degrade the little we have, to slander and to shunt the few people of stature we have, so that we should feel even smaller than we actually are, and thus to reduce our requests and demands to zero. . . .

We are firmly convinced that the greatest offender against the genuine friendship of peoples is the person who tries to disguise existing problems by flaunting real or imaginary achievements and thereby lets them [the problems] fester under the surface.

It is also our conviction that some of our problems exist simply because our higher authorities are unaware of them, thanks to those who are doing their best to sweep them under the rug.

Annex II
"Reunion" with the Ukraine
Excerpts from an Official History of
Transcarpathia, "Toward Happiness"

EDITOR'S NOTE. The official history of Transcarpathia was written by a committee of Russian and Ukrainian scholars, chaired by Sergei Aleksevich Mishchenko. The original text was published in 1973. It was translated into Hungarian and published in 1975 under the title *A boldogság felé* (Toward Happiness). In 1974, the book had won first prize in a national "scientific information competition" of the Soviet Information Society in Moscow. The few excerpts that follow are an illustration of the "scientific information" the book is disseminating among the Hungarians of the Carpatho-Ukraine.

Excerpts from *A boldogság felé: Kárpátontúl vázlatos története* (Uzhgorod, 1975), 3–4, 180–82.

For many centuries Transcarpathia had been forcibly separated from its [Ukrainian] motherland, and its working people were suffering under the relentless social, economic, political, and national oppression of Hungarian aristocrats, Austrian barons, Czech capitalists, and their "own" exploiters. Notwithstanding all this, however, the toilers have preserved their language and culture, as well as their feelings of unity with the Ukrainian people and their historical traditions. Through many centuries they have sustained in themselves the desire of reunification. This desire was intensified with every successive historical epoch, until it became an essential component of their very existence. . . . [Transcarpathia] had been inhabited from the first half of the first millenium by the ancestors of the East Slavs, the so-called White Croats, who were part of the proto-Russian Kievan Rus' state in the tenth and eleventh centuries. . . . [The White Croats in fact never lived in the Transcarpathian region; they moved to the Dalmatian coastline in the early seventh century. Cf. Francis Dvornik, *The Slavs: Their History and Civilization* (Boston, 1956), 26–28; and George Vernadsky, *The Origins of Russia* (Oxford, 1959), 82–84.] During the seventeenth and eighteenth centuries, the region's economic and cultural ties with Russia and the Ukraine have multiplied. As an example, numerous books from Moscow, St. Petersburg, Kiev, and L'vov have found their way into Transcarpathia, and many local people went to study in Russia and the Ukraine.

These developments have all contributed to the revival of those progressive Transcarpathian forces that were drawn to the Ukraine and to Russia.

The workers of Transcarpathia have contributed many glorious pages to the history of the struggle that was waged by the Ukrainian people against social and national oppression. This struggle became particularly conscious and purposeful after the Great October Socialist Revolution which opened a new chapter in the history of humanity. Under the leadership of the Communist party, the workers and the peasants were now fighting for the overthrow of the capitalist system and for their reunification with the Soviet Ukraine. This struggle ended in victory, for in October of 1944 the Red Army liberated Transcarpathia from under centuries of domination by its conquerors, and thereby this region returned permanently into the fold of the mother country.

The reunification of the Transcarpathian Ukraine with the Soviet Ukraine signified the triumph of historical justice. It was a turning point in the history of our region, which brilliantly exemplified the success of the Communist party's and the Soviet government's wise Leninist nationality policy.

Within the ranks of the family of Soviet peoples, and with their fraternal help, the economy and culture of this most recently gained area of the Soviet Ukraine began to prosper, while the toilers of Transcarpathia became the full-fledged proprietors of their land. . . .

The liberation of Transcarpathia by the Red Army and the great and selfless help of the fraternal peoples of the Soviet Union were both examples of the care extended by the Communist party and the Soviet government to the workers of Transcarpathia. The latter, in turn, were increasingly imbued with the knowledge that only within the confines of the Soviet Ukraine could the people of the region hope to achieve their national rebirth and their economic development.

In compliance with the wishes of the region's workers, the Soviet government undertook to negotiate with the Czechoslovak Republic the reunification of Transcarpathia with the Soviet Ukraine. On July 29, 1945, the Union of Soviet Socialist Republics and the Czechoslovak Republic concluded an agreement on the fate of the Transcarpathian Ukraine. This agreement pointed out that the "Transcarpathian Ukraine (known in the Czechoslovak Constitution as *Podkarpatská Rus*), which had become an autonomous part of the Czechoslovak Republic with the Treaty of Saint Germain of September 10, 1919, would now reunify with its ancient homeland, the Ukraine, and would become part of the Ukrainian Soviet Socialist Republic, in accordance with the expressed wishes of its people and on the basis of the friendly consensus of the high signatories."

The signing of the agreement of reunification with the Soviet Ukraine was greeted with enthusiasm by the Transcarpathian people at numerous meetings and mass gatherings. This was also emphasized in a letter by the citizens of Uzhgorod, dated June 30, 1945, which was drawn up at one of their mass meetings: "We are extremely happy that henceforth we will march within the Soviet Ukraine, hand in hand with the people of the Soviet Union, toward the shining peaks of a happy and joy-filled life, and thus achieve the fulfillment of our economic, national, and cultural goals." . . .

The reunification of the Transcarpathian Ukraine with Soviet Ukraine was the final act in the reunification process that gathered all Ukrainian lands into a unified Ukrainian Soviet state. Historical justice had triumphed. In consequence of the Soviet Communist party's Leninist nationality policy, and as a result of the increased power of the Soviet Union, the Transcarpathian workers' centuries-long heroic struggle thus ended with the region's liberation and its reunification with its motherland, the Soviet Union.

✳ *PART THREE*

Problems and Solutions

"In a national state there is no room for minority problems."
    Edvard Beneš, President of Czechoslovakia, in his *Foreign Affairs* article, "Postwar Czechoslovakia," 1946

"The participating States on whose territory national minorities exist will respect the right of persons belonging to such minorities to equality before the law, will afford them the full opportunity for the actual enjoyment of human rights and fundamental freedoms and will, in this manner, protect their legitimate interests in this sphere."
    Article VII of the "Declaration on Principles Guiding Relations between Participating States," Final Act, Helsinki, 1975

❋ 11

The Beneš Thesis: A Design for the Liquidation of National Minorities
Introduction

Vojtech Mastny

The diplomacy of World War II has been customarily regarded as the almost exclusive domain of the Great Powers. In Eastern Europe especially, myths about sinister deals among them at the expense of the small nations have survived with amazing persistency. Although there is much indeed to criticize in the wartime conduct of the Big Three, the Great Powers were by no means alone in their sins and mistakes. Others, far from being hapless pawns, did more than their share by indulging in policies which made a satisfactory postwar settlement difficult, if not impossible.

While the war continued, the Czechoslovak government-in-exile, presided over in London by Edvard Beneš, was perhaps the least troublesome of all the Eastern European allies. It kept on excellent terms with all the Great Powers, including the Soviet Union. During a visit to Moscow in December 1943, Beneš signed a treaty of friendship and postwar cooperation—the first such agreement between a small allied nation and the Soviet Union. Having first initiated this project and overcome successfully both Russian hesitations and British opposition, the Czechoslovak president was very proud of his accomplishment. Yet, the treaty always remained controversial. Especially after the Communist seizure of power in Czechoslovakia in 1948, there was speculation about the extent to which the 1943 agreement may have actually prepared the groundwork for that cataclysmic event of the Cold War. No reliable evidence has been published to document what transpired during the extensive discussions between Beneš and the Soviet leaders in December 1943. The president himself was the main source of information and he obviously disclosed only what he wanted to be known.

The Smutný documents provide the first direct and comprehensive account of the discussions among Beneš, Stalin, and Molotov in December 1943. Jaromír Smutný was a close intimate of Beneš from 1937 to the President's death in 1948. Thoroughly dedicated to the man whom he regarded as "the greatest Machiavelli our time," Smutný was not an uncritical admirer. Free from any political ambitions, he kept aloof from strife and intrigue in the Beneš "court." Safely established in the center of power, Smutný devoted much of his energy to keeping records of what was going on. Concealed from the eyes of his boss, he maintained a diary.

Jaromír Smutný attended the meeting as the head of the president's chancellery. All the documents are part of Smutný's literary estate which was deposited through the generosity of his widow, Mrs. Jaroslava Smutná, at the Archive of Russian and East European History and Culture at Columbia University. The bulk of Smutný's wartime papers, particularly his diaries, remained in Prague when he fled Czechoslovakia in June 1949—this time to escape from the Communist regime. He settled in London, in the same house where Beneš had set up his temporary headquarters in 1938. Then Smutný began organizing whatever papers he had managed to rescue, filling in gaps and preparing material for his memoirs. By the time he died in 1964, he had completed extensive portions of this work, although he had not given them the final touch. Two years later, selections from the 1939–41 diaries he had left in Prague appeared in a Czech-language publication which is an outstanding source for the history of World War II diplomacy. Of Smutný's London papers, those printed below were not included among the documents published in Prague.

Beneš's performance in Moscow hardly bears out the customary Western image of him as a skillful negotiator, a staunch democrat, and a man of compromise. But, the destruction of the myth does not make it any easier to understand the true motives of the man sometimes rightly considered as one of the most enigmatic politicians of his time. For it would be absurd to attribute his conduct to a lack of sophistication or to an excess of Russophile or any other sentiment.

The clue to Beneš's conduct should be sought in his overwhelming emphasis upon foreign policy; then, as ever, Beneš was a true believer in its primacy in the affairs of nations. This is the reason why he took such flexible views of what self-government and sovereignty meant. His policies had always been marked by that disproportion, but the impact of the war magnified it to the extreme. The crushing experience of Munich had led him not only to distrust the West—as has been frequently overemphasized—but also to greatly exaggerate the allegedly perennial German threat and, consequently, the need for Russian protection. Furthermore, his search for intimacy with the Soviet regime could not fail to affect adversely his own devotion to freedom and democracy, which he came to value considerably less than security. And, it is true that he had been predisposed in that direction before.

The president's self-righteous and narrow-minded nationalism is a disconcerting feature of his discussions with Molotov. His anti-German animus can perhaps be excused most easily—even his plan for the summary expulsion of the Sudeten Germans can be defended as an act of statesman-like wisdom. But there was no need for his demanding such pinpricks as the participation of Czechoslovak troops in the occupation of Germany. It is still more difficult to justify his effort to solicit from the unwilling Russians support for the expulsion of the Hungarian minority. Outright scandalous, however, was his demand that Hungary be occupied by the Red Army rather than by the Western Allies—just to guarantee that the hated neighbors would be crushed brutally enough.

The excerpts from President Beneš's writings that follow the excerpts from the Smutný papers illustrate Beneš's effort at presenting his postwar plans against Czechoslovakia's enemies as compatible with the humanistic ideals of Western civilization. Thus, the liquidation of national minorities by removing them forcibly is posited in his *Foreign Affairs* articles as a policy serving the national security of Czechoslovakia on the one hand, and, on the other, as a realization of lofty ideals of peace, progress, and democracy.

Annex I

*Excerpts from the Smutný Papers
Political Conversation between Beneš and Molotov
on December 14, 1943**

President Beneš: . . . I don't believe in a just and lasting peace. Peace will last long if we are ready to defend it. The Versailles agreement was not bad. The trouble was that neither you nor others were ready to defend it. . . . Our Germans are responsible for Munich, for the German invasion, and for everything that followed. They are the first to have taken responsibility for the war. War criminals from Germany itself are another story. But the punishment of our Germans is the big thing for us. . . .

The next question is the Hungarians. Many of our people say: They must be destroyed too. I myself am not so radical. A great power could talk like that, but we cannot carry out anything of that sort. Here, too, I want to adapt our policy to yours. An internal revolution must take place in Hungary in order to destroy feudalism. The British and the Americans are beginning to understand it. But they are afraid that the revolution in Hungary might be like the one after the last war—Béla Kun and all that. That's why the occupation of Hungary is so important. I think it is important that you also, not only the British and the Americans, share in it. I can imagine what would happen if the British alone were there. The Hungarian aristocrats would take them out for weekends and for hunting, tell them stories about how their democracy is the oldest in Europe and about their parliament. All that is lies, but the British would be impressed. It was the same after the last war. . . . That must not happen again; your participation in the occupation is very important to us. . . .

Molotov: The Hungarians must be punished, too. As far as the occupation is concerned, we have a shorter way to get there than the others, but the situation is still unclear and not topical. The British and the Americans are going to back the Poles. . . .

*Excerpted from Vojtech Mastny, "The Beneš-Stalin-Molotov Conversations in December 1943: New Documents," Jahrbücher für Geschichte Osteuropas, n.s. 20, no. 3 (September 1972): 376–402.

President Beneš: Of course, and the Poles might conduct a pro-Hungarian policy. There are also Yugoslavia and Romania, which I want to discuss later; for the time being, let's speak about our concern in regard to Hungary. . . . The minorities and their transfer. As you recall, I have also discussed this at the dinner with Marshal Stalin. He stated categorically: "We agree." That is very important to me. . . .

A Second Conversation between Beneš and Molotov on December 16, 1943

Beneš explains that we [Czechoslovakia] also want to relocate the Hungarians, or else exchange them for Slovaks from Hungary, and to redraw the frontier.

Molotov: All right. Have you submitted these plans to the Americans and the British?

Beneš: They know my opinion, but officially I haven't submitted them anything until I could agree with you. I don't have a good experience from the last war; there are many Magyarophiles among the British. They know it in principle, but first of all I wanted to know to what extent you would be supporting us. I discussed the matter twice with Roosevelt; I explained everything to him and during the last visit I wanted to make sure that he understood me correctly. Roosevelt is in favor. After I asked him whether he understood the meaning of what I told him about our treaty with Moscow, he replied: "I understand." In reply to the same question about the transfer, he said not only that he understood but also that the same solution should be applied in other countries. He hinted at Transylvania.

Molotov: Do you think that they honestly want it? [He refers to the promises of the British and the Americans in regard to the transfer.]

Beneš: That depends. I think they do, but then they say, how will you pay for it? Now, after the Teheran conference, they are going to be more agreeable.

Molotov: But tell me, what can you pay with? You have no colonies.

Protocol on the exchange of opinion between President Beneš and People's Commissar for Foreign Affairs V. Molotov on December 14 and 16, 1943, and among Dr. Beneš and Chairman of the Council of People's Commissars J. Stalin and V. Molotov on December 18, 1943

. . . 2. Exchange of opinion on postwar Germany and Hungary. Affirmed that consensus exists among Great Britain, the United States of America, and the Soviet Union concerning the necessity of taking all appropriate measures in order to prevent any attempt at a new aggression on the part of Germany. . . . Affirmed that Hungary carries a great responsibility for the war, particularly for the atrocities committed in this war against the population of the USSR and of the occupied territories, and that it must suffer the appropriate consequences. The territory of Hungary must be occupied, primarily by the Soviet army, which has a shorter way to get to Hungary than the other Allied armies. . . .

4. The problem with the population transfer. President Beneš explained that the transfer from the territory of Czechoslovakia of the German population, which has a great and original share in Germany's responsibility for the present war, is justified both in order to give justice to Czechoslovakia and in order to provide a guarantee against any further abuse of the German minority by the German Reich in the preparation of aggressive plans against peace and Slavdom. . . .

This problem concerns to a considerable extent also the Hungarian minority along the southern frontier of the Republic.

In the course of the discussion, Dr. Beneš explained that the British government in a confidential note had agreed in principle to the concept of the transfer of the minorities from Czechoslovakia and that President Roosevelt, too, had adopted a favorable position in this matter.

Affirmed that the government of the Soviet Union, having received from President Beneš a memorandum outlining the principles of the transfer, regards this vital problem of Czechoslovakia with full understanding and will give support to its solution. . . .

7(c). The transfer of the German and Hungarian populations from Czechoslovakia is approved in principle and Czechoslovakia is recognized internationally as the national state of the Czechs and the Slovaks. . . .

Annex II
Excerpts from Edvard Beneš's Writings
*The Organization of Postwar Europe (1942)**

The minority question will be one of the most momentous to be dealt with in connection with the new organization of Europe. National minorities are always—and in Central Europe especially—a real thorn in the side of individual nations. This is particularly true if they are German minorities. While other great nations—the English, French, Russians, and Spaniards—have sent their population surpluses to other continents, have opened up new regions, and at the same time have played a civilizing role, the Germans have often been content to send their colonists into neighboring countries, countries usually on the same cultural level as their own, sometimes even culturally ahead of them. They have become the agents for extending German interests and have prepared the ground for what we today describe as fifth columns. In other cases the German population has settled down permanently as a result of century-long German military and cultural pressure, so that today these German populations have an almost autochthonous character. In these territories, therefore, it was not possible in 1918 to create states that were linguistically and nationally homogeneous, unless by extensive transfers of population. This course was actually proposed—for instance, by the French sociologist Bernard Lavergne—but it was rejected as being apparently in contradiction to the idealistic tendencies governing the 1919 plans for a new Europe.

Instead, the course was chosen for defending minorities internationally. I would be the last to condemn the principles upon which this policy is based. But the mistake made from the beginning was in imposing protection of minorities only upon a few states and not on all those which had minorities. Thus it was really scandalous that despite Germany's record for wholesale and forcible Germanization of other nations in the course of previous centuries, she was not compelled to undertake to defend her minorities. It soon appeared, similarly, that a great mistake had been made in not making any provision

*Excerpted from Edvard Beneš, "The Organization of Postwar Europe," *Foreign Affairs* 20, no. 2 (January 1942): 235–39.

for protecting the national minorities in Italy. It was also unfortunate that the protection of minorities finally became a burden upon the states which supported them, while on the other hand those states which interfered with them actually received no punishment. Hungary violated her obligations towards her minorities from the very beginning. She did not give them schools or freedom of speech or of the press, and as a result was able over twenty years to denationalize thousands of Slovaks, Romanians, and Germans, all with entire impunity. Colonel Beck was able to declare that he no longer recognized the competence of the controlling organs of the League in minority questions—and the League was obliged to limit itself to a few platonic protests.

On the other hand, Czechoslovakia did not expect to be thanked for fulfilling her minority obligations, and did not wait to be thanked for doing so. I do not say that everything with us was perfect. I only say that in Europe, apart from Switzerland, we were the best [*Beneš's footnote:* Cf. the testimonial paid Czechoslovakia by Lord Cecil in his book, *A Great Experiment* (New York, 1941)], and that our policy was always governed by the principles of loyalty to engagements, tolerance, and good will. In spite of this, some of the German and Hungarian minorities in Czechoslovakia abused the justice which the Republic accorded them, trying under cover of our régime of law to disorganize the Republic and discredit it. For this work they received money from Germany and Hungary. In the name of minority rights, the Czechoslovak Republic was obliged to endure anti-state activities by a number of German political parties, by the Henlein press, and by subversive elements in the German higher schools. The propaganda of the minorities, stimulated by Nazi Germany, Fascist Italy, and reactionary Hungary, and spread by them abroad, finally created in Europe the impression that our minorities were suffering injustices. As a result, those who were trying to preserve peace at all costs found an excuse for sacrificing Czechoslovakia in the thesis that nothing immoral would be involved in her dismemberment as it would mean only the freeing of oppressed minorities from the Czechoslovak yoke.

In the end, things came to such an extraordinary pass that the totalitarian and dictator states—Germany, Hungary, and Italy—persecuted the minorities in their own territories and at the same time posed as the protectors of minorities in states which were really democratic. While denying their minorities any sort of freedom of expression, they cynically abused the freedom of the press and of assembly in the democratic states and shouted at the top of their voices to the whole world about the smallest possible difficulties that arose. The League of Nations, which was perfectly well informed regarding the actual state of affairs, did not move even a finger to set the record right when in 1938 the state which had respected the rights of minorities better than any other was held up before the world as an oppressor. I observe, therefore, though with regret, that the prewar system for the protection of minorities broke down.

The absurd state of affairs that I have just described cannot be renewed. Before we begin to define the rights of minorities we must define the rights of majorities and the obligation of minorities. Every nation has a right to live peaceably and freely within its state frontiers. If these frontiers are also national frontiers, all the better. But this is not the case in Central Europe; every Central European state has its minorities. In the present war, German minorities—which everywhere have served, partly passively, partly actively, as instruments for German imperialism—have actually become an international menace. No Central European state will again wish to risk what we, Jugoslavia, Rumania, or Poland have had to risk in the last few years.

I know of no formula for deciding minority questions in an ideal fashion. I do not recommend any method which involves brutality or violence. Perhaps in certain cases it will be possible by local alterations in the frontiers to diminish somewhat the minority population in individual states. Perhaps it will be necessary to undertake this time the transference of minority populations; Hitler himself has transferred German minorities from the Baltic and from Bessarabia. Germany, therefore, cannot *a priori* regard it as an injury to her if other states adopt the same methods with regard to German minorities. Possibly certain states, for reasons of national security, will find themselves obliged to institute some system of resettling their minorities within their own frontiers. This would be a painful operation and would involve many small injustices.

Certainly every nation in Central Europe will feel it right and proper to punish severely those members of its minorities who in these terrible years have been guilty of treachery, espionage, tyranny over the majority, terror, murder, and mass looting under the auspices of the German armies. All these crimes, and many more, have been committed, and today are being committed, on Poles in Poland, on

Czechoslovaks in Czechoslovakia, on Norwegians in Norway, on Belgians in Belgium, on Jugoslavs in Jugoslavia, on Hollanders in Holland, on Greeks in Greece. By the same principle every state will punish its own Quislings. Until all this has been carried out, until every state feels sure that its minorities no longer can aim a revolver against its national existence, we shall have to design measures for the protection of loyal minorities, for guaranteeing them their political and cultural rights, on the basis of absolute mutuality. But we cannot again institute the abnormal situation of privileged minorities in some states and of constantly oppressed minorities in others. Neither can we create a state of affairs in which certain larger states perpetually terrorize certain smaller states on the basis of the fact that the latter have a small section of population which speaks the same language.

Although it is impossible today to make definite proposals for solving the minority problems in detail, three general principles may be laid down:

(1) Even after this war it still will be impossible in Europe to create states which are nationally homogeneous, since there are cases in which certain countries cannot exist at all as states without a certain region of mixed populations (for instance, Czechoslovakia without the German and mixed districts in Bohemia and Moravia). However, such districts must be united only where really necessary and then on the smallest scale possible.

(2) It will be necessary after this war to carry out a transfer of populations on a very much larger scale than after the last war. This must be done in as humane manner as possible, internationally organized and internationally financed.

(3) The protection of minorities in the future should consist primarily in the defense of human democratic rights and not of national rights. Minorities in individual states must never again be given the character of internationally recognized political and legal units, with the possibility of again becoming sources of disturbance. On the other hand, it is necessary to facilitate emigration from one state to another, so that if national minorities do not want to live in a foreign state they may gradually unite with their own people in neighboring states.

Czechoslovakia Plans for Peace (1944)*

After the First World War, in accordance with the idealistic tendencies of the time, a clause in the Peace Treaty imposed upon the Czechoslovak Republic the protection of national minorities. . . . Experience has shown that the system established by the minorities treaties can be abused by an imperialistic state to promote its policies of expansion. Nazi Germany did just that. No nation—and least of all a small one like Czechoslovakia—can in the future afford a policy which would lay itself open to this sort of disruption by an alliance of enemy forces without and traitorous elements within. Czechoslovakia wishes to avoid any recurrence of the situation which led to Munich. She is therefore considering the transfer [of national minorities]. . . .

Ideas have not stood still. Our people participated in Europe's first religious and social revolution in the fifteenth century and always have been in the forefront of progressive European developments. . . . I am convinced that Czechoslovakia will overcome her initial difficulties in short order, solve her internal problems without severe disturbance, and take her place once more, strengthened and consolidated, in the van of European nations, a democratic and popular state in the truest sense of those all-important words. . . .

Postwar Czechoslovakia (1946)**

The choice is between the concept of a national state and the formally recognized Wilsonian concept of a state of nationalities, with all that involves. In a national state there is no room for minority problems. The rule applies just as much to the Germans as to the Hungarians in Czechoslovakia; and it concerns not only Czechoslovakia, but also Hungary, Jugoslavia, Rumania, and Poland. Even the Great Powers have recognized that in the interest of peace in Europe there remains no other solution but the removal of the Germans and Hungarians from Czechoslovakia. . . . The minority problem . . . must be solved finally and irrevocably on a purely national basis. . . .

Members of minorities who refuse to return to their national state

*Excerpted from Edvard Beneš, "Czechoslovakia Plans for Peace," *Foreign Affairs* 23, no. 1 (October 1944): 35–36.
**Excerpted from Edvard Beneš, "Postwar Czechoslovakia," *Foreign Affairs* 24, no. 3 (April 1946): 400–1, 404.

(for example, Slovaks who stay in Hungary and Hungarians who stay in Czechoslovakia) will be definitely sacrificed and given up to national assimilation in the other state. . . .

Since it is impossible to return either to the Munich territorial dictate or to accept a territorial revision in favor of the defeated countries, there is only one solution of the problem and that is the transfer.

Annex III
A Postscript:
"Progression" or "Retrogression"?

EDITOR'S NOTE. Apart from granting President Beneš an international forum for publicizing his ideas, Hamilton Fish Armstrong, editor of *Foreign Affairs,* also sympathized with these ideas. In the 1950s, in the course of my conversation with him in his New York office, Armstrong defended the Beneš policy of the ethnically homogeneous nation state achieved by population transfer as a "progression" from T. G. Masaryk's statemaking, contrary to my contention that it was, rather, a "retrogression." Armstrong also expressed these views in a letter of September 3, 1953. My point in this debate was that, in 1918, Czechoslovakia was founded with the promise of becoming "a sort of Switzerland." Therefore, the restoration of Czechoslovakia as a homogeneous nation state is a repudiation of one of the fundamental principles of its creation.

In the world emerging from the cataclysm of World War II, voices opposing the elimination of national minorities as a means of achieving homogeneous nation states were few and far between. An eloquent statement on behalf of a democratic concept of nations and states was that of P. de Azcárate, the Spanish-born former Director of the Minorities Question Section of the League of Nations (in *League of Nations and National Minorities: An Experiment* [Washington, D.C., 1945], 16–17):

> I am not ignorant of the fact that the transfer or interchange of population may be a practical means of readjustment between nationalities and frontiers in certain specific and clearly defined cases. But to consider it as an expedient applicable to all minorities seems to me outrageous. Such a

measure would necessitate the uprooting of great masses of peasant population from lands which their ancestors have cultivated perhaps for centuries, and the transfer of other no less considerable groups of urban
population from towns and cities where they and their forebears have lived
for generations. But serious as this uprooting would be, there is, in my
opinion, an even worse aspect of the forced transfer of populations. What
forces me categorically to reject this interchange as a general prescription
for the political ills caused by the existence of national minorities, is a
more lofty consideration. If human society were to accept the general
application of this method, it would admit, in the first place, its inability
to organize itself in a form in which peoples of different race, language
or nationality may live peaceably together and collaborate in an ordered
manner. Besides this, however, a precedent would be established which,
if generalized, would prove, *ad absurdum,* its own inconsistency. For after
all, these differences of race, language or nationality are only some of the
many differences inherent in every human society. And if we acknowledge
ourselves defeated by them, and have recourse to the barbarous and cruel
method of separating men, as though they were herds of sheep, into homogeneous national groups, in what way shall we solve other differences?
Would it not be tempting to eliminate political and social distinctions by
grouping men in such a way that all those with similar ideas or doctrines
should live together? Homogeneity never has been, nor ever can be, an
ideal for the organization of human societies. On the contrary, diversity
of mentalities, temperaments, aptitudes, ideas, beliefs, has always been
rightly considered as a source of material and moral prosperity and
strength in nations and states—provided, of course, that in these social
groups the rational principles of solidarity prevail over the primitive instincts of struggle and destruction.

Among the most outspoken critics of Beneš's policy of expulsion
was Oscar Jászi. He denied "the right of any state to experiment in
uprooting national minorities, which for centuries have lived and
worked on a territory which they regard as their beloved home." And
he deplored that "the successors of Masaryk" had adopted "the philosophy of Hitler and Stalin." (See his "Postwar Pacification in Europe," in *Federation: The Coming Structure of World Government,*
Howard O. Eaton, ed. [Norman, Oklahoma, 1944], 147–48; and his
"Danubia: Old and New," in *Proceedings of the American Philosophical Society,* XCIII, 1 [Philadelphia, 1949], 14.)

※ 12

The Tito Thesis:
A Principle of National Equality
and Its Application

Matthew Mestrovic

The Communist Party of Yugoslavia, formed at the Belgrade Congress in 1919, accepted Lenin's thesis on the national question.[1] In line with the Leninist ideology of the Third International, the party declared the principle of all peoples' equal right to self-determination and independent statehood, while at the same time stressing the international solidarity of the proletariat, transcending the division of mankind into separate national entities.

The Communist Party of Yugoslavia, formed from several small pre-World War I socialist parties and groups, was initially given a strong antinationalist bias by its predominantly Serbian leadership (Sima Marković, Filip Filipović, Kosta Novaković, Triša Kaclerović). Proclaiming as its aim the establishment of a "Soviet Yugoslav Republic," the Communist party accepted the concept of "Yugoslavism," the ideological rationale for the formation of the Kingdom of the Serbs, Croats, and Slovenes, "three tribes of a single nation" formed after World War I. But from the start the party also drew strong support from disgruntled non-Serbs under Serb hegemony, who believed that communism would not only bring social justice but also national freedom and equality.

Thus, clashing perceptions of the national question were present in the Yugoslav Communist movement from the beginning. The Yugoslav unitarist view uneasily coexisted with federalist and confederalist visions of the Yugoslav state.

In the 1920 elections for the Constituent Assembly, the Communist party showed strength in Macedonia, the Albanian-inhabited Kosovo, the Sandžak (predominantly Muslim), and Montenegro, regions where national dissatisfaction was pronounced but autochthonous national parties were now allowed to function. In Croatia-Slavonia, the independence-minded Croatian Republican Peasant Party of Stjepan Radić drew most of the Croat vote. The Communist party was not allowed to function and develop as a legal political movement. In 1921, the party was banned by the Law for the Defense of the State, and was forced into the political underground. During King Alexander's dictatorship (1929–34), the Communist party was almost completely destroyed by successful police infiltration and brutal repression. The number of party members dwindled to a mere thousand or so, most of them in prison.

Lack of clarity and consistency in Yugoslav Communist attitudes toward the national question reflected shifting Soviet views on Yugoslavia, dictated by Moscow's interests. As Yugoslavia became an important link in France's anti-Soviet *cordon sanitaire* policy, Moscow supported some of the centrifugal nationalisms, particularly that of the Croats. But though Moscow endorsed a breakup of Yugoslavia, it also maintained a modicum of ambivalence on this issue, which offered greater room for maneuver. The Yugoslav party, its line dictated by Moscow, thus had the tactical advantage of appealing both to integral Yugoslavism by advocating Leninist democratic centralism and proletarian internationalism, and at the same time to Croat, Macedonian, and other separatist nationalisms by stressing Communist commitment to national self-determination to the point of secession.

After 1935, the Comintern shift to popular front alliance with bourgeois and democratic parties against fascism, facilitated Communist infiltration of bourgeois parties. Antifascist respectability helped the Communists particularly in exerting growing influence over the youth. In 1941, when Yugoslavia was invaded by Nazi Germany and thus drawn into World War II, SKOJ (the Communist youth organization) had substantially more members than the party itself, which still numbered only about 8,000. All these advances (together with training of Yugoslav Communist military cadres in the Spanish Civil War) were preparatory steps which made the Communist party capable of launching a successful partisan uprising after Yugoslavia's German invasion and dismemberment in April 1941, and Hitler's attack on the Soviet Union in June 1941.

It was at their fifth land conference, in October 1940, that the Yugoslav Communists, under Tito's leadership, adopted a comprehensive platform regarding the national question under which they fought their national liberation struggle during World War II. Though the party did not propose the formation of a Yugoslav federation of seven national republics, its organizational structure was clearly inspired by the Soviet federal-national model, the party's provincial committees roughly corresponding to historical territorial entities: Slovenia, Croatia-Slavonia with Dalmatia, Bosnia-Hercegovina, Serbia, Montenegro, Vojvodina, and Macedonia.[2] As for the latter, the view had matured in the Comintern, headed by the Bulgarian Georgi Dimitrov, that the way to resolve Serbo-Bulgarian disputes over Macedonia was to recognize the Macedonian Slavs as a separate nation entitled to their own "state." The Albanians of Kosovo and the Hungarians and Germans of Vojvodina were promised "freedom and equality," and possibly vague and unclearly defined "autonomy." This was the federal plan generally adopted by the two wartime AVNOJ (Anti-Fascist Council of National Liberation) conferences in Bihać (November 1942) and in Jajce (November 1943) and formally implemented at the end of the war.

Yet, friction in the Yugoslav Communist movement regarding the national question persisted. Following the collapse and dismemberment of Yugoslavia in April 1941, while the Soviet-German pact was still in effect, there were some attempts, tolerated or perhaps even encouraged by Moscow, to establish an independent Communist party in the Axis-sponsored independent state of Croatia. Moscow also expelled Yugoslavia's ambassador representing the exiled royal government in London. But time was far too short to form a separate Croat party. In June 1941, the German attack on the Soviet Union was launched, Soviet diplomatic relations with the royal government in exile were resumed, and the Teheran Conference (December 1943) endorsed an Allied commitment to restore the prewar Yugoslav state. Yet, wartime Soviet diplomacy did not completely exclude the possibility of dividing and thus destroying Yugoslavia. At the 1944 Moscow conference between Churchill and Stalin, the day after the notorious percentages agreement to divide Southeastern Europe into spheres of influence, Foreign Ministers Eden and Molotov met to work out the details. Molotov wanted to increase Soviet influence in Yugoslavia from 50–50 to 60–40. At some point in the ensuing haggling, "Molotov hinted at the partition of Yugoslavia,"[4] but the British were not interested, insisting on Yugoslavia's territorial integrity and on equal influence for both the Western and Soviet sides.

In 1945, Belgrade having been taken by the advancing Soviet forces, Tito and his partisans gained the upper hand over the royalist Serbian Chetniks and implemented the Communist party plan for a federated Yugoslavia. According to Milovan Djilas, the actual borders of the six republics and two autonomous regions were drawn in a rather casual way during informal meetings of the top Communist leaders, Tito, Edvard Kardelj, Milovan Djilas, and Aleksandar Ranković.[5] It is also apparent from accounts by Djilas, Vladimir Dedijer, and others who were privy to discussions in top party councils, that there were sharp conceptual disagreements regarding both the effective power Yugoslavia's republics were to be granted and their borders. Andrija Hebrang, Croatia's wartime Communist party secretary, favored a broadly autonomous Communist Croatia in Yugoslavia as well as seemingly genuine collaboration with followers of the Croatian Peasant Party and even the Catholic Church. But, in 1944, Hebrang was removed from his central political position in Croatia and at the war's end was placed in charge of Yugoslavia's industrial development. In 1948, he was arrested and soon liquidated, on the dual—and bogus—charge of supporting Moscow in its dispute with the Yugoslav leadership and of having been a secret *Ustasha* mole in the top party leadership during the war.[6]

During the war Communist propaganda promised freedom and equality to all of Yugoslavia's "nations" and "nationalities" in order to win their support. But, after they seized power in restored Yugoslavia, it became apparent that Tito and his associates were subordinating the Yugoslav national question to party interests, as the Bolsheviks had done in the USSR. Yugoslavia was nominally a federal state of equal national republics and autonomous regions. The Yugoslav constitution of 1946 proclaimed the right of the republics to self-determination to the point of secession and equal rights for all, including the national minorities (see Annex I). But, in effect, Yugoslavia was a centralized state, ruled by a monolithic Communist party on the basis of the Leninist principle of democratic centralism that reduced the republics and autonomous provinces to mere administrative divisions. The conflict with Moscow that came into the open in 1948 further strengthened the centralist and unitary character of the new Yugoslavia.[7] The Yugoslav Communist leadership convincingly argued that maximum cohesion and unity was an imperative to withstand Soviet political and economic pressure, and possibly military intervention. Massive roundups of real and alleged "Cominformists" (among whom were Croat nationalists and other dissidents) helped mute all internal opposition.[8]

And yet, the federalist tendency in the party, with a confederalist and even separatist drift, was not permanently repressed and eliminated. In Croatia it reemerged with great force in the late 1960s following the fall of Aleksandar Ranković, the vice president and the effective head of the security apparatus, whose downfall signaled the temporary weakening and disarray of the secret police. Under younger leaders, such as Miko Tripalo, Dr. Savka Dabčević-Kučar, Pero Pirker, Srečko Bijelić, and others, the then dominant faction in the Croat Communist Central Committee fought for greater autonomy for the Socialist Republic of Croatia and the transformation of Yugoslavia into a genuine federation. On the fringe of the party, and outside its ranks, were nationalist elements grouped around the Matica Hrvatska and its various publications, notably the *Hrvatski tjednik* that wanted to go further to a real confederation. Eventually, in December 1971, Tito with the support of the military leaders and the old party cadres cracked down on the Croat ferment. Some 32,000 Croats inside and outside the party were purged.[9] Thousands were detained by the police or were sentenced to varying prison terms. Tito insisted on "strengthening democratic centralism and unity of the League of Communists of Yugoslavia."[10] But at the same time he permitted the enactment of the 1974 constitutional amendments which gave the republics broader autonomy, particularly in the economic domain, with the long-term unintended effect of fragmenting the Yugoslav economy into increasingly autarkic entities.

More recently, the Albanians became the principal threat to Yugoslavia's territorial integrity.[11] There were disturbances in 1968, and again in 1979, Tito's terminal year. Tito's policy of improvised repression and concessions did not stop growing Albanian dissatisfaction and nationalism. The Kosovo riots in 1981 were the worst disturbances Yugoslavia had experienced since the war. The demand of the

Kosovo demonstrators was a Kosovo republic, that is, that Kosovo be separated from Serbia and become Yugoslavia's seventh republic. The demand was rejected by Tito's successors in Belgrade out of fear of Serbian anger and longer-term implications. The Albanian aspirations threatened to reopen all the other national questions of Yugoslavia. This includes the dangerous problem of Macedonia. The recognition of the Macedonian Slavs as a separate nation did not satisfy the Bulgarians, who continue to lay historic and linguistic claims to the region. The intensity of Bulgarian demands seems to be related, at least in part, to fluctuations in Soviet-Yugoslav relations.

The Tito thesis of national equality was a Leninist principle that actually never prevailed as such in practice. Its application has been subject to whatever served the interests of the party. Tito and his associates made varying and often clashing promises required to ensure a Communist-led victory in the national liberation struggle.[12] After the war, the formal and theoretical right of "nations" and "nationalities" to freedom and equality, even independence through self-determination and secession, was recognized in the constitution. The various "nations" were granted their own republics, flags, governments, and other trappings of statehood, while the "nationalities" were better treated than national minorities (Hungarians, in particular) in other multinational states of the Danube region.[13] But the monolithic character of the ruling Communist party, the principle of Leninist democratic centralism, and the overriding power of the centrally controlled security apparatus, in practice negated much of the substance of "national" and "nationality" rights in federal and socialist Yugoslavia. In the late 1960s, the Croats pressed for broader autonomy which, in time, might have led to the transformation of Yugoslavia into a confederation of essentially sovereign republics. But this process was stopped in 1971 by Tito's "Karadjordjevo" coup.

It may be illusory to expect any permanent solution which would eliminate recurring tensions and clashes. The national contradictions in fact are so substantial and intractable that multinational Yugoslavia's historical viability itself remains an unanswered question.

Notes

1. The declaration issued by the Belgrade Congress virtually ignored the Yugoslav national problem, stressing instead the importance of the class strug-

gle in the newly established state. See Ferdo Čulinović, *Jugoslavija izmedju dva rata* (Zagreb, 1961), 197–99.

2. Dusan Lukač, *Radnički pokret u Jugoslaviji i nacionalno pitanje 1918–1941* (Belgrade, 1972); Pero Damjanović, Milovan Bosić, Dragica Lazarević, eds., *Peta zemaljska konferencija KPJ (19–23. oktobar 1940)* (Belgrade, 1980).

3. Franjo Tudman, *Nationalism in Contemporary Europe* (Boulder, Colo., 1981). See particularly Part III dealing with the national question in Yugoslavia.

4. Albert Resis, "The Churchill-Stalin Secret 'Percentages' Agreement on the Balkans, Moscow, October, 1944," *The American Historical Review* 83/2 (1978): 368–87.

5. Milovan Djilas, *Wartime* (New York, 1980).

6. Cf. Ivan Supek, *Crown Witness against Hebrang* (Chicago, 1983).

7. Cf. Krste Crvenkovski, *SKJ u samoupravnom drustvu, Medjunacionalni odnosi u samoupravnom drustvu* (Belgrade, 1967).

8. According to Radovan Radonjić official Yugoslav data indicates that those who "supported Stalin's views" (and were presumably imprisoned for them) numbered 55,663. Zagreb weekly *Danas*, August 16, 1983, 11–15.

9. Marko Veselica, *The Croatian National Question—Yugoslavia's Achilles' Heel* (London, 1981), 12.

10. Tito's remarks at the meeting of the Executive Committee of the Central Committee of the League of Communists of Croatia, July 4, 1971.

11. Cf. Elez Biberaj, "Kosove: The Struggle for Recognition," *The Albanian Problem in Yugoslavia: Two Views*, The Institute for the Study of Conflict, No. 137–38 (London, 1982).

12. Tito's article in wartime *Proleter*, December 1942, outlined the basic wartime stands on the national question of the Central Committee of the Communist Party of Yugoslavia. There are separate mentions of the Serbs, Croats, Slovenes, Montenegrins, Macedonians, Muslims, Albanians, Hungarians, and others, implying their recognition as separate nations entitled to distinct territorial states. The article stressed repeatedly that the national liberation struggle guarantees the "freedom, equality and brotherhood of all the nations of Yugoslavia." In the conclusion Tito repeated the Communist commitment to the principles proclaimed by the "great teachers and leaders—Lenin and Stalin," that is, "the right of every nation to self-determination to the point of secession." The victory of the partisans was to a considerable extent due to the stand of the Communists regarding the national question, their commitment to the freedom, equality, brotherhood, and even right to total national independence of all the nations of Yugoslavia.

13. See Chapter 9, above, on Hungarians under Yugoslav rule.

Annex I
*The Yugoslav Federal Constitution of 1946**

Article 1

The Federal Peoples' Republic of Yugoslavia is a federal peoples' state, republican in form, a community of peoples equal in rights who, on the basis of the right of self-determination, including the right of separation, have expressed their will to live together in a federative state. [The right of "nationalities" to "separation"— "secession," that is—was abolished by the 1974 Constitution. See for details Chapter 9.]

Article 13

National minorities in the Federal Peoples' Republic of Yugoslavia enjoy the right to and protection of their own cultural development and the free use of their own language.

Annex II
*Statute of the Autonomous Province of Vojvodina***

Article 1

The Autonomous Province of Vojvodina is a socio-political community within the Constituent Republic of Serbia.

The Autonomous Province of Vojvodina was set up as an autonomous unit in 1945 by a Decision of the People's Assembly of the People's Republic of Serbia, in accordance with the special features of its historical and cultural-educational development and the specific

*English text from James Kerr Pollock, ed., *Change and Crisis in European Government* (New York, 1947), 215, 218.
**English text from "Supplement 5" of a paper by Ernest Petriča of the Institute for National Minority Questions in Ljubljana prepared for the Seminar on the Multi-National Society, organized by the United Nations in cooperation with the Government of Yugoslavia, Ljubljana, 8 to 22 June 1965. United Nations, SO 235/3 (2) EUR 1965. Working Paper 12.

national structure of the population, in conformity with the will of the population of Vojvodina.

Article 32

The Hungarians, Slovaks, Rumanians, Ruthenians and other national minorities living on the territory of the Autonomous Province of Vojvodina are in all respects equal with other citizens, enjoy the same rights and duties provided for by the Constitution and the Law, and enjoy the full rights to use their native language, and to express and develop their culture and establish institutions ensuring these rights.

The national minorities are guaranteed, in accordance with the law, the rights to express themselves in their native language, using all modern media of information.

Annex III
International Relevance of the Yugoslav Experience
Excerpts from a Marxist Analysis by László Rehák*

The Yugoslav experience regarding minorities has considerable international relevance. The experience of Tito's Yugoslavia can be considered in the vanguard in this field . . . [and] transcends the region of which it is a part. . . .

After World War II the problem of national minorities was for all practical purposes excluded from international context. It was considered to be within the domestic jurisdiction of each country. Tito's Yugoslavia, while it considered the national minority question a domestic issue, to be handled in a socialist and humane way, always kept in view the long-range aspects and never opposed international agreements involving reciprocal commitments and obligations concerning nationality rights.

At the United Nations the minority question received at times little, at other times more attention. So far, the results are meager. . . . However, the time has passed when, as in 1946 at the Paris Peace

*Excerpts from László Rehák, *Kisebbségtől a nemzetiségig* (Belgrade, 1978), 100–4. On the Rehák analysis, see also Annex I in Chapter 9, above.

Conference, the American delegate Bedel-Smith could actually state in reference to the national minorities that: "A citizen of the United States of America has a hard time understanding why racial minorities want to maintain their distinctiveness when they have the option of assimilation." And the English delegate Lord Hood joined him on this question, stating: "I agree, our goal should be that the racial minorities should be assimilated by the countries in which they reside, and not that they should be able to maintain their distinctiveness."

[Also at the Paris Peace Conference, speaking on behalf of the Czechoslovak delegation,] Vlado Clementis said: "The national minorities are constant sources of friction between peoples and states. For this reason, Czechoslovakia hopes that with the expulsion of the German and Hungarian minorities it can become a purely national state. . . . In Czechoslovakia there is no politician, there is nobody, who believes that it is possible to return to the minority policies of the past, the impossibility of which has been demonstrated by experience."

At the Third Session of the Human Rights Commission, May–June 1948, on the motion of India, Great Britain, and bourgeois China, and supported by the United States of America, it was decided to leave out of the proposed Declaration on Human Rights the paragraph dealing with minorities. On this occasion, however, the delegate of Yugoslavia, Jože Vilfan, said: "The Commission must recognize that the melting pot conception is not applicable to Eastern Europe or Asia. . . . Yugoslavia's own experience is convincing testimony that the recognition of the rights of linguistic and cultural groups is important. . . . The rights of ethnic groups do not in every instance coincide with the rights of individuals, [therefore] cannot be protected solely by general declarations of individual rights."

While the Declaration on Human Rights does not contain a specific statement about the minority question, the UN General Assembly adopted a resolution on minorities the same day it adopted the Declaration (December 10, 1948). The resolution directs the Economic and Social Council and its organs, the Human Rights Commission and the Subcommittee on Prevention of Discrimination and Protection of Minorities to study minority problems systematically so that the United Nations would be capable of taking effective action for the protection of racial, national, religious, or linguistic minorities.

Based on the above resolution and at the behest of the subcommittee, the Commission on Human Rights adopted Article 27 in its International Covenant on Civil and Political Rights [to protect both individual and group rights of ethnic, religious, or linguistic minorities]. Article 27 was proposed by the Soviet Union, Yugoslavia, and Denmark and received the active support of many other states. . . . [For the text and a discussion of Article 27, see p. 109 in Chapter 6.]

✳ 13

Socialist Solutions—
Communist Realities
Introduction

Julian Schopflin

The claim is being advanced by the Communists of the Danube region that Marxist-Leninist nationality policy has brought—or, at least, is in the process of bringing—socialist solutions to the feuds and rivalries of the past. The evidence in support of these claims, unfortunately, is less than convincing.

Between the two world wars, the local Communist parties in the countries of the Danube region carried on a double struggle: the conventional class war as prescribed by Marx and Engels, and a parallel struggle for minority rights against their own national bourgeoisie, under the banner displaying the noble principles of Lenin and Stalin. In socialist and Communist circles great expectations were raised that, once this part of the world had undergone the hoped-for "socialist transformation," minority problems would be solved once and for all, on the basis of full cultural autonomy, economic fair shares, and even political representation. After all, did not the constitution of the Soviet Union declare the noblest, most liberal, principles: freedom of speech and assembly, right to publications, protection of indigenous cultures, and even the right of secession for national entities?

It should have been a warning signal for idealists that, already in the late 1930s—and even more obviously during World War II—the

Soviet Union was increasingly using minority conflicts as a ploy in its cynical power game. For instance, Transylvania was being offered, in turn, both to Hungarians and to Romanians, according to what seemed advantageous to the Soviet Union at the moment.

Since World War II, the constitutions of the Soviet satellites have all duly copied the Russian example, establishing in unequivocal terms the full rights of minorities in every respect. However, just as in the case of Soviet principles and practice, reality stands in stark, almost tragic, contrast to the noble sentiments enshrined in Communist constitutions.

The following significant interview with Edgár Balogh should be read in the context of a "looking-glass world" where words do not mean what they say—indeed, Lewis Carroll's playful story is shading into Orwell's "1984": a world of "doublespeak" and of constant "updating" of history.

Edgár Balogh is one of the "grand old men" of Hungarian minority politics and literature. His life and career are a telling example of minority fate in the Danube region. He was born in 1906 into a Hungarian family in Transylvania (present-day Romania, that is). In his early years, he was constantly on the move throughout the Habsburg Monarchy since his father was an administrative official in the Austro-Hungarian army. The family lived in Temesvár (today Timişoara), Trieste, Sarajevo, Kraków, and then settled, just before the outbreak of World War I, in Pozsony—Bratislava, that is, the future capital of Slovakia. Thus, young Edgár Balogh grew up in postwar Czechoslovakia and was one of the leaders of a broadly leftist social and cultural movement of the Hungarian minority, called *Sarló*. In the mid-1930s, having been forced (as a "native," in postwar legal terms, of Romania) to leave Czechoslovakia, he moved to Transylvania under Romanian rule. There he carried out his activities as writer, essayist, theoretician, and publicist, mostly in and around the highly respected left-wing Hungarian-language periodical *Korunk*. After World War II, he was appointed professor at the short-lived Hungarian university in Kolozsvár (Cluj). In the 1956 crackdown (following the scare caused to Hungary's Communist neighbors by the anti-Communist revolt in Budapest), he was arrested, with many other prominent Hungarian Communists in Romania, and spent several years in prison. After he was freed, he was reinstated as a university professor and now lives in retirement in Kolozsvár.

A man of encyclopedic knowledge, of wide reading, with an incisive, brilliant mind, he is the author of many books, countless essays, articles, and treatises. He has been a convinced Communist throughout his career; it seems that, in spite of all the vicissitudes and cruel disappointments of his life, he still maintains a belief in Marxism-Leninism. Or, at least, he makes use of Communist principles and phraseology—perhaps a kind of lip-service to the holy writ of Communism.

The interview he gave in 1978 to Pál E. Fehér of the periodical *Kritika* (published in Hungary), is a masterpiece of the devious Byzantine style and manner writers and politicians must use in Communist countries in order to speak out—loud but not clear. In a veiled way, he is voicing grievances and demanding justice; between the lines, he is exposing lies and misdeeds.

This approach demands from the writer a fairly lengthy double ritual. Repeated expressions of abject adulation are required for the imminent truths of Marxism-Leninism and for those who have trampled these truths into blood and mud, like Leonid Brezhnev or Nicolae Ceaușescu. The writer must couple this with a routine condemnation of everything that happens—or does not happen—in the "declining" West. He must contrast the perfect "solutions" of all problems, including minority conflicts, in the Soviet Union and its satellites, to the "oppression" of minorities in the Western world—Basques, Bretons, Catalans, Corsicans, and so on.

Only then, having performed this double duty, can he—very cautiously and in a deliberately obfuscating style—point out certain "misunderstandings" or "slight distortions" that have occurred (of course, only accidentally) regarding the safeguards and principles embodied in Communist constitutions. Thus we learn, between the lines, of the linguistic oppression of Hungarians in Romania, the systematic destruction of their schools and cultural institutions, the denial of opportunities to Hungarians in every walk of life, the blatant discrimination in economic matters, going against masses of people because they are Hungarian.

Knowing something of the corrupt and vicious regime of Ceaușescu and his cronies, we should recognize that Edgár Balogh has probably shown a measure of courage—the courage of despair. The theoretical convolutions of his writing, the careful weighing of words throughout the text, the flashes of his old debating skill, all this serves as a carefully fashioned framework for exposing the glaring injustices committed by Romanian chauvinism, the "cultural genocide" of the Hungarian minority in Transylvania.

The interview culminates in a demand for restitution, the implementation of constitutional safeguards, and in a subdued *cri de coeur* for the birthright of today's national minorities whose forebears lived for many centuries and where their descendants live now.

Excerpts from an Interview with Edgár Balogh

P.E.F.: *For the periodical* Kritika, *I would like to ask you a few questions concerning the current state of minority problems. Are we [in 1978] right in thinking that the recent meetings between János Kádár and Nicolae Ceauşescu may herald a Marxist-Leninist solution to the problem of nationalities?*

E.B.: Yes, I think there are hopes for a socialist solution. I have lived more than half my life—in fact, more than half a century—as a member of a minority, first in Czechoslovakia, then in Romania, so I hope I know what we are talking about. Yes, I agree that time and circumstances have put the question of minorities very much on the agenda. We must have an exchange of experiences, we need comparisons, to find a way toward this burning problem.

The liberation of colonial peoples has been going on now for more than three decades, and it is not quite complete yet. This historical process demands that the not-yet-independent nations in the capitalist West should also achieve their freedom. Furthermore, national minorities in the West should also gain full autonomy. Here, in the socialist East, we can be proud of how much better we have managed the questions of national independence and of coexistence between nations, than in the capitalist West.

The growing intensity—and, let us hope, an early solution—of the Basque and Catalan problems in the young Spanish democracy, the sharpening autonomist efforts by Bretons and Corsicans in France, the crisis in Northern Ireland, the conflicts between Walloons and Flemings in Belgium—all these testify to the inevitable conclusion that, following the great movements of emancipation in Asia and Africa, the problem of nationalities *within* the boundaries of the erst-while colonial powers is also demanding a solution. And not only in Western Europe; there are conflicts galore elsewhere [in the capitalist world], such as the confrontation of the Turks and Greeks in Cyprus, the Palestinian tragedy, the unsolved problems of the Kurds and of the American Indians.

In sharp contrast to this, we can observe the coming together and growing cooperation of nations controlled in principle by the pattern of the new Soviet constitution. Of course, we can see that economic and social developments do give rise to new claims, new demands, in the socialist world too, proving again that we have to exert constant vigilance while perfecting the heritage of Lenin.

It was Leonid Brezhnev himself, who, in his speech to the Supreme Soviet, gave proof of the vigilance of 140 million Great Russians, when he rejected the misguided conclusions of those who had argued that Leninist progress requires the abolition of national differences. He struck down the ideas aiming at the liquidation of different re-publics and autonomous areas of the Soviet Union and promulgating a uniform Soviet "nation" and abolishing the Council of Nationali-ties. . . .

Said Brezhnev, bearing witness to the inseparable unity of national independence and international solidarity: "The friendship of Soviet nationalities is indissoluble. In the course of building socialism, our nationalities come ever nearer to one another and their cultural life is a source of continuing mutual enrichment."

The natural demands of the present day are little different in those countries that set out on the course of socialist development later than the Soviet Union. Here, I can answer in a positive fashion the question you asked about the historic meetings of Nicolae Ceauşescu and János Kádár in the course of last year [1977]. The full moral weight of the Romanian Communist Party and of the Hungarian Socialist Workers' Party has been brought to bear on an agreement concerning the sig-nificance and role of national minorities in the two countries. Proof of this lies in the possibilities that can be realized by applying socialist integration to the problems of nationalities in our homelands.

According to the joint declaration issued after these meetings, the status of nationalities in both countries is based on equality before the law, on Marxist-Leninist ideology, and on the Charter of the

United Nations. The solution of all problems is facilitated by the fraternal relations of the two socialist countries. The true role of nationalities is that of a bridge between neighbors. In the spirit of principles, Romanians living in Hungary and Hungarians living in Romania should become active factors in socialist consolidation in Eastern Europe, nay, the heralds of a convergent development, in shining contrast to those retrograde phenomena, all those violations of human rights, that characterize the backwardness and internal contradictions of the capitalist world, particularly as regards the question of minorities.

P.E.F.: What are the traditions—the heritage with practical applications—of the scientific study of the problems of nationalities here in East-Central Europe? You, yourself, like most members of the leftist intelligentsia, have dealt with these problems in your work.

E.B.: It is no accident that the study of minorities—nowadays we prefer to call them nationalities—is being reborn today. After all, it had achieved some serious results already between the wars. All nations and nationalities have generated quite a library on the subject, but the first attempt at international—more precisely, intra-national—analysis and methodology based on scientific comparisons was made here in Transylvania.

I refer to the twenty-one uninterrupted years of the [Hungarian-language] fortnightly *Magyar Kisebbség* that was published in the small town of Lugos [in Romania] between 1922 and 1942. These twenty-one volumes are virtually the basis of studies of our nationality problems in a broader European context.

The periodical was founded and edited throughout its life by Elemér Jakabffy. He started his political career as a Hungarian conservative, but the impact of minority status in Transylvania gradually transformed him into a populist defender of minority rights and, finally, into an antifascist. True to his liberal beliefs, he also championed the cause of the Catalan and Basque minorities, declared his support for the Spanish democratic republic and condemned Franco's imperialistic chauvinism.

This [Hungarian-language] periodical, with its two supplements— *Die Stimme der Minderheiten* in German and *La voix des minorités* in French—supported the cause of minorities throughout its existence. Furthermore, Jakabffy, a member of the Romanian parliament, championed the rights of minorities at the League of Nations, attending several conferences in Geneva. He and his collaborators protested against the arbitrary arrest of a leader of the Slovene minority in Mussolini's fascist Italy (who happened to be also president of the League of Nations' conferences on minorities); they opposed the racist ideology and anti-Semitism of Hitler; at home [in Romania], they condemned the oppressive policies of Romanian feudal capitalism, but in the same spirit pilloried the totalitarian sympathies emerging within the ranks of the Hungarian minority in Romania.

The study of minorities was carried on at the same time in Czechoslovakia and Hungary, too. (It would be worthwile, for instance, to disinter the juridical, sociological, and statistical writings of Masaryk's pupils and followers.) However, only *Magyar Kisebbség,* pursuing the inner logic of its struggle, came to appreciate the Marxist-Leninist approach and Soviet practice in the treatment of minorities. One of its contributors, Imre Mikó, as early as 1932, quoted Lenin's views on the minority problem in a treatise on the nationality question in Transylvania. The journal championed, in the same spirit, the rights of Ukrainians and Belorussians oppressed in prewar Poland, as well as the rights of Poles in Eastern Germany.

After World War II, a truly socialist analysis of the nationality problems in the Danube Valley had only appeared in the sixties. In Czechoslovakia, Yugoslava, and Romania, scores of sociologists, writers and publicists have published treatises, commentaries, and articles on the problem. And, in 1974, the Seminar on Minorities, organized by the United Nations in Ohrid (Yugoslavia), elevated the subject from a regional topic to a worldwide one. Finally, in 1975, the Helsinki Agreements dealt with minority rights, both in legal terms and in terms of fundamental human rights. Thus the minorities of socialist southeast Europe—Slovenes, Slovaks, and Romanians in Hungary, Turks in Bulgaria, Germans in Romania, and of course, the most numerous among minorities, the Hungarians in Czechoslovakia, Romania and Yugoslavia—have since been internationally placed on the same legal platform as the minorities of the capitalist countries and of the ex-colonial world.

P.E.F.: How do you assess recent literature dealing with the problem of nationalities using the Marxist approach, taking into consideration the experience of socialist countries in this field?

E.B.: The question of nationalities has, in fact, become a worldwide problem. As *Magyar Nemzet* [a Hungarian daily published in

Budapest] wrote: "Internationalism aims at supporting and nurturing ethnic minorities, not at doing away with them. The Soviet Union is the shining example, proving that nationalities, minorities, or ethnic groups can only achieve their full fruition, their complete equality of rights, in the era of socialist internationalism." The article was inspired by the publication of two important books in Hungary, dealing with the historical, social, and political aspects of minority problems: *Nationalities and the Minority Problem in Western Europe* by Rudolf Joó, and *Minorities—Nationalities* by László Kővágó. Both books [in Hungarian], written in the wake of the Ohrid conference, treated the matter on the basis of international equality before the law. Drawing comparisons with the socialist achievements, they pointed out the unsettled conditions in the capitalist countries. Joó surveys the reappearance of minority problems in Western Europe, ever since the sixties, in particular under the impact of the anti-colonial liberation movements. The author gives many examples of attempts at forcible absorption (or the even more dangerous policies aiming at assimilation) on the one hand, and minority movements on the other, demanding the right to equality and autonomy. He draws attention to the policies of Western Communist parties which have been calling for the joint struggle of majority and minority workers to obtain these rights.

A word about assimilation. Individual cases occur everywhere and all the time; there is nothing wrong with this. It is one of the fundamental human rights, if it is voluntary. On the other hand, we must condemn "racist" attitudes that attempt to prevent the free choice of people to belong where they wish. Therefore, forcible assimilation of a national minority, bent on breaking up a historical entity, is a crime against the inalienable rights of communities.

Joó's book also reveals the glaring differences in minority policies among certain Western European states. Yet, the exemplary behavior of Switzerland or Finland can hardly counterbalance the oppressive policies pursued in France or in Sweden. The unitary concept of the "French nation" denied the right to autonomy to three Latin groups (Occitans, Catalans, and Corsicans), two German fragments (Alsatians and ethnic Germans), to the Celtic Bretons, and the Basques. Twelve million non-French people are being forced into "Frenchness." In Sweden, it is true, only forty thousand Finns are subjected to forcible assimilation through monolingual [Swedish] schooling, in sharp contrast to the privileged position of the Swedish minority in Finland. But, it is not the quantities that count!

Kővágó's book is a virtual catechism of the study of nationalities. After assessing the history of the problem, leading up to its emergence at the United Nations, he clarifies the nature and types of various minorities, offering a more precise definition of the south-east European variant. Pinning down the tendency toward a worldwide awakening of ethnic self-assertion, he correctly recognizes that only the Marxist-Leninist principles and practices of the socialist countries offer satisfactory solutions: "It is largely thanks to the efforts of certain socialist countries, that the question of minorities appears, increasingly, in international agreements. It is to their credit that the United Nations is gradually becoming the world forum for settling nationality problems." To prove his point, he quotes a Hungarian document submitted to the UN-sponsored Ohrid seminar on minorities, and he praises the manner in which the Hungarian Peoples' Republic has so generously settled the rights and freedoms of its minorities (admittedly smaller in numbers—and, therefore, also a smaller problem—than in other countries).

East and West equally reject nowadays "racist" discrimination against languages, ethnic absorption through forcible assimilation, all forms of minority liquidation, although, in Western bourgeois nation-state systems, there is still much to be put right. Moreover, their bad examples may still have some influence even in our own socialist system. That is why we must become fully aware of the potentialities of our own socialist solution, and must spread our message thereof throughout the world. Our moral authority relies on our rational treatment of the problem, on our recognition that only equal rights can serve as a basis for a fraternal community of nations.

P.E.F.: In your view, how does actual practice reflect these theoretical clarifications? We know that daily life can throw up new problems, even though we are following the right principles.

E.B.: We should never forget that the problem of nationality has two aspects: On the one hand, it affects the minority and, on the other, the majority. We expect the solutions, both in the moral and the legal sense, to come from common patriotism, from national harmony, supported by both sides. This dual approach is essential to generating mutual trust, a friendly atmosphere. The majority must always be reassured that minority rights would not hurt its ultimate sovereignty, indeed its existence (for, history has countless examples of minority grievances covering up hostile intentions against the majority). The majority must become convinced that the well-being and prosperity of a minority actually benefits the free and peaceful development of the state as a whole. The minority, in turn, must recognize that the full flowering of its national life—certainly in the troubled Danube region, but probably elsewhere, too—can only be achieved through constantly improving mutual understanding, and not through chauvinistic resistance.

The present boundaries in Europe were largely created through wars in the course of the emergence of nation-states. Conflicting territorial claims were inevitable following the collapse of the Habsburg Empire. Serbs and Romanians wanted to join their independent compatriots; Czechs, Slovaks, Hungarians desired their own sovereign countries. The Hungarian Soviet Republic in 1919 did make an attempt at a federal Danubian union. Following its debacle, national minorities had to suffer a double oppression. They were oppressed as workers by the bourgeoisie and oppressed as national minorities by the "master races."

Nevertheless, the newly found independence had its beneficial effects too. Social, economic, and cultural changes—as in the case of the Slovaks, or the Romanians of Transylvania—meant overcoming the backwardness of centuries. And, among the Hungarian minorities in the new countries, there were quite a few people who rejected the idea of a "Greater Hungary." They fully recognized the rights of Slovaks or Romanians to national rebirth and fought for a common front, uniting all democratic forces of both the majorities and the minorities. Alas, we know that these movements carried a moral weight only against the onslaughts of chauvinism. It was only following World War II that a way was opened toward a peaceful solution of minority problems.

It would be particularly interesting to study the reasons why the postwar revolutionary transformation of our countries toward socialism has taken place within the old frontiers of prewar bourgeois nation-states. Here, historic inevitability preserved the smaller sovereign states, whereas in Russia it favored the great international federation of the Soviet Union. Be that as it may, our frontiers proved to be foundations for peace and socialist development. Therefore, it is self-evident that full recognition of these frontiers and acceptance of the judgment of history is an essential precondition for the full establishment of minority rights, alongside the majority nations which became socialist societies themselves.

Already before the war, Titulescu, the liberal bourgeois political leader in Romania, spoke of the "spiritualization" of frontiers. Count Mihály Károlyi, the "grand old man" of the Hungarian left, championed a Danubian confederation. After the war, Petru Groza, Prime Minister of Romania, suggested a Hungarian-Romanian customs union. Now, when the great socialist transformation in both countries has reached a stage of consolidation, the demand for frontier adjustments only surfaces occasionally in the provocative propaganda of dissidents in the West. Our tasks are to improve the relations within these frontiers and between neighboring socialist countries—that is the way to do away with outstanding minority problems.

Sometimes it is a subject for debate whether the problem of nationalities has achieved its perfect solution in our socialist countries of the Danube Valley, or not. In my view, this is just a play on words. It is a great achievement that the fascist *Herrenvolk* concept, racist discrimination, the pitting of majorities against minorities, and vice versa, are things of the past. The emergence of people's democracies also has meant liberation for our minorities (except the short-lived deportation of Hungarians from Czechoslovakia). The constitution of every single socialist country proclaims national equality, the right to one's own language and culture, rejects any and every kind of discrimination among citizens. These principles are thus the guiding lights of public life in our countries. Members of all nationalities are represented in our public administrations. The minorities can enjoy their own press, theaters, and schools. Their villages and towns share the fruits of scientific and technical advancement.

However, proudly as we may contrast the achievements of our socialist system with the forcible assimilation and cunning attempts at absorption going on in the West, we must admit that our resistance to similar remnants of our past is not as explicit as it ought to be. We can still find certain inconsistencies in our everyday life—deviations, that is, from the Soviet solution. In other words, the settlement of the nationality question is not quite complete. Not yet. In this respect, I agree with those who say that this question, like many other problems of socialist construction, can only be solved in a continuing manner.

What I really mean is that the infiltration of the French "nation-state" idea is still noticeable in our countries. In the last century this idea became the inspiration of nationalist movements throughout Europe. In the Danube region, however, it produced double-edged results. For instance, in Hungary, the Law of Nationalities of 1868 abolished all national discrimination. Yet, at the same time, the concept of the unitary "Hungarian political nation" created the artificial notion of individual "Slovak-speaking Hungarians" or "Romanian-speaking Hungarians," instead of safeguarding the rights of these minorities as collective communities. It was in this way that a "liberal" law opened the door to a more-or-less coercive assimilation of the minorities by the Hungarian majority.

Today, during the creative phase of socialist development, we still have to face certain "bourgeois" features of nationalism. After all, this phase has had to solve quite a few problems that should have been the task of capitalism. It is no wonder, therefore, that the seemingly attractive—though essentially contradictory—nineteenth-century French idea of the "nation-state" resurfaced in our part of the world, clashing with the Soviet internationalist theory and practice.

May I quote some examples from Romania? There was a time when the interpretation of the concept of "Romanian socialist nation" was not fully clarified and the dangers of misinterpretation were looming large. But then János Fazekas, Deputy Prime Minister, clarified the question in the classic Marxist-Leninist manner at a party congress. According to him, the Hungarian minority in Romania cannot be simply incorporated in the "Romanian socialist nation," because the Hungarians are members of a separate "entity," a different "ethnic community." As such, the Hungarians have their own specific characteristics and a different ethos. Yet, one essential feature is also their indissoluble unity with the Romanian nation within the same socialist state.

This important pronouncement thus substituted the concept of "Romanian socialist nationality" in place of the "Romanian socialist nation." So, at one stroke, the unnatural consequences of an assumed danger of incorporation into the majority were averted. Hungarians in Romania from then on could shake off the nightmare of absorption and could look forward to a promising future of joint patriotism.

A dispute at the Writers Association of Romania—on the subject of the existence or nonexistence of Hungarian literature in Romania—

had a similar outcome. Chauvinistic ideas may always arise from the subconscious; so, someone suggested that instead of "Hungarian writers of Romania" we should call them "Romanian authors writing in Hungarian." This would have meant a distortion of what rightfully stands for "Romanian" with a separate history and national consciousness. Furthermore, it would have forced upon us an artificial homogeneity, a slide back to the bourgeois interpretation of the abstract French idea of citizenship. It would have also ruined the important role of a "bridge" between socialist states to be played by Hungarian and Romanian literature. Fortunately, Romanian and Hungarian writers clarified the question offering thus another example of a truly democratic exchange of views, the only authentic one in a truly socialist context.

These examples, showing the socialist vigilance of Communists in Romania, do not mean that Romania is the only socialist country where the rejection of the "nation-state" is necessary. In Hungary, in contrast to the exemplary nationality policy of the state, one can sometimes note in the press the formalistic French equation of state and nation. We have also been witnessing in Czechoslovakia the painful process through which two nations and several nationalities have struggled to achieve a satisfactory coexistence within the same socialist state.

Painfully, but we are moving everywhere in the Danube region toward the establishment of community rights for all nationalities. This follows logically from the acceptance of the concept of "socialist nationality" in a socialist society. In Hungary, this development has led to the democratic associations of South Slav, German, Romanian, and Slovak nationalities; in Czechoslovakia, to the cultural association of Hungarians, in Romania to the workers' councils of Hungarians, Germans and Serbs. Doubtless there are many more stages to come in the course of this development. Socialist integration will dissolve the ideological remnants of the still existing tendencies toward forcible assimilation or willful isolation. Progress toward Communism will open further vistas of coexistence between Socialist nations and nationalities as well as between our fraternal socialist states.

P.E.F.: How would you assess the state of self-knowledge among our nations?

E.B.: The various constitutions of our socialist countries safeguard the free use of every citizen's own language. By means of the press, publishing, theaters, schools, and cultural associations, the state ensures the equality of development for all nationalities. Also planned economic development in our countries, the distribution of industry, serves the whole community equally, without bias regarding national minority areas. This is in sharp contrast with the practices in the capitalist world, both past and present; there, it is usually the less developed and very often the minority areas that are disadvantaged, either owing to lack of planning or to deliberate discrimination.

In our socialist world there might occur now and then certain events eliciting local or individual complaints. This is being counterbalanced by those fundamental achievements which allow the self-development of every nationality. Nevertheless, when we are digging deeper, analyzing the key questions of language and culture, like schooling and scientific work, our conditions do reveal certain unsolved problems. It is, fortunately, our common socialist development, and our fraternal coexistence, that make such an analysis at all possible.

First and foremost, we must clarify the physiological and psychological role played by the mother tongue. What is its essence and how does it relate to any other languages? The mother tongue is the tool for forming concepts from early, instinctual beginnings to the grasping of the most complex configurations. Through the language of literature, politics, administration, science, a person reaches full understanding of the world, and it is the mother tongue that shapes all these thinking processes. All other languages that may be desirable in a working life—like the language of the majority and of course the great world languages—can be learned properly only by an adjustment to the conceptual thinking developed through the medium of the mother tongue. To come to the main point: Every single child in a minority group should be able to study at *every* level of schooling in his own language. Only in this way would he be enabled to conceptualize the differences between languages and thus to make another language his own. In normal circumstances, every young person in a minority should carry on his studies in his own language, from nursery school to university. We have statistics galore to prove that in this manner he will be able to learn the majority language more easily, more correctly, and also better understand the concepts learned in a "foreign" language.

The complexity of higher education nowadays makes it impossible to ensure training in the mother tongue for every nationality in every field. However, under the ideal circumstances suggested above, at this higher stage the student would already be effectively bilingual and suffer no hardships in his further development. Furthermore, lectureships in minority languages at higher institutions could ensure parallel teachings of scientific and professional terminologies in minority languages. That would greatly help the working masses of minority origin. The ever-increasing priority given to technical education makes the need of such minority-language lectureships the more urgent at the universities run in the majority language. This way, the supply of properly trained teachers at minority technical colleges would be ensured; also the exchange of information and experience in the various technical fields would be considerably improved countrywide. On top of that, without a full command of the mother tongue at every level, a nationality cannot properly fulfill its role in bridge-building between neighboring countries.

We have to mention all this because—among the thousand-and-one problems of socialist development—the cultivation of mother tongues at the highest levels, the historical necessity of bilingualism, and the rightful national minority claims of the working masses have not yet aroused enough spontaneity in the higher spheres of planning. Year by year, we find increasing numbers of young people of minority origin who (owing perhaps partly to their parents' negligence but mainly to the lack of a satisfactory network of schools) must continue their studies in another language. Thus, sadly, they will never reach a higher level either in their mother tongue or in the language of their studies; their education will remain at a low level and their contribution to society remain unsatisfactory. They cannot render useful service to their own people, and their ability to communicate with another culture will not develop either; thus their value to the majority will also diminish.

Deliberate assimilation is against the official policy of our socialist countries. However, it is not enough to brandish our constitutional minority rights. We must work for the recognition of our common interests in this respect. Only this way can we remain faithful to the "unity of theory and practice" preached by Lenin.

Furthermore, a language is not only a means of communication, but also a treasure-house of wisdom accumulated through the centuries. It is the bond between people and their environment; a witness to human development. Therefore it is also a tool for documentation and explanation. It should be the means of exploring and explaining the land of one's birth, its geography, ethnology, and place-names; of safeguarding the heritage, the eminent achievements of the people; of knowing its living literature, as well as deciphering the message of ancient gravestones.

We owe all this to our future. A minority can only become a creative factor in the new historical period if it is in full possession of its own libraries, museums and collections, places of worship, its institutions for the study of literature and history. We have a respectable number of experts among every nationality in Central and Eastern Europe, and the results of their work regularly appear in minority periodicals. In Yugoslavia, I can refer to the Institute of Hungarology in Novi Sad (Újvidék); in Romania, to the scientific journal of the Transylvanian Saxons in Sibiu (Nagyszeben); the Hungarian-language *A Hét* in Bucharest, the *Korunk* in Cluj (Kolozsvár); in Slovakia, to the seminar held in 1977 by *Irodalmi Szemle* in Bratislava (Pozsony) under the title "Nationality and Science."

However, this desirable self-knowledge of our national minorities has so far found expression largely in the framework of literary and linguistic studies only. Studies in folklore, in science, or in cultural subjects in the broadest sense are still an unfulfilled promise. Neither can we see the very desirable cooperation between the academies of our socialist countries. If a timely change does not occur in this field, blanks will arise on our map of the Danube Valley—the treasures of whole regions, of individual ethnic groups will sink into oblivion.

It cannot be emphasized strongly enough that national self-knowledge at a scientific level, the history of nations (which is the basis of socialist consciousness), and their comparative study, is an essential factor in that "bridge-building" between nations I have mentioned. If we make proper use of the principle of internationalism in this immense field, we can counteract all tendencies toward self-isolation and their hidden chauvinistic threats.

A problem of greatest importance arises from the social changes precipitated by industrialization and urbanization: demographic shifts (affecting both majorities and minorities), population movements, the emergence of isolated groups, as well as an increase in areas of mixed populations. This process cannot be stopped and we must take stock of the consequences. How does it affect the survival of minorities?

Who is to assess the new tasks? It is in the universal—national and international—interest that all the necessary services to mixed populations, to transferred ethnic groups, should be organized and directed by the state. This is a constitutional duty. In the past, the ecclesiastical network of the Greek Orthodox church used to follow Serb, Romanian, or Macedonian emigrants moving west; in the opposite direction, the churches and schools of the Calvinist faith followed eastward the Hungarian settlers in Moldavia and Wallachia. Nowadays, only a minority nationality firmly integrated into the political community of the state as a whole can perform such social tasks. A complete new organization is required in order to satisfy the needs of minority groups moving into urban areas, into new industrial complexes. Assessment of their social stratification, their requirements for schools and institutions, the safeguarding of use of their own language—through their newspapers, theaters, amateur groups—is an urgent task. New growing forms of coexistence, new exchanges between different cultures, new links in the chain of socialist integration may thus arise to the immense benefit of all. Surely all this is in the national interest in order to strengthen inner cohesion, not to mention the necessity of setting new examples in true internationalism.

It is everybody's turn to show a good example. "We have realized in our country, on a small scale, what you are going to realize on a much larger scale in your countries," declared Lenin in 1919, at the Congress of Eastern Communist parties. Since then, millions in Asia and Africa, in their newly independent countries, are nurturing their national languages and cultures by following the example of Soviet nationality policies. The limelight now is upon us, the socialist countries which have arisen since 1945. Our future, the future of majority nations as well as that of their minorities, depends on the growth of our successful coexistence. Also, our prestige in the world will grow only to the extent that internationalism will be the guiding light of our nations. Only the strengthening of coexistence among us will bring the full fruition of equal rights for all of us. This is the only way to avoid national conflict in the course of socialist integration.

P.E.F.: What is your view of the practical question: How can people speaking the same language, but living behind different frontiers, best enhance the cultivation of their common language and common tradition, best deal with their present problems, best engage in the "bridge-building" you have mentioned?

E.B.: Just as the building of socialism in one country is a question of internal politics, so is the settlement of the nationality question. It cannot be solved by external force, by intervention, by sloganizing, or by provocation. In particular, it ill behooves the capitalist West to attempt such an interference. After all, they are unable or unwilling to ensure free development even to their own national minorities. Their hidden or indeed open aim is forcible assimilation, to create thereby a pliable raw material for their class rule. The sovereignty of socialist states cannot and must not tolerate any such interference in the affairs of majorities and minorities. The autochthonous forms of party life and state building must be based on common agreements, on international socialist cooperation. We all agree that mutual economic help among socialist states is the best means for progress toward communism. By the same token, any cultural flowering based on such economic structure is dependent on our mutual help and cooperation.

Socialist legality is against any action aimed at retarding or hurting the development of nations and nationalities. Socialist coexistence and cooperation are regulated by the principle of full equality. These simple facts elevate the socialist world to the exceptional position where it can serve as an example to all oppressed peoples of the world, offering the hope of a better future for all national minorities. Our coexistence, our mutual help, our solutions based on peaceful agreements serve as moral imperatives, going beyond simple observance of equality before the law. They also serve as a visible counterforce against attempts at assimilation, against irredentism, against terrorism (as a last resort of an oppressed minority). They are, besides, the strongest possible arguments supporting the worldwide endeavors for peace of the Soviet Union, the peaceful settlement of problems in the Third World and, in the last analysis, the noble humanism of the UN charter. These principles should apply to the Irish problem or that of the peoples of Palestine, the Kurds or the Quechua Indians. All solutions must be based on humanism and the common interest of all peoples of the world.

It is therefore of universal importance, part of our responsibilities toward the whole world, that our achievements in the field of nationality policies should be jointly assessed, the results exchanged in writing or at conferences. The successes of coexistence between majority and minorities, the "bridge-building" efforts across frontiers, the ever-increasing inner cohesion of socialist states, allow us to tackle new tasks set for us by new claims, new developments.

We can reduce the risk of any kind of imperialist intervention, if we can strengthen socialist integration by perfecting the solutions of our nationality problems. It is essential to draw the poison fangs of chauvinistic remnants lingering under the surface among both minorities and majorities. This way we can elevate the Danube Valley into a shining beacon for the brotherhood of peoples.

This is the main task of the resurrected minority studies, now called in their new socialist form: nationality studies. We must find the methods that may open new vistas of further development. Only thus can we make practical reality of the noble pronouncement made in 1971 by Nicolae Ceauşescu, party secretary and leading statesman of the Romanian Socialist Republic (which, on the strength of the numbers and importance of its minorities, is destined to show a supreme example): "Romanians and Hungarians have been living in the same cities, in the same villages, for hundreds of years—they will live together there for thousands of years!"

EDITOR'S NOTE. Hungarian friends, who met Edgár Balogh in the course of his visits to Budapest recently, described him as a disillusioned man, pessimistic of Hungarian-Romanian relations, and of the Hungarian minorities' situation in general. S.B.

✳ 14

Communist Hungary and the Hungarian Minorities

Pierre Kende

Following the Communist takeover, the Hungarians have found themselves in a unique position among the nations of the Soviet bloc. During the Stalinist years, the people of Hungary were not only forbidden to concern themselves with the fate of the Hungarian minorities, they were virtually forbidden even to recognize their existence. This curtailment, in national terms, was somewhat similar to East Germany's position vis-à-vis West Germany. However, in Germany's case, although the nation was split in two, both parts were in national terms "majorities," and only the smaller eastern part was under Stalinist rule.

In Hungary's case, four factors emerged after World War II to create a position uniquely detrimental to national interests: (1) Hungary's military defeat as an ally of Nazi Germany, aggravated by the moral burden of Hungary's complicity in the holocaust of Hungary's Jews following the country's Nazi occupation in March 1944; (2) Hungarians are not Slavs; (3) a residue of the prewar anti-Hungarian so-called "Little Entente" attitude of Hungary's neighbors still existed; and (4) the Soviet Union's interest in the status quo that was established after World War II in Central and Eastern Europe.

Let us look at these four factors one by one.

Hungary emerged from the war on the losers' side. It was also saddled by the victors with the opprobrium of a "guilty nation." This circumstance would probably bestow a status of inferiority on any

country—as exemplified by West Germany—even if it was in possession of its full sovereignty.[1] In comparison with the Germans, in the
case of the Hungarians an additional aggravating factor has been the
total Soviet overlordship. In Hungary, every official statement regarding the country's stance as a nation had to bear the heavy hand
of Soviet censorship already during the transitional phase of the coalition regime between 1945 and 1947.

In the past, a country defeated in war could at least complain about
the aftermath of defeat. There has hardly been any precedent in history of a defeated nation having been deprived of even the *jus mur-
murandi*. The Soviet rulers forbade precisely this right to the
Hungarian people. On the other hand, the Soviet occupying power,
and its stooge, the Hungarian Communist party, had never demanded
a moral self-examination from the defeated people. Communist ideology as such—especially the variant made in Moscow—is concep-
tually incapable of such an exercise. The Soviet occupiers demanded
only a verbal condemnation of the "criminal past," and even this
consisted of rather formalistic repetitions of slogans. Soul-searching
of a true kind could have only been possible in an atmosphere dominated by Christian, or humanistic, ethics. The postwar regimes, however, did everything to ward off such an ethical approach.[2]

The effects of the Hungarians not being of Slavic nationality are
not too difficult to assess. It is true that some of the Slavic countries
themselves suffered territorial losses whenever their geography came
into conflict with the expansionist Soviet power (see, for example, the
annexation of the eastern provinces of Poland and of Carpatho-
Ruthenia from Czechoslovakia). Slavic losses, however, were com-
pensated by Slavic gains: annexations of territories, or expulsion of
populations, or both. All the boundary changes and population expulsions were at the expense of non-Slavic peoples, mainly Germans
and Hungarians, or, on a minor scale, Romanians (in Bessarabia and
Dobrudja).

The Little Entente complex is manifested in Hungary's neighbors'
exaggerated censure of Hungarians. The Czechs and Slovaks maintained that Hungary played a decisive role in the dismemberment of
their republic in 1938–39. The Yugoslavs, with more justification,
have not forgotten that, in 1941, the Hungarians attacked them,
jointly with the Germans, only weeks after the signing of a treaty of

"eternal friendship." The Romanians cultivate the fear that Hungarian troops may one day again march into Transylvania as they did following the Second Vienna Award in 1940.

In the face of such emotional reactions on the part of Hungary's neighbors, it is difficult indeed to probe the situation of Hungarian minorities in Hungary's neighboring countries calmly. A mere expression of interest by Hungarians in the fate of their compatriots in these countries is identified with territorial revisionism of the interwar Horthy era. Conversely, Hungarian suspicion toward the neighboring countries lingers on. Thus, planted in a thicket of emotions, a sort of Little Entente complex exists on both sides.[3]

The Soviet interest in maintaining the territorial status quo is the most decisive of all adverse factors affecting the Hungarians. Also, in this context, the Hungarians are involved in the territorial conflict between Romania and the Soviet Union. For years the Romanian and the Soviet governments have been playing a rather curious and somewhat comical game of doubletalk concerning Transylvania and Bessarabia. Should the Romanians bring up the loss of Bessarabia, the Soviets would allude to the Romanian annexation of Transylvania; should the Soviets hint at "violations of Marxist-Leninist principles of nationality policies" in Transylvania, the Romanians would bring up the case of Bessarabia as the same violation of that sacred Marxist-Leninist principle. Thus, any Hungarian initiative on behalf of the Hungarian minority in Transylvania would be inevitably intertwined with Soviet-Romanian relations.

The tension between the Communist state and the Hungarian people today is only to a small extent affected by realistic considerations of what could be done for the Hungarian minorities. Officially, the Communist party behaves in a passive manner, while the people at large believe that, whatever the circumstances, something could be done and ought to be done.

In order to analyze the development of this dichotomy between party and people, one has to distinguish three main phases in the postwar political scene in Hungary. The first period is that of coalition governments, 1945–47 (or 1948, depending on one's interpretation of when the full control of the Communist party had been established). It was followed by a long period of slavish imitation of Soviet ideology and phraseology. This second period started under Mátyás Rákosi and, apart from the short break culminating in the revolution of 1956, it continued under the Kádár regime into the early 1960s. The current third period of ideological "loosening-up" and the post-revolutionary consolidation of the Kádár regime, began in the mid-sixties. But, as far as the reassertion of national interests goes, a real "opening" can be dated only from the seventies.

The coalition period sharply differed from the other two, insofar as Soviet-oriented official internationalism was not yet government policy. Therefore, certain national claims and grievances were freely voiced on the stage of higher politics. Politicians belonging mainly to the Independent Smallholders Party—but others also—were spokesmen of national causes. In that period even the Communist party, no matter for what kind of tactical reasons, had occasionally showed interest in certain questions of Hungarian national concern.

The center of national concern in this phase was the position the Hungarian government should take at the Paris Peace Conference. Also, an issue of great urgency was the threat of expulsion of Hungarians from Czechoslovakia. Public opinion viewed the peace negotiations with the most profound pessimism. Branded as "Hitler's last satellite," Hungary could hardly propound all the claims she would have liked to. Even the most justified territorial claims had to be tempered. The restitution of the pre-Munich 1938 frontiers had been settled for the most part in the armistice protocols and at the Potsdam Conference, thereby the Hungarians could only hope to be able to make a few modest propositions at the Peace Conference in 1946.

It had to be taken for granted that the new Soviet-Hungarian frontier would be sacrosanct. Also, any rectification of the frontier with Tito's Yugoslavia was out of the question. The Hungarian-Czechoslovak frontier may have looked less inviolable in view of Slovakia's pro-Nazi record, but President Beneš and Czech Communist party chief, Klement Gottwald, had done their best (or worst) before the Peace Conference to ensure that any territorial modifications would only be to Hungary's detriment. All that was still left open was the boundary issue with Romania concerning northern Transylvania. In fact, this was the only issue in which the Hungarians could hope for some success. After all, Romania was Hungary's only rival who had stolen a march only by a short head, by switching sides from Hitler to the victorious Grand Alliance.[4]

The non-Communist elements in the coalition government—above all, the Smallholders, supported by the pro-Allied wing in the wartime foreign service—urged determined action in the Romanian matter.[5] The Communists were reserved, probably due to a lack of clear instructions from Moscow. At the Peace Conference, however, it turned out that the Soviet Union rigidly refused even the smallest change of the prewar frontiers that might have been justifiable on the basis of a contiguous Hungarian population spilling over from Hungary into Romania.

Sensing, even before the Peace Conference, an unfavorable decision, the Hungarian Communists adopted a rather skillful rhetorical stance. Hungary, they said, could expect favorable or unfavorable treatment, depending on the country's internal development in the "right" or "wrong" direction.[6] So, the unfavorable outcome, they said after the Peace Conference, was the result of "reactionary forces," hinting at the Smallholders Party, the primary target of their strategy to wreck the coalition government.

In the matter of the expulsion of Hungarians from Czechoslovakia, the Communists were occasionally active. They probably were so because the initiative for expulsion originated in Prague rather than in Moscow. In any case, this was the only occasion when the Hungarian Communist party gave postwar support to an issue which has stirred up national indignation.[7] Also, this was the only issue involving the Hungarian minorities which was reported fully by the Hungarian media. Only occasional rumors circulated about the massacres of Hungarians by Romanians in reoccupied northern Transylvania, or about the vengeance wrought upon the Hungarian population in the Vojvodina by Tito's partisans. Even today, the Hungarian public is largely ignorant about these dreadful events.

During that baleful first postwar period, all the elements leading to popular frustration on account of national humiliation were already at hand: the sufferings of the occupation, the embargo on uttering justifiable national grievances, the barriers to expressing national sentiments, the settlement of frontiers by dictates, and an almost complete severance of all contacts between Hungary and the Hungarian minorities in the neighboring countries.

While the Communist party was not yet in total control, it did at least show some sensitivity toward the "new Trianon" inflicted on the

Hungarian people. Once the party consolidated its power on the Soviet model, it lost interest in popular national causes altogether. After 1948, the country was forced to take actions in the anti-Western Soviet "peace" campaign, in the condemnation of Tito's "treason." In general, the Soviet model has prevailed in Hungary as in the other countries of the Soviet bloc. The only hope in that Communist era of so-called "new patriotism" was the promise that, once the socialist transformation was completed, the problems of the national minorities in the Danube region would be automatically solved under the sign of socialist equality and Communist fraternity. No details had been spelled out as to how this happy outcome would be achieved.

The Communist policy of "new patriotism" aimed at inculcating the Hungarians with Soviet-centered loyalty to replace Hungarian national consciousness. In the spirit of Soviet ideology, this was considered socialist patriotism in the service of "proletarian internationalism." The essence of this "internationalism" was unconditional loyalty to Moscow, constant glorification of Soviet policies, endless quotations from the catechisms of Lenin and Stalin concerning past, present, and future, and, last but not least, forcible Russification, which included rewriting Hungary's history: even the intervention by Emperor Nicholas I as Austria's ally against the Hungarian revolution of 1848/49 was sugar-coated by the contention that the tsarist officer corps actually sympathized with the Hungarian cause and secretly helped the Hungarians.[8]

The "patriotism" of the Communist party in Hungary had nothing to do with the real interests of the nation. In this respect, the Hungarian Communist leadership had certainly been unique in postwar Eastern Europe. Only the East German leadership was similarly engaged in extinguishing national feelings of its own people. But, unlike in Hungary, that did not affect the nation as a whole.

Among Hungary's Communist leaders of that time the only exception was Imre Nagy—not only as the prime minister of the 1956 revolution but also as the head of the government between 1953 and 1955. His government program of 1953, as well as his personal style (he was of Hungarian peasant origin), created a link with the true feelings of the Hungarian people. He let the people know that he too realized the crippling effects of Stalinism, not only in the material sphere but also in the spiritual self-esteem of the nation. It came as no surprise that in 1956 the people in revolt against the hated regime followed Nagy as their leader. Although he too, on account of his years in exile in the Soviet Union, was a so-called "Muscovite" Communist, Imre Nagy was regarded by the people as a fellow Hungarian.

By 1948, the Stalinist regime, headed by Mátyás Rákosi, established total Communist control in Hungary. This regime was opposed to anything that had to do with the sentiments of the nation. The struggle for personal survival throttled discussions of the fate of the nation even inside the harrassed and frightened families. Contact with relatives or friends beyond the frontiers was completely cut off during the period. National dismemberment became complete. The fate of Hungarians in Transylvania, Slovakia, Yugoslavia, and in the Soviet Ukraine was not known. The Hungarian fatherland had neither personal nor cultural contacts with the Hungarian minorities. The socialism of Lenin and Stalin, far from abolishing frontiers between nations, created, in fact, unscaleable barriers. A whole generation of Hungarians grew up on both sides of Hungary's borders in complete igorance of one another.

Only after Stalin's death, with the Soviet-Yugoslav thaw and Khrushchev's de-Stalinization, did this hermetic isolation begin to loosen up among the Soviet satellites. And, of course, the 1956 Revolution in Hungary has been another powerful factor in restoring the sense of unity among Hungarians deprived of national sovereignty.

One of the first demands of the revolutionary youths was the restitution of national sovereignty. The revolution was a collective experience of the whole society, with the insignificant exception of those few who remained loyal to the Soviet Union, including members of the political police. The Hungarian Revolution of 1956 was a *national* uprising. The people found their own selves again, regaining, for however short a time, freedom of speech and action. The revolutionary government of Imre Nagy expressed the will of the people. For a few days, even János Kádár supported the revolution in his capacity as spokesman of a reorganized Communist party, which collaborated with the non-Communist parties in a coalition government.[9]

The brief and tragic episode of the 1956 Revolution allowed no time for the formation of all aspects of national aspirations. It was the frightened fantasy of neighboring Communist states to accuse the Hungarian revolution of reviving demands for frontier revisions. It is, of course, very likely that a sovereign Hungary, putting into practice the principles of 1956, would have handled the grievances of the Hungarian minorities differently from the Stalinist regime, or, for that matter, the subsequent Kádár regime. In fact, the Hungarian minorities were watching Hungary's struggle in 1956 with bated breath and hoping against hope for a change in the fatherland's behavior toward them.

The first decade of the Kádár regime showed no change in Communist behavior. The governing party, reconstructed for the single purpose of serving the restoration of Soviet power, fully adopted the spirit of the prerevolutionary Rákosi regime. If there was any difference between the two, it consisted in the Kádár regime taking even more absurd positions on issues of popular concern. The Kádár regime branded the 1956 Revolution as a "fascist counterrevolution"— a sure way to alienate itself from the nation. The artificially recreated Communist party actually prided itself on having issued the invitation to the Soviet armed forces. They had the gall to call their suppression of the revolution a "second liberation"—showing total contempt for public opinion both inside and outside of Hungary.

The Soviet invasion and its consequences caused a national bloodletting of huge dimensions.[10] Crushed in mind and body, the nation was paralyzed. The 1960s and 1970s, however, brought a radical change. It is no exaggeration to say that, particularly toward the last years of the seventies, Hungarian national consciousness erupted anew with an unforeseen force and liveliness. Following a gap of thirty years, the national will to life reasserted itself in a resumed continuity with the nation's past. Inevitably, fundamental questions affecting the state and the nation were raised once more. Not unlike in 1956, the great changes originated from below, from society itself, not from the regime. Nevertheless, there were a few supporting factors for which the regime should be given credit. With the Kádár regime's so-called consolidation, came subtle changes in the methods of exercising Communist party power.

To characterize the new situation, several factors seem to be of equal importance: the rise of a new generation, freed of the paralyzing burdens of the past; the opening of the frontiers, both toward neighboring countries and the West for individual travel as well as government-sponsored cultural exchanges; the loosening of the zeal of constant mass mobilization and of wholesale ideological compulsion by Communist party and state—in sum, a more objective and more professional governance. As a result, the paralyzing atmosphere of constant fear and uncertainty about life in general has greatly diminished throughout the society.[11]

In official foreign policy, however, hardly anything has changed with regard to world politics or in relations with Hungary's neighbors. The Hungarian government was sticking closely to the Soviet line, without any deviation. The most flagrant case of this subservience was the Hungarian participation in the invasion of Czechoslovakia in 1968. Toward Hungary's other neighbors, too, the behavior of the Communist state and party closely mirrors the relations with the Soviet Union. There has not been a single instance in which the state has demonstrated any kind of independence from the Soviet Union.

This may not mean that the Kádár regime is completely indifferent to the fate of Hungarian minorities in the neighboring states. For example, the Hungarian government has been doing its level best to satisfy the cultural requirements of Hungary's own very small Romanian, Slovak, and German minorities, evidently in support of its moral claim for reciprocation.[12] And, behind the scenes, the Communist rulers of Hungary allegedly do try to communicate their interest in minority matters, particularly to their Romanian and Czechoslovak comrades. However, Kádár's meeting in 1977 with Romania's Nicolae Ceaușescu had no effect on Romanian policy.

Since the seventies, official Hungarian attitudes have noticeably changed regarding public opinion, due, it is believed, to the influence of certain members of the party leadership. Beyond the official silence one can detect a certain tolerance for protesting voices coming from broad ranges of public opinion. In any case since the mid-seventies, there has been no serious massive harassment of those who have raised their voices on behalf of the Hungarian minorities. A few literary and historical essays on the subject have, in fact, been published although in periodicals rather than in the daily newspapers. And a somewhat subdued press campaign took place, presumably with official blessings, on two occasions: in 1981, against the forcible Slovakization of Hungarian historical family names, part of the Slovak effort to erase Hungarian history from the land which is today Slovakia;[13] and, in 1982, against a scurrilous Hungarian-hating book by Ion Lăncrănjan, published in Bucharest on Transylvania's past and present.[14]

As if to counterbalance these concessions to popular frustration, in 1983 the old Communist slogan of "struggle against bourgeois nationalism" reappeared in the Hungarian party program.[15] But, as a newspaperman from Budapest has privately explained the official attitude to Hungarian minority issues: "The principal newspapers are instructed to keep their mouths shut. . . . [On the other hand,] editors of not too important publications do not get any specific directives; matters are left to their survival instinct. . . . The press has no right to strike an attitude that is incompatible with the policies of the state. . . . Yet, only the country's trustworthiness in the Soviet bloc is of overriding importance: its loyalty to the Soviet alliance."[16] In other words, the Little Entente syndrome surrounding Hungary still prevails. However, officially, proletarian internationalism rules.

The pressure of public opinion is an entirely new phenomenon in Communist Hungary. In contrast to the past, it does affect, willy-nilly, the actions of the regime, at least to the extent that officials can no longer sweep issues under the rug. It demonstrates the bankruptcy of official internationalism, the failure of efforts of four decades aimed at purging Hungarian society of patriotic interest in problems affecting the existence of the Hungarian state and the Hungarian people.

Many people believe that the present patriotic-nationalist ferment is largely due to actions by writers and poets, and above all to the efforts of the late Gyula Illyés, for years the "grand old man" of Hungarian letters. Illyés's role in awakening the national consciousness has been, no doubt, of paramount importance. In 1977, he issued a clarion call in a newspaper article on the persecution of Hungarians in Transylvania.[17] Characteristically, the article did not mention by name either Transylvania or Romania. But everybody knew, both at home and abroad, what he was talking about.

The Illyés article made a profound impression on the Hungarian public. Also, it triggered angry Romanian attacks against Illyés personally and the Hungarians generally.[18] Until his death in April 1983, Illyés spoke up on every possible occasion about the burning issues of Hungarian minorities in both Transylvania and Slovakia. Since his freedom of speech at home was limited, he used the freedom of the West, both in Europe and America, to raise his voice against oppression.[19] With his defiant stand, Gyula Illyés became the unchallenged spokesman of the true spirit of the Hungarian people. However, it would be oversimplification to attribute the sea-change in public opinion to one person alone. Since the seventies, other factors, too, have contributed to the rise of a new national spirit. Among them, the most decisive has been, for the younger generations especially, the liberalization of foreign travel.

The years since the late sixties have been a veritable age of discovery. First, hundreds of thousands, then millions of Hungarians became acquainted with the forbidden world around them. Particularly significant has been the resumption of links with Hungarians in the neighboring states. An age of discovery usually begets legends. According to one of them, there were Hungarians of the younger generation who did not realize that the Székelys (Szeklers) of Transylvania were Hungarians. True or not, up to the sixties hardly anybody in Hungary could learn anything about the conditions of the Székelys, or indeed of any other Hungarian population across the borders. With the exception of a handful of stray visitors, or a few families living along the borders, the Hungarians of Hungary were kept in complete ignorance about the life of Hungarians in Transylvania, in Slovakia, or in Yugoslavia. Mass tourism since the late sixties radically changed the situation. There is hardly any family in Hungary without relatives or acquaintances living beyond the present state boundaries. Upsetting accounts of the fate of Hungarian minorities have quickly spread in the wake of personal experiences of Hungarians traveling in the neighboring countries—with the exception of the Soviet Carpatho-Ukraine which remains closed to Hungarian tourism.

The articulation of the "discovery" of the Hungarian minorities has been the work of men of letters. Ethnologists and folklorists, in particular, have been active during the course of this explosion of national interest. A whole generation of young Hungarians has made pilgrimages, especially to Transylvania, in search of roots and traditions. An interesting element in this movement of "discoveries" has been the fact that, as a result of industrialization and the modernization of agriculture, traditional village life has almost completely disappeared in Hungary proper, while many villages in the Székely land of Transylvania still offer a picture of the Hungarian village of the past.

This cultural immersion in the Hungarian past has merged with the campaign for the defense of Hungarian minorities. An additional factor buttressing the trend has been the constantly worsening situation of the Hungarian minority. Also, no less important, has been the simultaneous appearance of a loosely organized democratic opposition in Hungary and the greater opportunities for publicity. The Hungarian diaspora in the West, too, has played a part in this fermentation at home. It has been an encouraging development since the seventies that Hungarians at home have been able to maintain a lively contact with Hungarian intellectual circles and literary groups in the West.

The distress signals of the Hungarian minorities, mainly from Romania and Slovakia, have been taken up by two oppositional groups in Hungary. One is the group of writers who are following in the footsteps of the erstwhile populist movement of the thirties, whose outstanding spokesman is the writer Sándor Csoóri.[20] The other one is the democratic reformist opposition with its prolific samizdat publications. The cause of the Hungarian minorities unites the two groups in a loose coalition. Their ranks have been reinforced mainly by historians. A number of young philosophers who have emigrated from Transylvania have also made their influence felt. The pacifist character of these movements must be strongly stressed. There are no Hungarian secret societies or terrorist groups, Armenian or Palestinian style, although much anger has been building up in Hungarian society on account of the fate of their compatriots across the borders.

The reawakening of the Hungarian national conscience is by no means concentrated solely on the issue of the minorities. A further, and no less significant, characteristic of this movement has been the liberation of historiography from the grips of ideology. Poland and Hungary are unique in this respect among the countries of the Soviet bloc. In Hungary, the historians, with few exceptions, have en bloc turned their backs on the role in which the propaganda machine of the party had previously cast them. They have resumed the scholarly task of detached investigation of facts. The public, in turn, has expressed its craving for the truth.

The history of World War II, memoirs and a host of other types of reminiscences, as well as works about the Austro-Hungarian Monarchy have become the popular vogue of the reading public. The new generation, in particular, wants to know what really happened to their country. They demand to know the facts—and their causes—deliberately denied to them by Marxist pseudo-history. The demand is the greater since in school textbooks Marxist pseudo-history is still the rule.

The confluence of truth in historiography and of public interest in uncensored truth in general is the most significant aspect of the re-awakened national consciousness. The movement is a peaceful one, but not without tension. It is marked by clashes with officialdom and censorship. Many stormy scenes have occurred at various meetings with young intellectuals, supported by the public, demanding accurate information and the truth about the nation's past and present. There has been improvement in the regime's attitude, but the thirst for public information is still largely being satisfied by nongovernmental sources: in private conversations, in "free universities" organized by opposition groups, and by books and periodicals brought in from the West.

The younger generations maintain a healthy attitude of disbelief and suspicion toward anything official. One speaker, at a particularly passionate encounter, burst out: "Since 1948 a deliberate policy of ruthless destruction has been carried out in order to eliminate our sense of history."[21] This "ruthless destruction" was mainly the work of official historiography. Up until the Revolution of 1956, it followed Soviet-style Marxism. In the decade following the Soviet suppression of the revolution, official historiography adopted a kind of apolitical economist trend. This may have been a shade better in terms of a more scientific approach, but it still lacked any relevance to national problems. However, in the seventies, this apolitical economist trend in historiography opened the road toward more courageous expressions of truth in general.[22]

It would be a mistake to be overoptimistic about the present situation. The straitjacket on Hungary's foreign policy and the arbitrary self-legitimation of Communist party rule has maintained barriers against the wave of popular frustration. Only a few safety valves are being kept open to lessen the pressure of dissatisfaction. Yet, for the government to yield at all to the pressure of public opinion is certainly a new phenomenon.

One of the main weaknesses of the Kádár regime is its failure to offer any kind of tangible results in support of the Hungarian minorities. The old rhetoric about the "bridge role" and the "socialist solution" has become threadbare and obsolete. Nobody believes in a genuine friendship with the neighboring Communist countries. The party leadership is fully aware of that. They do not believe in it, either. But they seem to be powerless to improve Hungary's position in the Soviet bloc. More recently, some "openness" (to use Mikhail Gorbachev's slogan) has been noticeable in matters pertaining to the problems of Hungarian minorities. (See Annex V below.) A new official attitude may be in the making. If so, it remains to be seen whether it is capable of achieving tangible results.

Notes

1. See on this subject, Pierre Kende, "Reflections on Hungarian History," *The Review* (1959).
2. In the context of the tragedy of Jewry, this problem has been dealt with by István Bibó. His essay on the subject will shortly appear in English translation.
3. In 1982, a mild critical remark by Gyula Illyés, pointing at the cultural difficulties the Hungarians are having in the Vojvodina, stirred up a protest even in relatively tolerant Yugoslavia with charges of Horthy-era "revisionism" levied against Illyés. See Annex II in Chapter 9, above.
4. Cf. Chapter 4, above, for details on the Paris Peace Conference of 1946.
5. V. J. Lahav, "Szovjet politika Erdélyben, 1940–1946," *Irodalmi Újság* (January–February 1979).
6. Ibid.
7. Cf. Sándor Balogh, *A népi demokratikus Magyarország külpolitikája, 1945–1947* (Budapest, 1982), 127–28.
8. A street was named in Budapest after the tsarist Russian officer Gussev who was alleged to have conspired with the Hungarians in 1849 and to have been executed for his activities. Later on it transpired that Gussev was the fictional creation of a Hungarian writer, a Communist exile in Moscow before 1945.
9. See, in particular, Kádár's speech on the Hungarian people's "glorious uprising," November 1, 1956, in Melvin J. Lasky, ed. *The Hungarian Revolution: A White Book* (London, 1957), 179–80.
10. By the end of 1956, about 2 percent of the country's total population fled abroad. About one-fourth eventually returned when conditions improved, but tens of thousands were, in the meantime, imprisoned, and the exact number of those executed has never been established.

11. Cf. Pierre Kende, *Qu'est-ce que le "Kadarisme"?* (Paris, 1983).

12. See György Aczél, "National Minority Rights: The Law of Socialism," *The New Hungarian Quarterly* 25/95 (Autumn 1984): 6–10.

13. Péter Hanák, "Címeres furcsaságok," *Élet és Irodalom* February 21, 1981.

14. "Situation Report on Romania," *Radio Free Europe Research,* vol. 8, no. 1 (Munich, 1982), 25–26.

15. Public report on the meeting of the Central Committee of the Hungarian Socialist Workers' Party, April 12–14, 1983.

16. Quoted from a private letter received from a journalist friend in Budapest.

17. Gyula Illyés, "Válasz Herdernek és Adynak," *Magyar Nemzet,* December 25, 1977, and January 1, 1978.

18. Illyés was attacked by the President of the Romanian Academy of Political Science in a Bucharest newspaper. Illyés's reply, in spite of its very moderate language, was suppressed by the Hungarian regime. Its text was published in *Magyar Füzetek,* no. 5 (1979).

19. Illyés wrote an introduction to a book by Kálmán Janics, published abroad, on the postwar persecution of Hungarians in Czechoslovakia between 1945 and 1948 (Munich, 1979; English version, New York, 1982).

20. Many publications containing Csoóri's articles were confiscated. He clashed with officialdom on account of his introduction to Miklós Duray's autobiography on growing up as a Hungarian in postwar Czechoslovakia, published in New York in 1983. See "The Duray Affair" in Annex I of Chapter 8, above.

21. *Forrás,* no. 9 (1979). The complete material of the conference at Lakitelek appeared in the same issue of the magazine published in Kecskemét.

22. On the trends of Hungarian historiography after 1956, see András Kovács, "Két kiegyezés," *Magyar Füzetek,* no. 12 (1983). Cf. Istvan Deak, "Introduction," Chapter 15, below.

Annex I
"Revisionism" and "Fascist Propaganda"*

EDITOR'S NOTE. After World War I, the principal aim of Hungary's foreign policy under the Horthy regime was the revision of the Treaty of Trianon. After World War II, on the demand of Czechoslovakia,

*The texts of the amendment and argument are quoted from *Foreign Relations of the United States, 1946* (Washington, D.C., 1969) 4:727.

the Treaty of Paris banned "revisionism," equating it with "fascist propaganda."

The Czechoslovak amendment, added to Article 4 of the Peace Treaty, and the Czechoslovak argument supporting this amendment, reads as follows:

Hungary also binds herself to dissolve all organizations existing on her territory whose aim is to disseminate revisionism openly or secretly, and to prohibit in future the existence and activity of such organizations as aim at spreading revisionism or exciting a hostile attitude to Czechoslovakia among Hungarians.

Czechoslovakia also considers it necessary to forbid not only hostile propaganda by Hungary but every other activity tending to threaten the security of other states. It is equally essential to prohibit not only fascist propaganda but also its correlative "revisionism," which would continue to be aimed against and to threaten Czechoslovakia.

Annex II
"Bridge Role" and "Socialist Solution"

EDITOR'S NOTE. Under the Kádár regime Hungary's policy vis-à-vis her neighbors with Hungarian populations has emphasized "bridge role" and "socialist solution." These twin principles were spelled out most memorably in the course of an interview Kádár gave to Harry Schleicher of the *Frankfurter Rundschau* in 1977 on the eve of his official visit to Bonn. The interview was published in the June 30, 1977, issue of the West-German paper, as well as in the July 3, 1977, issue of the Hungarian Communist party paper *Népszabadság* in Budapest. The English translation that follows is based on the Hungarian version.

Schleicher: In the course of their history, the Hungarian people have lost the possibility of national integration in a unitary state. One consequence of this is the existence of Hungarian minorities in all neighboring states. Do you think that people may simply lose their right to a national state? Will the Hungarian people resign themselves to this state of affairs? What is the situation of Hungarian minorities? What can Hungary do to improve their situation?

Kádár: It is an accident of history—not only in Europe but in many other parts of the world too—that minority groups are living beyond the frontiers of their nation-state. This gives rise to problems everywhere. These problems require the close attention of the countries concerned and bestow great responsibility on their governments.

In the twentieth century one cannot solve minority problems by the methods of the nineteenth century. The only possible way ahead in Europe is by increasing cooperation between peoples. Only socialism will be capable of finally solving the nationality question by ensuring unfettered development of the society as a whole—including the national minorities.

In Europe today, we can only reach a solution to the problems of nationalities and of minorities by making use of the lessons of history, not by harping on a "glorious past." The ruling classes of the past, by their policies of chauvinism, hatred toward minorities, and revanchism caused untold damage to the Hungarian nation, almost imperilling its existence.

Our government follows a radically different line. Our efforts are directed at attaining our people's aims—national in content, but in the framework of socialism. Of course, we want to ensure that our own [ethnic] minorities [in Hungary] can enjoy equal opportunities to flourish. It is our desire that national minorities—in Hungary as well as in the neighboring countries—should create a *bridge* between countries and peoples.

It is well known that large numbers of Hungarians live not only in our neighboring countries but in other European countries too—indeed, all over the world. It is the official policy of the Hungarian People's Republic to take it for granted that Hungarian minorities should fully integrate themselves in the life of their states. At the same time, we also take it for granted that they should be free to express their love and attachment to the mother country, the ancestral homeland—always within the limits of loyalty and permissibility. This is the purpose of countless agreements with many other states in order to facilitate travel and cultural contacts and to foster common folk traditions.

The signatories of the Helsinki Final Act were unanimously agreed on the inviolability of present-day frontiers. This alone can ensure peace and security in the world. In the course of this historic conference we too have expressed our conviction that this principle is the common interest of the thirty-five participants, being a pledge for peaceful coexistence.

Annex III
Hungary at the Madrid Conference

EDITOR'S NOTE. The Madrid follow-up conference, reviewing adherence to the provisions of the Helsinki Final Act, dragged on for almost three years (1980–83). Paragraph 11 of its Concluding Document reaffirmed the rights of national minorities. The Hungarian Minister of Foreign Affairs, Péter Várkonyi, addressing the closing session on September 8, 1983, praised the achievements of the conference consonant with the peace policy of the Soviet bloc but kept silent about Paragraph 11 (below). Nor did the Hungarian delegation take public notice during the conference of the memoranda submitted on behalf of the Hungarian minorities in Romania and Czechoslovakia (for the text of some of these memoranda, see the annexes in Chapters 7 and 8, above).

---

11. [The Participating States] stress also the importance of constant progress in ensuring the respect for and actual enjoyment of the rights of persons belonging to national minorities as well as protecting their legitimate interests as provided for in the [Helsinki] Final Act.

Annex IV
Voice of the Hungarian Democratic Opposition

EDITOR'S NOTE. Several groups of the illegal Hungarian democratic opposition issued a joint statement in Budapest on March 12, 1984. They expressed their solidarity with a Polish-Czechoslovak joint declaration of KOR [Committee in Defense of Labor in Poland], Solidarity, and Charter 77, dated February 12, 1984, demanding release of political prisoners and democratization of the countries of Eastern Europe, as well as the right of these countries to independence and freedom. In addition to joining these demands of other East European nations in the Soviet orbit of power, the Hungarian democratic opposition's statement called attention to "what is the most burning concern of all Hungarians: the suppression of the rights of national minorities in Eastern Europe." Their statement on this particular issue reads as follows:*

Our Czechoslovak friends certainly know of the discriminations inflicted in their own country upon the oppressed Hungarian minority. What is happening to the Transylvanian Hungarians is also common knowledge. We not only demand an end to these discriminations, but we support the right of the Hungarian minorities to cultural autonomy. We subscribe to their right and ability to administer their specific affairs under their own future institutions, which are to be democratically established. We appeal to all East European believers in justice and fairness to stand up against nationalism, against the instruments of forcible assimilation through policies in the field of education, population settlement, and regional economic development. Only by eliminating these practices can the friendship between our peoples become truly sincere. This friendship is our desire, no less than the long-awaited freedom of our countries and peace without humiliation.

The Hungarian democratic opposition also issued an appeal to the European Cultural Forum (one of the so-called Helsinki follow-up conferences) meeting in Budapest in the fall of 1985. Covering a broad range of subjects related to both cultural and political freedoms in Communist Hungary, the appeal called attention to the plight of the Hungarian minorities. It suggested that, if all other means of help to the Hungarians in the neighboring countries would fail, the Hungarian government should seek redress of the Hungarian grievances by "turning to international forums."**

*For the full text of the Hungarian statement, see *Irodalmi Újság* 35/2 (1984).
**For the full text of the appeal, see *Irodalmi Újság* 37:1 (1986).

Dated 15 October 1985, the appeal was signed by the following representatives of the democratic opposition: Péter Bokros, Gábor Demszky, Zoltán Endreffy, György Gadó, Béla Gondos, Miklós Haraszti, András Kardos, János Kenedi, János Kis, György Konrád, György Krassó, Tamás Molnár, András Nagy, Jenő Nagy, Tibor Pákh, György Petri, Sándor Radnóti, László Rajk, Ottilia Solt, Pál Szalai, Miklós Gáspár Tamás, Mihály Vajda.

Annex V
"Nationality Democracy" vs. "Majority Nationalism" A New Course?

EDITOR'S NOTE. Hungary's Communist Party regime is beginning to acknowledge publicly the existence of the Hungarian minority problem. In addition to domestic publicity, the problem occasionally is given international publicity as well. For instance, the official English language periodical, *The New Hungarian Quarterly,* has recently dealt, gingerly though quite openly, with the problem of Hungarian minorities in the neighboring countries.

Mátyás Szűrös, the Party's Central Committee secretary in charge of foreign relations, discussed "the role played by national minorities in détente." He called for recognizing "the dual loyalty of national minorities to do good in the interests of better understanding among the nations." He was critical of "curtailment of the collective political and cultural rights of national minorities" and of "any limitation of direct communication with the mother country."[1]

In the same issue of *The New Hungarian Quarterly,* Rudolf Joó, a research fellow at the recently established Institute for Hungarian Studies, published a comprehensive outline on "national minority policies." The following excerpts cover some of the principal ideas of his article.[2]

The state should not only recognize the fact of ethnic variety, it should also establish the most favourable conditions for the survival and development of minorities. This includes such collective rights as an educational system in the native tongue, a bilingual or multi-lingual public administration, the establishment of government institutions dealing with the nationality problem and the establishment of autonomous regions.

The socialist construction of government that developed from the second half of the forties in Central and South-Eastern Europe produced numerous original, and indeed pioneering, institutions of equality of nationalities, which differed in extent and form from country to country, occasionally even from nationality to nationality. . . . However, that era was one in which the process of establishing the general institutions of nationality democracy coincided with a growing domination of the anti-democratic exercise of power. . . . It is not surprising, therefore, that in the political situation that had developed, some of the measures directed at ethnic equality remained on the statutes, being simply unredeemed promises and never the social reality.

The current changes in science and technology, such as the electronic revolution now taking place (including the spread of computers, video programmes, cable television, and satellite broadcast) establish theoretical opportunities for group survival and community organization in addition to chances of the complete assimilation of minorities and thus their concomitant disintegration. . . . Predictably, . . . a uniform general condition to all, will continue to democratically provide modern means for developing these minorities' national identity. Similarly, the type of political structure that is permeated by majority nationalism is likely to continue to reduce those possibilities.

In a similar vein, the problem of national minorities has been brought up by Hungary's delegate at the third Helsinki review conference which began its deliberations in Vienna in November 1986. Without naming any one of the neighboring countries, László Demus, a high-ranking official of the Hungarian Foreign Ministry, expressed Hungary's concern for "the fate of Hungarians living beyond our boundaries." He condemned "any form of nationalism," but in particular "one of its worst forms: forcible assimilation."

Meanwhile, the head of the Hungarian delegation, Ambassador André Erdős, announced that Hungary is joining two proposals initiated by Yugoslavia and Canada, respectively, advocating more effective protection of the rights of national minorities. It is worth mentioning that Hungary was the only Soviet-bloc country to cosponsor such a proposal, endorsed by the United States.

In March 1987, Mátyás Szűrös, emerging as the principal Hungarian governmental spokesman for national minority rights, spoke of Hungary's deep interest in international minority protection at a meeting in New York of the Institute for East-West Security Studies. Hungary, he said, regards safeguarding of "unhampered contacts" between national minorities and their mother country as a "fundamental human right."

Departing from the practice of dealing with the delicate minority issues in general terms, a formal Hungarian Government statement, April 2, 1987, accused President Ceauşescu's Romanian Government of actions that "caused disturbance in the cooperation between the two neighboring Socialist countries and damaged the fundamental interests of both the Hungarian and Romanian peoples." The unusual public altercation on a government level between the two countries was provoked by Romanian condemnation of a 3-volume scholarly work on the history of Transylvania published by the Hungarians.

Notes

1. Mátyás Szűrös, "Hungary and Détente in Europe," *The New Hungarian Quarterly,* vol. 27, no. 103 (1986): 13–14.
2. Rudolf Joó, "Approaches to National Minority Policy," ibid., 40–46 passim. For a full text of the Hungarian official interventions at the Helsinki follow-up conference at Vienna in behalf of the national minorities, see *The New Hungarian Quarterly,* no. 106 (1987), 125–30.

✳ 15

The Past as an Obstacle to Danubian Reconciliation: Introduction

Istvan Deak

Central and Eastern European nationalism first arose in the late eighteenth century under the multiple impact of the Enlightenment, early Romanticism, and the Jacobin revolution. As a result of these influences, national elites in the region began discarding Latin and German as the languages of official and scholarly communication, replacing these cosmopolitan languages with reformed versions of the local vernacular. At the same time, the long process of social, administrative, economic, and political modernization was begun.

In the Carpathian Basin, the dominant Hungarian nobility gradually transformed itself from a feudal corporation into a national elite; it also began to Magyarize Hungary's cities, long inhabited by non-Hungarian elements, mostly Germans. At the same time, the peasants were co-opted, at least in theory, into the body of the nation as full-fledged citizens. Membership into the "natio Hungarica" had once meant simple identification, irrespective of one's mother tongue, with the group interests of the country's ruling elite. Now membership in the Hungarian nation required ready identification with the political, cultural, and linguistic goals of the Hungarian national leadership.

By the 1840s, Hungarian had become the official language of Hungary (if not yet in the Habsburg-administered Transylvania), whereas the languages of the other nationalities—spoken at that time still by more than half of the country's population—were treated as tolerated local dialects. Thus, such modern Marxist-Leninist states as Romania and Czechoslovakia, or rather Slovakia, are merely reviving the practice of nineteenth-century liberal nationalism when they claim that all of the inhabitants of their country are Romanians or Slovaks, respectively, even though some of these "Romanians" and "Slovaks" speak a different language. It was also not today's Slovak and Romanian Communist historians who started the practice of calling nearly every important figure in their countries' pasts a "Slovak" or a "Romanian," irrespective of his or her self-identification and mother tongue.

The early nineteenth-century Hungarian national revival proved to be contagious in the Danube region, and by 1848 Hungarian nationalism was confronted with the awakened vigorous nationalism of the Serbs, Croats, Romanians, and Slovaks. In this respect, the Revolution of 1848 was a genuine watershed. Before that year liberal nationalists confidently expected the simultaneous triumph and harmonious cooperation of all national movements. The revolution taught them otherwise. It became clear that ethnic boundaries and national goals were hopelessly intermingled in the region, and simultaneous outbursts of lofty patriotic idealism could not but lead to bloodshed.

Peace in Central Europe was restored by the non-national Habsburg army, whose German, Slavic, Romanian, and even Hungarian soldiers understood, however obscurely, that a supranationalistic idea had to override—or at least supplement—national considerations if the peoples of the Danube region were to live and prosper. That idea was embodied in the Habsburg emperor-king, as well as the *Pax Austriaca*.

The Austrian peace could not last forever. Conflicting national claims had gravely weakened the Monarchy's political structure well before its demise. In fact, after the Compromise of 1867, only the Austrian half of the Monarchy was a true multinational empire; the Hungarian half had (with the exception of Croatia-Slavonia) become a typical European nation-state, with one dominant nationality claiming to embody the nation and to have the right to determine the policies of the state.

World War I brought a complete reversal in the political fortunes of the nations in the Danube region and with it, a diligent rewriting of history. The same elementary student in Transylvania, who in 1918 had been told that the Hungarians were a race of heroes and the Romanians a race of cunning cowards, was taught precisely the opposite in 1919. The interwar period and World War II saw a fatal exacerbation of nationalist radicalism and aggressiveness, ending with the extermination or expulsion of the two great *Kulturvölker* of Eastern Europe, the Germans and the Jews, and the decimation of several other ethnic groups. Small wonder that communism in Eastern Europe was greeted with relief even by some among those who otherwise did not sympathize with Communist ideas. Now, it seemed, universal reconciliation would become possible under the aegis of a new, more humane ideology.

The conditions were indeed favorable. All of Eastern Europe was in ruins; the old ruling classes had been badly discredited, and communism seemed to offer the prospect of true equality not only among social classes but also among impoverished nations. Yet it soon became clear that some nations were definitely more equal than others. By the end of the war, Czechoslovakia, Yugoslavia and Romania managed to join the ranks of the victors, the Yugoslavs with some justification, but the others more through diplomacy and obfuscation of their largely collaborationist wartime behavior. The Hungarians, on the other hand, came out of the war as absolute losers.

With the Communist takeover of Eastern Europe between 1945 and 1948 came the need to rethink the past for yet another time. During the Stalin years, the Hungarians did this rethinking most energetically, engaging in an orgy of self-accusation without parallel anywhere in Central and Eastern Europe. Hungarian Stalinist historiography condemned the whole of the Hungarian past, excepting only a few "progressive" episodes like the Jacobin conspiracy of the early 1790s and the Revolution of 1848, and a few progressive individuals like Louis Kossuth, who had managed, from time to time, to rise above their own "class limitations." History was presented as an epic struggle between a vicious ruling class that included even rich peasants and a heroic but regularly defeated lower class; defeated, that is, until the Soviet liberation of 1945.

Soviet Stalinist historiography was always nationalist to a degree, extolling the virtues of great national leaders who resolutely fought the foreign invaders as well as disruptive domestic feudal elements.

When he praised such modernizing and centralizing tyrants as Aleksandr Nevsky, Ivan the Terrible, and Peter the Great, Stalin attempted to legitimize his own tyranny and that of his party bureaucracy. Hungarian Stalinist historiography also claimed to be patriotic, and it went to some length in praising the historic alliance between such great national leaders as János Hunyadi and Ferenc Rákóczi II on the one hand and the common people on the other. But, since Hungary could not boast many successful national leaders, and inasmuch as Hungary's kings had been foreigners at least since the sixteenth century, Hungarian historiography in the 1950s ended up being extremely critical of almost everybody in Hungarian history.

Hungary's neighbors never went to the same lengths of self-accusation, perhaps because they had emerged victorious from both world wars. Czech, Slovak, Romanian, or South Slav Stalinist textbook writers also dealt with the "historic guilt" of native exploiters, but, from the very start, these historians placed a great deal of the blame on the shoulders of foreigners. It seemed that "progressive" Romanian, Czech, Slovak, or South Slav forces had always waged a "resolute struggle" against the German, Austrian, Hungarian, or Ottoman oppressors. If the struggle failed, these historians explained, it was because the native nobility or bourgeoisie had betrayed the national cause. This meant, of course, that the native elites at least could have joined the common national struggle, which is a far cry from the Hungarian Stalinist claim of categorical hostility of interest between social classes.

Following the death of Stalin, a more radical national rehabilitation began in the East European countries. The number of historic native enemies and traitors grew smaller and smaller as more and more members of the historic elite were made to join the ranks of the "progressives." Concurrently, the "foreign" (including the Hungarian) exploiters of the Slovaks and Romanians were made to shoulder an ever-increasing part of the historical guilt.

It is remarkable, and perhaps a hopeful sign for the future, that at least one state in the region continues, officially at least, in the nonnational tradition once cultivated, under a very different regime, by the Habsburg Monarchy. That state is Communist Yugoslavia. Theoretically, in its very "nationality," Yugoslav is a sort of denial of separate Serbian, Croatian, Slovene, and other nationalist claims. Genetically, despite its historical nationalist background, the regional-ethnic term "Yugoslav" stands close to the non-national term "Austrian" of the Habsburg past.

In Hungary, in Stalinist times, there was a complete subservience to all Marxist-Leninist tenets and commands of the Soviet Union. The peace treaties ending World War I and World War II were never criticized, and textbooks were careful not to mention the Hungarian names of cities that had been part of Hungary prior to 1918 but now belonged to other countries. The subservience to the commands of the Soviet Union went so far that the Hungarian textbooks referred to *Sub*-Carpathia (a Hungarian province until the end of World War I when it became annexed by Czechoslovakia, and since World War II, part of the Soviet Union) exclusively by its new Soviet name, *Trans*-Carpathia, as if the fact of Soviet annexation had physically lifted the province and carried it, from the Hungarian point of view, to the far side of the Carpathian Mountains.

From Stalinist subservience, the change to a sophisticated, liberal, and liberated historiography came rather drastically in Hungary in the 1960s. One of the results has been that while in the 1950s nationalism was taboo, now it is merely unfashionable among the best Hungarian historians. All of this has made for an often very reliable Hungarian historiography; its shortcomings are mainly in the realm of contemporary history, which is why it does not quite satisfy the public. Another reason for continued dissatisfaction is that the public in general has become increasingly nationalistic. Confronted, as they are in particular, with radical Romanian and Slovak nationalism, many Hungarians clamor for a radical nationalism of their own. Furthermore, a genuine Hungarian problem is the status of Hungarians living in Romania, Czechoslovakia, Yugoslavia, and the Soviet Union, a problem that is crying out for a frank debate.

Hungarians expect nationalism to come more from their historians than from their government. This is partly because their own government is not free, but also because Central and East European nationalism has always been profoundly historical; national claims, in many instances, are based on traditional rights and historical precedents. Furthermore, in Communist countries historians and intellectuals in general perform many public functions which in other countries are normally performed by political parties and pressure groups. Yet, in Hungary's case, even if the historians were willing to follow the popular trend, they would be restrained by the government which is more reluctant to offend its socialist neighbors than the latter are to offend Hungary.

Is the nationality situation in the Danube region worse or better than it was, say, a half century ago? It is better if one considers the tone of official Communist pronouncements, the relative moderation of some governments (that of Hungary in particular), and the apolitical and non-nationalistic attitudes and tendencies among the younger generations. There is also, of course, the presence of the Soviet army as a peacekeeping force. But the *Pax Sovietica,* although a powerful restraint, is also an obstacle to genuine reconciliation in Eastern Europe. One might even argue that the readiness of the Soviet Union to use one Warsaw Pact country against another (as was the case of Romania and Czechoslovakia against Hungary in 1956, and of practically the entire Soviet bloc against Czechoslovakia in 1968) exacerbates national conflict. But even if this were not the case—and the Czechoslovak people probably do not resent their Polish or Hungarian neighbors for the invasion of 1968—there still remains the lack of candor in all interstate and international Communist party relations.

The absence of genuine diplomatic contacts and negotiations among the small socialist countries must perpetuate or even increase mutual resentment. There is, for instance, no bipartisan commission to revise and coordinate the history textbooks of neighboring countries, as has been the case between France and West Germany for several decades. The clash of historical interpretations and the mutual assignment of blame continues unchecked. And yet, the situation is far from hopeless. It is good to remember from time to time that much of the internecine hostility in Central and Eastern Europe has always been orchestrated from above, and that the peoples of the region have often been more tolerant of one another than their leaders have wanted them to be. Genuine international cooperation, even federation, are things that many millions of people in the region would certainly love to try.

Lajos Für's essay on "Hungarian History as Taught by Hungary's Neighbors" (below) is a testimony to both the enduring success of nationalism in the Danube region and to the failure of Marxism-Leninism as an ideology imbued with internationalist spirit. Furthermore, the essay is a testimony to the manifest inability of Communist societies to create the much vaunted "new man," characterized, among other things, by brotherly affection for his fellow Communists in other countries. The essay also sheds light on the several varieties of communism in the Danube region. On the one hand is a state like Romania, which is unable to provide its subjects with even a modicum of freedom and material comfort and therefore employs the time-honored political device of chauvinism as a substitute for bread and liberty. On the other hand is a state like Yugoslavia, able and willing to offer a relatively greater degree of freedom, and thus prosperity as well, to its citizens and seemingly for that reason ready to use nationalism only sparingly as a political weapon.

The extremist character of Romanian nationalism is very probably also caused by Romania's relative isolation and independence within the Soviet bloc; still it seems as if the degree of official nationalism stands in inverse proportion to the quality of life in a given country. Ironically, Romania and Hungary have been military and ideological allies for the last forty-odd years, first as satellites of Nazi Germany and then as satellites of the Soviet Union. Yet this fact is scarcely reflected in the Romanian schoolbooks' treatment of Hungarian history. On the other hand, Yugoslavia and Hungary have been outright political and military enemies during much of the Nazi and Stalinist periods. Yet the Yugoslav treatment of the Hungarian past and of relations between Hungarians and South Slavs is more judicious. The irony is compounded by the fact that, despite their formal alliance, the Romanian and Hungarian publics have been hostile to each other for several decades, while the Hungarian public has always tended to admire the Yugoslavs, their formal enemies.

Romanian nationalism and, to a somewhat lesser extent, Slovak nationalism are extreme cases, as Lajos Für's essay reveals. But even in Communist countries like Yugoslavia or Hungary where relative political moderation prevails, history textbooks are unable to tackle with sincerity the delicate questions of ethnic relations so as to advance the cause of Danubian reconciliation. There is a certain lack of candor even in the case of independent Yugoslavia, a condition dictated at least in part by the requirements of Marxist-Leninist ideology. For, Communist ideology does claim that the triumph of communism inevitably places relations between nations on a loftier level, free of artificially created hatreds of bourgeois imperialism. Thus, if chauvinism raises its ugly head, it can only be due to a conscious or unconscious misinterpretation of the teachings of Marxism-Leninism.

The fact of the matter is that few people in Eastern Europe, even in governmental circles, believe in Marxism-Leninism, while most East Europeans sincerely believe in the moral and spiritual primacy of their nationality, or at least in the justice of their national grievance. The balance in history textbooks is definitely tilting toward the triumph of nationalist sentiments, while it continues to be necessary to camouflage these sentiments with the slogans of official Marxist internationalist ideology. Take, for example, the ever more aggressively voiced Romanian argument that in the history of their nation nearly everyone, from princes and boyar landowners down to landless peasants, has always fought for progress and national unification. Such a claim flies directly in the face of the Marxist thesis about irreconcilable antagonisms between the exploiters and the exploited. The Romanian textbooks solve the dilemma by claiming that the exploiters of the Romanian nation were foreigners—Austrians, Hungarians, Ottomans, or Russians—whereas the freedom fighters were invariably of Romanian stock.

To be sure, the present Communist regimes of the Danube region inherited a rich nationalist tradition. Furthermore, the nationalism of the Communist history textbooks discussed by Lajos Für is, on the whole, less radical than that of interwar regimes. But it is also true that no earlier regime in Central and Eastern Europe was as badly entangled in conflicting ideological pretensions as are the Communist regimes today.

Hungarian History as Taught by Hungary's Neighbors by Lajos Für*

Under the impact of forces that shaped the Danube region's history, the Hungarians became a dispersed nation, with almost every third Hungarian living beyond the boundaries of Hungary today. Some of them live in faraway lands, scattered all over the globe. But, most of these Hungarians live just across the borders of Hungary proper. They did not move; the boundaries of the Danube states have moved. How

*This edited English version is an abbreviated adaptation of the Hungarian original.

is Hungarian history taught to the children of these Hungarian national minorities?

This review deals with Hungarian-language textbooks in use in grade schools and middle schools in neighboring Romania, Czechoslovakia, and Yugoslavia; those in Soviet Carpatho-Ukraine are referred to only perfunctorily (however, for some details, see Annex II in Chapter 10, above). Furthermore, our review is limited to Hungarian history from the mid-fifteenth century, selectively covering only events of major importance. Ancient and medieval history is thus excluded. It should be briefly noted, however, that interpretations of those earlier periods of the past are sources of some of the most appalling romantic illusions and nationalist falsifications. Views pertaining to the very distant past feed much of the antagonism among the Danube peoples today. It suffices to point out the emotional conflicts stirred up by the theory of Daco-Romanian continuity[1] or by the recently invented theories of Slovak ethnogenesis.[2] The purpose of these and other highly speculative interpretations is simply to deny the Hungarians their rightful place and role in the history of the Danube region.[3]

Leaving aside disputes about the remote and often obscure past, what follows are views taught by Hungary's neighbors on Hungarian history of more recent and better documented times.

The fifteenth century ushered in momentous upheavals in the history of the Danube region. The Moslem Turks were pitting their might against the Christian forces of the European continent, while the Habsburgs, on their way to Central European hegemony, were aspiring to the Czech and Hungarian thrones. Central and southeastern Europe became the battlefield of conflicts between powers more tenacious and merciless than those of earlier times. The medieval Hungarian state stood up to the pressures of the mounting crisis better than the other countries of the region. In fact, in the era of the Hunyadis, Hungary reached such heights of success that it appeared as if it were able to overcome both its internal and external problems. What do the Hungarian-language textbooks of the neighboring states teach about this era of Hungarian history?

"The Turks endangered equally the Serbs, Hungarians, and Romanians, therefore these three neighboring peoples struggled against them with combined forces," declares one of the Yugoslav textbooks.

It is followed by appreciation of János Hunyadi. He is considered as belonging to all three peoples, with emphasis on his uncertain ethnic ancestry: "Already as a young man he had fought as a mercenary and later as the commander of mercenaries against the Turks in Serbia . . . soon obtained large estates in the Banat and Transylvania and also received high offices in Hungary."[4] This is true. However, the Banat, Transylvania, and Hungary are dealt with as if they were three wholly distinct countries, although they were integral parts of the kingdom of Hungary.

The Transylvanian student in Romania is taught something else about János Hunyadi:

> In those difficult times, an individual of great merit became quite famous. His name was János (Jancu) and he was the son of a Romanian tribal leader. . . . On account of his brave deeds, the Hungarian king gave him many estates as well as the castle of Vajdahunyad. The boy learned how to handle weapons in Italy. When he returned to Transylvania he understood how great a danger was the Turkish oppression for the Romanians and the other peoples living in this part of Europe. After he had quickly demonstrated his military skills and leadership capacity . . . he was elected as the voivode of Transylvania. . . . He maintained close and friendly ties with the rulers of Wallachia and Moldavia. They too were endangered by the destruction caused by the Turks and it was possible to contain the Turkish danger only collectively, along the entire length of the Danube. Hunyadi successfully destroyed that Turkish army which penetrated into Transylvania. Also, when the Turks overran Wallachia, he rushed to help the Romanians there and was victorious in a great battle fought at the Jalomita River. . . . The Turks then realized that the Romanians represented a great force, while united under the command of a heroic ruler. . . . Thus, the combined forces of the Transylvanian, Wallachian, and Moldavian Romanians, under the leadership of János Hunyadi, defended the freedom of our people and that of all the peoples of Europe. Hunyadi died soon after this victory and was buried in the church of Alba Julia, with the following inscription on his headstone: "The light of the world has gone out."[5]

One should add that the previous edition (1966) of the same textbook mentioned that, in addition to the office of "voivode," Hunyadi also held the title of "Governor of Hungary"; and that Hunyadi's bravery inspired the Romanians, Hungarians, and the other Danube peoples, who then stood as "a living wall" to block the advance of the Turks.[6] However, two years later (1968) the same textbook spoke of the peoples of the "three Romanian countries" only, namely Transylvania, Moldavia, and Wallachia.

The student studying in a Hungarian-language school in Czechoslovakia learns precious little about János Hunyadi. The textbook speaks of Hungary's "inner anarchy" which "provided an outstanding opportunity" for the Turks to attack the Hungarian kingdom. János Hunyadi is identified as "the great nemesis of the Turks," who "temporarily stopped the Turkish conquest of Hungary." The second half of the same sentence already deals with his son, Matthias Corvinus, Hungary's king, with similar laconic pithiness.

Matthias Corvinus was one of the greatest rulers of the Danube region and one of the better known rulers of Europe's Renaissance era. He receives no proper recognition by the Slovak textbook—except that, under his rule, "the Slovaks, Czechs, Serbs, and Romanians fought together with the Hungarians," and that, in his famous Black Army, there were many Czech and Slovak Hussites, as well as Serbs and Romanians. The Slovak text lists his victories against the Turks, but stresses the renewed "inner anarchy" in Hungary after his death.[7] Attention is paid to the outstanding cultural accomplishments of his age, but under the curious heading: "Humanism and Renaissance in Hungary, Bohemia, and Slovakia." In fact, Slovakia, as such, did not exist at that time; it was part of Hungary.

The Slovak textbook discusses the concurrent spread of the Czech Hussite movement in Hungary. By limiting it to the territory of present Slovakia, the text creates the impression as if this significant progressive movement of Central Europe had been an exclusively Czech and Slovak national affair.[8] In fact, the teachings of Jan Hus transcended linguistic and national boundaries, providing plenty of work for the inquisitors of the Catholic church everywhere in Hungary, not only among Slovaks.

The Yugoslav textbook deals with the era of King Matthias in some detail, but the Romanian textbook does not mention it at all. However, the texts of all countries deal at great length with the subsequent peasant war in Hungary, led by György Dózsa. The Czechoslovak summary is the most exact and detailed, stressing the struggle of the Hungarian peasantry against their oppressors. The Yugoslav presentation, consistent with its general conception, emphasizes the common destiny of the Danubian peasantry. It also mentions that the formerly faction-ridden aristocracy became united: "They were all united when it came to dealing with the poor people; it did not make any difference if these were Hungarian, Serb, or Romanian."[9] However, the title of the chapter divides the Hungarian state into nationalistic sounding parts: Peasant Uprisings in Hungary, Transylvania, and Vojvodina." Even greater falsehood is reflected by the chapter title of the corresponding Romanian text: "The György Dózsa-Led Transylvanian Peasant War." The student is told that in terms of his ancestry, Dózsa was a Székely—a Hungarian, that is. However, a picture of Dózsa based on a contemporary etching spells his name in Romanian as "GHE. DOJA," giving the impression that he was a Romanian. On the other hand, the text emphasizes the exclusively Hungarian character of the aristocracy arrayed against the peasants.

All texts properly connect the defeat of the peasant uprising with Hungary's defeat in the battle of Mohács in 1526. The Romanian text, however, separates Transylvania from Hungary, as if it existed as a Romanian state. Following the Turkish conquest of Hungary, the text says, "The Transylvanian Voivode remained an independent state; it was obliged only—just as Moldavia and Wallachia—to pay taxes to the Turks. Its name became the Principality of Transylvania." It is well known that Transylvania had been part of the Hungarian kingdom since the eleventh century and that it remained under Hungarian rule even during the Turkish period, from 1526 to 1686.

After Mohács, three hundred years of Hungarian history are passed over in silence in the Romanian textbook. Only in connection with the 1848 revolutions does the Transylvanian student find out, once again, something about Hungary. Until then, Transylvania is dealt with as one of the "three Romanian countries," without ever mentioning Hungary. On the other hand, the reign of less than one year of the Wallachian Michael the Brave in Transylvania (1600–1601) is described in glowing terms in a separate chapter. For the first time, says the text, the "three Romanian countries" were united under one ruler, in fulfillment of the Romanian people's "desires for liberty and union."[10] Meanwhile, the names of Transylvania's Hungarian princes, those of Bethlen, the Rákóczis, and so on, are not even mentioned. After Michael the Brave, the next name mentioned is again a Romanian: Horia-Closca, the leader in 1848 of peasant uprisings in Transylvania.[11]

The Slovak textbook discusses these three hundred years in some detail:

> The Turks ruled over a large part of the territory of Hungary for 150 years. . . . Transylvania was a vassal principality of the Turks; nonetheless, it had great political significance. In point of fact, Transylvania functioned as a counterweight to the politics of the Habsburgs; for one half of a century it served as the basis of the struggle for independence and was the center of Hungarian cultural development.

The text also describes in detail, and in proper historical perspective, the times of István Bocskai. But the location of the wars of the Transylvanian Hungarian princes against the Habsburgs in northern Hungary is referred to in present-day terms as "Slovakia."

The Yugoslav textbook dramatizes the tragic consequences of the defeat at Mohács: "The Hungarian-Croatian kingdom has ceased to exist. . . . While the peoples of Europe could develop freely, our peoples (the South Slavs as well as the Hungarians) were forced to conduct a constant bloody struggle just to sustain ourselves."[13] But what about Transylvania? According to one of the Yugoslav maps, it was swallowed up in the shaded areas indicating the extent of the Turkish dominions, just as were the Balkans and North Africa. The cartographer, incorrectly, included in these Turkish dominions the greater part of northern Hungary as well.[14]

In the same textbook, the discussion of the Zrinyi family is no less curious. After the peace of Vasvár (1664), we read, the Danubian hope in the Habsburgs as liberators was disappointed and "one part of the dissatisfied Croatian and Hungarian aristocracy decided to depose the House of Habsburg. The most powerful Croatian aristocrats, including Miklós Zrinyi, the Croatian governor, his brother Péter, as well as Péter's brother-in-law, Frankopán, together with some Hungarian aristocrats, organized a conspiracy." It is true, the Zrinyi family was of Croatian origin and Miklós Zrinyi's ancestral home was in Croatia. However, he was also one of the greatest Hungarians of his age. A Hungarian poet and a military leader, an outstanding theoretician of war, the master of Hungarian Baroque literature, his models were his Hungarian-Croatian great-grandfather, the "hero of Szigetvár," and the great Hungarian Renaissance king, Matthias Corvinus. He stood for independence of the Danube peoples. It is most unfortunate to deny him his proper place in Danubian history.

Let us move on to 1848, the era of European bourgeois revolutions and struggles for national independence. We know that the Hungarian leadership of 1848, incapable of freeing itself from the nationalist bourgeois nation-state conception, was unwilling to make timely concessions to historic Hungary's non-Magyar nationalities. On the other hand, these nationalities—blinded by nationalist fervor and misled by Habsburg promises—became a major support of reaction against the revolutions of 1848.

How do the textbooks tackle these complex issues? The Romanian text deals with the revolution in Transylvania in a separate chapter: The Romanians, hearing of the Hungarian revolution, "hoped that the day of truth had come also for the Romanians. The Hungarian government, however, planned to make Transylvania part of Hungary." The Hungarians wanted to take Transylvania away? From whom? In 1711, following the defeat of the Rákóczi-led war for independence, the Habsburgs, in order to divide the strength of the rebellious country, had placed Transylvania under the direct control of Vienna, together with the southern military defense districts, as an autonomous province. Thus, in 1848, the Hungarian government simply wished to reunite Transylvania and make it a part of Hungary again.

The Hungarians of Transylvania enthusiastically supported, of course, the reunion with their mother country. Furthermore, as the Hungarian historian, Zoltán I. Tóth, an ardent advocate of Hungarian-Romanian reconciliation, pointed out: "The demand for union in 1848 was a question of progress. Would Transylvania support the revolution or the counterrevolution? The issue of union at that time therefore also meant whether progress or reaction would be dominant in Transylvania."[15] And a Hungarian Communist writer-politician, József Révai, hardly guilty of nationalist sentiments, expressed a similar view:

That revolutionary Hungary did not grant autonomy to the Serbs and did not give up its desire for union with Transylvania, cannot be faulted even from the perspective of ninety years. The connection of the national movement of the Slavic and Romanian peoples with Habsburg reaction and tsarism was at that time a living and painful fact. . . . Revolutionary Hungary could not permit that the counterrevolution should find a home under the cover of Slav and Romanian autonomy.[16]

A gallery of the great personalities of the "Transylvanian revolution" of 1848 is presented by the Romanian textbook. This includes a picture of Sándor Petőfi, the Hungarian revolutionary poet, but in a shocking company: Simon Bărnuţiu and Stefan Ludwig Roth. Bărnuţiu and Roth both collaborated with Vienna, the former as leader of the Romanians, and the latter as leader of the Saxons of Transylvania. The caption with these pictures is worth quoting: "When they became aware of the intentions of the Hungarian government [namely, of its desire to make Transylvania part of Hungary], the Romanians decided to attain for themselves social equality and national liberty. Numerous educated individuals, enthusiastic and patriotic youth, such as Avram Jancu, Georghe Bariţiu, Simon Bărnuţiu, and Eftimie Murgu stood at the head of the movement." It would be difficult to create more confusion about historical reality or to confound and obscure more thoroughly the conflicting forces of the 1848 revolution. So it comes as no surprise that among the leaders of the revolution who, following their defeat in 1849, sought refuge in foreign lands, the name of Lajos Kossuth is not even mentioned, while on the other hand it is pointed out that the Romanian exiles "continued the struggle for the freedom and unity of the Romanians."[17]

After all of this, it is refreshing to meet relative objectivity in the Czechoslovak textbooks. Discussing the eras of enlightenment and reform ushering in the revolution, the text lists the leading Hungarian figures of that age (Bessenyei, Csokonai, Kölcsey, Vörösmarty, Széchenyi, Kossuth, Deák, Eötvös, and so forth). It is, however, somewhat disappointing that the book deals in an offhand manner with the Hungarian revolution itself. A strangely brief summary oddly stresses the Croatian Jellasić's attack against the Hungarian revolution: "In point of fact the Hungarian war of independence started with this attack. Almost a year-long military and political struggle ensued, until Görgey surrendered on August 13, 1849, on the plains of Világos to the reactionary Austrian and tsarist armies. With this the Hungarian war of independence came to an end." And that's the end of the Slovak account of the Hungarian revolution as well.

More detailed, on the other hand, is the Slovak account of the conflict between Hungarians and the Slovaks during the revolution of 1848–49. The text deals with the "Slovak volunteers who attacked the Hungarian revolution" and who were "joined by the Czechs." It frankly admits, however, that the leadership of these volunteers was entrusted to Austrian army officers, and the Slovak troops became "the tools of the Austrian reaction."[18]

In the well-illustrated coverage of the Hungarian revolution by the Yugoslav textbook, Petőfi's picture is prominently displayed.[19] He is followed by Táncsics, Štúr, Jancu, Kossuth, Jellasić, and the brave Hungarian general of Serbian descent, Damjanich. The explanatory note puts this mixed company of revolutionaries and reactionaries into some order by correctly identifying who was who. On the other hand, the book discusses the events of the revolution in territorial units corresponding to present-day national boundaries. Thus, events of the "upper northern regions" of Austria and Hungary appear under the heading: "Revolution in Bohemia and Slovakia." In the chapter entitled "The Revolutionary Movements of the Romanians in 1848," Transylvania is treated in conjunction with Moldavia and Wallachia, and only Romanian movements are chronicled. The events in the Vojvodina region are also separated from their Hungarian context and are presented in conjunction with the Slovenian and Croatian happenings. As a result, closely related events of that time, forming a historic unit, are shorn of their true meaning.

Territorial arbitrariness notwithstanding, every fact in the Yugoslav textbook is verifiable. The participants and the national groups are evaluated in a manner consistent with historical truth. And judgments concerning positions taken by the Hungarian revolutionary government in nationality matters are moderate, as the following samples indicate: "Kossuth struggled with an honest fervor for the liberty and independence of the Hungarian people against Austria; however, he did not acknowledge the same right for the Serbians, Romanians, and Slovaks living on the territory of Hungary at that time. Thus, he alienated these peoples from the Hungarian revolution and struggle for independence." When the House of Habsburg was dethroned in Hungary, the Yugoslav text continues, and the revolutionary democrats obtained a larger role, "they enacted the first nationality law in Europe; however, this no longer satisfied either the Serbians or the Romanians." The text does not stress the conflicts by making one-sided reproaches. Rather, grief over lost opportunities of cooperation is the leading theme.

The Austro-Hungarian Compromise of 1867, and related problems of the dualist monarchy, are dealt with from the same biased or moderate points of view as the other issues examined thus far.

The Romanian textbook does not even mention the Compromise itself, but begins to cover late nineteenth-century Danubian history with the struggles for independence of 1877–78 in the Balkans, describing them at length and in glowing terms, in particular the Romanian people's endeavors to "liberate Transylvania from Austrian oppression." No mention is made of the fact that with the Austro-Hungarian Compromise of 1867, the historic union of Hungary and Transylvania was restored. In conjunction with World War I, Transylvania is mentioned once again. "Neutral Romania," so the textbook says, "stipulated that it would enter the war only if it could achieve the unity of the state, including the liberation of Transylvania. This ancient desire of the Romanian people was identical with the desires of the Poles, Serbs, Czechs, and other peoples oppressed by Austria-Hungary, Turkey or Germany."[20] The Slovaks, Croats, Slovenes, Bulgarians, Albanians, Ukrainians, Latvians, Lithuanians, Estonians, and Finns are not mentioned by name among the oppressed peoples, and tsarist Russia is strangely missing from the list of oppressors. The story of the dual monarchy's dissolution is also muddled: "In 1916 the Romanian army could not oust Austro-Hungarian rule from Transylvania. . . . In the fall of 1918 this empire began to disintegrate. All of the nationalities oppressed by Austria-Hungary—the Romanians, Czechs, Poles, Hungarians [sic], Serbs—revolted. The Hungarians, Czechs, and Poles established their own independent states. The Serbs and the Romanians joined the already independent parts of their countries."[21] This strange listing suggests that the Hungarians have been "liberated" from the "oppression" of their own country. Also, among the liberated peoples, the Slovaks, Croats, Slovenes, and Ruthenians, are not mentioned by name.

The Slovak textbook is substantially more objective in dealing with the dualist era, although within the confines of a dogmatic Marxist point of view, as in this sentence: "With the dualist compromise, the Austrian aristocracy and bourgeoisie—disregarding the legal claims of other nations—unjustly shared power with the Hungarian aristocracy." The text, however, recognizes capitalist development, civil rights, freedom of enterprise, freedom of opinion, and so on, in the Czech lands of the dualist monarchy. Also, while stressing dualist Hungary's continued "half feudal status,"[22] it calls the Compromise, from a Hungarian point of view, a "realistic one" which contributed to vast capitalistic development.[23]

The Yugoslav textbooks, too, are quite objective on the topic of the age of Austro-Hungarian dualism. The negative aspects are summed up as follows: "With the Compromise the ruling class of the two most powerful nations (the German and Hungarian) assured their power over the other peoples of the multinational Austro-Hungarian Monarchy." Thus, more than half of the population "remained deprived of its national rights," and the unsolved nationality question embroiled the Monarchy in crisis situations until the time of its dissolution.[24] But the positive aspects are not ignored. The 1867 Compromise "contributed to the ordering of the inner situation. The capitalist transformation made headway, . . . the bourgeoisie and the working class also developed. The system of parliamentary constitutionalism was solidified, which was based upon the achievements of bourgeois democracy." However, the economic circumstances developed unevenly and this "intensified the national, social, and political contradictions of the Monarchy."[25]

A moderate tone also characterizes the section on the dissolution of the Habsburg Monarchy. As a consequence of the defeats suffered on the battlefields, the Yugoslav text reads, "the old Habsburg Monarchy was falling apart. Its dissolution provided impetus to the movements of separation and self-determination of the former subject nationalities. The Czechs, Slovaks, Poles, Croatians, Serbians, Romanians, and other peoples established national councils which directed these movements resulting from the dismemberment of the Austro-Hungarian Monarchy toward the goal of establishing national states."[26]

All textbooks, including those of the Carpatho-Ukraine,[27] declare, on the one hand, that World War I resulted in a revolutionary new world order and, on the other, that it was a war of the imperialist great powers. Both aspects are most succinctly expressed by the Czechoslovak text: "The imperialist and unjust character of World War I is indisputable. . . . The opposing alliance systems were struggling for realignment of the world and [at the same time] they wished to suppress the momentum of revolutionary forces."[28] The Yugoslav textbook calls the war "predatory and unjust," but also points out that for the smaller nations, especially for the small Slavic peoples, it was a "just" war of "self defense."[29]

This supposedly Marxist interpretation of "self defense" serves as an ideological prop for approving the territorial changes which followed the war. All textbooks suggest that the changes were proper fruits of victory, and well deserved results of valiant battles fought at a great human cost. Only the Yugoslav text speaks of a "dictated peace" and in vague terms even implies that within the newly drawn frontiers unresolved nationality problems continued to exist.[30]

With the two world wars and the subsequent peace settlement historic Hungary and the supremacy of Hungarians in the Danube region came to an end. It is crucial for a true Danubian reconciliation that the interpretations of the past should not hinder the peace of the present, that distorted views should not poison the historical consciousness of the Danubian people. Distorted views of the common past are especially hurtful to the Hungarians, dismembered nation as they are. For the Hungarians, it is of crucial importance that their common past with their neighbors, which lasted for a thousand years, should not be the victim of recent resentments of the nationalist age. The "millennium" of the Hungarian state is by no means a history of the Hungarian people alone. Historic Hungary was the home of many peoples and the birthplace of several nations of today.[31] In the schools of the Danubian countries this common past should be taught in a common way. However, today, Danubian history is taught in five different ways to the five peoples who share a common past. Moreover, the Hungarian people are taught their own history in five different ways since they live in five different states today. Apart from discrediting Danubian historical scholarship, these contradictory interpretations are harmful to peaceful coexistence among the Danubian people.

With the coming to power of the working classes in the people's democracies after World War II, Marxism-Leninism has been made into a dominant ideology of the Danube region. All of us profess tenets of dialectical materialism in our interpretation of the past. Supposedly, the historians, the teachers, and the textbook writers are all Marxists. Their historical consciousness, despite their divergent national characteristics and viewpoints, should be built upon identical socialist foundations. As scholars, we may have disagreements, but children's textbooks are not the proper forum for debating them.

We have often heard that the Hungarian minorities in the four countries of our neighbors could serve as "bridges" among the peoples of the Danube region. This nice metaphor has, unfortunately, turned into an empty slogan. Let us not destroy the bridges built by our common past. Rather, let us strengthen them by an authentic and fair interpretation of our common historical experience.

Notes

1. Cf. I. I. Russo, *Etnogeneza romanilôr* (Bucharest, 1981); Ion Joratiu Crissan, *Burebista and His Time* (Bucharest, 1978); *Relations between the Autochthonous and Migratory Populations* (Bucharest, 1978).

2. Cf. Peter Ratkoš, *Pramene k dejinám velkej Moravy* (Bratislava, 1964); Jan Dekan, *Moravia Magna* (Bratislava, 1980).

3. Editor's Note. Linking Great Moravia to present-day Slovakia is the Slovak parallel to the Romanian Daco-Roman theory of continuity. Similar nationalist myths are being now nurtured by Soviet historiography, proclaiming today's Transcarpathia part of an ancient Ukrainian homeland. The myth-making tendencies of Hungary's neighbors are being challenged by Hungarian historians who are anxious to replace myths concerning the early history of the Danube region with verifiable facts of modern research based on archeological excavations, historical source criticism, linguistic scholarship, and so forth. The Hungarian historian Péter Hanák has summed up the problem succinctly in the course of a roundtable discussion broadcast by Hungarian Radio and published, in 1979, in the first issue of a new Budapest periodical, *História*, whose aim is to promote enlightened historical education of the general public. Addressing himself to one of the currently most controversial questions, namely, "Who were the people who lived in the Carpathian Basin before the Hungarian conquest?," Hanák said: "No continuity between the peoples of the former Roman provinces of the Roman Empire and the peoples living there 500 years later, in the ninth century, can be demonstrated. The ideas of continuity—whether with reference to the Huns, the Great Moravian Empire, or the Dacians—have all been invented . . . by romantic historiographies of the early nineteenth century, to awaken the nation, foster beliefs in a heroic past. . . . But scholarship has advanced since, beyond myths and romantic idealizations."

4. *Történelem az elemi iskolák VI. osztálya számára* (Novi Sad, 1967), 185–86.

5. *Hazánk története: Tankönyv a IV. osztály számára* (Bucharest, 1968), 110–12.

6. Ibid. (1966), 60–62.

7. *Csehszlovákia története: Tankönyv a középiskolák második és harmadik osztálya számára* (Bratislava, 1966), 80, 186–87.

8. Ibid., 71–74.

9. *Történelem az elemi iskolák VII. osztálya számára* (Subotica, 1966), 123–26.

10. *Hazánk története*, 123–26.

11. Ibid., 145–46.

12. *Csehszlovákia története*, 104.

13. *Történelem az elemi iskolák VI. osztálya számára*, 191.

14. Ibid., 199.

15. Zoltán I. Tóth, *Magyarok és románok*, ed. Dániel Csatári (Budapest, 1966), 208.

16. József Révai, *Marxizmus, népiesség, magyarság*, 3d ed. (Budapest, 1949), 208.

17. *Hazánk története*, 165–67.

18. *Csehszlovákia története*, 146–47.

19. *Történelem az elemi iskolák VI. osztálya számára*, 191.

20. *Hazánk története*, 183, 203.

21. Ibid., 208.

22. *Csehszlovákia története*, 154–55.

23. Ibid., 178.

24. *Történelem az elemi iskolák VI. osztálya számára*, 108–9.

25. Ibid., 112–36.

26. Ibid., 184–85.

27. *Az újkor története; II. rész. Középiskolai tankönyv* (Kiev-Uzhgorod, 1966), 261.

28. *Csehszlovákia története*, 206.

29. *Történelem az elemi iskolák VIII. osztálya számára* (Novi Sad, 1966), 15.

30. Ibid., 42.

31. For more on this subject, see above, Chapter 1, "State- and Nation-Building in Central Europe."

✳ 16

The Future of the Hungarian Minorities

Stephen Borsody

Fair solutions of national conflicts in the Danube region are a matter of "mutual willingness" to recognize the equality of rights to national self-determination—so argued István Bibó, foremost political ideologist of Hungary's postpartition era, in one of his best known essays hauntingly titled, "The Misery of the East-European Small States."[1] Since World War II, however, the general trend has been further away from "mutual willingness" to recognize the equality of rights to national self-determination. One of the newest characteristics of Danubian state-building has been the legitimization of the homogeneous nation-state solution. It regards expulsion and assimilation as legitimate means of solving national minority problems. This policy was only partially successful in its postwar implementation.[2] But the idea itself affected the treatment of national minorities almost everywhere in the Danube region. Ethnic justice seems to be even less respected today than it was before World War II. And, ironically, this situation has come about despite the fact that the Danube region has been under the rule of Communists who, theoretically, are committed to Marxist-Leninist principles of national equality and self-determination.

Yugoslavia alone among the Communist countries with Hungarian minorities has provided for the Hungarians a relatively tolerable home under the shield of Marxist-Leninist nationality policy. Yugoslavia also separated itself from the Soviet Union's postwar creation, the Soviet bloc. Thus, paradoxically, the Soviet-propagated Marxist-Leninist nationality policy has actually been proven more welcome in independent Communist Yugoslavia than in the Soviet bloc itself, including the Soviet Union's own territorial acquisition in the Danube region, the Carpatho-Ukraine.

Postwar Communist Hungary alone among the countries of the Soviet bloc has been ruled by a regime which ostentatiously indulged in antinational indoctrination. The Communist regime in Hungary was forcibly feeding its people humiliating doctrines of national inferiority. Hungarians were taught to regard themselves as a "guilty nation," a "fascist nation," and to behave accordingly, unlearning in particular such nationalist bad habits as poking their noses into the internal affairs of their neighbors ruling over Hungarian minorities.

In 1956, postwar Hungarian bitterness and frustration erupted in a national uprising. Soviet armed intervention crushed the Hungarian Revolution of 1956. Unexpectedly, however, out of the postwar and postrevolutionary humiliations, a liberalized regime emerged under János Kádár. Kádár's Hungary is often thought of as a showcase nation of the Soviet bloc—"Russia's Hong Kong," as Budapest slang calls it. It is relatively prosperous, displaying relative freedoms which are uncommon in the Soviet bloc. Yet, along with a newly-found sense of national pride and self-esteem, a sense of national tragedy is tormenting the Hungarians. This time, it is caused not so much by Russian occupation—unwelcome as that may be—but by the constantly worsening conditions of the Hungarian minorities, particularly in Romania and Czechoslovakia.[3]

With some measure of national autonomy in Hungary regained, the Hungarian public has been inevitably reawakened to the plight of the Hungarian minorities. In a sense, it is a reawakened Hungarian "revisionism" which Hungary's neighbors had hoped to silence forever. However, though triggered by injustices of the peace settlement and unfair treatment of the minorities, as was pre-World War II revisionism, Hungarian concern today for the nation as a whole resolutely denies any affinity with the chauvinistic revisionist propaganda of the Horthy era. The new nationalism of socialist Hungary reflects the postwar democratization of Hungarian society. Its appeal is to universal human rights, its aim is to spread peacefully the principles of national equality and international solidarity among the peoples of the Danube region.

With the Soviet Union as the pillar of the territorial status quo, it would be more illusory than ever for the Hungarians to advocate boundary revisions. In fact, the nationalist obsession with boundary revision expired with the Horthy regime. Yet, there is no mood of resignation either—no willingness to accept discrimination against Hungarians as a permanent feature of the Hungarian future. The national mood in Hungary is a mixture of acute resentment and vague hope that in one way or another fairness may prevail, someday, somehow. In a way, many events of the contemporary world incite such hopes. From even more desperate situations than the Hungarians find themselves in today, peoples in different parts of the world have lived to see their national aspirations fulfilled since World War II. Former colonial peoples, some even lacking collectively developed longings to become nations, have been granted rights of national self-determination. Changes closer to home, in areas with more similarity to the problems of the Danube region, may serve as an encouragement, too. Franco-German reconciliation in particular, which made the European Community possible in the West, is seen by many Hungarians as a positive precedent illustrating how deepseated nationalist hostilities can be superseded by regional peace. And, closest to home, the Yugoslav example of a relatively tolerant nationality policy is taken as a sign that national minority life in the Danube region—even under the existing status quo—should not necessarily be made unbearable by the ruling majority.

The communiqués of international meetings between Communist countries of the Danube region speak only of fraternal harmony. It cannot be known, therefore, in what way Hungary's Communist regime is trying behind the facade of proletarian internationalism to induce its fraternal Communist neighbors to ease the nationalist pressures on the Hungarian minorities. But, in Hungary itself, the Communist regime has lately somewhat eased the ban on public discussion of Hungarian minority problems, which prompted Party ideologues to warn against Hungarian minority issues becoming "priority" national concerns.

One long overdue concession is in the field of scholarship. An Institute for Hungarian Studies began its work recently at the National Széchenyi Library. It will continue the study of the Hungarian diaspora in the West which, unlike the Hungarian minorities, was never a forbidden topic. In addition, the Institute is also scheduled to begin a systematic survey of the status of the indigenous Hungarian minorities in the neighboring countries which, although comprising over one-fourth of the nation, for nearly forty years has been an area of total neglect. (On signs of change in the Hungarian official attitude, see Annex V of chapter 14.)

Publicity of the plight of the Hungarian minorities remains scrupulously restricted. On the other hand, what still is not mentionable publicly has been a lively topic of long standing in Hungarian underground literature. One of the Hungarian semi-underground writers of international renown, György Konrád, in one of his works published abroad, has recently given a good description of how Hungarians of the democratic-reformist generation see themselves today as a nation:

> The three medieval kingdoms of Central Europe—the Polish, the Czech, and the Hungarian—had been apparently the work of peoples who could master great perseverance in the art of survival. Each of them in different ways has paid dearly for its independence. If after centuries of effort they are still unsuccessful, this proves only that their stubborn struggle for self-determination is to be continued until they win it.
>
> It would be nonsense and lacking in historical understanding, for instance, to assume that the Hungarian people, after shaking off the supremacy of so many other powers, would ever sink into a slumber of surrender and do nothing against their present, or future, occupiers. The Hungarian people, not unlike other people, will not rest until they win their self-determination in the Carpathian Basin. They wish to face all their neighbors with friendly strength, not submitting themselves to any of them, not subduing any of them either, but living with all of them in natural reciprocity and cooperation. . . .
>
> The Hungarian state has been the principal aim of the entire history of the Hungarians: If not a kingdom, at least a principality; if not the country as a whole, at least Transylvania; if not the Carpathian Basin as a whole, at least the center of it; if not with full sovereignty, at least with partial sovereignty. They made deals with the Turks, Germans, Russians; they made compromises; but never exclusively under duress or with hatred. Even if it is half-way independence only, there should be a Hungarian state. Wherever Hungarians live, they should be free to speak Hungarian; the authority in charge of their affairs should be Hungarian.[4]

In plain political prose: What the Hungarian minorities need for their survival is autonomy. For, only autonomy can safeguard a national minority collectively against the majority nationality in charge of the powers of the state. Experience teaches only too convincingly that, in a national conflict situation, individuals without collective safeguards are helpless victims of oppression.

Today none of the four countries that have annexed territories with either homogeneous or mixed Hungarian populations have recognized the *collective* national rights of the Hungarian minorities, let alone their claim to territorial autonomy. Two of the four countries, Yugoslavia and the Soviet Union, declare themselves as multinational states. Constitutionally, both are unions of "nations and nationalities." Yet, neither of them specifically acknowledges the Hungarian nationality's right to autonomy. The Hungarians are granted minority rights only within larger autonomous or centralized regions ruled by the majority—in Vojvodina by the Serbs, and in Transcarpathia by the Ukrainians. In the other two countries, Czechoslovakia and Romania, the situation is worse—even theoretically. Both declare themselves outright as national states—of the Czechs and Slovaks, and of the Romanians, respectively. The Hungarians are relegated to newly concocted categories whose very names stress only the ties to the state authority under which the Hungarians live rather than the nationality to which they belong.

The Hungarians in Romania are defined as a "co-inhabiting nationality," and those in Czechoslovakia as "citizens of Hungarian national origins." In the 1950s, under Soviet pressure, Romania granted autonomy of sorts to the Hungarians of Transylvania, only to abolish it when Soviet occupation troops were withdrawn as a reward for Romania's loyalty to the Soviets at the time of the Hungarian Revolution of 1956. Ever since, the Romanians have embarked on an ultra-nationalistic course, leaving no doubts about their ultimate goal of liquidating the Hungarians as a national collective. The Slovak treatment of the Hungarian minority in Czechoslovakia is becoming ever more akin to that of the Romanians. Still mourning their failure to expel the Hungarians forthwith after World War II (the way the Czechs did their German rivals), the Slovaks are working hard to make the Hungarians disappear by assimilation. Their method, cultural pauperization of the minority, nowadays called "cultural genocide," is in many ways reminiscent of the assimilation methods pre-World War I Hungary practiced—except that the Hungarian state of the nineteenth-century European liberal capitalist era operated without the instruments of oppression the Communist totalitarian states of Eastern Europe have at their disposal today.

Danubian dissidents of the majority nationalities often argue that the Hungarian minorities' demand for autonomy is for something the majorities themselves would like to enjoy. This is sidetracking the issue of national minority oppression. Of course no democratic autonomy is conceivable under a totalitarian regime. On the other hand, even in a one-party totalitarian society, ethnic autonomy of any sort could offer some protection to a minority nationality against the ruling majority. Both majorities and minorities are suffering oppression in the Danube region today. But this does not lessen the national majorities' power to oppress national minorities. If anything, the totalitarian state enhances it.

Whatever their definition or status, the Hungarian minorities in all four countries of the Danube region are targets of "patriotic" indoctrination, exhorting them to be loyal to the "common fatherland," which means loyalty to Romania, Czechoslovakia, Yugoslavia, and the Soviet Union. But patriotic propaganda is a poor weapon against the potential disloyalty of national minorities. Communist claims of ethnic fairness in most states of the Danube region are too unreal to be taken seriously. Unless the state is reasonably fair to a national minority—as is the case with Yugoslavia's treatment of its Hungarian minority—propaganda of the "socialist solution" will not win the minorities' loyalty to the state.

Communist parties of the Danube region, while pledging allegiance to the state and nation, are also ideologically committed to "proletarian internationalism" and "bridge-building" among neighboring countries. The national minorities (or "nationalities," according to Communist terminology which shuns as reactionary the term "minorities") are supposed to play a prominent role in the Marxist-Leninist program of "bridge-building."

The idea that Hungarian minorities may serve as "bridges" among the peoples of the Danube region is an attractive one. The "bridge" role may even suit the new line in Hungarian thinking about nationalism. National thinking today, not unlike traditional nationalism, embraces the entire scene of Hungary's history in the Danube region. It serves the cause of Hungarian national unity. However, instead of reclaiming the privileged position of the past for the Hungarians, the new thinking envisages reconciliation, ethnic equality, regional cooperation. The Hungarian people, whether in Hungary or in the neighboring states, feel as one nation. But in order to live as one nation they also have to live in peace with their neighbors in the Danube region. The theoretical search for an answer to this complex regional problem is not confined to the official Marxist-Leninist "bridge" ideology. Another approach to it, by way of a revival of Oscar Jászi's federalist legacy, is the old idea of a Danubian federation. In a Communist country, it is an unusual way, too, considering Jászi's well-known anti-Marxist and anti-Soviet record. A democratic Danubian federation may not be easier to realize today than it was after World War I when Jászi tried it in vain in the turmoil of Austria-Hungary's collapse. But its spirit is alive and gaining intellectual popularity in Hungary today under the Communist approved ideological slogan of "Danubian patriotism."[5] It is a beautiful idea. Whether it can help to overcome the divisive forces of Danubian nationalism and resolve the painful problem of Hungarian minorities is a different question.

Today, the national minorities are sources of conflict rather than bridges of understanding. They could become bridge-builders of Danubian peace only if the national majorities could agree on the building plan of a Danubian regional union. The trouble today with the implementation of the official "bridge" program stems from the nationalist climate of the nation-state system and from the glaring imbalance in the distribution of national minorities among the Danubian states. The Hungarians, with large ethnic minorities of their own people in the neighboring states, feel compelled by their sense of national unity to seek regional cooperation. On the other hand, ethnic minorities of the neighboring peoples in Hungary today are so insignificant, in comparison to the size of Hungarian minorities in the neighboring states, that there is no compelling national incentive on the part of Hungary's neighbors to foster reciprocal ethnic tolerance in the spirit of regional patriotism.

Under the existing circumstances, the prospects for the national survival of the Hungarian minorities are far from encouraging. Yet, in this age of worldwide nationalist agitation, it is unlikely that the Hungarian national minorities will meekly succumb to denationalization and politely disappear. Also, there is growing pressure on the Hungarian Communist regime to do more than just repeat the "proletarian internationalist" slogans of "bridge-building," while lumping the Hungarian minorities together with all the Hungarians "abroad," as if there were no differences between Hungarians across the borders in the Danube region and those in Australia or the United States. Whether a change from public silence to open concern in the Hungarian government's attitude—if at all tolerated by the Russians—could directly bring about a change of attitude among Hungary's Danubian neighbors is not at all certain. But, if combined with international attention to the oppression of Hungarian minorities, it may perhaps in some cases put pressure on the oppressors to mend their ways. International publicity may well turn out to be a more effective remedy than proletarian internationalism.

Dictates following defeats in two world wars created the present Hungarian problem, but dictates cannot solve it. It may ultimately be solved by peaceful evolution, provided historical circumstances allow the Danube region to outgrow its ethnocentric intolerance and develop into a community of nations, similar to the one which, however slowly, is breaking new ground for peace through reconciliation and cooperation on a regional scale in Western Europe.

Meanwhile, unpredictable as events in the Communist world often are, the possibility of a change for the better under Soviet Russian auspices should not be ruled out. After all, it was Stalin's intervention against President Beneš's anti-minority policy that stopped the persecution of Hungarians in Czechoslovakia after World War II.[6] It was along the same lines of Marxist-Leninist nationality policy that, for a while in the 1950s, the Hungarians of Transylvania were granted, on Soviet prodding, autonomy by the ruling Romanians. And Yugoslavia's Tito (trained in the Soviet way of thinking) showed respect for the Marxist-Leninist principles by advocating a tolerant minority policy toward the Hungarians, both before and after Belgrade's break with Moscow.[7]

The "socialist world," as the East European Communists are fond of calling the Soviet bloc, is theoretically committed to treating national minorities according to principles of democratic equality. Theoretically, territorial autonomy is the very essence of the Marxist-Leninist nationality policy. In the Soviet Union, it has been translated into practice—at least to the extent that Soviet Russian realities are compatible with such democratic theories. The question in the Danube region is whether the Soviet leaders would consider it in their interest to follow the divide-and-rule routine, as others have done before, or to choose to become true peacemakers and throw their weight in favor of reconciliation, something no one has done before. Admittedly, the latter is only a pious hope because, regrettably, the Soviets are more likely to follow the former course.

Yet, if not spontaneous changes in Communist attitudes, perhaps a change in the international climate outside the "socialist world" may influence the Soviets and the nations in their orbit to tackle the Hungarian nationality problem more equitably. For the time being though this too must seem as just another pious hope.

After World War II, President Beneš's campaign against the national minorities carried the day in the world of the victors. From his wartime argument that the "fascist" national minorities destroyed "democratic" Czechoslovakia, he developed a general theory, maintaining that national minorities are a threat to peace and should be liquidated. The emotions of the moment at that time precluded any rational discussion of the issues involved. The tangled nationality problems of Central Europe were even less objectively tackled after World War II than they had been after World War I.[8]

But even with wartime emotions subsiding, the anti-minority position has found unintentional support in the human rights movement of postwar years. Dominated as that movement has been by former colonial peoples, the worldwide agitation for human rights has concerned itself almost exclusively with oppression of non-whites by whites, while by and large ignoring national conflicts among whites. This is the reverse of the post-World War I situation, when the rights of the colonial peoples were conveniently ignored amidst Western humanistic agitation for the liberation of Europe's oppressed nations.

Another tilting of human rights toward special interests has come with the Western emphasis on free emigration. Israel, anxious to increase Jewish ethnic strength in the hostile Arab Middle East, regards Eastern Europe—more specifically the Soviet Union—as the most promising place from which to attract immigrants. The United States vigorously supports this effort. In fact, the American Trade Act of 1974 tied most-favored-nation treatment to free emigration as an assurance of the "continued dedication of the United States to fundamental human rights." West Germany likewise has become an energetic supporter of free emigration, regarding it a top human rights issue. Plagued by a postwar manpower shortage, repatriation of the remaining German ethnic minorities from Eastern Europe became a popular German national objective. This is a truly radical change considering that, before World War II, the Germans, more than anybody else in Europe, had kept protection of the national minorities on the agenda of international interest.

The United Nations dropped from its organization the prewar League of Nations' machinery for international protection of national minorities.[9] This was not due merely to postwar anti-minority arguments, but also to the idea that national minority rights are actually part of human rights. The human rights approach to national rights may sound correct in principle, but in practice a lack of explicit commitment to national minority protection invariably favors the majority. For instance, in a recent U.N. Human Rights Commission-sponsored comprehensive study on minority rights, in a six-point definition of minority protection five points dealt with no need or undesirability of minority protection, from the point of view of the majority nations.[10]

With the Helsinki accords of 1975, the national minority issue has at least been nominally restored to the agenda of international interest. The Helsinki Final Act explicitly declared respect for national minority rights. At the time of the founding of the United Nations, right after World War II, such a declaration would have been inconceivable. It is disappointing, however, that the follow-up conferences on the Helsinki accords have so far ignored the human rights complaints of the Hungarian minorities. For the time being, although the Hungarians are Europe's largest minority, to the world at large the Hungarian nationality problem does not appear to exist.

The Communist revolution after World War II, with all its promises of internationalism, has proven itself no less nationalistic than the bourgeois nationalist revolutions after World War I. The Danube region is deadlocked in nationalist discord, which is not the work of local nationalist intractability alone.

The peace settlements after both world wars contributed greatly to convincing Hungary's neighbors that the annexation of large territories inhabited by Hungarians is just and fair.[11] They have treated these territories as their own exclusive national domains. Their efforts— since World War II in particular—to eliminate the Hungarian presence from these territories by forcible assimilation, dispersal, and colonization have been relentless. Even the vestiges of the past are not spared. Historical falsifications aimed at denying Hungarian realities abound.[12] Under such a climate of ethnocentric nationalism, no sense of fairness which might advance reconciliation is likely to grow inside the Danube region. Perhaps only impartial assistance from the outside can end the nationalist feuds that have for so long frustrated the rule of justice and peace among the Danubian peoples in general, and between the Hungarians and their neighbors in particular. For the time being, however, no effective source of such impartial assistance from the outside is in sight. The Hungarians, majority and minority alike, must fend for themselves.

Twice in the past, crippled but undaunted, the Hungarians survived long periods of foreign rule and temporary territorial partitions. The first such period, following the sixteenth-century catastrophe of the Ottoman Turkish conquest, lasted for one hundred and fifty years. The second one, following an ambiguous liberation from the Turks, lasted even longer under the dominion of the German Habsburgs. In our time, the Hungarian state, though greatly diminished in size, has so far survived the heavy hand of Soviet Russian suzerainty remarkably well. The question is whether the Hungarian minorities—struggling against the threats to the preservation of their national identity in Romania, Czechoslovakia, Yugoslavia, and the Soviet Ukraine—will survive the twentieth-century adversities of Hungarian history.

In a world concerned with nuclear holocaust, the future of the Hungarian minorities may appear as a matter of small concern indeed. The dimensions and ramifications of the Hungarian problem as a whole, however, are far from negligible. They affect, as they have for a long time, all the peoples and states in and around the Danube region—and thus the policies of the Great Powers as well. In the light of past experiences, humanitarian considerations apart, to ignore any of the unresolved problems of this explosive region would seem rather unwise.

Notes

1. István Bibó, *A keleteurópai kisállamok nyomorúsága* (Budapest, 1946); reprinted in István Bibó, *Harmadik út* (London, 1960), 110–67, and also in Bibó's collected works published by the European Protestant Hungarian Free University (Bern, 1981–), 1:202–51. An English edition of ex-

cerpts from István Bibó's principal writings, including the above quoted essay, is in preparation.

2. For the Beneš thesis on the homogeneous nation-state, see Chapter 11, above. Also, on the implementation of his thesis, see Chapters 4 and 5, above.

3. For further details on Communist Hungary's attitude toward the Hungarian minorities, see Chapter 14, above.

4. György Konrád, "A magyar út," *Magyar Füzetek,* no. 12 (1983): 78. The text quoted here in the editor's translation differs slightly from the one in Richard Allen's translation from the Hungarian in György Konrád, *Antipolitics* (New York, 1984), 150–51.

5. Péter Hanák, *Jászi Oszkár dunai patriotizmusa* (Budapest, 1985), and his Introduction to the Hungarian translation of Jászi's *The Dissolution of the Habsburg Monarchy* (Budapest, 1983), 53. Also, on the theme of new Hungarian nationalism, see István [Stephen] Borsody, "A magyar nacionalizmus demokratizálása," *Új Látóhatár,* 32/3–4 (1982): 311–22.

6. See page 6 of my preface to *Czechoslovak Policy and the Hungarian Minority, 1945–1948* (New York, 1982), an English version of Kálmán Janics's book, *A hontalanság évei.*

7. For the Tito thesis, see Chapter 12, above.

8. In the perspective of twentieth-century world history, I have dealt with the problems of peace in the Danube region in my book, *The Tragedy of Central Europe: Nazi and Soviet Conquest and Aftermath,* rev. and updated ed. (New Haven, 1980), originally published under the title *The Triumph of Tyranny: The Nazi and Soviet Conquest of Central Europe* (London, 1960).

9. For an evaluation of the League of Nations' and the United Nations' attitudes toward national minorities, see Chapter 6, above.

10. Special Report by the Sub-Commission on the Prevention of Discrimination and Protection of Minorities of the UN Human Rights Commission, compiled under the direction of Francesco Capotorti: *Study on the Rights of Persons Belonging to Ethnic, Religious, and Linguistic Minorities* (New York, 1979), 5–6.

11. In Western archives (in the United States in particular), there are plenty of papers indicating Western misgivings about the nation-state order in the Danube region, either from the point of view of international stability or because of unfairness in drawing the national boundaries. The standard excuse, however, in explaining the role of the Great Powers as arbiters of peacemaking has been to refer to the Danubian peoples' intractability. This view was first formulated after World War I by Charles Seymour, chief of the Austro-Hungarian Division of the American Peace Commission: "The nationalities . . . [had been] bursting with nationalistic ambitions . . . if they preferred disunion no one could deny them" (Charles Seymour, "The End

of an Empire: Remnants of Austria-Hungary," in Edward Mandel House and Charles Seymour, eds., *What Really Happened at Paris* [New York, 1921], 90.) This view, which has found wide acceptance, conveniently glosses over an essential point in Danubian peacemaking presided over by the Great Powers as final arbiters. Namely, that territorial promises and awards by the Great Powers to the small victor nations at the expense of their defeated rivals a priori excluded any incentive on their part to practice mutual fairness and to seek regional union.

12. For conflicting views on Hungary's history, see Chapter 15, above.

✳ *APPENDIX*

1. Statistics
2. Maps
3. Chronology
4. Selected Bibliography

✳ 1. STATISTICS

The Hungarians and Their Neighbors 1851–2000

Zoltán Dávid

The first official census of Hungary's population according to "mother tongue" took place in 1851. Assessment and publication of its data has never been completed. Nevertheless, we do get from it a picture of Hungary's ethnic composition at mid-nineteenth century. The census was carried out in the so-called "Bach era" under Austrian civil authority, in the wake of the Hungarian defeat in the War of Independence of 1848–49. There is general agreement that the data are far from accurate. Most likely, only the number of Germans is accurate, while that of Magyar-speaking Hungarians is the least reliable. True to the anti-Hungarian spirit of the Bach era, the census counted Hungarians and Székelys in Transylvania as two separate categories, thereby reducing the number of Hungarians to the lowest possible figure—just as Romanian censuses under Ceauşescu have been doing since 1977.

Following the Austro-Hungarian Compromise of 1867, an independent Hungarian Statistical Office was established in Budapest. Its first general census was carried out in 1869. However, for "political reasons" (as it was in fact officially confirmed without further explanation) this census disregarded the languages spoken by the peoples of Hungary. The first ethnic census producing data on the basis of mother tongue did not take place until 1880, thirty years after the

1851 census. Thereafter such censuses were carried out regularly every ten years.

Statistical inquiry requires first of all clarification of principles, and this raises particular problems and difficulties when it comes to collecting data on language and nationality. It is the census takers' task to assess the state of ethnic self-awareness in respondents, which is a tricky operation considering the often unclear, illogical, politically charged, and emotionally biased state of mind of many respondents. Theoretically, the concepts of nation, nationality, race, origin, language, and culture seem to have clear collective meaning. But in practice, as far as individual people are concerned, these concepts may be differently perceived—to say nothing of the individual attitudes of the census takers themselves. Of course, these problems arise only in countries with more than one language and one nationality. And historic Hungary was such a country, as are all the states created since World War I in the Danube region.

Certain regions of historic Hungary were ethnically perhaps the most complex places in the world when census taking according to mother tongue began in the nineteenth century. People speaking different languages, when living in close communities or larger areas, preserved their "mother tongue" for centuries. Their ethnic status was clear and the censuses reflected it quite reliably. Problems and dangers of distortion arose in the boundary areas between neighboring groups, along the so-called "language frontiers," and also in villages with mixed populations. Then, too, in towns everyday life demanded bilingualism which, in nineteenth-century Hungary, sooner or later turned into the exclusive use of the dominant state language: the Hungarian. Hungary's capital, Budapest, was a characteristic example of rapid language change. Up to the middle of the nineteenth century, the majority of inhabitants were German-speaking. Then, with the influx of Hungarian-speaking people into the capital—and under the impact of the political ambiance following the Compromise of 1867—Budapest became by the end of the nineteenth century almost completely Hungarian-speaking. Similar processes took place in other originally German-speaking towns of Hungary. Magyarization was also significantly assisted by the rapid assimilation of immigrant Jews in the capital and other towns. In the countryside, too, many bilingual villages—in particular those along the Hungarian-Slovak language frontier—became Hungarian-speaking; the area of Kassa (Košice) stands out as an example of such a rural language change.

Hungarian statisticians distinguished themselves by refining the methods of census taking according to mother tongue. They also made great efforts to ensure the impartiality of ethnic census. They took pride in the high standards of methodology in their data collection. The work of the Hungarian Statistical Office was held in great esteem internationally. Nevertheless, in the spirit of the age of nationalism, the official reports on the decennial censuses extolled the expansion of the Hungarian language, thereby casting undeserved doubts on the objectivity of Hungarian statistics. There were increasingly violent attacks condemning Hungarian statistics, staged mainly by Czechs, concerned as they were about the stagnation—indeed, decline—of Slovaks in Hungary. The primary Czech argument against Hungarian statistics was that many people who spoke Hungarian were actually not of Hungarian nationality. The criticism disseminated by Czechs in publications abroad began to influence world opinion against alleged Magyarization in Hungary. On the other hand, Hungarian statisticians did nothing to defend their integrity.

The criticisms were, in part at least, justifiable. However, distortions of Hungarian ethnic statistics, if they occurred, were not caused by political pressure on the Hungarian Statistical Office, nor were they the result of deliberate falsification. The Hungarian Statistical Office was not an instrument of Magyarization. Many people living, so to speak, on the borderline of two languages made their own decisions when they declared themselves Hungarians. After all, this was the language of the Hungarian state. Ever since Hungary's partitions in the twentieth century, similar distortions (not to speak of worse offenses) can be found galore in the census-taking practices of Hungary's neighbors. All this, of course, works now to the detriment of the Hungarians.

The peace treaties after World War I amply demonstrated the importance of nationality statistics. In drawing the new state boundaries, Hungary's rivals proclaimed the primacy of the ethnic principle over the historical one. However, willful distortions of the ethnic principles resulted in not only the partition of the Hungarian state but of the Hungarian nation as well. And, paradoxically, it was the carefully registered data concerning mother tongues collected by the Hungarian censuses that were used by Hungary's neighbors against the Hungarians. Data favoring the Hungarians, however, were ignored by the peacemakers. In consequence, after World War I more than three million Hungarians, one out of every three, were incorporated into the newly created or enlarged states surrounding Hungary.

One of the arguments in support of the new boundaries was that quite a few non-Hungarians were left within the borders of diminished Hungary. This claim was anything but fair. For instance, by the Treaty of Trianon, 1,664,000 Hungarians were allotted to the enlarged state of Romania, but only 23,000 Romanians remained in Trianon Hungary. Substantial ethnic disproportions in the distribution of postwar minorities were also created for the benefit of Trianon Hungary's two other neighbors, Czechoslovakia and Yugoslavia.

In analyzing the censuses taken in Trianon Hungary, it should be pointed out that during the peace negotiations about 350,000 Hungarians fled to Hungary from the new states. Of those, 200,000 came from Romania, 100,000 from Czechoslovakia, and 50,000 from Yugoslavia. The ethnic behavior of non-Hungarians left in truncated Hungary varied greatly. For instance, in the first postwar census of 1920, entire Slovak-inhabited villages declared themselves Hungarian, while in others Slovak national consciousness had been awakened.

A new postwar task of Hungarian statisticians was the study of the fate of the three million so-called minority Hungarians in the neighboring states. From 1920 onward, the successor states, too, held decennial censuses—and it was now the Hungarians' turn to become critical of ethnic data collected according to mother tongue by Hungary's neighbors. In Czechoslovakia, for instance, the 1921 census listed only 739,000 Hungarians, in contrast to the 1,055,000 registered in the same area by the last census under Hungarian administration in 1910. One ploy applied by the Czechoslovak census to reduce the number of Hungarians was to separate persons of Jewish religion from the Hungarian-speaking population. This resulted in a considerable Hungarian loss, particularly in towns. Of course, smaller Hungarian groups living in non-Hungarian environments began to shrink or disappear in all the successor states, while bilingual citizens in the town often switched their nationality to the new rulers' tongue, which became the state language. Also, a major loss for the Hungarian minorities was the flight of civil servants to Hungary. But, even after all these factors are taken into consideration, Hungarian criticism of ethnic censuses in the neighboring states was not without foundation.

Still another new task confronting Hungarian statisticians came with the revision of the Trianon frontiers between 1938 and 1941, when Hungary regained some of her lost territories. In 1941, the Hungarian Statistical Office set in motion extensive preparations for a census in the enlarged country. Count Pál Teleki, prime minister at the time and a recognized expert in national minority affairs, intervened several times to ensure fairness in collecting ethnic data. Nevertheless a number of factors hampered the work of the Statistical Office. Particularly important at that time was to ensure complete objectivity regarding the German minority affected by Nazi propaganda. Another sensitive aspect was the attitude of Slovaks, Serbs, and Romanians who—after two decades of belonging to the majority in their own nation-states—found themselves again in a minority status under Hungarian rule.

According to the 1941 census, the total population of enlarged Hungary was 12,146,000. A careful analysis of the ethnic data reveals that about 489,000 persons of non-Hungarian mother tongue declared Hungarian as their nationality. Among Croats, 91 percent declared themselves to be Hungarian, while 35 percent among Slovaks and 25 percent among Germans did the same thing. The ratio was the lowest among Serbs and Ruthenians, 3 percent, while among Romanians it was 4 percent.

After World War II, the Paris Peace Conference ignored Hungary's effort to make the frontiers more consonant with ethnic realities in the Danube region. Hungary, denounced by her neighbors as "Hitler's last satellite," was treated as a nation not deserving fairness. The Trianon frontiers were restored without much ado in this second partition. Czechoslovakia in fact was granted an additional "bridgehead" across the Danube from Bratislava, consisting of four villages with exclusively Hungarian populations.

After World War II, the restoration of frontiers led to a much greater movement of peoples than that following the boundary changes in 1918–20, mainly because of the expulsion of millions of Germans. As for the Hungarians, about 125,000 fled from Romania, 30,000 from Czechoslovakia, and 30,000 from Yugoslavia, in the wake of vicious postwar persecutions. In the course of a "population exchange," about 87,000 Hungarians were forced to leave their ancestral homes in present-day Slovakia. According to Hungarian statistics, 59,774 Slovaks were transferred more or less voluntarily from Hungary to Czechoslovakia (some Slovak sources claim 73,273 repatriated Slovaks). The Potsdam Conference—on Czechoslovakia's request—ordered the expulsion of Germans from Hungary (to make room for the Hungarians earmarked for total expulsion from Czechoslovakia, a design that foundered ultimately). There are no official data in Hungarian statistics on the number of Germans transferred from Hungary. It can, however, be estimated that, out of the 475,491 Germans (according to the 1941 census), about 225,000 were forced to leave Hungary.

The first post-World War II Hungarian census, carried out in 1949, bore a strong imprint of the "homogeneous nation-state" spirit of the times. Large numbers of bilingual Germans and a smaller number of Slovaks who were spared transfer or expulsion declared themselves as Hungarians. Thus, the total number of non-Hungarians was reduced to 129,000, and Hungary's population became 98.6 percent Hungarian. By 1970, the number of non-Hungarians increased to 170,000, but that was still only 1.5 percent of the total population.

The interest of Hungarian statisticians goes beyond the boundaries of present-day Hungary—partly because of the large numbers of Hungarians living in the neighboring states, but also because of historical involvement with ethnic relations in the Carpathian Basin as a whole. The continuing analysis of ethnic statistics of the Carpathian Basin since the breakup of historic Hungary is made easier by the fact that the areas annexed by Hungary's neighbors still constitute more-or-less separate entities within the new state boundaries. The area annexed by Austria is today the province of Burgenland. Slovakia remains distinct from the Czech lands of Bohemia and Moravia within Czechoslovakia. Ruthenia today is a Transcarpathian province of the Ukraine within the Soviet Union. In Romania, administrative changes did not erase the boundaries of Transylvania and adjacent territories once belonging to Hungary. So far, no political change has been able to wipe out the natural boundaries of the Carpathian Mountains. Only in Yugoslavia, changes in borders between Serbia and Croatia need to be taken into consideration in analyzing post-partition ethnic statistics of historic Hungary.

As our tables below show, according to official censuses carried out in the countries of the Carpathian Basin, the proportion of Hungarians in the area of historic Hungary decreased between 1910 and 1980 from 54.5 percent to 50.5 percent. In our tables we had to introduce "estimates" in order to take into account the chauvinistic practices affecting census taking. In most instances, official statistical data in the Danube region cannot be accepted without reservations. Thus, against the total of 2,887,000 Hungarians shown in official censuses of Hungary's neighbors, one can safely estimate the actual Hungarian minority population to stand at 3.4 million (see table 4). Adding this to the bulk of the Hungarians living in Hungary, the total number of Hungarians in the Danube region today amounts to an estimated 14 million. They are the second largest national ethnic group of the region, topped only by the Romanians. But what does the future hold for the Hungarians?

According to the 1980 census, Hungary's population was 10,709,463. This shows a net increase of 387,364 (3.8 percent) against the census of 1970. Although the increase is 0.2 percent higher than in the 1960–1970 decade, it is only half of the increase of the 1949–1960 statistical decade. Furthermore, if the period since 1975 is registered by years beyond 1980, a steady decline is noticeable, leading to actual losses rather than gains in the last few years. The natural increase was 63,138 in 1975 (6 percent); 53,165 in 1976 (5 percent); 45,543 in 1977 (4.3 percent); 28,039 in 1978 (2.7 percent); 23,535 in 1979 (2.2 percent); 3,318 in 1980 (0.3 percent); but *minus* 1,867 in 1981 (−0.2 percent); *minus* 10,759 in 1982 (−1 percent); and *minus* 21,240 in 1983 (−2 percent). In addition to falling birth rates, emigration is a prominent factor among the causes of the recent decreases. Furthermore, in order to maintain the economic gains of recent years, all signs seem to indicate that Hungary is not going to embark on a successful campaign for more children. It is even questionable whether Hungary reduced to its present size would be economically capable of sustaining any further population growth. The density of population in Hungary already is one of the highest in Europe. Thus, looking into the future, a decrease in population—or, at best, stagnation—is most likely to continue in Hungary through the year 2000.

From the viewpoint of the year 2000, the state of the Hungarians in the neighboring countries is not promising either—there, too, stagnation at best may be expected.

In Czechoslovakia, according to the 1980 census, there were 579,200 people of Hungarian nationality. While between 1961 and 1970 the number of Hungarians increased by 39,000, in the last decade the increase was only 7,000. At the same time, the total population of Czechoslovakia increased by 4 percent between 1961 and 1970, and by 6.5 percent between 1970 and 1980. The decline of Czechoslovakia's Hungarians is due partly to the decline of opportunities and standards of education in the Hungarian mother tongue. It is a well-known fact that the language of schooling bears upon people's nationality. Another reason is the method of census taking. The official instruction at the last census was to list as Slovaks all pupils attending Slovak schools. All these and other pressures are reflected in the statistical discrepancies between "nationality" and "mother tongue" of respondents: the number of people who declared themselves Hungarian by "nationality" was fifty thousand fewer than that of those who claimed Hungarian as their "mother tongue." Incidentally, the erratic fluctuation in the numbers of Hungarians in the two postwar censuses has no demographic significance; it is the result of the Slovak nationalist "re-Slovakization" campaign, stopped following the Communist takeover in 1948 (see Table 4a).

In our estimate, the number of Hungarians living in Czechoslovakia today is about 750,000, or even 1 million, counting the bilingual "borderline" population of towns as well as the people of unquestionably Hungarian origin who figure as Slovaks in the official statistics. Yet, by the indicators we are using in our forecast, we cannot envisage an increase in Czechoslovakia's Hungarian population. In our estimate, a decline to 640,000 by the year 2000 seems more likely. At the same time the number of Slovaks will probably reach over 5 million, representing the second highest increase (slightly behind the Romanians) among the peoples of the Carpathian Basin during the period since World War I.

In Trans-Carpathia of the Soviet Ukraine, the situation of the Hungarians seems somewhat better. True, according to the last census, their increase was only half of what could have been expected: only

3 percent as against 7.3 percent in the preceding decade. Unexpectedly, however—and contrary to the general pattern—more people declared themselves Hungarians by "nationality" (171,000) than by "mother tongue" (163,134). We do not know the reason. In any case, our indicators suggest that by the year 2000 one may expect 200,000 Hungarians in Trans-Carpathia among a total population of 1,100,000.

In Romania, the last census gave the number of people of Hungarian nationality as 1,670,568. This is an increase of 51,000 over the previous decade, but only one-third of what might have been expected. According to official statistics, since the 1956–1966 decade, the natural increase of Hungarians in Romania came practically to a halt. The total number of Romanians between 1956 and 1977 increased by 4 million (26 percent). During the same period, the Hungarian population grew only by a total of 17,000 (1 percent), whereas projections based on natural increase expected a gain of nearly 400,000. In view of what goes on in Romanian census taking, the actual number of Hungarians today can be safely estimated at 2 million. This corresponds to less than 10 percent of Romania's total population of over 22 million, but is close to 30 percent of the population in the Romanian territories annexed from Hungary (Transylvania proper and adjacent western areas).

Of course, despite their strong national consciousness and the great tradition of their Transylvanian-Hungarian culture, erosion by assimilation is a constant threat to Romania's Hungarian minority. One of the unfavorable factors is that 47 percent of Hungarians today live in towns where they are subject to increasing pressures of Romanization. Mixed marriages, the growing suppression of education in the Hungarian mother tongue, the loss of day-to-day contacts with the Hungarian community in a Romanian environment—all these assimilatory forces have a much stronger impact in towns than in the villages. Another unfavorable circumstance is the official policy of industrialization, bypassing as it does the Hungarian areas thereby forcing the Hungarian workers to move into purely Romanian regions of the country. In Hungarian areas where industries have been set up, Romanian employees are usually recruited to run them. As a consequence, the economically disadvantaged Hungarian villages can hardly maintain their existing population levels, let alone increase them. It is particularly the younger generation that is being attracted

to the towns or to newly established industrial centers in the Romanian regions. And the farther they have to move from their places of
birth, the more difficult it becomes for them to safeguard their Hungarian tongue and the Hungarian national consciousness.

Taking into account all these factors, one cannot forecast a number
greater than 2.2 million Hungarians living in Romania by the year
2000. One must envisage that at least 200,000 Hungarians will be
absorbed into the fast-growing ruling Romanian nationality. By the
turn of the century, there may be a total of half a million assimilated
Romanians of Hungarian origin. Certainly, knowing the tendency of
Romanian statistics, one can expect only a very small officially recognized increase of Hungarians.

In Yugoslavia, statistically speaking, the situation of the Hungarian
minority is the worst among Hungary's neighbors. On the other hand,
official policy toward the Hungarian minority is the most advantageous. To take the statistics first: In 1961, a total of 504,368 people
of Hungarian nationality were counted. By 1971, this number dropped
to 477,374. The 1981 census showed a further decrease: only 426,865
(minus 1.9 percent) were counted, against a total population of
22,418,331 in Yugoslavia. Since 1961, the total Hungarian loss is
77,503 (minus 10.6 percent). The decrease itself is no surprise, though
it is greater than expected.

The main reason for the decrease is emigration. Yugoslavia's Hungarians may decide more easily than Hungarians in other states to
emigrate because they are less deeply rooted there. Their land was
almost completely devastated by the Turkish wars of the sixteenth
and seventeenth centuries. After liberation from Turkish rule, this
region was only partially repopulated by Hungarian peasants, because
the Habsburg administration preferred German and Slav settlers in
this so-called military border zone. It has also been said that the
Titoist, relatively liberal, Yugoslav nationality policy plays a role in
the decline of the Hungarian minority. The idea behind this assumption is that oppression, not liberalism, increases a minority's strength.
However, this theory is highly debatable. It is more likely that, in
addition to emigration, ambition for economic success through assimilation is the principal cause of the Hungarian population decrease.
As for the future: the decrease most likely is going to continue and
by 2000 the number of Hungarians may be down to about 390,000.

1. *Historic Hungary**

Population figures for Hungarians and non-Hungarians in historic Hungary (without Croatia-Slavonia) according to official censuses taken since 1851.

(a) In thousands

Year	Hungarians	Romanians	Slovaks	Serbs-Croats	Ruthenes	Germans	Others	Total
1851	4,527	2,163	1,690	446	355	1,367	572	11,120
1869	6,207	2,322	1,826	495	448	1,816	105	13,219
1880	6,404	2,403	1,855	640	353	1,871	233	13,749
1890	7,358	2,589	1,897	689	380	1,990	260	15,163
1900	8,652	2,799	2,002	629	425	1,999	332	16,838
1910	9,944	2,948	1,946	657	464	1,903	402	18,264

(b) In percents

Year	Hungarians	Romanians	Slovaks	Serbs-Croats	Ruthenes	Germans	Others	Total
1851	40.7	19.5	15.2	4.0	3.2	12.3	5.2	100.0
1869	46.9	17.6	13.8	3.8	3.4	13.7	0.8	100.0
1880	46.6	17.5	13.5	4.6	2.6	13.6	1.6	100.0
1890	48.5	17.1	12.5	4.6	2.5	13.1	1.7	100.0
1900	51.4	16.6	11.9	3.7	2.5	11.9	2.0	100.0
1910	54.5	16.1	10.7	3.6	2.5	10.4	2.2	100.0

*Editor's Note: The statistical tables that follow illustrate the demographic history of Hungarians and their neighbors from the first official ethnic census of 1851 to the estimated figures for the year 2000. Both the text above, a shortened version of a longer, mostly unpublished, study by the Hungarian author, and the tables below are the editor's arrangements.

2. Historic Hungary Partitioned

Population figures for Hungarians and non-Hungarians in the territories of former historic Hungary (without Croatia-Slavonia) according to official censuses taken since 1920, with estimates for 2000.

(a) In thousands

Year	Hungarians	Romanians	Slovaks	Serbs-Croats	Ruthenes	Germans	Others	Total
1920	9,634	3,016	2,225	649	470	1,797	679	18,470
1930	10,480	3,274	2,583	715	567	1,763	791	20,153
1950	11,507	3,842	3,673	1,006	626	630	503	21,787
1960	12,474	4,144	3,663	1,134	746	663	577	23,401
1970	12,915	4,648	3,975	1,191	872	660	582	24,843
1980	13,448	5,320	4,356	1,467	980	651	427	26,649
2000 est.	13,400	6,550	5,100	1,650	Ukrainians 1,120	600	530	28,950

(b) In percents

Year	Hungarians	Romanians	Slovaks	Serbs-Croats	Ruthenes	Germans	Others	Total
1920	52.2	16.3	12.0	3.5	2.6	9.7	3.7	100.0
1930	52.0	16.2	12.9	3.6	2.8	8.6	3.9	100.0
1950	52.8	17.6	16.9	4.6	2.9	2.8	2.4	100.0
1960	53.3	17.7	15.6	4.9	3.2	2.8	2.5	100.0
1970	52.0	18.7	16.0	4.7	3.5	2.7	2.4	100.0
1980	50.5	19.9	16.3	5.5	3.8	2.4	1.6	100.0
2000 est.	46.2	22.7	17.8	5.6	Ukrainians 3.9	2.0	1.8	100.0

3. *The Hungarians Partitioned*

Population figures (in thousands) for Hungarians living in Hungary and in the neighboring states.

(a) According to official censuses since 1920

Year	Total	Living in Hungary	Percent	In neighboring states	Percent
1920	9,634	7,157	74.3	2,477	25.7
1930	10,480	8,001	76.4	2,479	23.6
1950	11,507	9,076	78.9	2,431	21.1
1960	12,474	9,786	78.5	2,688	21.5
1970	12,915	10,166	78.8	2,749	21.2
1980	13,448	10,580	78.7	2,868	21.3

(b) According to estimates from World War I through 2000

Year	Total	Living in Hungary	Percent	In neighboring states	Percent
1918/19	10,307	6,807	66.0	3,500	34.0
1980	13,950	10,580	75.8	3,370	24.2
2000	13,430	10,000	74.5	3,430	25.5

4. *The Hungarians of Hungary's Neighbors*

Population figures (in thousands) for the Hungarian minorities living in the territories annexed by Romania, Czechoslovakia, Yugoslavia, and the Soviet Ukraine.

(a) According to official censuses since 1920

Year	Romania	Czechoslovakia	Yugoslavia	Soviet Ukraine	Total
1920	1,322	739	391	—	2,452
1930	1,353	708	400	—	2,461
1950	1,482	355	449	140	2,426
1960	1,559	518	459	146	2,552
1970	1,597	554	439	152	2,742
1980	1,670	628	426	163	2,887

(b) According to estimates from 1980 to 2000

Year	Romania	Czechoslovakia	Yugoslavia	Soviet Ukraine	Total
1980	2,000	750	450	170	3,370
2000	2,200	640	390	200	3,430

✳ 2. MAPS

Hungary and the Hungarians

Lajos Palovics

1. Hungary's historical boundaries

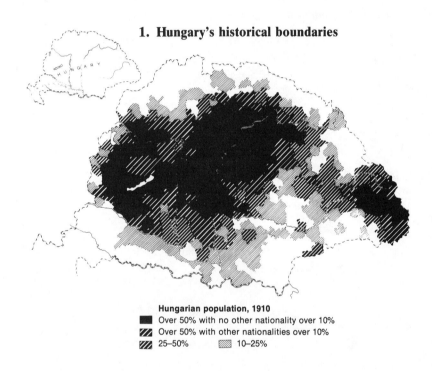

Hungarian population, 1910
▪ Over 50% with no other nationality over 10%
▨ Over 50% with other nationalities over 10%
▨ 25–50%   ▨ 10–25%

Boundary changes since World War I are superimposed on an ethnic map based on the 1910 census. The sole purpose of this method is to relate Hungary's partition to the division and the resulting ethnic losses of the Hungarian people.

2. Hungary's boundaries after World War I (1920)

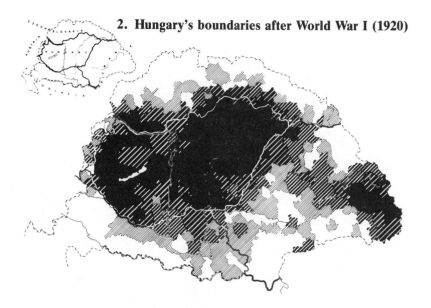

3. Hungary's boundaries after the two Vienna Awards (1938, 1940) and the occupation of Subcarpathia (1939) and Vojvodina (1941)

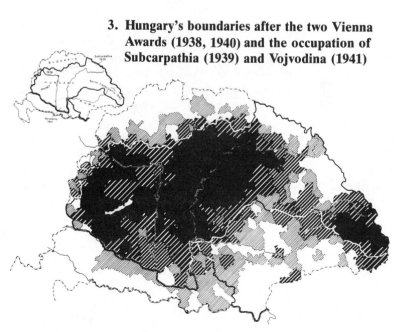

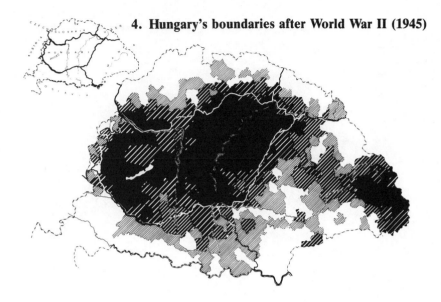

4. Hungary's boundaries after World War II (1945)

EDITOR'S NOTE. Nationalist rivalry in the Danube region is a contest for both the size of land and the number of people. Ever since World War I, the drawing of boundaries between nation-states has been the central issue of Danubian international relations. It has often been pointed out that no boundaries could ever be drawn to the satisfaction of all concerned. Yet there are boundaries which reflect more fairly and those which reflect less fairly ethnic realities.

Rather sketchily, the above maps illustrate boundary changes from an ethnic point of view. Real peace, of course, may be achieved only by overcoming the nationalist preoccupation with boundaries. As long as territorial jealousy dominates international relations, no civilized community of nations is conceivable in the Danube region.

✳ 3. CHRONOLOGY

Hungary's Partition and the Hungarian Minorities since World War I*

Iván K. Szűcs

A. Regional Survey

1914 July 28. Austria-Hungary declares war on Serbia, thereby precipitating the outbreak of World War I

1916 August 17. The Allies pledge Transylvania to Romania as a reward for entering the war on their side

1917 July 20. Members of the Yugoslav Committee in exile sign the Pact of Corfu on the future formation of a Yugoslav state

1918 June 28. France recognizes the Czecho-Slovak National Council in exile as "first basis" of a future Czecho-Slovak government

August 9. Great Britain recognizes the Czecho-Slovak Council in exile as "present trustee" of the Czecho-Slovak government

September 2. The United States recognizes the Czecho-Slovak Council in exile as "de facto belligerent" government

---

*EDITOR'S NOTE. Throughout the Chronology—in the Regional Survey in particular—the Hungarian author's text has been significantly supplemented and edited for publication in the West.

October 3. Austria-Hungary, in a joint note with Germany and Turkey, appeals to President Wilson to initiate general peace negotiations on the basis of the Fourteen Points

October 6. In Zagreb, a National Council is formed by Serbs, Croats, and Slovenes with the aim of uniting them in a South Slav state

October 25. In Hungary, a National Council under the presidency of Mihály Károlyi is formed to establish the country's independence, conclude a treaty of peace, and carry out democratic reforms including the recognition of the country's non-Hungarian nationalities' right to autonomy under a federal system

October 27. Austria-Hungary sues for an armistice

October 28. In Prague, the Czech National Council declares the independence of the Czech lands within a Czecho-Slovak state

October 29. In Zagreb, the National Assembly declares Croatia's secession from Hungary

October 30. In Turčiansky Sv. Martin (Túrócszentmárton, Hungary), a Slovak Assembly declares the secession of the Slovaks from Hungary and their union with the Czechs in a Czecho-Slovak state

November 5. Armies of the Kingdom of Serbia begin to occupy the South Slav-inhabited territories of Hungary

November 8. Military formations set up by the provisional Czechoslovak government begin to occupy the Slovak-inhabited northern territories of Hungary

November 12. The Ruthenian People's Council of America (formed in July 1918) declares Ruthenia's secession from Hungary and its union with Czecho-Slovakia

November 12–14. On behalf of the Hungarian National Council, Oszkár Jászi negotiates in Arad with president Iuliu Maniu and other members of the Romanian National Council of Transylvania; the Romanians reject the offer of autonomy and demand independence

December 1. In Paris, Prince Regent Alexander of Serbia

proclaims the formation of the Kingdom of Serbs, Croats, and Slovenes (later known as Yugoslavia)
December 1–2. In Alba Iulia (Gyulafehérvár, Hungary), an assembly convoked by the Romanian National Council of Transylvania declares union with the Kingdom of Romania while promising the non-Romanians of Transylvania equality and national freedom with cultural autonomy
December 2. Armies of the Kingdom of Romania cross the Hungarian border and begin to occupy Transylvania
1919 January 11. In Bucharest, the Romanian government proclaims the annexation of Transylvania
January 12. Opening of the Paris Peace Conference
March 20. The Allied Supreme Council orders further Hungarian withdrawal from territories to be occupied by Romania. Unwilling to obey this order, handed to him in the so-called "Vyx note," Károlyi resigns as president of the Hungarian Republic; the democratic republican regime collapses
March 21. A Republic of Councils on the Soviet model is formed in Hungary under the leadership of Béla Kun. In the hope of Soviet help, the new regime organizes armed resistance to defy Allied territorial dispositions
April. Romanian and Czech armies attack the Hungarian Republic of Councils. A counteroffensive by the Hungarian Red Army drives the Czechs out of Hungary and Eastern Slovakia
June 17. The Allied Supreme Council orders the Hungarian Red Army troops to retire behind the provisional frontiers decreed by the Paris Peace Conference. Unsuccessful against the Romanians, Kun's crumbling Communist regime obeys the Allied order
August 1. Fall of the Hungarian Republic of Councils, followed by a counterrevolution, restoring the kingdom under Admiral Miklós Horthy as regent
1920 June 4. Signing of the Peace Treaty of Trianon with Hungary, executing the partition of Hungary
August 14 through June 7, 1921. Signing of treaties among

Czechoslovakia, Yugoslavia, and Romania (the Little Entente countries) to counteract Hungary's revisionist policy

1924　January 25. France signs a treaty of alliance with Czechoslovakia, followed by similar treaties with Romania (January 10, 1926) and Yugoslavia (November 11, 1927)

1927　April 5. Italy signs a treaty of friendship and cooperation with Hungary

1929　January 1. Royal dictatorship is proclaimed in Yugoslavia, torn by conflict between Serbs and Croats

1933　With Hitler's appointment as chancellor, the campaign for treaty revision is radicalized under Nazi Germany leadership

1935　May 2. France concludes a treaty of mutual assistance with the Soviet Union.

　　　May 16. Czechoslovakia signs a treaty of mutual assistance with the USSR, thereby joining the Franco-Soviet treaty

　　　December. T. G. Masaryk, one of the principal architects of postwar Central Europe, retires and is succeeded by Edvard Beneš as President of Czechoslovakia

1937　September 14. T. G. Masaryk dies

1938　March. Following Hitler's annexation of Austria, there is a mounting crisis in Czechoslovakia, precipitated by Sudeten German demands for autonomy

　　　September 30. With the signing of the Four-power Munich Agreement, the breakup of Czechoslovakia begins

　　　October 14. Hungary adheres to the Anti-Comintern Pact (Tripartite Pact, as it is called later)

　　　November 2. The first Vienna Award of the Axis powers returns the Hungarian-inhabited territories of Czechoslovakia to Hungary

1939　March 14. Slovakia proclaimed an independent state

　　　March 15. Bohemia and Moravia is annexed by Nazi Germany, Carpatho-Ukraine by Hungary

　　　August 23. Signing of the Nazi-Soviet Pact, followed, September 1, by Hitler's invasion of Poland and the outbreak of World War II. Poland is defeated and divided

1940 June. The USSR regains Bessarabia and northern Bukovina from Romania

August 20. The second Vienna Award of the Axis powers returns most of the Hungarian-inhabited territories of Romania to Hungary by partitioning Transylvania

1941 March. A Serbian-led coup in Belgrade revokes Yugoslavia's adherence to the Tripartite Pact, whereupon Hitler demands free passage for German troops through Hungary and invades Yugoslavia. Regent Horthy yields to German demand. In protest, April 3, Hungary's Prime Minister Pál Teleki commits suicide. Hungary regains the Vojvodina and other territories from dismembered Yugoslavia. Croatia is proclaimed an independent state.

June 21. Hitler invades the Soviet Union

June 22. Romania attacks the Soviet Union

June 23. Slovakia enters the war against the Soviet Union. Croatia declares war on the Soviet Union.

June 27. Hungary joins the war against the Soviet Union

1944 March 19. Nazi Germany occupies Hungary to forestall the country's leaving the war against the Soviet Union

August 23. Romania leaves the war against the Soviet Union and declares war on Nazi Germany

October 15. Regent Horthy announces Hungary's withdrawal from the war, whereupon the Germans install a Nazi puppet regime in Budapest under Ferenc Szálasi, soon to be removed with the retreating Germans to Western Hungary

December 22. In eastern Hungary, liberated from the Nazis by the Soviet Union, a Hungarian provisional national assembly and government is formed in Debrecen

December 23. The Provisional Government of Hungary declares war on Nazi Germany

1945 February 4–12. The Yalta Conference, while pledging "free and unfettered elections," actually ushers in the establishment of pro-Soviet governments in a divided Europe

March 6. Petru Groza's government is formed in Romania, expanding Communist control over the country

March 7. A Yugoslav provisional government is set up with dominant Communist participation under Tito's leadership

April 3. A national front government is appointed by President Beneš in Czechoslovakia with Communist participation

July 17–August 2. The Potsdam Conference, while reiterating the pledges of the Yalta agreements, fails to halt the process of Europe's partition into Eastern Soviet and Western democratic spheres

1946   July 29. The Peace Conference convenes in Paris

1947   February 10. Five treaties of peace are signed in Paris; Hungary's second partition is confirmed

May 31. Collapse of the democratically elected coalition government in Hungary, leading to total Communist takeover within a year

September 22–23. At a meeting at Szklarska Poreba, Poland, the Soviet-controlled Cominform (Information Bureau of the Communist parties) is set up with headquarters in Belgrade

1948   February 25. Communist takeover in Czechoslovakia. Beneš remains president until June 7, and dies September 3

June 27. Break between Tito and Stalin; Yugoslavia is expelled from the Cominform and becomes the first Communist state free of Soviet control

1949   January 25. The Soviet bloc's economic organization is set up under the Soviet controlled Comecon (Council of Mutual Economic Assistance)

1953   March 5. Stalin dies

May 11–15. At a meeting in Warsaw, the Soviet bloc's military alliance, called the Warsaw Treaty, is formed under Soviet command

June. In East Berlin, Soviet occupation troops crush an uprising of German workers

1955   May. East-West negotiations for a peace treaty with Austria are completed under the terms of Austria's neutralization

1956   February. Nikita Khrushchev's denunciation of Stalin at the Twentieth Party Congress, followed by "de-Stalinization"

October. Crisis in Poland. Władysław Gomulka is returned to power amidst widespread unrest

October 23. Triggered by the anti-regime revolt in Poland, sympathy demonstrations in Budapest lead to a national uprising against Soviet rule in Hungary

November 1. Prime Minister Imre Nagy, as head of the revolutionary coalition government, declares Hungary's neutrality. Hungary leaves the Warsaw Treaty and asks the UN to deal with the "question of Hungary's neutrality and the defense of that neutrality by the four Great Powers." November 4. Soviet military intervention crushes the Hungarian Revolution. János Kádár forms a new Communist government in Hungary under Soviet occupation

1968 The "Prague Spring"

April 10. The Czechoslovak Communist party publishes its Action Program to achieve "socialism with a human face"

August 20. Soviet military intervention stops the reform movement and places Czechoslovakia under Soviet occupation. Birth of the "Brezhnev doctrine," justifying intervention

1969 The "New Economic Mechanism" is launched in Hungary, advancing the country's "liberalization" without changing the Communist party's monopoly of power

1975 July 30–August 1. The final meeting of the Conference on Security and Cooperation in Europe is held in Helsinki; a declaration of the "Final Act" includes the affirmation of the rights of national minorities

1977 In Czechoslovakia, the Charter 77 civil rights movement is launched by Czech dissidents

1978 The first Helsinki review conference in Belgrade discusses human rights, including those of national equality

1980 August. In Poland, the free trade union "Solidarity" is legalized, only to be outlawed in December 1981 under General Jaruzelski's military dictatorship

1983 The second Helsinki review conference in Madrid in its closing document reiterates the safeguarding of the rights of national minorities.

356 IVÁN K. SZŰCS

The Soviet-backed Jaruzelski regime in Poland eases some
of its martial law measures, but the Solidarity trade union
remains outlawed

1984 October 23. On the anniversary of the 1956 Hungarian Revolution, several Polish underground organizations issue a
joint proclamation reiterating the 1981 call by the Solidarity free trade union for international unity of workers of
Eastern Europe

1985 August. On the tenth anniversary of the Helsinki Final Act,
Czechoslovakia's Charter 77 spokesmen declare that there
is "no reason to celebrate" because Europe has slipped
into "a new cold war." In support of détente, an earlier
statement by the Czech human rights group appeals for
East-West negotiations to disband the Warsaw Pact and
NATO to be followed by "withdrawal of American and
Soviet troops from the territories of their European allies"

1986 June. At a Warsaw Pact meeting in Budapest, Mikhail S.
Gorbachev, the new Soviet leader, expresses tolerance and
even some admiration for Hungary's market-oriented economic policies. He said: "We are pleased with the successes of our friends and strive to take over everything that
may be useful for our country." However, he also stresses
the need for closer political and economic cooperation
among Soviet-bloc countries, which was interpreted as a
Soviet warning against closer ties between the bloc-coun-
tries and the West

July. At the congress of the Polish Communist Party in Warsaw, Mikhail Gorbachev reiterates (July 1) the Soviet
pledge of support against any attempts to "wrench a country away from the socialist community." In an Independence Day editorial (July 4), *The New York Times*
denounces the Gorbachev statement as a reaffirmation of
the Brezhnev doctrine, which is "the Soviet declaration of
Eastern Europe's non-independence"

October. On the thirtieth anniversary of the Hungarian revolution of 1956, a joint proclamation is issued in Budapest,
Warsaw, Prague, and East Berlin signed by 122 prominent

Soviet-bloc Europeans from Hungary (54), Poland (28), Czechoslovakia (24), and East Germany (16). Three Romanian dissidents join later. The first document of its kind, the proclamation says: "We declare our joint determination to struggle for political democracy in our countries, pluralism based on the principles of self-government, peaceful reunification of divided Europe and its democratic integration as well as the rights of all minorities"

November. The third Helsinki review conference opens in Vienna. In the course of discussions on human rights, László Demus, a member of Hungary's delegation, expresses Hungary's concern for "the fate of Hungarians living beyond our boundaries," condemns "any form of nationalism," in particular "one of its worst forms: forcible assimilation"

1987 May 26. In the course of an official visit to Bucharest, Mikhail Gorbachev reminds the Romanians of the Leninist teaching to treat nationalities with "delicacy and carefulness"

B. Hungarians in Romania

1920 June. Under the provisions of the Peace Treaty of Trianon, Romania annexes from Hungary an area of 102,000 sq. km. with a total population of 3.5 million of which (according to the 1910 census) 1,664,000 are Hungarians.

Napkelet, the first literary magazine of the Hungarians in Romania, is launched at Kolozsvár (Cluj); editor: Árpád Paál

1921 January 23. An appeal is published by prominent Hungarian writers at Kolozsvár (Cluj) denouncing chauvinism and urging peaceful coexistence with the Romanian people

March 19. Hungarian bishops of the Roman Catholic, Calvinist, and Unitarian churches take the oath of allegiance to the state of Romania

June 5. The Hungarian People's Party is founded at a meeting in Bánffyhunyad (Huedin); president: Lajos Albrecht; secretary: Károly Kós

July 6. With the aim to secure nationwide political representation of the Hungarians in Romania, the Hungarian Association is established at Kolozsvár (Cluj); presidents: Samu Jósika and Gusztáv Maller; secretary: Károly Kós

July. The literary periodical *Pásztortűz* is launched at Kolozsvár (Cluj); editor: Sándor Reményik

1922   February 12. A second political party, the Hungarian National Party, is founded

December 28. The two political parties of the Hungarians in Romania are merged into the National Hungarian Party.

The political review *Magyar Kisebbség* is launched by Elemér Jakabffy at Lugos (Lugoj); achieving international recognition, it will continue publication until 1942

1923   March 29. Promulgation of the new Romanian Constitution, guaranteeing equality before the law to all citizens of the country, but without specifying the minority rights pledged in the 1918 Alba Iulia declaration or those guaranteed by the Paris peace treaties

1924   June 26. The Primary Education Act places the regions inhabited by national minorities under special administration and provides special benefits for Romanian teachers engaged in educating persons "denationalized by alien elements"

The Hungarian publishing house *Erdélyi Szépmíves Céh* is founded at Kolozsvár (Cluj)

The periodical *Géniusz* is started at Arad; editor: Zoltán Franyó

1925   The law on private education makes obligatory the teaching of the Romanian language, as well as of Romania's geography, history, and constitution in Romanian; teachers have to pass Romanian language examinations

1926   The progressive literary magazine *Korunk* is launched at Kolozsvár (Cluj) by László Dienes; editor from 1929: Gábor Gaál

July 18. On the initiative of János Kemény, the literary society *Erdélyi Helikon* is established at a meeting of Hungarian writers at the Kemény castle in Marosvécs

1927 April 22. The so-called statute of cults deprives the churches of their autonomy and places them under state supervision

Summer. The left wing of the National Hungarian Party secedes and organizes itself again as a Hungarian People's Party; leaders: Endre Antalffy, Károly Molter, Károly Kós, Géza Tabéry. On the extreme left, Hungarian Communists are active in the underground Communist party of Romania

1928 Foundation of the periodical *Erdélyi Helikon,* which will remain until 1944 the representative literary organ of the Transylvanian Hungarian writers; its successive editors: Lajos Áprili, Miklós Bánffy, Károly Kós, Aladár Kuncz, and László Kovács

1930 According to the Romanian census, there are 1,425,507 people of Hungarian "nationality" (7.9 percent of the country's total population), while 1,554,525 (8.6 percent) claim Hungarian as their "mother tongue"

September 2. The Hungarian party of Transylvania files complaint at the League of Nations against the "cultural zones" for violating the provisions of the Paris peace treaties on the protection of minority rights

1932 January 10. An editorial in the newspaper *Ellenzék,* under the title, "Let's Build a Bridge," urges reconciliation with the Romanian people

September. *Falvak Népe,* a paper intended for the Hungarian peasantry, is launched by János Demeter but is suppressed in February 1933 because of its radical political coloration

1934 August. The progressive opposition within the Hungarian Party of Romania constitutes itself into the National Union of Hungarian Workers (MADOSZ)

1935 September 25. The National Union of Hungarian Workers and the Romanian Ploughmen's Front hold a joint conference

December 6. The Democratic Bloc of Romania, the Ploughmen's Front, the National Union of Hungarian Workers, and the Independent Socialist party form an antifascist democratic front

1936 A new trade law dissolves the Hungarian industrial corporations and assigns their property to the state-managed chambers of industry

1937 October 2–4. At a meeting at Marosvásárhely (Tirgu Mureş), representatives of the Hungarian youth of Transylvania adopt an antifascist resolution urging collaboration with Romanian democratic elements

November 14. The National Union of Hungarian Workers, member of the antifascist democratic front, holds a mass meeting at Brassó (Braşov)

1938 Royal dictatorship under King Karol II is proclaimed. All political parties are disbanded. Rights of Romania's national minorities are further curtailed contrary to the provisions on international protection of minority rights

May 4. To create the impression that the new Constitution is concerned with minority rights, a high commission for the minorities is appointed at the Romanian prime minister's office; it is later converted into a Ministry for Minority affairs

August 14. The Public Administration act, dividing the country into ten provinces, secures the ethnic predominance of Romanians within each unit

1939 February 11. In response to the rising international crisis, a Hungarian People's Community is formed under the auspices of the Front of National Rebirth; president: Miklós Bánffy; secretary: Imre Makó

June 27. Hungary's Council of Ministers declares: "Should Romania fulfill the Soviet Union's territorial demands of June 26, it must also comply with Hungary's territorial claims"

1940 August 16–23. Direct negotiations between Hungary and Romania on frontier rectification end in failure

August 30. The Second Vienna Award returns to Hungary northern Transylvania and other territories annexed by Romania after World War I; of the total population of 2,185,546 transferred to Hungary, 51.4 percent are Hungarians and 42.1 percent Romanians

September. Hungarian troops occupy the territories reannexed from Romania

November 1. A nonparty group of Transylvanian members of the Hungarian Parliament is formed in Budapest, headed by Gábor Paál

December 14. The nonparty group of Hungarian Transylvanian deputies is dissolved and the Transylvanian Party is formed; president: Géza Ember; secretary-general: Béla Teleki

In the course of boundary changes between Hungary and Romania, 200,000 Romanians leave Hungary and some 60,000 Hungarians move to Hungary from areas remaining under Romanian rule

1941 June. 800 Communists are arrested by the Hungarian authorities in the repossessed territories

Repatriation to Hungary of ca. 13,500 Székelys who settled in Bukovina in the eighteenth century

1944 August 23. The Soviet Red Army breaks through the German-Romanian frontier at Jaşi; Romania sues for an armistice

August 25. Romania declares war on Germany

September 12. Romania concludes an armistice with the Soviet Union; according to the armistice, Transylvania, "or the greater part of thereof," will be returned to Romania

September 16. A memorandum of Transylvanian Hungarians, presented by Miklós Bánffy to Regent Horthy, urges Hungary to conclude an armistice

September 23. The Soviet Red Army crosses the Hungarian-Romanian frontier

October. Romanian administration is restored in the territories reannexed by Romania.

Terrorist commandos of the Peasant Party, the so-called Maniu gardists, commit a series of massacres in Hungarian villages

October 16. *Világosság,* the first postwar Hungarian paper of Transylvania under restored Romanian rule is published at Kolozsvár (Cluj); editor Edgár Balogh (Communist)

At a meeting in Brassó (Braşov), a National Union of Hungarian Workers of Transylvania is formed; president Gyárfás Kurkó (Communist). *Népi Egység* (People's Union), is launched

October 25. Soviet military administration is temporarily restored in northern Transylvania to stop the anti-Hungarian atrocities

1945   February 6. The Statute of Nationalities decrees that all citizens of Romania, regardless of race, language, nationality, and religion, are equal

March 6. Petru Groza (Communist), leader of the agrarian socialist Ploughmen's Front, forms a new government and pledges fair treatment of the national minorities

March 9. Romanian administration is restored throughout the reannexed territories

March 23. Decree on the land reform is promulgated; some 300,000 Hungarian small land holders in Transylvania are hard hit

March 30. The Citizenship Act leaves some 200,000 Hungarians in an uncertain status; thousands of them are forced to leave Transylvania

April 2. A decree issued in Kolozsvár (Cluj) orders the legal use of minority languages. Bilingual signs are made obligatory for the postal service and railways

May 29. A Hungarian university, the Bólyai State University, is ordered to be organized in Kolozsvár (Cluj). In November, its medical faculty is transferred to Marosvásárhely (Tirgu Mureş)

1946   February 4. The *Székely Állami Szinház* (Székely State Theater) opens at Marosvásárhely (Tirgu Mureş)

June 18. The Hungarian People's Union of Romania, at its Congress at Székelyudvarhely (Odorheiu-Silvaniei), reports that 1,680 Hungarian primary schools and 127 secondary schools are functioning in Transylvania and other territories under Romanian rule

June 22. The literary weekly *Útunk* is started; editor Gábor Gaál

November 19. The Hungarian People's Union receives 670,000 votes at the general elections and is represented by 29 Hungarian deputies in the Romanian parliament

1947 February 10. Signing of the peace treaty with Hungary in Paris. Pre-1938 boundaries are restored, but citizens of Romania, regardless of race, language, religion, or nationality, are to have equal rights, full enjoyment of human rights, fundamental freedoms, including free expression of opinion in the press and other organs of information and in public meetings, as well as freedom of religion and freedom of assembly. However, even the relatively tolerant Groza government carried out these provisions only on a limited scale

June. Obligatory language examinations for railwaymen of Hungarian nationality are abolished

August. Hungarian schools for the Hungarians of Moldavia (the Csángós) are established; these schools will be abolished in the 1950s

December 5. According to a language decree, judges and lay assessors must speak the minority language wherever thirty percent or more of the population is non-Romanian speaking

December 30. King Michael abdicates; Romania is proclaimed a republic

1948 January. According to the official census there are 1,499,851 Hungarians (9.4 percent of the total population) living in Romania

March 6. The first "people's democratic" (Communist) Constitution is promulgated

August 3. The new education law secularizes schools and introduces seven-year compulsory education

September. The Hungarian Opera of Kolozsvár (Cluj) reopens

1949 June 21. Áron Márton, Hungarian Roman Catholic bishop, is imprisoned. He will be released in 1955 but will remain under house arrest until 1967

October. Accused of high treason, the leaders of the Hungarian People's Union are tried and sentenced to imprisonment. They will be set free in 1955, except the union's president, Gyárfás Kurkó, who will be released only in 1965

1952   September 24. Promulgation of the new People's Democratic Constitution; four counties with solidly Hungarian (Székely) population are united in a Hungarian Autonomous Region and granted some measure of self-government

1953   The Hungarian People's Union is dissolved. *Igaz Szó,* a literary periodical, begins publication

1956   October. Sympathy demonstrations with the Hungarian Revolution in many parts of Transylvania; mass arrests, deportations, and imprisonments of Hungarians follow

1957   The prewar progressive periodical *Korunk* resumes publication in Kolozsvár (Cluj)

1958   As a reward for Romania's loyalty to the Soviet Union during the Hungarian Revolution, Soviet troops are withdrawn from Romania. A new wave of oppression of the minority nationalities begins

1959   February 22. The Bólyai Hungarian University of Kolozsvár is united with the Babeş Romanian University also of Kolozsvár (Cluj). Hungarian schools throughout the country are united with Romanian schools

1960   December 24. The territory of the Hungarian Autonomous Province is revised and renamed Maros-Hungarian Autonomous Region. By comprising fewer Hungarians and more Romanians, the ratio of Hungarians is reduced from 77.3 percent to 62 percent, leading to a gradual liquidation of the autonomy of the province

1962   April. The socialist reorganization of agriculture, discriminatory to the Hungarians, is completed

1965   March 22. Nicolae Ceauşescu is elected First Secretary of the Central Committee of the Romanian Communist Party

August 21. A new Constitution of the Socialist Republic of Romania is promulgated, stating that "Romania is a nation-state in which also nationalities are living"

1966 According to the official census, 1,653,873 persons' mother tongue is Hungarian, while 1,619,592 declare themselves of Hungarian nationality

1968 February 16. Romania's Great National Assembly suppresses the Maros Hungarian Autonomous Region

November 15. A Council of Workers of Hungarian Nationality is formed, but with no legal status to represent the Hungarian nationality

1969 September. The department of Hungarian language and literature is reopened at the University of Bucharest

November. Romanian television begins to broadcast in Hungarian. In Bucharest, the *Kriterion* publishing house is founded for the non-Romanian nationalities with a branch editorial office in Cluj-Napoca (Kolozsvár's new name in Romanian)

1970 October. *A Hét*, a Hungarian weekly, begins publication in Bucharest

1971 June. Zoltán Komócsin, a member of the Central Committee of the Hungarian Socialist Workers' Party, declares in Budapest that "Hungary is interested in the fate of the Hungarian national minority in Romania"

July. In a speech dealing with "ideological, political and cultural-educational" questions, Ceauşescu declares: "We can have only one history, one conception of history"

1973 May 19. An educational reform act is published, favoring Romanian as the language of education

1974 Claiming shortage of paper, a decree on the press reduces the size of newspapers; the minority press is hardest hit

November. A law on protection of the nation's cultural assets declares that cultural heritage is "the property of the people." Centuries-old documents of the Hungarian Roman Catholic, Calvinist, and Unitarian churches, as well as of the Hungarian and Saxon towns, are threatened by sequestration by the state. The government's forcible assimilation policy against national minorities is gaining momentum

1975 A decree makes it obligatory for foreign visitors in Romania to stay in hotels; it is aimed, in particular, against Hungarians visiting relatives and friends in Transylvania

1977 June 15–16. Meeting between János Kádár and Nicolae Ceauşescu in Debrecen (Hungary) and Nagyvárad (Oradea, Romania). The joint communiqué declares that minority "nationalities living in the two neighboring states should increasingly play the role of a bridge in the interest of rapprochement between the Hungarian and Romanian people"

1978 The Western press publishes letters by Károly Király, a prominent Hungarian member of the Romanian Communist party. Addressed to the party leadership, the Király letters protest against the oppression of the Hungarian minority. Király is denounced by the Romanian party authorities and forced into internal exile

1981 December. An underground periodical, *Ellenpontok,* of Hungarian intellectuals is launched

1982 September. Editors of *Ellenpontok* submit a memorandum to the Madrid conference reviewing adherence to the provisions of the Helsinki Final Act; elaborating on oppressive policies of the Romanian government, the memorandum calls for the formation of an international commission to examine the situation in Transylvania

1983 May. Attila Ara-Kovács, one of the authors of the Madrid memorandum, is expelled from Romania.

1984 July. Károly Tóth, another author of the Madrid memorandum, is expelled from Romania.

1985 September. Géza Szőcs, the third author of the Madrid Memorandum, submits a petition to the Central Committee of the Romanian Communist party, demanding redress of Hungarian grievances on the basis of proposals drafted by the editors of the samizdat periodical *Ellenpontok* in 1982. The petition also demands the release of all political prisoners, including Ernő Borbély, a professor of philosophy, and László Búzás, an economist, serving seven- and six-year sentences, respectively

1986 August. Géza Szőcs is expelled from Romania

C. Hungarians in Czechoslovakia

1920 June. Under the provisions of the Peace Treaty of Trianon, Czechoslovakia annexes 63,999 sq. km. of Hungary's territory with a total population of 3.5 million of which (according to the 1910 census) 1,071,000 are Hungarians

July. A Hungarian People's Association is formed at Komárom (Komárno), but the authorities, by refusing to ratify its statutes, prevent it from functioning. A Hungarian Society for Promoting the Theatrical Art in Slovakia, formed at the same time, will receive official authorization five years later (in 1925)

1922 February. The Associated Hungarian Opposition Parties of Slovakia, with headquarters in Losonc (Lučenec), open their central office in Kassa (Košice); the organization comprises the National Christian Socialist Party, the National Hungarian Smallholders' and Farmers' Party, and the Hungarian People's League of Czechoslovakia

June 1. *Prágai Magyar Hírlap,* principal newspaper of the Hungarians in Czechoslovakia, begins publication in Prague.

Leftist exiles from Horthy Hungary start publishing the daily *Reggel* in Bratislava (Pozsony)

1923 March 23. Defense of the Republic Act is promulgated, enabling the Czechoslovak authorities to curtail the rights of the opposition; newspapers can be confiscated and suppressed for shorter or longer periods of time according to the severity of the case

1924 The "Kazinczy Társaság," to rally the forces of Hungarian literary life, and its Book-lovers' Club, to promote Hungarian book publishing, are founded in Kassa (Košice)

1925 Parliamentary elections are held in which Hungarian parties are for the first time allowed nationwide participation. The

National Christian Socialist Party and the Hungarian National Party gain a total of 237,000 votes and send 10 deputies and 6 senators to the Prague Parliament. Czechoslovak parties, such as the Agrarian and Socialist parties, also receive Hungarian votes. The Hungarian Cultural Society of Slovakia is founded with headquarters at Komárom, but the authorities delay its ratification till 1928. The Association of Hungarian University Students is founded with chapters in Prague, Brno, and Bratislava (Pozsony)

1928   January 28–29. The country's Social Democratic parties, including Hungarian Social Democrats, proclaim their unity at their congress in Prague

August 3–13. At the Gombaszög camping of Hungarian scouts, young intellectuals start *Sarló,* a leftist youth movement with Communist overtones. Also, the Communist party of Czechoslovakia has a Hungarian section of some significance.

Summer. The Association of Hungarian Choral Societies, with headquarters in Bratislava, starts operations with five great song festivals. The Hungarian Society of Physical Education is founded

1929   *Vetés,* periodical of Hungarian university students at Bratislava, publishes the program of "Sarló" drawn up by Edgár Balogh, a Communist

1930   Increase of technical education for Hungarian youth is demanded. According to official statistics, among the 4,166 classes of the country's technical schools only 9 are taught in Hungarian; by virtue of their numbers, the Hungarians would be entitled to at least 300 classes

December. The official census reveals that there are 719,569 Hungarians in Czechoslovakia

1931   As a concession to demands for a Hungarian university, a Hungarian Scientific Academy is founded in Bratislava with a gift by President Masaryk, hence its name: Masaryk Academy; it has no university status or functions

1933   October. Law on the suppression and dissolution of political parties is enacted; its target: the activities of the opposition parties and their press

To replace the defunct *Reggel*, the daily *Magyar Újság*, financed by the Czechoslovak government, is launched in Bratislava

1935 Three leading cultural societies (Toldy Circle, Kazinczy Society, and Jókai Club) are united in a Hungarian Literary Association of Czechoslovakia

Magyar Nap, a daily of the Communist party of Czechoslovakia, begins publication in Moravská Ostrava

1936 May. The State Security Act is promulgated to watch over the "untrustworthy" (i.e., minority) citizens

June. The National Christian Socialist Party and the Hungarian National Party are merged into a United Hungary Party; its leaders: János Esterházy and Andor Jaross, as well as Géza Szüllő, a foreign policy expert

1937 February 18. Government declaration on the fair treatment of minorities, followed by promises of a "Minority Statute." It is in response to growing agitation by the Sudeten Germans, led by Konrad Henlein

Hungarian grievances are centered on lack of cultural autonomy. An example in the field of education: among 239 middle grade schools, with 1,841 classes, only 13, with 135 classes are Hungarian administered; by virtue of their numbers, the Hungarians would be entitled to at least 40 autonomous middle grade schools

1938 Rapidly growing domestic and international crisis. The Hungarians, too, are campaigning for more language rights but without emulating the Nazi pattern of Sudeten German political radicalism. Hungarian "activists," supporting the government, take an antifascist stand

March 21. In districts with a Hungarian ethnic majority, villages are granted the right to use Hungarian as an official language

July. Lord Runciman arrives at Prague as the British government's "unofficial mediator," but fails to ease the growing Sudeten German crisis

September 29. The Four-power Munich Agreement yields to Hitler's demand for the annexation of the Sudeten Germans, but leaves the Hungarian question in Czechoslovakia unresolved

October. Direct talks between Czechoslovakia and Hungary fail to reach agreement on frontier rectification according to ethnic principles

November 2. The First Vienna Award of the Axis powers: Hungary regains an area of 11,927 sq. km. from Czechoslovakia with 869,299 inhabitants of whom 86.5 percent are Hungarians and 9.8 percent Slovaks. The Hungarian minority in Slovakia is reduced to less than 100,000; the number of Slovaks in Hungary is increased by about 200,000

1939 Slovakia becomes an independent state under Hitler's auspices

1941 December 18. The Slovak National Assembly votes for the deportation of Slovakia's Jews; the only vote against it is cast by János Esterházy, representative of the Hungarian minority in Slovakia

1944 November 23. The London-based Czechoslovak government-in-exile petitions the Great Powers to approve the expulsion of the Hungarian minority from Slovakia

1945 April 5. The program of the postwar Czechoslovak government is made public in Košice (Kassa). Declaring the Hungarians responsible for the dismemberment of Czechoslovakia, it deprives them of citizenship rights; so-called "active antifascists" are exempted, but only following an investigation of their political past from the point of view of Slovak national interests

May 18. A decree of the Slovak National Council excludes the Hungarians from membership in all political parties (with the exception of the "active antifascists"). Another decree bans all Hungarian printed matter in Slovakia

May 30. All civil servants, including professors and teachers, of Hungarian nationality are summarily dismissed by a

decree of the Slovak National Council. Subsequently, most
of them will be expelled from the country

August 21. The Potsdam Conference rejects the request of
the Czechoslovak government for summary expulsion of
the Hungarians from Czechoslovakia but approves a population exchange

1946 February 27. Agreement between Hungary and Czechoslovakia on population exchange

June 17. The Slovak National Council issues a decree on "re-
Slovakization" of Hungarians of presumed Slovak origin

November 19. Deportation begins of Hungarians from the
solidly Hungarian Csallóköz region to the depopulated Sudetenland. The compulsory resettlement lasts until February 25, 1947

1947 February. Signing in Paris of the Treaty of Peace with Hungary. The 1938 frontiers are restored; three additional
Hungarian villages, the so-called Bratislava bridgehead,
are annexed by Czechoslovakia

September. János Esterházy, a prisoner of the Russians, is
sentenced in absence by a Bratislava court to death by
hanging for "treason." His death sentence commuted for
life, he dies in 1957 in a Czechoslovak prison

1948 February. Following the Communist takeover in Prague, *Új
Szó,* a newspaper in Hungarian, begins publication in Bratislava

October 12. A decree of the Czechoslovak Council of Ministers restores the citizenship and civil rights of Hungarians

November 28. The Hungarians settled in the Sudetenland are
allowed to return to their original places of residence in
Slovakia

1949 March 5. Formation in Bratislava of CSEMADOK, the Cultural Association of Hungarian Workers of Czechoslovakia

September 1. Instruction in Hungarian begins in primary
schools

1950 March 31. According to the census, carried out under a continuing reign of terror in Slovakia, only 367,733 people are
registered as Hungarians in Czechoslovakia

September 1. The first postwar Hungarian secondary school opens in Komárno. Also, a Hungarian department is established at the Teacher's Training College in Bratislava

1952 July 1. Bilingualism is decreed in the Hungarian-inhabited areas of southern Slovakia

1953 A Hungarian publishing house begins operations in Bratislava (Pozsony). A Hungarian regional theater is founded in Komárno (Komárom)

1954 April 8. The Central Committee of the Slovak Communist party declares the re-Slovakization decree of 1946 null and void

1959 February 5. Decreed that acts of Parliament and other provisions of law are to be made public in the Hungarian language

November. *Irodalmi Szemle* begins publication

1960 September 1. Visa requirements for travel between Hungary and Czechoslovakia are abolished

1961 March 1. According to the census, there are 533,934 Hungarians living in Czechoslovakia. The 230,000 increase since the last census is due to the 1954 annulment of the 1946 re-Slovakization decree

1968 January. The "Prague Spring" is ushered in by a decision of the Plenum of the Czechoslovak Communist party on the necessity of democratization

March 12. In accordance with the January Plenum decision, CSEMADOK, representing the Hungarians in Slovakia, submits a proposal for solving the nationality question

April 1. A proposal on solving the nationality question drawn up at the request of the Slovak Communist party by the Hungarian branch of the Slovak Writers' Union is published in Bratislava. The Hungarian proposal calls for self-management of educational affairs, founding of a Hungarian scientific institute, a Hungarian central library, and an independent Hungarian publishing house

April 10. The Czechoslovak Communist party's Action Program is made public. In addition to solving the relations between Czechs and Slovaks, the program also deals with the solution of the national minorities' question; its thesis: "The nationalities shall be entitled to self-government in matters concerning them"

August 21. Soviet military intervention stops the Communist reform movement

September 8. At a CSEMADOK meeting, Gustváv Husák, the emerging new Communist leader, promises recognition of the right to autonomy by speedy promulgation of a Nationalities' Act

October 17. The Slovak National Assembly adopts the Nationalities' Act but without the provision of cultural autonomy. It approves only the formation of a Nationalities' Council, which includes representatives of the nationalities

October 28. On the fiftieth anniversary of Czechoslovakia's founding, the new federal constitution recognizes two equal republics: one for the Czechs, the other for the Slovaks

November 23–24. Conference of the Hungarian intellectuals makes new proposals on the nationality question in the Slovak Socialist Republic of Czechoslovakia

December 7. A Hungarian Youth Association is allowed to be set up in Bratislava

1969 January. The "Madách Hungarian Book and Newspaper Publishing Company" begins operations in Bratislava

László Dobos becomes a Hungarian member of the first government of the Slovak Socialist Republic as Minister without Portfolio. The newly formed Slovak Trade Union Council disregards the legally stipulated principle of proportional representation of the minority nationalities

March 17. CSEMADOK holds an extraordinary meeting under its new president, László Dobos, and passes a resolution to function not merely as a cultural but also as a socio-political association representing the Hungarian minority as a whole

April 8. Council of Nationalities is formed as an advisory organ of the Slovak government; among its fifteen members there are five Hungarians

1970 April 29. Minister without Portfolio László Dobos resigns; his post in the government is abolished. Also Rezső Szabó, Hungarian Vice-President of the Slovak National Council, is relieved of his post

June. The Hungarian regional theater of Kassa (Košice) begins performances

December 1. According to the census there are 621,588 persons in Czechoslovakia whose "mother tongue" is Hungarian and 572,568 whose "nationality" is Hungarian. The census also reveals that 422 communities have lost their Hungarian majority

1971 March 29. CSEMADOK president László Dobos resigns his post. An additional twenty-five members of the leadership are dismissed. CSEMADOK is forced to give up its coveted status as a socio-political organization representing the Hungarians in Slovakia

Teaching of the Slovak language in Hungarian kindergartens and in the first two grades of general schools is made obligatory. Slovak-language courses in all Hungarian schools are increased

1972 April 15–16. At its general meeting, CSEMADOK nullifies its 1969 resolution on cultural autonomy. CSEMADOK is excluded from the National Front of Slovakia and is placed under the authority of the Slovak Ministry of Culture

1975 It is disclosed that during the past five years government investments in Hungarian-populated southern regions of Slovakia have been 70 to 75 percent less than in other parts of the country

1976 Slovakia's central educational authorities are planning to reduce by fifty percent the enrollment of pupils in Hungarian schools

1978 The Committee for the Defense of the Rights of the Hungarian Minority in Czechoslovakia, an underground civil rights organization, is founded; its leading member: Miklós Duray

1979 Slovakia's new Educational Act provides that each administrative district can have only one Hungarian secondary school

Kálmán Janics's book, *Hontalanság évei*, on postwar persecution of Hungarians in Czechoslovakia is published in Munich by the Bern-based European Protestant Hungarian Free University; an English version of the book, *Czechoslovak Policy and the Hungarian Minority: 1945–1948*, is published in New York in 1982

1980 November. According to the census, the number of Hungarians living in Slovakia is down to 559,800

1981 A comprehensive memorandum on the situation of the Hungarians in Slovakia is prepared by the Committee for the Defense of the Rights of the Hungarian Minority in Czechoslovakia. It is published in Paris in 1982 by Dialogues Européens in Hungarian only, *Szlovákiai jelentés. A magyar kisebbség állapotáról*

1982 November 10. Miklós Duray is arrested and charged with slandering the Republic at home and abroad

1983 January 31. The Duray trial begins in Bratislava

February 24. Duray is set free without a verdict

1984 February–March. Massive Hungarian protests against the planned Slovak school reform bill

April 2. Yielding to Hungarian protests, the Slovak National Council revises the school reform draft

May 10. Duray is rearrested under reinstated charges of "activities contrary to the interests of the state"

1985 May 10. After a year in detention without a trial, Duray is set free with all charges dropped under the provisions of a general amnesty issued on the fortieth anniversary of VE-day

1986 March 8. In Bratislava, buildings and offices of Hungarian cultural institutions are vandalized.

March 27. Charter 77 condemns the anti-Hungarian "acts of terrorism"

D. The Hungarians in Yugoslavia

1920 June. Under the provisions of the Peace Treaty of Trianon, Yugoslavia annexes 21,000 sq. km. of Hungary's territory with a population of 1.6 million of which (according to the 1910 census) 465,000 are Hungarians

August. Under the law on secularization of education, 751 privately run Hungarian schools are closed and their property seized without compensation

1921 January. According to the census, 467,568 Hungarians are living in Yugoslavia

1922 September. At Zenta, the National Hungarian Party of Yugoslavia is formed

1929 January 6. A royal dictatorship under King Alexander I is instituted. All political parties are disbanded and Parliament dissolved. The Hungarian minority is left without a party and parliamentary representation

October 3. With Pan-Serb national interests in mind, Yugoslavia is divided into ten administrative units. Vojvodina is incorporated into the Danube Banat. The ratio of Hungarians in this new administrative unit decreases from 27.2 to 18.3 percent

1931 November. The new trade law bans the use of Hungarian public signs and labels in the Danube Banat

1932 In Újvidék (Novi Sad), *Kalangya,* a literary review, is started

1933 March 14. Self-government of villages is restored and municipal elections are held, thus the Hungarians regain some voice in communal affairs

1934 In Szabadka (Subotica), *Híd,* a literary and artistic periodical is started

September. A parallel Hungarian branch is set up at the Belgrade Teachers' Training College; it will be closed in 1935, but reopened in 1937

1937 September. The participation of at least 300 members is required for the formation of purchasing, marketing, and consumer cooperatives; this new law discriminates against the many small Hungarian communities

1938 February. A law issued by the Ministry of Justice, in conjunction with the Ministries of Agriculture, Home Affairs, and National Defense, restricting the sale of real estate, prevents the Hungarians from acquiring new properties and in some areas dispossesses them for alleged reasons of national security

1939 June. Under a by-law on municipal administration, Hungarians are barred from training courses for municipal officials in the Danube Banat

1940 March. An Association of Hungarian Cultural Societies of Croatia is formed with headquarters at Zagreb, while the overwhelming majority of Hungarians living in the Danube Banat remains deprived of such an organization

1941 March. A military coup in Belgrade brings a Serb nationalist regime to power which opposes Yugoslavia's joining the Tripartite Pact of the Axis powers. After demanding free passage of German troops through Hungary, Hitler invades Yugoslavia and dismembers it.
April 11. Hungary occupies the Bácska, the Baranya triangle, and the Mura region. A territory of 11,417 sq. km. with a population of 1,025,508, of which 36.6 percent are Hungarians, is reannexed by Hungary

1942 January 4. Hungarian gendarmerie and army units commit massacres in Újvidék, Zsábla, and surrounding areas; Yugoslavs and Jews are the victims

1945 Yugoslavia is liberated by the Soviet Red Army and Tito's partisans. Yugoslavs take revenge for the Újvidék-Zsábla massacres
June. A Hungarian Cultural Association is founded in Újvidék; its task is to organize cultural societies, libraries, book publishing and distribution, and to participate in managing Hungarian educational affairs. *Magyar Szó*, a Hungarian-language daily of the Yugoslav Communist party, is licensed
August. The law on land reform and settlement is enacted. Some 50,000 Serbs with their families are settled in the Vojvodina

September. In the newly constituted province of Vojvodina, 34,782 pupils are enrolled in 732 Hungarian elementary schools and 6,082 in eight secondary schools

In Szabadka, the Hungarian Theater of Vojvodina is opened; in 1951, it will be merged with the Croatian People's Theater

1946 The Yugoslav Federal Constitution promulgates the principle of national equality

October. At the Teachers' Training College of Újvidék, a Hungarian department is opened

1947 February. The Peace Treaty with Hungary signed in Paris restores the pre-1938 frontiers

1948 According to the census, there are 496,492 Hungarians in Yugoslavia

In the Republic of Croatia, a Hungarian Cultural and Educational Association is founded, later called the Association of Hungarians in Croatia

1949 November. Újvidék (Novi Sad) Radio starts broadcasting in Hungarian

1952 January. The Hungarian Literary Society, a division of the Cultural Council of Vojvodina is founded in Újvidék (Novi Sad)

Magyar Képes Újság, a biweekly, is started in Zagreb

1953 The census reveals that 502,175 Hungarians live in Yugoslavia

1958 The Seventh Congress of the Yugoslav Communist party confirms the policy toward the nationalities based on the principle of national equality

1961 According to the census, the number of Hungarians reaches 504,368 in Yugoslavia

1962 May 13. The new statute of the Autonomous Province of Vojvodina enters into force; minority rights include the official use of nationality languages

1964 January. The Hungarian Philological Society of Yugoslavia is founded in Szabadka (Subotica)

1965 *Új Symposion,* a Hungarian avant-garde periodical, begins publication

1966 February. Visa requirements for travel between Hungary and Yugoslavia are abolished

1967   The Forum Hungarian Publishing House is founded in Újvidék (Novi Sad)
1968   According to official statistics, the ratio of white- to blue-collar workers among Hungarians is 18:82, whereas among the country's South Slavs it is 30:70
1969   February. An Institute of Hungarology is founded at the University of Újvidék (Novi Sad)
1974   The new Yugoslav Federal Constitution reconfirms the principle of equal rights of "nations" and "nationalities" in the Socialist Federal Republic of Yugoslavia
1975   Communal Hungarian Educational and Cultural agencies are formed in villages with mixed populations in Slovenia. Also, a nationality commission is established at the Slovenian House of Representatives
1977   April. A resolution of the House of Representatives of the Socialist Federal Republic of Slovenia guarantees the equality of languages in both private and public life
1978   Statistics of the 1977–78 academic year show that there are 172 Hungarian schools with 33,200 pupils, whereas in 1953–54 there had been 285 such schools with 50,000 pupils. Also, the census registers a steady decline in the number of Hungarians in Yugoslavia over the last two decades
1981   According to the census, the country's Hungarian population has fallen to 427,000
1984   May. The editor and the entire editorial staff of *Új Symposion* is dismissed under charges of "ideological insensitivity and political immaturity"

E. Hungarians in Sub- and Trans-Carpathia

1920   Under the provisions of the Peace Treaty of Trianon, of the over one million Hungarians who were incorporated into Czechoslovakia, about 150,000 are in the autonomous territory of Subcarpathian Ruthenia (*Podkarpatská Rus*)
1924   Barred from the elections of 1920, the Hungarians now send representatives to the Prague Parliament for the first time
1928   The Hungarian Cultural Society of Sub-Carpathia, a division of the Hungarian Cultural Society of Slovakia, is founded

1934   Hungarian Association of Choral Societies of Sub-Carpathia
       is founded
1938   November 2. Under the provisions of the First Vienna Award,
       the predominantly Hungarian areas of Sub-Carpathia are
       returned to Hungary, including the capital Užhorod
       (Ungvár) where the Hungarians are a minority
1939   March 15. Hungary annexes the entire territory of Subcar-
       pathian Ruthenia: 12,171 sq. km. with 496,000 inhabitants
       including 63,000 Hungarians (12.7 percent of the total pop-
       ulation)
1940   July 23. A bill on the autonomy of Ruthenia, submitted by
       Prime Minister Pál Teleki, is withdrawn
1944   October. The liberation of Ruthenia by the Soviet Army is
       completed
       November 26. At Mukačevo (Munkács), the formation of
       Carpatho-Ukraine is proclaimed. The name of Sub-Car-
       pathia is changed to Trans-Carpathia
1945   June 29. By virtue of an agreement with Cechoslovakia, the
       USSR annexes the Carpatho-Ukraine
       A Hungarian edition of the Ukrainian *Zakarpatska Pravda*
       is published, called *Kárpáti Igaz Szó*
       A Hungarian section of the Textbook Publishing House of
       the Ukrainian Republic at Uzhgorod (Ungvár) is set up
1946   January 22. Carpatho-Ukraine becomes a district (*oblast*) of
       the Ukrainian Soviet Socialist Republic with Uzhgorod as
       its capital
1947   February. The Peace Treaty of Paris confirms the annexation
       of the Carpatho-Ukraine by the Soviet Union
       September. Teaching in Hungarian begins in the general
       schools of the Hungarian-inhabited areas of the Carpatho-
       Ukraine
1953   Two Hungarian secondary schools open, in Nagydobrony and
       Beregszász
1959   According to the census, there are 154,738 Hungarians in the
       Carpatho-Ukraine
       At Uzhgorod (Ungvár) a Hungarian cultural magazine, *Kár-
       pátok,* is launched; it is suspended after the appearance of
       the first issue

1963 September. At the University of Uzhgorod, a Hungarian department is opened
1966 The Transcarpathian regional television begins broadcasting a Hungarian program
1967 *Forrás Stúdió*, a magazine of young writers, is founded
1969 According to educational statistics, there are 93 Hungarian schools operating in the Carpatho-Ukraine: 17 four-grade, 58 eight-grade, and 18 secondary schools, with a total of 22,807 pupils and 1,433 teachers. A Hungarian theatrical group at Beregszász (Berehovo) is made into a "people's theater"
1970 According to the census, there are 166,000 Hungarians living in the USSR—their overwhelming majority in the Carpatho-Ukraine
1971 Following an attack by *Kárpáti Igaz Szó*, denouncing the writers of *Forrás Stúdió* as "alienated" from society, the magazine is suppressed; *József Attila Stúdió*, under the control of *Kárpáti Igaz Szo*, takes its place
1980 According to the census, the population of the Carpatho-Ukraine is 1,157,400, of which 171,000 are Hungarians

❋ 4. SELECTED BIBLIOGRAPHY

The Central European Problem and the Hungarian Question

Thomas Szendrey

1. Bibliographies

Bakó, Elemér. *A Guide to Hungarian Studies*. 2 vols. Stanford, 1973.

Bakó, Elemér, and William Sólyom-Fekete. *Hungarians in Rumania and Transylvania: A Bibliographical List of Publications in Hungarian and West European Languages Compiled from the Holdings of the Library of Congress*. Washington, D.C., 1969.

Bentley, G. Carter. *Ethnicity and Nationality: A Bibliographic Guide*. Seattle, 1981.

Carlton, Robert G., and Paul L. Horecky. *The U.S.S.R. and Eastern Europe: Periodicals in Western Languages*. Washington, D.C., 1964.

Deutsch, Karl W., and Richard L. Merritt. *Nationalism: An Interdisciplinary Bibliography, 1933–1965*. Cambridge, Mass., 1966.

Hammond, Thomas. *Soviet Foreign Relations and World Communism: A Selected Annotated Bibliography of 7,000 Books in 30 Languages*. Princeton, 1965.

Horak, Stephen M. *East European National Minorities, 1919–1980: A Handbook*. Littleton, Colo., 1985.

———. *Russia, the U.S.S.R. and Eastern Europe: A Bibliographic Guide to English Language Publications, 1964–1974*. Littleton, Colo., 1978.

———. *Russia, the U.S.S.R. and Eastern Europe: A Bibliographic Guide to English Language Publications, 1975–1980*. Littleton, Colo., 1982.

Horecky, Paul L. *East Central Europe: A Guide to Basic Publications.* Chicago, 1969.

Society of the Hungarian Quarterly. *A Companion to Hungarian Studies.* Budapest, 1943.

Spath, Manfred, and Werner Philipp. *Bibliography of Articles on East European and Russian History Selected from English Language Periodicals.* Berlin, 1981.

Walker, Gregory. *Official Publications of the Soviet Union and Eastern Europe 1945–1980: A Select Annotated Bibliography.* London, 1982.

2. Memoirs

Andrássy, Gyula. *Diplomacy and the War.* London, 1921.

Bandholtz, Harry. *An Undiplomatic Diary.* New York, 1933.

Beneš, Edvard. *Memoirs of Dr. Edvard Beneš.* London, 1954.

———. *My War Memoirs.* London, 1928.

Bonsal, Stephen. *Suitors and Suppliants: The Little Nations at Versailles.* New York, 1946.

Churchill, Winston S. *The Second World War.* 6 vols. Cambridge, Mass., 1949.

Clemenceau, Georges. *Grandeur and Misery of Victory.* New York, 1930.

Gafencu, Grigore. *Last Days of Europe.* New Haven, 1948.

Horthy, Nicholas. *Memoirs.* New York, 1957.

House, Edward Mandell, and Charles Seymour, eds. *What Really Happened at Paris: The Story of the Peace Conference, 1918–1919.* New York, 1921.

Kállay, Nicholas. *Hungarian Premier: A Personal Account of a Nation's Struggle in the Second World War.* London, 1954.

Károlyi, Mihály. *Faith without Illusion: Memoirs of Mihály Károlyi.* London, 1956.

———. *Fighting the World: The Struggle for Peace.* New York, 1925.

Lansing, Robert. *The Peace Negotiations: A Personal Narrative.* Boston, 1921.

Lloyd-George, David. *Memoirs of the Peace Conference.* 2 vols. New Haven, 1939.

———. *The Truth about the Peace Treaties.* 3 vols. London, 1938.

Masaryk, Thomas. *The Making of a State.* New York, 1927.

Nagy, Ferenc. *The Struggle behind the Iron Curtain.* New York, 1948.
Nagy, Imre. *On Communism.* New York, 1957.
Nicolson, Harold. *Peacemaking 1919.* London, 1933.
Rothermere, Harold. *My Campaign for Hungary.* London, 1932.
Schöpflin, Gyula (Julian). *Szélkiáltó: Emlékezések.* Paris, 1983.
Tardieu, André. *La Paix.* Paris, 1921.

3. General Works

Armstrong, John A. *Nations before Nationalism.* Chapel Hill, 1982.
Balogh, Eva S. "Nationality Problems of the Hungarian Soviet Republic." In *Hungary in Revolution, 1918–1919,* edited by Ivan Volgyes. Lincoln, 1971.
Banac, Ivo, et al., ed. *Nation and Ideology: Essays in Honor of Wayne S. Vucinich.* New York, 1981.
Bartlett, E. A. *The Tragedy of Central Europe.* London, 1923.
Besemeres, John F. *Socialist Population and Politics: The Political Implications of Demographic Trends in the USSR and Eastern Europe.* White Plains, 1980.
Bethlen, Stephen. *The Treaty of Trianon and European Peace.* London, 1934.
Borsody, Stephen. "Hungary in the Habsburg Monarchy." In *Society in Change,* edited by S. B. and A. H. Vardy. New York, 1983.
———. "Hungary's Road to Trianon." In *Essays on World War I,* edited by Béla K. Király, et al. New York, 1982.
———. *The Tragedy of Central Europe: Nazi and Soviet Conquest and Aftermath.* Rev. ed. New Haven, 1980.
Brunner, George, and Boris Meissner, eds. *Nationalitäten-Probleme in der SowjetUnion und Osteuropa.* Cologne, 1982.
Brzezinski, Zbigniew. *The Soviet Bloc: Unity and Conflict.* Rev. ed. Cambridge, Mass., 1976.
Buergenthal, Thomas, ed. *Human Rights, International Law and the Helsinki Accord.* Montclair, N.J., 1977.
Burks, R. V. *The Dynamics of Communism in Eastern Europe.* Princeton, 1961.
Campbell, John C. *American Policy toward Communist Eastern Europe: The Choices Ahead.* Minneapolis, 1965.
Capotorti, Francesco. *Study on the Rights of Persons Belonging to Ethnic, Religious and Linguistic Minorities.* New York, 1979.

Carr, E. H. *Nationalism and After.* London, 1945.

Connor, Walker. *The National Question in Marxist-Leninist Theory and Strategy.* Princeton, 1984.

Crane, John O. *The Little Entente.* New York, 1931.

Csatári, Dániel. *Dans la tourmente.* Budapest, 1974.

Dávid, Zoltán. "A magyar nemzetiségi statisztika múltja és jelene." *Valóság* 23, no. 8 (1980): 87–101.

Deák, Francis. *Hungary at the Paris Peace Conference.* New York, 1942.

Deák, Francis, and Dezső Újváry, eds. *Papers and Documents Relating to the Foreign Relations of Hungary.* 2 vols. Budapest, 1939–46.

Deak, Istvan. *The Lawful Revolution: Louis Kossuth and the Hungarians.* New York, 1979.

————. "Hungary," in H. Rogger and E. Weber, *The European Right.* London, 1965.

Dvornik, Francis. *The Making of Central and Eastern Europe.* London, 1949.

Erös, J. "Hungary," in S. J. Woolf, ed., *European Fascism.* London, 1968.

Fejtő, François. *Behind the Rape of Hungary.* New York, 1957.

————. *A History of the People's Democracies.* Harmonsworth, 1974.

Gati, Charles. *Hungary and the Soviet Bloc.* Durham, 1986.

————, ed. *The International Politics of Eastern Europe.* New York, 1976.

Gower, Robert. *The Hungarian Minorities in the Succession States.* London, 1937.

Halecki, Oscar. *Borderlands of Western Civilization.* New York, 1952.

Hanak, Harry. *Great Britain and Austria-Hungary during the First World War.* London, 1962.

Hartl, Hans. *Nationalitätenprobleme im heutigen Südosteuropa.* Munich, 1973.

Hill, Norman. *Claims to Territory in International Law and Relations.* New York, 1945.

Hungary. Külügyminisztérium. *The Hungarian Peace Negotiations.* 3 vols. Budapest, 1920–21.

Janowsky, Oscar. *Nationalities and National Minorities.* New York, 1945.

Jászi, Oscar. *The Dissolution of the Habsburg Monarchy.* Chicago, 1929.

————. *Revolution and Counter-Revolution in Hungary.* London, 1924.

————. *Magyar kálvária, magyar feltámadás.* Vienna, 1920. New ed. Munich, 1969.

————. *A Monarchia jövője. A dualizmus bukása és a Dunai Egyesült Államok.* Budapest, 1918.

————. *A nemzeti államok kialakulása és a nemzetiségi kérdés.* Budapest, 1912.

Juhász, Gyula. *Magyarország külpolitikája, 1919–1945.* 2d ed. Budapest, 1975.

Kann, Robert. *The Multinational Empire: Nationalism and National Reform in the Habsburg Monarchy 1848–1918.* New York, 1950.

Kende, Pierre. *Normalization Processes in Soviet-dominated Central Europe: Hungary, Czechoslovakia, Poland.* Cologne, 1982.

————, and K. Pomian, eds. *1956: Varsovie-Budapest: la deuxième revolution d'Octobre.* Paris, 1978.

————, and Z. Strmiska, eds. *Egalité et inégalités en Europe de 'Est.* Paris, 1984.

Kertesz, Stephen D., ed. *The Last European Peace Conference, 1946* [Documents supplementing the volume below]. Lanham, 1985.

————. *Between Russia and the West: Hungary and the Illusions of Peacemaking, 1945–1947.* Notre Dame, 1984.

————. *Diplomacy in a Whirlpool: Hungary between Nazi Germany and Soviet Russia.* Notre Dame, 1953.

King, Robert. *Nationalities under Communism.* Cambridge, Mass., 1973.

Király, Béla K., and Paul Jonás, eds. *The Hungarian Revolution of 1956 in Retrospect.* New York, 1978.

Király, Béla K. et al., eds. *Essays on World War I: Total War and Peacemaking, A Case Study on Trianon.* New York, 1982.

Klein, George, and Milan J. Reban, eds. *The Politics of Ethnicity in Eastern Europe.* New York, 1981.

Kolarz, Walter. *Myths and Realities in Eastern Europe.* London, 1946.

Komjáthy, Anthony. *The Crises of France's East Central European Diplomacy, 1933–1938.* New York, 1976.

Konrád, George (György). *Antipolitics,* translated by Richard E. Allen. New York, 1984.

Kovrig, Bennett. *Communism in Hungary: From Kun to Kádár.* Stanford, 1979.

———. *The Myth of Liberation: East Central Europe in U.S. Diplomacy and Politics since 1941.* Baltimore, 1973.

Krejci, Jaroslav, and Vitezslav Velimsky. *Ethnic and Political Nations in Europe.* New York, 1981.

Lauterpacht, H. *International Law and Human Rights.* New York, 1950.

Lendvai, Paul. *Eagles in Cobwebs: Nationalism and Communism in the Balkans.* Garden City, N.Y., 1969.

Low, Alfred. *Lenin on the Question of Nationality.* New York, 1958.

———. *The Soviet Hungarian Republic and the Paris Peace Conference.* Philadelphia, 1963.

Luard, Evan, ed. *The International Protection of Human Rights.* London, 1967.

Lukacs, John. *The Great Powers and Eastern Europe.* New York, 1953.

Macartney, C. A. *Hungary: A Short History.* Edinburgh, 1962.

———. *Hungary and her Successors.* London, 1937.

———. *National States and National Minorities.* London, 1934.

———. *October Fifteenth: A History of Modern Hungary, 1929–1945.* 2 vols. Edinburgh, 1961.

Macartney, C. A., and A. W. Palmer. *Independent Eastern Europe.* London, 1962.

Machray, Robert. *The Little Entente.* London, 1929.

Mair, L. P. *The Protection of Minorities. The Working and Scope of the Minorities Treaties under the League of Nations.* London, 1928.

Mamatey, Victor. *The United States and East Central Europe, 1914–1918.* Princeton, 1957.

Mastny, Vojtech. *Russia's Road to the Cold War: Diplomacy, Warfare, and the Politics of Communism, 1941–45.* New York, 1979.

Mayer, Arno J. *Politics and Diplomacy of Peacemaking: Containment and Counterrevolution at Versailles, 1918–1919.* New York, 1967.

Méray, Tibor. *Nagy Imre élete és halála.* Munich, 1978.

Mitrany, David. *Marx against the Peasant.* London, 1951.

Molony, William. *Nationality and the Peace Treaties.* New York, 1934.

Nagy, Zsuzsa L. *A párizsi békekonferencia és Magyarország.* Budapest, 1965.

———. *The United States and the Danubian Basin.* Budapest, 1975.

Niederhauser, Emil. *The Rise of Nationality in Eastern Europe.* Budapest, 1982.

Pearson, Raymond. *National Minorities in Eastern Europe, 1848–1944.* New York, 1983.

Pétroff, Thomas. *Les minorités nationales en Europe centrale et orientale.* Paris, 1935.

Rothschild, Joseph. *Ethnopolitics: A Conceptual Framework.* New York, 1981.

Saucerman, Sophia. *International Transfers of Territory in Europe.* Washington, D.C., 1937.

Schechtman, Joseph. *Postwar Population Transfers in Europe, 1945–1955.* Philadelphia, 1962.

Schöpflin, George. "Opposition and Para-Opposition: Critical Currents in Hungary, 1968–78," in *Opposition in Eastern Europe,* edited by Rudolf L. Tőkés. Baltimore, 1979.

———, ed. *The Soviet Union and Eastern Europe: A Handbook.* London, 1970.

———. "National Minorities under Communism in Eastern Europe." In *Eastern Europe in Transition,* edited by Kurt London. Baltimore, 1966.

Seton-Watson, Hugh. *The East European Revolution.* New York, 1951.

———. *Eastern Europe between the Wars, 1918–1941.* New York, 1962.

———. *Nationalism and Communism: Essays 1946–1963.* New York, 1964.

———. *Nations and States: An Inquiry into the Origins of Nations and the Politics of Nationalism.* London, 1977.

Seton-Watson, Hugh and Christopher. *The Making of a New Europe: R. W. Seton-Watson and the Last Years of Austria-Hungary.* Seattle, 1981.

Shoup, Paul S. *The East European and Soviet Data Handbook: Political, Social, and Developmental Indicators, 1945–1975.* New York, 1981.

Skilling, H. Gordon. *Communism National and International: Eastern Europe after Stalin.* Toronto, 1964.

Stalin, Joseph. *Marxism and the National and Colonial Question.* New York, 1942.

Stone, Julius. *International Guarantees of Minority Rights: Procedures of the Council of the League of Nations in Theory and Practice.* London, 1932.

Sugar, Peter F., ed. *Native Fascism in the Successor States, 1918–1945.* Santa Barbara, 1971.

Sugar, Peter, and Ivo Lederer. *Nationalism in Eastern Europe.* Seattle, 1969.

Szabó, Imre. Cultural Rights. Translated by Gábor Pulay and Gedeon Dienes. Leiden, 1974.

Szekfű, Jules. *État et nation.* Paris, 1945.

Teleki, Paul. *The Evolution of Hungary and its Place in European History.* New York, 1923.

Temperley, H. W. *A History of the Peace Conference of Paris.* 6 vols. London, 1920–24.

Terry, Sarah M., ed. *Soviet Policy in Eastern Europe.* New Haven, 1984.

Váli, Ferenc. *Rift and Revolt in Hungary: Nationalism vs. Communism.* Cambridge, Mass., 1961.

Várdy, Steven B. *Modern Hungarian Historiography.* New York, 1976.

———, and Ágnes H. Várdy, eds. *Society in Change: Studies in Honor of Béla K. Király.* New York, 1983.

Varsányi, Julius. *Border Is Fate.* Adelaide-Sydney, 1982.

Wirsing, Robert W. *Protection of Ethnic Minorities: Comparative Perspectives.* New York, 1981.

Zeman, Z. A. B. *The Breakup of the Habsburg Empire 1914–1918.* London, 1961.

Zinner, Paul E. *Revolution in Hungary.* New York, 1962.

———. *National Communism and Popular Revolt in Eastern Europe.* New York, 1956.

4. Transylvania and Romania

Ajtay, József. *The Transylvanian Question.* London, 1921.

Braham, Randolph L. *Education in Romania: A Decade of Change.* Washington, D.C., 1972.

Cabot, John Moore. *The Racial Conflict in Transylvania.* Boston, 1926.

Cadzow, John, Andrew Ludányi, and Louis J. Éltető, eds. *Transylvania: The Roots of Ethnic Conflict.* Kent, Ohio, 1983.

Daicoviciu, Constantin, et al., eds. *Rumania.* Bucharest, 1959.

Deér, József, and László Gáldi, eds. *Magyarok és románok*. 2 vols. Budapest, 1943–1944.

Dragomir, Sylvius. *The Ethnical Minorities in Transylvania*. Geneva, 1927.

Fischer-Galati, Stephen, ed. *Romania*. New York, 1956.

Giurescu, Constantin. *Transylvania in the History of Romania*. London, 1970.

Hitchins, Keith. *The Romanian National Movement in Transylvania, 1790–1849*. Cambridge, Mass., 1969.

Horváth, Eugene. *Transylvania and the History of the Roumanians*. Budapest, 1935.

Illyés, Elemér. *National Minorities in Romania: Change in Transylvania*. New York, 1982.

Ionesco, Ghita. *Communism in Rumania 1944–1962*. London, 1964.

Makkai, Ladislas. *Histoire du Transylvanie*. Paris, 1946.

Markham, Reuben H. *Romania under the Soviet Yoke*. Boston, 1949.

Mitrany, David. *Greater Rumania: A Study in National Ideals*. London, 1917.

Nelson, Daniel N. *Romania in the 1980's*. Boulder, Colo., 1981.

Oldson, William. *The Historical and Nationalist Thought of Nicolae Iorga*. New York, 1973.

Rura, Michael J. *Reinterpretation of History as a Method of Furthering Communism in Rumania*. Washington, D.C., 1961.

Schöpflin, George. *The Hungarians of Rumania*. London, 1978.

Seton-Watson, R. W. *A History of the Roumanians*. Cambridge, 1934.

———. *Roumania and the Great War*. London, 1915.

———. *Transylvania: A Key Problem*. Oxford, 1943.

———. *Treaty Revision and the Hungarian Frontiers*. London, 1934.

Spector, Sherman. *Rumania at the Paris Peace Conference*. New York, 1962.

Szász, Zsombor. *The Minorities in Roumanian Transylvania*. London, 1927.

Váli, Ferenc A. "Transylvania and the Hungarian Minority." *Journal of International Affairs* 20, no. 1 (1966): 32–44.

5. The Hungarians and Czechoslovakia

Borsody, István (Stephen). *Magyar-szlovák kiegyezés*. Budapest, 1945.

————, ed. *Magyarok Csehszlovákiában, 1918–1938*. Budapest, 1938.

Chaszar, Edward. *Decision in Vienna: The Czechoslovak-Hungarian Border Dispute of 1938*. Astor Park, Fla., 1978.

Clementis, V. *La quéstion des hongrois de Tchécoslovaquie*. Paris, 1946.

Friedman, Otto. *The Breakup of Czech Democracy*. London, 1950.

Hoensch, J. K. *Der ungarische Revisionismus und die Zerschlagung der Tschechoslowakei*. Tübingen, 1967.

Janics, Kálmán. *Czechoslovak Policy and the Hungarian Minority, 1945–1948*. English version adapted from Hungarian by Stephen Borsody. New York, 1982.

Jelinek, Yeshayahu. *The Parish Republic: Hlinka's Slovak People's Party, 1939–1945*. New York, 1976.

Kirschbaum, J. M. *Slovakia, Nation at the Crossroads of Central Europe*. New York, 1966.

Kővágó, József, ed. *The Cities of the Hungarian Linguistic Territory in Slovakia*. Budapest, 1946.

Masaryk, Tomáš Garrigue. *Česka otázka*. Prague, 1894.

————. *Nová Evropa*. Prague, 1920.

Mastny, Vojtech. *Czechoslovakia: Crisis in World Communism*. New York, 1972.

Mikus, Joseph A. *Slovakia and the Slovaks*. Washington, D.C., 1977.

Odlozilik, Ottokar. *Masaryk's Idea of Democracy*. New York, 1952.

Perman, D. *The Shaping of the Czechoslovak State*. Leiden, 1962.

Rechcigl, Miloslav, Jr., ed. *Czechoslovakia: Past and Present*. 2 vols. The Hague, 1968.

Révay, István. "Die Magyaren in der Tschechoslowakei." In *Handbuch der Europäischen Volskgruppen*, edited by M. Straka. Vienna, 1970.

Seton-Watson, R. W. *A History of the Czechs and Slovaks*. London, 1943.

————. *Masaryk in England*. London, 1943.

————. *Slovakia Then and Now: A Political Survey*. London, 1931.

Szporluk, Roman. *The Political Thought of Thomas G. Masaryk*. New York, 1981.

Zsolnay, V. von. "Die Lage der Madjaren in der Slowakei." *Zeitschrift für Ostforschung* 16 (1967): 326–41.

6. The Hungarians and Yugoslavia

Banac, Ivo. *The National Question in Yugoslavia: Origins, History, Politics.* Ithaca, 1984.

Bertsch, Gary K. *Nation-Building in Yugoslavia: A Study of Political Integration and Attitudinal Consensus.* Beverly Hills, 1971.

Campbell, John C. *Tito's Separate Road: America and Yugoslavia in World Politics.* New York, 1967.

Cohen, Leonard, and Paul Warwick. *Political Cohesion in a Fragile Mosaic: The Yugoslav Experience.* Boulder, Colo., 1983.

Djilas, Milovan. *Parts of a Lifetime.* New York, 1975.

————. *Tito: The Story from the Inside.* New York, 1980.

Dragnich, Alex. *The First Yugoslavia: Search for a Viable Political System.* Stanford, 1983.

Fisher, Jack C. *Yugoslavia—A Multi-National State: Regional Difference and Administrative Response.* San Francisco, 1966.

Hoffman, George W., and Fred Warner Neal. *Yugoslavia and the New Communism.* New York, 1962.

Hondius, Frederik W. *The Yugoslav Community of Nations.* The Hague, 1968.

Lederer, Ivo J. *Yugoslavia at the Paris Peace Conference: A Study in Frontiermaking.* New Haven, 1963.

Mestrovic, Matthew, et al. *Yugoslavia in Crisis: The Political and Economic Dimensions.* London, 1983.

Rehák, László. *A kisebbségek Jugoszláviában.* Novi Sad, 1967.

————. *Kisebbségtől a nemzetiségig.* Novi Sad, 1978.

Shoup, Paul. *Communism and the Yugoslav National Question.* New York, 1968.

Stankovic, Slobodan. *The End of the Tito Era: Yugoslavia's Dilemmas.* Stanford, 1981.

Tihany, Leslie C. *The Baranya Dispute: Diplomacy in the Vortex of Ideologies, 1918–1921.* New York, 1978.

Zaninovich, M. George. *The Development of Socialist Yugoslavia in Integration and Community Building in Eastern Europe.* Baltimore, 1968.

7. The Hungarians and the Carpatho-Ukraine

Arsentyev, N. V., et al. *A boldogság felé*. Uzhgorod, 1975.

Jászi, Oscar. "The Problem of Sub-Carpathian Ruthenia." *Czechoslovakia*, edited by R. J. Kerner. Berkeley, 1949.

Magocsi, Paul. *History of the Rusyns*. Vienna, 1983.

————. *The Shaping of a National Identity: Subcarpathian Rus', 1848–1948*. Cambridge, Mass., 1978.

Nemec, Frantisek, and Vladimir Moudry. *The Soviet Seizure of Subcarpathian Ruthenia*. Toronto, 1955. Reprint, Westport, Conn., 1981.

Skultéty, Csaba. "A kárpátaljai magyarság szellemi élete." In *Magyar Mérleg*, edited by Éva Saáry, vol. 3, pp. 121–42. Zurich, 1983.

Váradi-Sternberg, János. *Utak, találkozások, emberek*. Uzhgorod, 1974.

The Contributors

Works of the contributors relevant to this volume's subject are listed under "Selected Bibliography," above.

EVA S. BALOGH is an associate of Brevis Press. She received her Ph.D. from Yale University where she taught history as an assistant professor and was dean of Morse College. She served as managing editor of the Yale Russian and East European Publications in 1978–80.

STEPHEN BORSODY is professor emeritus of history, Chatham College. His academic degrees in law, political science, and history are from Charles University in Prague and the University of Budapest. A native of Northern Hungary, which became part of Czechoslovakia after World War I, he was a Hungarian journalist and diplomat before becoming a college professor in the United States.

JOHN C. CAMPBELL, a senior fellow and director of political studies at the Council on Foreign Relations in New York City (now retired), served a dozen years in the State Department in Washington and has written extensively on Eastern Europe, the Middle East, and American foreign policy. His Ph.D. is from Harvard University.

ZOLTÁN DÁVID, director of Archives at the Hungarian Bureau of Statistics in Budapest (retired), is author of studies on population movements in the Danube region and on Hungarian demography of the twentieth century. He received his doctorate in law at the University of Budapest.

ISTVAN DEAK is a professor of history at Columbia University in New York City. He was a journalist and librarian in Budapest, Paris, and Munich. He received his Ph.D. from Columbia University and served as director of the University's Institute on East Central Europe in 1967–78 and 1979–80. His book, *The Lawful Revolution: Louis Kossuth and the Hungarians, 1848–1849,* won The Lionel Trilling Book Award of Columbia College.

FRANÇOIS FEJTŐ, a historian, writer, and journalist, is a former deputy editor-in-chief of Agence France Press in charge of Communist and East European affairs. Before moving to Paris in the 1930s, he was an editor of the Socialist daily *Népszava* in Budapest. A lecturer at the Institute d'Études Politiques in Paris, he received a Ph.D. degree from the University of Paris at Nanterre. Several of his books have been translated into English.

LAJOS FÜR is a Hungarian historian of the post-World War II era. An expert on agrarian history and nationality affairs, he lives in Budapest.

KÁLMÁN JANICS, a physician and sociologist living in Slovakia, is among the few Hungarians of the older generation with a higher education who survived the postwar expulsion of national minorities from Czechoslovakia. He is the author of several studies on national minority problems.

PIERRE KENDE is a senior research fellow at the École des Hautes Études en Sciences Sociales, Paris. He received his doctorate in sociology from the Sorbonne. Author of studies on Communist affairs, he is founder of Dialogues Européens and an editor of its periodical, *Magyar Füzetek,* promoting publication of East European dissident writers in the West. He left Hungary in 1956.

BENNETT KOVRIG is a professor of political science and chairman of the Department of Political Economy at the University of Toronto. After studies at the University of Toronto, he attended the London School of Economics and Political Science, and received his Ph.D. from the University of London. He is the author of several works on Central and Eastern Europe.

ANDREW LUDANYI, a professor of political science at Ohio Northern University, received his Ph.D. at Louisiana State University. A recent Fulbright and IREX scholar at the Gorky State Library in Budapest, he is currently engaged in studying the Communist national minority policies of Hungary.

VOJTECH MASTNY is a research professor of the Center for International Relations at Boston University and a visiting professor at Johns Hopkins University School of Advanced International Studies in Washington. A graduate of Charles University in Prague and Oxford University in England, he received his Ph.D. from Columbia University. Among other distinctions he has earned as a scholar, his dissertation, "The Czechs under Nazi Rule: The Failure of National Resistance," won the Clarke F. Ansley Award.

MATTHEW MESTROVIC is a professor of history at Fairleigh Dickinson University at Teaneck, New Jersey. He received his Ph.D. from Columbia University. Author and lecturer, he is also active in Croatian public life abroad and is currently president of the Executive Committee of the Croatian National Congress.

ZSUZSA L. NAGY is a senior research fellow at the Institute of History of the Hungarian Academy of Science in Budapest. In addition to studies on peacemaking after World War I and on prewar Hungarian liberalism, she has written extensively on the liberal bourgeois opposition in Hungary between the two world wars.

LAJOS PALOVICS, a cartographer living in Budapest, has published several important maps on ethnographic and other issues of Hungary and of Central Europe.

GEORGE SCHÖPFLIN teaches East European politics at the London School of Economics and the School of Slavonic and East European Studies, University of London. He has written widely on a variety of East European topics, notably questions of ethnicity. His most recent book is on "Politics in Eastern Europe."

JULIAN SCHOPFLIN, a writer and translator, was program director of Hungarian Radio in Budapest, 1945–49. He entered diplomatic service as Hungary's envoy to Sweden, 1949–50. After settling in England as a political exile, he was lecturer at the North East Polytechnic in London.

THOMAS SZENDREY is a professor of history at Gannon University, Pennsylvania. He received his Ph.D. from St. John's University. His publications are in the field of European intellectual history and the philosophy of history.

IVÁN K. SZŰCS is the pseudonym of a young Hungarian historian living in Budapest who is specializing in the study of Hungarian minorities in the Danube region.

FERENC A. VÁLI (1905–1984) was professor of international relations at the University of Massachusetts at Amherst. He received his doctorate in law from the University of Budapest and his Ph.D. from the University of London. He entered Hungarian government service after World War II. Imprisoned on political charges in 1951, he was released at the time of the Hungarian Revolution in 1956 and immigrated to the United States in 1957. An expert on international and minority law, his writings covered a variety of issues.

STEVEN BELA VARDY is a professor of history at Duquesne University and an adjunct professor at the University of Pittsburgh. He received his Ph.D. from Indiana University. His publications are in the field of historiography and on Hungarian immigration to the United States.

Index